Rituals of the Light Within

A Compendium of Writings from the Magical
Work of Elizabeth Anderton Fox

Rituals of the Light Within

A Compendium of Writings from the Magical Work of Elizabeth Anderton Fox

Megalithica Books
Stafford England

Editor: Leni Hester
Layout: Taylor Ellwood
Cover Design: Storm Constantine

ISBN: 978-0-9955117-3-6
Catalogue Number: MB0187

Set in Papyrus and Book Antiqua

A Megalithica Books Publication
An imprint of Immanion Press
http://www.immanion-press.com

Dedication

For my two mentors and friends:
Dolores Ashcroft Nowicki
Director of Studies of the Servants of the Light School
and
Gary L. Stewart
Knight Commander of the Order Militia Crucifera Evangelica
Imperator of the Confraternity of the Rose Cross
Sovereign Grand Master of the British Martinist Order

With my thanks for their constant support and encouragement
over the years.

also
In memory of my late husband John A.B. Fox, a true Servant of
the Light, without whose partnership and initiative these rituals
would never have been written.

Table of Contents

Introduction

'Rituals of the Light Within' is a collection of writings, composed between 1982 and 2015. They were primarily designed for use by small and large groups in workshop settings. In putting them in print it is hoped that they will prove useful to others and interesting as reading material.

A major part of our training and work in esoteric study is undertaken in our everyday experiences of life, as we all know some of these are enjoyable and some stressful and often painful. However, an inner experience is equally as effective for learning as is an outer one; it is this principle, which underlies the use of ritual and guided visualisations. Experiences had and people met in the inner world of the mind can be as vivid and as memorable as any physical plane experience. For each of us everything takes place within the theatre of our own mind. Dreams and imagination can give us experiences, which have a strong influence on our lives afterwards - even so can ritual and meditation experiences change and enrich our lives.

Over the years some of the rituals have been, and continue to be, used by both the OMCE and SOL with my permission. They may therefore be familiar to some members of both.

The rituals are based on a wide range of spiritual and esoteric teachings. They contain elements of the Kabbalah as used in Western mystery teachings. They also use traditional teachings from astrology, science, tarot, astronomy and many wisdom traditions. Above all they are a reflection of a personal spiritual journey. They are based on personal experiences of the Light which shines within each and every one of us.

Circle of Unity Ritual

All participants wear white robes if possible, all enter and are seated in a circle, there should be only the number of seats in the circle for the participants, they enter in the following order:

Outer Guard, Earth, Man, Birth, Child, Body, Priest, Mind, Secular, Past, Beginning, Outer, Space, Centre, Below, Dark, Inner Guard, Cosmos, Woman, Death, Elder, Spirit, Priestess, Soul, Sacred, Future, Ending, Inner, Time, Circumference, Above and Light.

The Outer Guard leads, all follow and circle the Temple to their seat, starting with Outer Guard in the West. <u>Note</u>. The Temple is only circled once, some on entry some on exit, depending on position in the circle.

Where possible the pairs should be male/female:

Outer Guard	*Inner Guard*
Earth	*Cosmos*
Man	*Woman*
Birth	*Death*
Child	*Elder*
Body	*Spirit*
Priest	*Priestess*
Mind	*Soul*
Secular	*Sacred*
Past	*Future*
Beginning	*Ending*
Outer	*Inner*
Space	*Time*
Centre	*Circumference*
Below	*Above*
Dark	*Light*

Requirements

Two large candles, two boxes of matches and two candle snuffers, one for each of the Guardians, also small tables to hold these items.
A singing bowl, bell or gong, which is struck by the <u>OUTER GUARD</u> except for the first time when it is struck by <u>LIGHT.</u>
CD player and disc for music.

Ritual

OUTER GUARD
(Turn on music for entry. Aleph Processional)
(Admit all participants)

INNER GUARD
(Turn off music when all seated.)
(NOTE. Each speaker rises to speak and sits upon returning to their seat. Both go straight to centre and return straight to their seats. The two of each pair should rise together.)

OUTER GUARD
I stand in the West of this Temple and seal its portal from all intruders. *(Turns and seals the doorway.)* I stand guard upon the material plane that the Companions of the Light may meet in peace and security.
(Lights candle)

INNER GUARD
I stand in the East of this Temple and keep watch upon the inner planes, that only those who are of the Light may join us and partake in our celebration of unity.
(Lights candle)

OUTER GUARD AND INNER GUARD
(Walk towards each other meeting in the centre of the circle, they face each other and join hands. They say together)
We are security.
(LIGHT sounds singing bowl)
(Both turn and walk back to their places.)

EARTH
I am the small blue planet on which you stand, I turn through the cycles of the days and years, ever returning to my beginning. I am the cradle of nature by whose bounty all your necessities are met and supplied. I am the ground beneath your feet, the cool rivers and streams and the mysterious depths of the oceans and seas. Over my face flow the heat and the cold of the seasons, the warmth of the sun and the sweet refreshing rains. I am your

earthly home, your nurse, your cradle, your life's stage and at the end I receive your mortal remains which are but myself reformed.

COSMOS

I am the vast Cosmos in which you dwell. Your planet, sun and galaxy are your home in the limitless expanses of space. In my realms they are but as a dewdrop in the waters of Earth. Mine are all the shining stars in your night sky, which are but as candle flames in the limitless darkness of space. Mine are the worlds and galaxies beyond the beyond for I exist without end or beginning, endless are the turnings of my wheels of creation, yet am I but one of the Universes, which exist within the infolding of the One.

EARTH AND COSMOS

(Walk towards each other meeting in the centre of the circle, they face each other and join hands. They say together)
We are worlds.
(OUTER GUARD sounds singing bowl)
(Both turn and walk back to their places.)

MAN

I am Man of the family of humanity. I am the son of Earth, I mould and fashion it according to my will. Mine are the towns and cities, the temples and palaces and the great and humble homes of the people. The fields and forests are the work of my hand, I cultivate, create and fashion all the manifold works according to our needs. I make of the earth a garden and a paradise. Yet do I also make of it a hell, for in my greed and ambition I destroy and kill. I make war and conflict and bring pain and suffering to my fellows.

I am a child of Earth and live my life according to earthly things, yet too I lift up my eyes to the heavens and am the observer of the universe. I am the creator of beauty and seek out the secrets of nature that I may understand and know them. I am the eternal seeker.

I am the son of my Father and the Father of my Son, I am the protector and lover of my Wife and the perpetuator of the generations.

WOMAN

I am the Woman of the family of humanity. I am the daughter of Earth, I am the companion and the mate of Man. Mine are the hands which light the hearth fire, I nourish and nurture my family and see that they are clothed and fed. I bring beauty and grace to the society of men and at my knee is the seed of learning and kindness sown in the hearts of my children.

Mine is the voice of the peacemaker and I calm the aggression in the heart of Man. My hands bind the wounds they inflict upon each other and comfort the bereaved when the battle is done.

I am the daughter of my Mother and the Mother of my Daughter, I am the beloved and the lover of my Husband and I am the nurturer of the generations.

MAN AND WOMAN

(Walk towards each other meeting in the centre of the circle, they face each other and join hands. They say together;
We are love.
(OUTER GUARD sounds singing bowl)
(Both turn and walk back to their places.)

BIRTH

I am the bringer forth of new life. I watch over the conception and development of new vehicles for the manifestation of the life force, I bring forth young at the appointed time when the mystery of generation has accomplished its task. I assist the child from the womb, the bird from the egg, the frog from the spawn and animals from the bodies of their Mothers. To each species I give the means of nourishment of the young, to each according to their need and their circumstance. I am the first cry which draws the breath of life into the new vehicle prepared for it, I am the butterfly which emerges from the chrysalis, the new born of all species and the eternal miracle of life upon Earth.

DEATH

I am the bringer of peace to the sick and the aged, I take back the outworn and the damaged and return them again to the cauldron of life. I see that none are tried beyond their strength to endure and set a limit to each existence. I am the final liberator and mine is the gift of ending.

Know that I am but the doorway, which releases life, so that it may return anew. Fear me not for my portals lead only to freedom and return.

BIRTH AND DEATH
(Walk towards each other meeting in the centre of the circle, they face each other and join hands. They say together)
We are life.
(OUTER GUARD sounds singing bowl)
(Both turn and walk back to their places.)

CHILD
I am the Child of the family of humanity. I am the beloved of my parents and their hope for the future. I carry the history of my species within each cell of my body. I am the link in the chain of the generations, which stretches down the centuries. I am life renewed, the fresh beginning of the young, the strength and potency of the newly mature and the fulfilment of the promise of my ancestors. I bring my energy and enthusiasm to the development of my race, the building of its knowledge and the development of its culture.

ELDER
I am the mature Elder of the family of humanity, I have lived the life of my people and garnered the wisdom which comes from the experiences of life. I give counsel and advice in the decisions that govern our prosperity and safety. I am the teacher of the young and the wise one to whom all come seeking comfort for their hearts unease.

CHILD AND ELDER
(Walk towards each other meeting in the centre of the circle, they face each other and join hands. They say together)
We are experience.
(OUTER GUARD sounds singing bowl)
(Both turn and walk back to their places.)

BODY
I am the body vehicle which enables Man and Woman to

experience in the material world. My senses are the communicators by which they share their knowledge and know each other.

I am magnificently adapted for life on Earth, I respond to heat and cold, hunger and thirst, fear and courage, sight and sound, scent and touch. My senses and feelings are the informants of your needs. Care for me and I will be a house of comfort all your life long. I am a creation of the Creator, respect and treat me as such. Make of me a sacred Temple and remember that I am given into your charge for your joy and instruction and abuse me not. I am made of the Earth for the housing of life, there is a time and a term to my existence, when life moves on relinquish me with grace and gratitude.

SPIRIT

I am that invisible essence which lives within you, I am the beat of your heart and the breath of your life, I flow in every nerve and sinew, animate every muscle and organ, I am your energy and your desire. I am the force which flows through all living things. I am life. I flow through plant and animal, insect and bird, fish and the creatures of the deep, and men and women of all races and all times. I am eternal for only my vehicles die and change.

BODY AND SPIRIT
(Walk towards each other meeting in the centre of the circle, they face each other and join hands. They say together)
We are life manifest.
(OUTER GUARD sounds singing bowl)
(Both turn and walk back to their places.)

PRIEST

I am the man who becomes the Priest of my people, for I listen to the unsung and look at the unseen. I lift my eyes to the heavens seeking the Creator of Creation. My heart searches in the depths of the unknown, I yearn to know the source from whence my spirit came and enter the depths of the sacred Mysteries.

I am a solace to the stricken and a comforter to the lost and the bewildered. I bring forth the powers of the unseen and wield them in the service of God and Man. I lift up my eyes to the everlasting and bow in awe before the works of the Divine.

PRIESTESS
I am the woman who becomes the Priestess of my people, for I walk the paths of the sacred and the Mystery. Mine are the pathways of the spirit and I am the voice of the messengers of the Gods who speak to those who would listen and hear.

I tend the eternal flame of the spirit and its symbolic representation which ever shines within the precincts of the Temple. I am the mediator and the seeress, the words of my tongue are an inspiration and a prophecy. I bring intuition, grace and beauty to the service of the Most High.

PRIEST AND PRIESTESS
(Walk towards each other meeting in the centre of the circle, they face each other and join hands. They say together)
We are service.
(OUTER GUARD sounds singing bowl)
(Both turn and walk back to their places.)

MIND
I am Mind, mine is the realm of intelligence, the guiding principle of the life of humanity. Within me are the secret places of inspiration and wisdom. I hold the key to the store of memory, I am the guardian of the archives of the past and the recorder of the acts of the present. The pearl of consciousness is the jewel in my crown for within me dwells the knowledge that "I am."

SOUL
I am Soul, the companion and the parent of Mind. I carry the flame of the Divine Spark which is ever the reminder to humanity of its origin in Divinity. I am the voice of that nameless longing that ever seeks to return to its Source, I am that which knows when Mind knows not. Body, Spirit and Mind are children of the Earth but I am the Child of Eternity.

MIND AND SOUL
(Walk towards each other meeting in the centre of the circle, they face each other and join hands. They say together)

We are immortality.
(OUTER GUARD sounds singing bowl)
(Both turn and walk back to their places.)

SECULAR
I am all things of the secular world, I am the mundane tasks of daily life, the necessities imposed upon humanity by the needs of the body. I am labour and toil, yet too am I the pleasures of the body. I am your dwelling place, the beauty with which you surround yourself, the works of art and of music, which beautifies the material world. I am your history and your future, I am the life of mankind upon Earth, I am the good and the bad, the cruel and the kind, the wonderful and the appalling – I am war and peace.

SACRED
I am everything which reaches beyond the material world. I am the words of the Mystic and the prayers of the Saint. I am the sacred which touches the heart and uplifts the being of humanity beyond the stars. I am the aspiration, which inspires the building of great Temples and the devotion which brings dedication of life to the Work of the Most High.

I am the quiet in the sacred sanctuary and the awe, which touches the soul when it melts into Oneness with the Divine.

SECULAR AND SACRED
(Walk towards each other meeting in the centre of the circle, they face each other and join hands. They say together)
We are reality.
(OUTER GUARD sounds singing bowl)
(Both turn and walk back to their places.)

PAST
I am the Past, I am all that has been from the beginning of time. I am the turmoil and power of the creation of worlds. I am the first cell that stirred into life and the developed complexities of all life forms. I am the history of humanity, its accomplishments and failures and the wonders it has brought into being. I am the world you see about you which is the creation of your ancestors. I am your songs and your stories, which are your celebration of

your past. I am your memories of this life time and the echoes which resonate in the depths of your soul that are the lessons learned from the experiences of your long journey.

FUTURE

I am the Future, the great unborn of that which is yet to be. I am hope and aspiration, I am the as yet un-manifest effects of your present and your past. I am what will be in the fullness of Time. I am light travelling from a distant star in its own present into your future when some astronomer yet unborn will receive it as a dim glow in an eye whose ancestors are yet to be. I am all potential, I am endless possibilities, I am eternal and infinite - or brief as the next breath which fails to be.

PAST AND FUTURE

(Walk towards each other meeting in the centre of the circle, they face each other and join hands. They say together)
 We are now.
(OUTER GUARD sounds singing bowl)
(Both turn and walk back to their places.)

BEGINNING

I am the Beginning, the first moment of an exploding Universe. I am the first link in the chain of becoming. I am the meeting of male and female in the instant of conception. Mine is that spark of inspiration, which lights up the mind of artist, scientist or composer. I am the first step from the unknown to the known, I am decision, choice and the initiator of all action.

ENDING

I am Ending, the last moment of accomplishment when all is brought to fruition. I am the results of all effort and the final page of the book of life. I am welcome when the present has been hard and painful, I am resented when the present has been joyful and good. Yet I am unavoidable and inevitable for all things of Earth have their season and their passing. Yet am I not without fruit for within me is ever the seed of tomorrow and renewal.

BEGINNING AND ENDING
(Walk towards each other meeting in the centre of the circle, they face each other and join hands. They say together;
We are eternity.
(OUTER GUARD sounds singing bowl)
(Both turn and walk back to their places.)

OUTER
I am the Outer, the world you perceive with the body senses. I am the farthest galaxy and the smallest particle. I am the stage of Earth on which you play out the events and purposes of your life, here you find fame or infamy, praise or blame, wealth or poverty, success or failure.

Here you can fulfil your ambitions, achieve your desires and make your contribution to your society and world. Here you can make or break the achievements of a lifetime.

INNER
I am the Inner, the hidden secret world, which exists within your mind. I am your emotions and your feelings, your desires and your appetites. I am too the still small voice which speaks to you from your soul. I am that other concealed dimension where mind may touch mind, memory stir memory and the immaterial universe may be entered and known. I am the visions of splendour which inspire and enlighten, I am the knowledge of the unknowable which only the soul may perceive, I am the Teacher who has trod this way before you and who now whispers advice and guidance in the silence of meditation.

OUTER AND INNER
(Walk towards each other meeting in the centre of the circle, they face each other and join hands. They say together)
We are identical.
(OUTER GUARD sounds singing bowl)
(Both turn and walk back to their places.)

SPACE
I am Space, the distance between here and there. I am what appears to separate you from others. I am great to the small and small to the great for I am the creation of your perception. Even

as the atom knows not its neighbour, even so are the galaxies strangers to each other across the vast expanses of my realms. I seem to be empty but this is just the failure of your senses to perceive – for how can you know that which you lack the ability to observe? Nothing in the Universe is a vacuum, even so am I a mystery.

TIME

I am Time, the distance between now and then. I am the length of your life span, the distance between birth and death. I am slow to the suffering and speedy to the joyous for I am the creation of your perception. I am the means by which you measure the coming and going of night and day, the changing of the seasons and the turning of the heavens. I am a tool of your own making, mistake me not for an immutable law.

SPACE AND TIME

(Walk towards each other meeting in the centre of the circle, they face each other and join hands. They say together)
We are illusion.
(OUTER GUARD sounds singing bowl)
(Both turn and walk back to their places.)

CENTRE

I am the centre of the circle of becoming, the white hot point at the centre of a star, the celestial body which rules over its solar system, the sovereign who rules over his country, the father who guides his family and the nucleus within each molecule of matter. I am the focal point of consciousness, that elusive centre from which the individual looks out upon the world, I am too that consciousness which turns inwards to the centre of its being and finds it looks out upon another world, another dimension and another reality.

CIRCUMFERENCE

I am the Circumference, I mark the boundary of the circle of becoming. I set the limit to a world, you walk upon my line each step you take upon the Earth. I mark too the limit of the visible Universe, yet ever recede as you seek to know me. The Centre and I are twin brothers who cannot be separated one from the other, without him I could not exist for there would be nowhere from whence to define my boundaries. Without me he could not exist for a centre must needs have a dimension to define.

CENTRE AND CIRCUMFERENCE
(Walk towards each other meeting in the centre of the circle, they face each other and join hands. They say together)
We are everywhere.
(OUTER GUARD sounds singing bowl)
(Both turn and walk back to their places.)

BELOW
I am the Below, the starting point for your observation of your world. Look at what is below you and find the same patterns as you see within yourself. You are a cell in the body of humanity, even as an individual cell is a part of your body. The blood in your arteries and veins flows in the same patterns you see in the trees above you and the rivers and streams which nourish your world. The deeper you look, the more the patterns repeat, you are the above to the microscopic below. Plants know life and animals know consciousness even as you yourself know consciousness, the pattern is the same but the quality is different, of what is your own consciousness the Below?

ABOVE
I am the Above, the sky which rises above Earth, the atmosphere which encapsulates life. I am the starry heavens which shine above the darkness of night. I am the archetypal patterns built into the matrix of creation. I am Mind that designs and builds the manifold worlds and life forms. I am Consciousness freed from the restrictions of the body. I am the Powers which humanity calls Gods. I am that to which you aspire; if you would know my nature look into yourself for you are the below of my above. All things are part of the same Creation, all things interact upon each other, nothing moves in the Above or the Below but that it is cause or effect for its own Below and Above.

BELOW AND ABOVE
(Walk towards each other meeting in the centre of the circle, they face each other and join hands. They say together)

We are reflections.
(OUTER GUARD sounds singing bowl)
(Both turn and walk back to their places.)

DARK
I am the Dark, I am the opposite side of the circle of Light. I am the soft darkness of night, which shelters and protects, I am the veil which conceals the unknowable. I am the Universe you do not know exists for your eyes are unable to perceive it. Yet, would you say there is no sound because <u>your</u> ears are unable to hear it? Be not deceived into thinking nought is because your senses do not reveal the concealed.

I have been called evil because my cloak has been used to mask the acts and deeds of twisted harmful men and women – the evil lies within themselves and is revealed as well in darkness as the brightest day.

I am the soft darkness of a restful sleep, the sheltering arm over the newly born, the welcome end to labouring day. I am the veil of night which, drawn across the sky, shows forth the mighty panorama of the stars. Remember this, that only when you know the deepest dark of dark, can you know too the brightest light of Light.

LIGHT
I am the Light, I am the opposite side of the circle of Darkness. I am the brilliant light of day, which illuminates, warms and sustains all life on Earth. I am the light by which all beauty stirs the heart; all colour, form and texture delights the mind and all knowledge is gained and revealed in books and every manner of communication.

I am the Light of Truth and Wisdom, which comes to those who seek the secret ways, I am the Light which ever beckons onward and draws the human soul to walk the sacred path. Long are the days and tortuous the ways, hard the lessons learned and tests to overcome, but then at last comes dawn and the growing soul awakes. Then from the darkness of the human mind shines forth the Light, which never shone from source nor sun nor star, but radiates through inner worlds sublime, the living essence of the worlds Divine, the shining eternal font from whence your soul was born. Remember this - that only when this inner Light shall shine within undimmed shall you be free to rise to the Above and in your turn look down on this Below and take the hand of those who also strive to grow and in true love say " We are One".

DARK AND LIGHT
(Walk towards each other meeting in the centre of the circle, they face each other and join hands. They say together)
We are One.
(OUTER GUARD sounds singing bowl)
(Both turn and walk back to their places.)

INNER GUARD
Our circle is complete, may the Inner Worlds be safely sealed and the knowledge we have gained be held within us. Let us now acknowledge our Unity and depart.

OUTER GUARD
(Turns to West and unseals the Temple. Faces East again)
The outer portal is open and unsealed, let us depart in Unity and peace.

INNER GUARD
(Turn on music for exit. Opera Savage, Vangelis)

LIGHT
(Moves to stand in front of ABOVE next to him/her, they clasp hands and say)
We are One.
(LIGHT moves on to CIRCUMFERENCE and they clasp hands and say)
We are One.
(This is repeated round the circle, each moving on to the next person, when LIGHT reaches the OUTER GUARD he/she exits the Temple, OUTER GUARD being the last to leave. OUTER GUARD extinguishes candles before exiting)

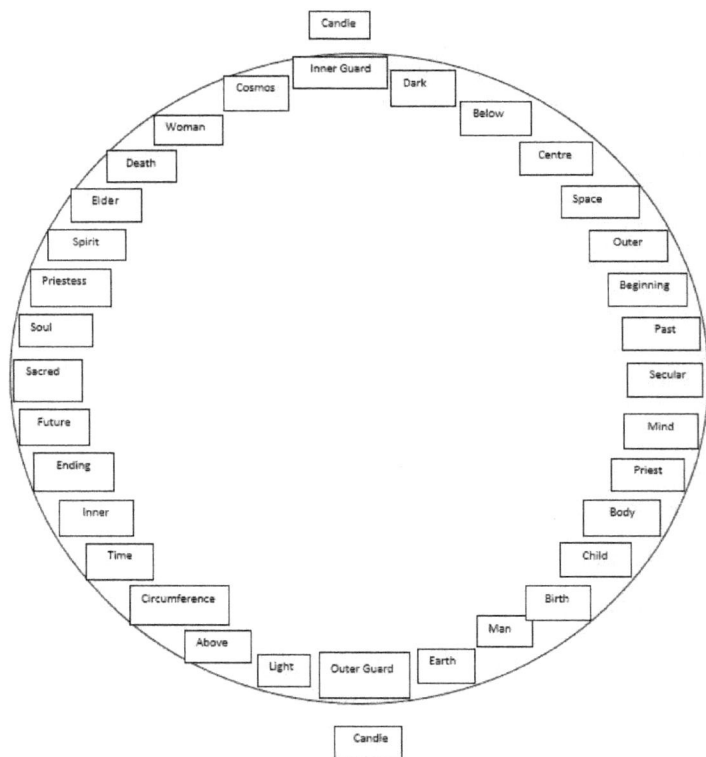

Candle

Inner Guard
Cosmos — Dark
Woman — Below
Death — Centre
Elder — Space
Spirit — Outer
Priestess — Beginning
Soul — Past
Sacred — Secular
Future — Mind
Ending — Priest
Inner — Body
Time — Child
Circumference — Birth
Above — Man
Light — Outer Guard — Earth

Candle

22

Doorways of the Fool Ritual

TEMPLE REQUIREMENTS

Chairs for the fourteen pillars of the doorways
Small table each for the Priest and Priestess
Bag for the Fool
Gifts of the Fool, small crystals are ideal
Sword each for the Priest and Priestess
Lamp and staff for the Hermit
Taper and candle snuffer for the Fool
A candle and holder for each officer of the pillars of the doorways

TEMPLE ARRANGEMENTS.

The Fool is outside the door of the Temple
The Hermit is inside the Temple near the door
Officers of the Pillars of the Doorways are seated as in plan each holds a lit candle
The Priest and the Priestess have Temple equipment on their tables, at minimum a lit candle on each table and a sword
Lighting is as low as possible
Note. It is safer to use electric candles

Ritual

All those who are not taking Office are admitted by THE HERMIT.
The Officers of the PILLARS OF THE DOORWAYS enter in pairs from the West, each carrying a candle and proceed to their places in order;
THE PRIESTESS and THE PRIEST
THE MOON and THE SUN
JUSTICE and JUDGMENT
DEATH and THE DEVIL
THE TOWER and THE CHARIOT
THE EMPRESS and THE EMPEROR
THE LOVERS and THE WORLD
All are seated at the same time taking their signal from the Priest and Priestess.
There are a few moments of silence.

THE FOOL
(Knocks nine times on the outside of the door in three series of three knocks. The first and second set of knocks are met by SILENCE)

THE HERMIT
(Loudly)
Who comes?

THE FOOL
One who seeks his lost home.

THE HERMIT
Say from whence you came and what manner of place you seek.

THE FOOL
That I know not, for it is lost from my memory. In the darkness I spin and turn and only the spark of my being lightens the void. I seek a resting place and the companions I knew in the before time.

THE HERMIT
This door you may enter and here find companions. Yet is it not your lost home for none remain here but are gone hence again upon the long journey.

THE FOOL
My heart aches for a resting place. I would accept entry through your doorway though it be but a short pause in my wandering.

THE HERMIT
Entry beyond this first doorway is of my giving but you must seek those who will be willing to grant you passage through the next. Say what do you bring with you as token to pass this door?

THE FOOL
I bring naught but myself and the bag I carry in my hand. This is all my treasure for it holds my memory of my lost home and within it are the tokens with which I will pay the guardians of the doorways.

THE HERMIT
No payment is asked or taken. Give your tokens only as gifts. The door can only be opened by the correct key. Tell me, what is the key which unlocks my door?

THE FOOL
The key which unlocks your door is desire.

THE HERMIT
(Opens the door and taking the Fool by the hand draws him gently within.)

THE FOOL
(Takes Token from bag and hands it to the Hermit)
This Token I give to you with my thanks for this opportunity to pass your door.

THE HERMIT
Come, I will show you the second doorway and introduce you to those who guard the pillars of the doorway.
(Leads the Fool to the Second Doorway.)

THE WORLD
Greetings stranger. What do you seek?

THE FOOL
I seek entry into your world that I may have companionship and learn that which is necessary for me to return to my true home.

THE WORLD
I guard the right-hand pillar of the doorway between the manifest and the un-manifest. Once you have passed my doorway there is no return until you have passed all the doorways within manifestation. Do you undertake to complete the journey within my realm?

THE FOOL
I so undertake and to seal my good faith I give you this Token.
(Gives Token to The World)

THE WORLD
Your pledge is noted and received.

THE LOVERS
My pillar of the doorway into manifestation is man and woman joined in the partnership of love. Without their assistance you cannot enter through this doorway. By their blending they will build the body which will be your vehicle into manifestation and experience of earth.

Between you and the lovers there will build links of power to draw you through the doorway.

Say, what is the key you bring to unlock it?

THE FOOL
The key which I bring is the Wheel of Fortune, spun by the great ones of the four elements. Freely I place myself upon the wheel that I may know the good and the bad, the light and the dark and the manifold paths of life.
(Gives Token to the Lovers.)

This token I give you in acknowledgment of your opening of the door into manifestation.

THE HERMIT
Now are you born upon earth and must meet those who rule this realm.
(Draws The Fool through the second doorway and leads to the Third Doorway.)

THE EMPEROR
I am the ruler of the right hand pillar of the doorway of earth. Mine are the powers of the masculine force, virile and strong. In my hands is the sceptre, which rules and directs.

He who passes this doorway must accept my sovereignty and acknowledge my powers in himself and his world.

THE EMPRESS
I am the ruler of the left hand pillar of the doorway of earth. My powers are those of fertility and fecundity of man and nature. I nurture the seed of life and bring it to birth and maturity. Those who pass my door must respect my domain of nature in

themselves and the earth.

Say, what key do you carry which will unlock our doorway?

THE FOOL
The key which I carry is that of strength. With confidence in my own ability and independence I will acknowledge the rightful authority of the Emperor. With purity of intention, courage and compassion will I acknowledge the ruler-ship of the Empress.
(The Fool gives tokens to the Emperor and Empress)

These tokens I give you in recognition of your authority and ruler-ship.

THE HERMIT
(Leads The Fool through the Third Doorway and leads to the Fourth Doorway)

THE CHARIOT
I am the right hand pillar of the fourth doorway. My powers are those of the ones who have achieved stability in their earth life.

I control the chariot of triumph and success. The positive and negative forces are harnessed to my will and in my hands are ruler-ship and authority.

THE TOWER
I am the left hand pillar of the fourth doorway. I remind you that nothing is permanent. The achievements of earth have their end inherent in their beginnings. Conflict and disruption are ever present and nothing is ultimately secure. All things must change even as the strongest tower of man is destroyed by the powers of nature.

Do you have within you the key to our doorway?

THE FOOL
The key which I bring to this doorway is that of temperance. By this key I will hold the balance between stability and change. Strengthened by the ability to adapt and flexibility of mind, I will walk through your doorway between the twin pillars of the opposing forces.
(The Fool gives Tokens to the Chariot and the Tower)

These Tokens I give you in acknowledgment of your powers of creation and destruction.

THE HERMIT
(Leads The Fool through the Fourth and to the Fifth Doorway)

THE DEVIL
I am the right hand pillar of the Fifth Doorway. I have been called the Devil and the personification of evil but my powers you submit to of your own will.

Mine are the chains which bind you to the material world. Wealth and possessions will I give you and the soporifics of sensuality and excess. Linger in my realm and look no further for satisfaction and purpose.

DEATH
I am the left hand pillar of the fifth doorway. It is fear of me which guards this gate. To pass through this doorway you must surrender all you have gained of material possessions. I am death of all you have known, embrace me and I will give you oblivion and transformation.

Tell me, have you the key of courage with which to unlock this doorway?

THE FOOL
The key to your doorway is the view of the Hanged Man. Seeing thus I know that your oblivion is only the surrender of the known and your transformation is birth into another time and another space.
(The Fool gives Tokens to the Devil and Death)

These tokens I give you as gifts in remembrance of my freedom from fear of you and my passage through your doorway.

THE HERMIT
(Leads The Fool through the Fifth Doorway and to the Sixth)

JUDGMENT
I am the right hand pillar of the sixth doorway. Your courage in passing the fifth doorway I acknowledge but I challenge your

right to pass mine.

Judgment is the name of my pillar. Those who pass through this doorway must go naked in spirit before the Great Ones. Looking back they must see truly their own self and acknowledge their failures and their accomplishments. Looking forward they must see and understand their own destiny, then rise unafraid to embrace and attain it.

JUSTICE

I am the left hand pillar of the sixth doorway. My name is justice and I am your guardian and your hope. Before me all things are seen in truth and the ways of your heart are open to my view. Your path is one of learning and of growth. It is not your errors and your failures which tip the balance of my scales but the sincerity of your purpose and the clarity of your vision.

The key to our doorway is engraved with the names of truth, balance and dedication. Tell me, may we deliver it with safety into your hand?

THE FOOL

Within me I bear the symbols of my right to receive your key. About my waist is the serpent-cincture denoting the eternity of attainment in the spirit. In my right hand the wand through which I transmit the powers and gifts of the spirit and by my left hand are these given to the earth.

Before me are the symbols of the elements of earth which are mine to control. By the sword will I direct the power of the word. The cup I will fill to sustain all. By my rod shall justice prevail and the pentacle shall signify my dominion.

By the authority and power of the Magician I claim your key.

(The Fool gives Tokens to Judgment and Justice)

These tokens I give you in recognition of your sovereignty over me.

THE HERMIT

(Leads The Fool through the Sixth Doorway and to the Seventh approaching from the East.)

THE SUN

I am the right hand pillar of the seventh doorway. I am the sun which warms and nurtures you, I am the source of your physical vehicle and the light of your world. In my rays are energy, health and beneficence. The times and the tides of your life are bounded by my journeyings. I am your creator and sustainer and the fountain head of all life. I am also your inner light and the illuminator of your pathway. I am the herald of your future in the bright depths of the eternal.

THE MOON

I am the left hand pillar of the seventh doorway. I am the moon, daughter of the sun and you see me only by his light. My power is over the deep places of mind and all nature ebbs and flows to the rhythms of my coming and going. Mine are the secret powers which beckon yet warn and the potent forces of the feminine in woman and nature.

I am the reflector and the reflection and in my image are all mysteries perceived.

Tell me, what key do you bring to pass through this doorway?

THE FOOL

The key which I bring is the star of hope and of promise. By its light will I perceive truth and come to know fully my own nature. The star eternal beckons me on through your doorway. It's rising before me is a hope and a promise. It speaks to me of my long past and my far future. By its light I am led onward to the great initiation and the completion of my journey.
(The Fool gives Tokens to the Sun and the Moon)

These tokens I give you in gratitude for your blessings and your light.

THE HERMIT

(Leads The Fool through the Seventh Doorway and to the Eighth)

THE PRIEST

I am the right hand pillar of the last doorway. I am Priest of your temple pathway. I am your teacher, guide and counsellor. I have watched over you in the days of your journey and spoken to you as the still voice in the silence. Mine is the hand which you have clasped in the dark moments of your despair. Mine too is the hand which sets the light in the sanctuary before you.

THE PRIESTESS
I am the left hand pillar of the last doorway. I am Priestess of the hidden sanctuary and guardian of the veil between the worlds.
I am woman, who opens the doorway into life and who is also the opener and the guardian of its final portal. Mine is the hand which will lead you through this doorway and set your feet upon the causeway of eternity. Tell me, what is the key to our doorway?

THE FOOL
I come empty handed to your doorway. All that I had I have given and I hold no more keys. Therefore must I plead your aid and compassion to permit me entry through your doorway that I may complete my tasks in manifestation and continue my quest for my true home.

THE PRIEST
Yet one key is left to you. Your entry through this doorway is not in our gift. We may prevent your finding the key but once it is in your hand no power of ours may hinder your use of it. This key cannot be given, for he who would use it must be capable of finding it.

THE PRIESTESS
Look into your memory and remember. For you have walked the pathways of earth and used the keys of its doorways. Tell me - have you learned nothing from this journey?

THE FOOL
I am indeed the fool, for I have not seen that which is plain before my eyes nor understood until this moment all that I have unlocked by passing through the doorways.

I am myself the key.

By this knowledge I claim my freedom, by my right as a divine child of the universe I bid you open your doorway.

I have lingered over long on earth and I must once more

walk the causeway of the stars. The depths of the void are my pathways and only in the heart of the eternal is my resting place.

THE PRIEST

We rejoice in your victory. Walk now into your future wearing the sandals of wisdom and the cloak of self-knowledge.
(The Priest and Priestess put the sandals and the cloak upon The Fool.)

THE PRIESTESS

We honour the light within you and enfold you in our love and our blessing. Go forth into your freedom.
(The Priest and Priestess form an arch with their swords and each holding a hand of the Fool draw him through their Doorway.)

MUSICIAN
(Music is played for the exit of The Fool and all participating.)

THE HERMIT
(Comes forward and meets The Fool and escorts him from the Temple.)

THE HERMIT
(Brings each to the Priest and Priestess through the Doorways in the following order. The Priest and Priestess draw them through their doorway, each pair then leaves the Temple as directed by the Hermit. All other participants leave in the same manner).
THE LOVERS and THE WORLD
THE EMPRESS and THE EMPEROR
THE TOWER and THE CHARIOT
DEATH and THE DEVIL
JUSTICE and JUDGMENT
THE SUN and THE MOON
Finally the Hermit passes between the Priest and Priestess and all three leave the Temple)

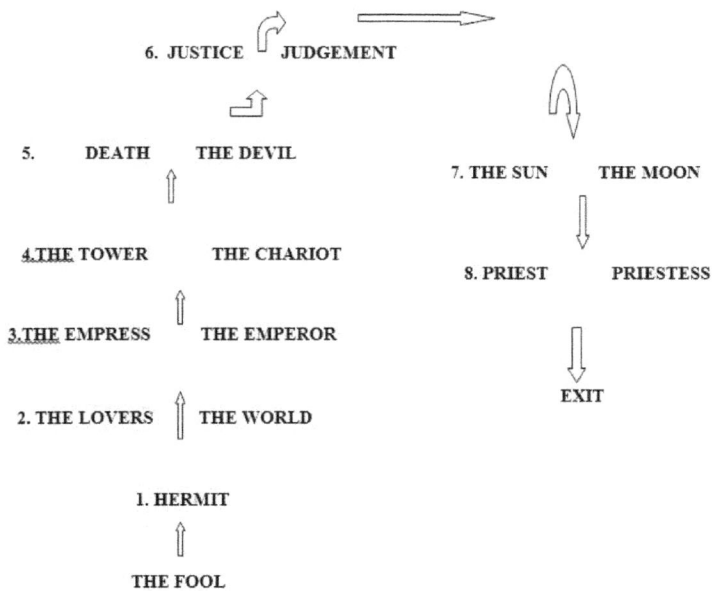

6. JUSTICE   JUDGEMENT

5.   DEATH   THE DEVIL

7. THE SUN   THE MOON

4.THE TOWER   THE CHARIOT

8. PRIEST   PRIESTESS

3.THE EMPRESS   THE EMPEROR

2. THE LOVERS   THE WORLD

EXIT

1. HERMIT

THE FOOL

Zodiac Ritual

TEMPLE ARRANGEMENT

The Temple is arranged in a circle with the entrance in the West.

The Temple is in full light until lowered to just sufficient for safety and for reading scripts.

The stations of the Four Watchers are outside the circle in the four cross quarter directions.

The Traveller is outside the Temple.

Polaris' station is in the centre of the circle with a large candle on a tall stand before him/her.

Time's station is to the East of Polaris, near to the centre.

Space' station is West of Polaris, near to the centre.

TEMPLE REQUIREMENTS

Sufficient seats arranged in a circle for all attending (less eight)

Seats in the four cross quarters for the Four Watchers.

Seats in the centre of the circle for Space, Time and Polaris.

(Polaris requires a seat without any back so that he/she may face in different directions, revolving if possible. Time faces East, Space faces West)

Tape recorder and music.

Four tall candles for the Four Watchers.

Tall candle and stand for Polaris.

Matches and candle snuffers at the four stations of the Watchers and Polaris.

Five boxes of matches.

Five Candle Snuffers.

SPACE wears a dark blue robe.

TIME wears a light blue robe.

POLARIS wears a white robe.

SUN wears a gold robe.

MOON wears a silver robe.

THE TRAVELLER wears a red robe with floating over cover of silver.

OFFICERS OF THE RITUAL

THE TRAVELLER / A Comet

TIME male

SPACE female

POLARIS
WATCHER OF THE EAST
WATCHER OF THE WEST
WATCHER OF THE SOUTH
WATCHER OF THE NORTH

NOTE. The Stations of the Watchers are placed as the position of their stars in the sky, they watch over a hemisphere of space, not a direction as on Earth.

SUN	*male*
MOON	*female*
ARIES	*male*
TAURUS	*male*
GEMINI	*female*
CANCER	*female*
LEO	*male*
VIRGO	*female*
LIBRA	*female*
SCORPIO	*male*
SAGITTARIUS	*male*
CAPRICORN	*female*
AQUARIUS	*male*
PISCES	*female*
GUARDIAN / MUSICIAN	

Ritual

The entry is in silence.
NOTE. Each Officer rises when speaking.

  The Four Watchers enter first in order North, East, South and West. They circle the Temple each stopping at their appointed place, outside the circle in the cross quarter positions.

  The Moon enters next followed by Virgo, Leo, Cancer, Gemini, Taurus, Aries, Sun, Pisces, Aquarius, Capricorn, Sagittarius, Scorpio and Libra. They circle the Temple, each stopping at their appointed place.

  The Upholders of Power (all those not taking an Office) enter and circle the Temple to the remaining places in the circle.

  All are then seated.

  Space, Time, Polaris and The Traveller enter in their appointed time in the ritual.

SPACE
(Allow a few moments for everyone to settle and the Temple to become silent. Enter and circle the Temple three times, slowly in silence, stopping just short of completing the third circle and stand facing the Watcher of the North.

Extend one arm fully forwards, finger pointing above the Watcher.)

Raphael whose Star is Regulus, come forth from the Void and spread Thy wings of protection about the northern sphere of space.

Lower arm so finger points at the Watcher of the North.

SPACE
Watcher of the North, by the Light of Regulus and with the strength of Raphael, watch well. The heavens above us are in your care, see that no enemies of Light disturb our peace.
Do you guard well?

WATCHER OF THE NORTH
I guard well
(Light candle)

SPACE
(Drop arm, turn and continue the circle until facing the Watcher of the West, extend one arm fully forwards, finger pointing above the Watcher)

Oriel whose star is Antares, come forth from the Void and spread Thy wings of protection about the western sphere of space.

(Lower arm so finger points at the Watcher of the West)

Watcher of the West, by the Light of Antares and with the strength of Oriel, watch well. The heavens behind us are in your care, see that no enemies of Light disturb our peace.

Do you guard well?

WATCHER OF THE WEST
I guard well.
(Light candle)

SPACE
(Drop arm, turn and continue the circle until facing the Watcher of the

South, extend one arm fully forwards, finger pointing above the Watcher.)

Gabriel whose star is Formalhaut, come forth from the Void and spread Thy wings of protection about the southern sphere of space.

(Lower arm so finger points at the Watcher of the South)

Watcher of the South, by the Light of Formalhaut and with the strength of Gabriel, watch well. The heavens beneath us are in your care, see that no enemies of Light disturb our peace.

Do you guard well?

WATCHER OF THE SOUTH.
I guard well.
(Light candle)

SPACE
(Drop arm, turn and continue the circle until facing the Watcher of the East, extend one arm fully forwards, finger pointing above the Watcher)

Michael whose star is Aldebaran, come forth from the Void and spread Thy wings of protection about the eastern sphere of space.

(Lower arm so finger points at the Watcher of the East)

Watcher of the East, by the Light of Aldebaran and with the strength of Michael, watch well. The heavens before us are in your care, see that no enemies of Light disturb our peace.

Do you guard well?

WATCHER OF THE EAST.
I guard well.
(Light candle)

SPACE
(Drop arm, continue around the circle and approach station from west and be seated)

TIME
(Enter, circle to the East and stand facing The Sun.)

In the East I set the Solar Orb, Ruler of the Skies of Earth, source of all life and vitality. Definer of the bounds of Time,

Lord of the Aeons, Keeper of the Limits of the Ages and pivot of the wandering stars.

In your bright presence the hours of the day are set and when the face of the Earth turns from you the darkness of night descends.

Great One of Light, illumine our work and set the paths of your children in our sky.

(When Sun rises, step behind and follow just behind as Sun circles the Temple)

SUN

(Rise, circle the Temple slowly, define the place of each Planet by facing outwards from the circle, extending the arm and pointing upwards)

The paths of the Planets I inscribe in the heavens that their course may be set and their influence defined.

(Between Sun and Aries)

Here I set Mercury, to rule the mind, activity and communication.

(Between Taurus and Gemini)

Here I set Venus, to rule love, beauty and harmony.

(Between Cancer and Leo)

Here I set Mars, to rule action, force and achievement.

(Between Virgo and Moon)

Here I set Jupiter to rule justice, humour and wisdom.

(Directly facing Moon)

Here I set Moon to rule the soul, emotions and dreams.

(Between Moon and Libra)

Here I set Saturn to rule patience, caution and order.

(Between Scorpio and Sagittarius)

Here I set Uranus to rule invention, discovery and insight.

(Between Capricorn and Aquarius)

Here I set Neptune to rule ideals, visions and tides.

(Between Pisces and Sun)

Here I set Pluto to rule change, mutation and new growth.

(Return to station, face the circle, spread out both arms to indicate the entire Temple)

Here I set Earth to rule experience, reality and life.

As was said by Thrice Greatest Hermes;

"It is true, certain, and without falsehood, that whatever is below is like that which is above; and that which is above is like that which is below: to accomplish the one wonderful work."

And again he said;

"Its Father is the Sun, its Mother is the Moon; the Wind carries it in its womb; and its nurse is the Earth. This Thing is the Father of all perfect things in the world."

TIME
(Rise and step in front of Sun, turn and face West.)

Even as Dawn heralds the Sun's rising, so too does his sky journey mark the hours of the day.

MUSICIAN
(Lower the lights slowly as Sun and time circle to the West. Leave sufficient light for reading and safety)

TIME
(Turn, take Sun's hand and together circle sun-wise to the West and face Moon)

The day is done and the Moon rises. Now let her silver light rule the night sky.

MOON, SUN AND TIME
(Moon rises, Sun takes her seat, Time takes Moon's hand and they circle the Temple together to the East, both face West)

MOON
I am the silver mirror of Sun's hidden light, my changing face reflects the flow of time. From crescent shape to full, and back to crescent once again, I wax and wane, till hidden behind the shadow of the Earth my face grows dark and gives full radiance of the night unto the stars.

MOON AND TIME
(Moon sits in the chair of Sun. Time returns to station and sits)

SPACE
(Rise and circle the Temple to the entrance to greet Polaris)

POLARIS AND SPACE
(Enter Polaris, Space leads Polaris round the Temple, gradually circle in to the centre)

SPACE

I place you here to hold steady the central pillar of the sky.
Around you eternally circles the vast panorama of the Universe.
Yours is the unmoving centre of the dance of the stars through time.

POLARIS

(Light candle)

Steady, fixed and firm I am the hub of the turning wheel of the heavens.

I mark the Northern Pole for all on Earth. Travellers - look up and let me guide you home.

(Polaris sits. During the ritual Polaris turns to follow the movements of Space, Sun and The Traveller as they move round the Temple)

SPACE

(Move to the East, then follow the circle, sun-wise, marking each Zodiac station by facing the Officer and pointing in their direction with arm held straight out)

Here I place the constellation of Aries which brings courage, independence and will.

Here I place the constellation of Taurus which brings determination, endurance and success.

Here I place the constellation of Gemini which brings action, intellect and versatility.

Here I place the constellation of Cancer which brings tenacity, caring and sensitivity.

Here I place the constellation of Leo which brings authority, command and dominion.

Here I place the constellation of Virgo which brings order, industry and efficiency.

Here I place the constellation of Libra which brings harmony, balance and intuition.

Here I place the constellation of Scorpio which brings persistence, discretion and transformation.

Here I place the constellation of Sagittarius which brings devotion, ideals and philosophy.

Here I place the constellation of Capricorn which brings caution, patience and practicality.

Here I place the constellation of Aquarius which brings art, innovation and invention.

Here I place the constellation of Pisces which brings sacrifice, mysticism and understanding.

SPACE
(Turn and face into the circle)
The stars are set in their courses, the planets in their orbits and the Sun enthroned in authority and splendour.

So is our Temple now a microcosm of the macrocosm, a true theatre of the heavens.

TIME
(Rises)
Day and night, month and year, age and aeon are set and defined.

SPACE AND TIME
(Space returns to station and both are seated)

MUSICIAN
(Few minutes of dramatic music Ennio Morricone "The Mission" River Track 12)

THE TRAVELLER
(Enter quickly and dramatically, circle the Temple and stop in front of The Sun in the West)

MUSICIAN
(Stop music)

THE TRAVELLER
Great One of Light, your power has drawn me hence from the far depths of the Universe – I travel the outermost arms of the Galaxy and the concealed mysteries of space – you who are the end and the beginning of my journey - can you tell me its purpose?

SUN
Traveller, you follow a solitary path through the cosmos and I am but the last pivot upon which your journey turns. I know not

what powers draw you away from me again nor what befalls you in the long ages before you once more return to me.

I know only that you are The Traveller and blaze a trail of glory across my skies. Ask the purpose of your journey of my Daughter the Moon for she is wise and Priestess of many Mysteries.

THE TRAVELLER
(Circle the Temple and stand in front of Moon in the East)
Lady Moon, I am The Traveller, drawn from the depths of space by your Father the Sun. He says he knows not the purpose of my journey and bids me seek my answer in your wisdom and your Mysteries.

MOON
Traveller, I have seen your light approaching from afar and known you for one who comes from a place my Brother and Sister planets and I will never know. For we are bound to our Father Sun and follow the rhythms of his celestial path, marking the times and tides for those of Earth. We are the markers of their days and nights, the powers and influences which shape their fate; we are their guides and beacons of their destiny, their shining symbols in the sea of space. How then would I know of your purpose and your journey?

THE TRAVELLER
Lady Moon – what you say is true, yet your Father Sun spoke of you as Priestess of the Mysteries, does not your inner vision show you true and tell you the answer that I ask of you?

MOON
Traveller – it is not from me that you should seek this answer but from yourself. You follow a solitary path in search of experience and your own wisdom. Yet are you a child of the Universe and it is the duty of the wise ones to instruct you. Seek those who are the spirits of the stars and learn of their wisdom that you may acquire your own.

THE TRAVELLER
Lady Moon this I will do.

(Circle the Temple to stand in front of Aries, continuing after each has spoken to the next Officer of the Zodiac signs)
Lord of Aries give me of your wisdom.

ARIES
Traveller – I am the beginning of all beginnings, I am the Time of the before-time.

I was there in the darkness and turmoil of creation, I was the golden rain which fell before the bright waters came.

I am the mouth and the tail of the serpent of time, I mark the death of the old and the birth of the new.

I am the seed and the first stirrings of springtime, in my time all things are renewed.

In me is your beginning and childhood, mine are the days of your youth and the first sweet blossoming of life. Rejoice in the sap that is rising and dance the sweet rhythm of spring. Drink deep of the blessings I bring you and grow strong for the journey ahead.

Yet remember that life is a circle, that the sweetest of joys must all pass, and the darkest despair has an ending and the door of your death leads to birth.

As a symbol I give to remind you, the ring which both binds and makes free, for its gold is a troth and a promise and to freedom and love is the key.

THE TRAVELLER
Lord of Taurus give me of your wisdom.

TAURUS
Traveller – I stood guard at the dawn of the ages, at the birth of the Earth I was there. I was fire in the first volcano and the red flow of its lava my blood. My roar was the sound of creation and my seed the foundation of life. I was slain that the land might be fertile and I arose that all creatures might live.

Stubborn, determined and steadfast, I will show you the way to stand firm. Solid, sensuous and earthy, I will keep you well-grounded on Earth.

Yet the symbol I give to remind you is sacred as well as profane, at its centre is the secret chamber where lies the key to your heart. So walk all the twists of the labyrinth, all the trials

43

and the joys of your life, and come at the final accounting to stand tall in the Truth of the Light.

THE TRAVELLER
Lady of Gemini give me of your wisdom.

GEMINI
Traveller – I watched your approach from afar and I see your weariness, yet can I give you no rest from your journey.

Know that earth life forever dances over the black and white squares of polarity, which are upon the floor of the Temple of the Twelve Pillars.

I am your right hand path and your left hand path, your good and your evil. I am the twin pillars between which you must find balance.

I am the right hand face and the left hand face of life, only when you see my full countenance will you be free.

I give you a symbol to remind you of this. Upon your left foot I place a slipper of silver and upon your right foot I place a slipper of gold. Shod thus with the twin slippers of the opposites shall you dance to the eternal rhythm of Life.

THE TRAVELLER
Lady of Cancer give me of your wisdom.

CANCER
Traveller – I am the celestial doorway through which humanity enters into life. I am your harsh school of experience and the hard shell which protects you.

I am the hearth of your home and the fire of your heart. Find me at the height of your happiness and in the depths of your despair.

I am the bitter sea of the Mother and her fountain of compassion. Seek her in the oceans of your passion and sing to her the songs of your bliss.

The pearl is my symbol to remind you of this, its beauty is born of the tears of your pain and its wisdom is gained through your trials and your grief. But remember too that the purpose of your journey is also for the joy of it, the very joy of it, the joy of being.

THE TRAVELLER
Lord of Leo give me of your wisdom.

LEO
Traveller – I am the King of all I see, I am the heart centre of everything.

I have walked down the days of your history and strode through the tales of your myth. I am Adam, Adonis, Apollo and Osiris, Horus and Ra. I am Moses, Jesus and Arthur and all heroes, saviours and kings.

I am splendour and light and glory. Look into your own heart and see my reflection – for my Light and your Light are of the one Source. Carry the Light on your travels that no being and no place shall know darkness.

The symbol I give you is the golden crown of ruler-ship that you may remember this task.

THE TRAVELLER
Lady of Virgo give me of your wisdom.

VIRGO
Traveller – I am the lush green grass of the meadow and the gold of the harvest. I am the bright blossom of springtime and the ripe fruits of autumn. Mine is the fair face of the maiden and the child that is born of her love. I am beauty and the bright star of the morning.

If you would drink of my cup of plenty, taste the bitter as well as the sweet. For remember, all are my children and all serve them who sit at my feet.

The symbol I give to remind you is the Golden Egg of infinite potential. Within it lie hidden the seeds of your life and of your immortality.

THE TRAVELLER
Lady of Libra give me of your wisdom.

LIBRA
Traveller – I am the scales of justice and the balance between your head and your heart. I am the wisdom born of intelligence that tempers the rashness of unrestrained emotion. I am the love

and the feeling that fertilises and restrains the sterile power of cold reason.

Whatever your deeds upon your journey, weigh them against the feather of Truth and the purity of your heart, that your thoughts and your acts may be worthy. Keep the scales balanced, so that you fall not into the extremes of neither the left hand path nor the right hand path.

I give you as a symbol to remind you of this the bridge of the rainbow which is both pure white Light and all colour.

THE TRAVELLER
Lord of Scorpio give me of your wisdom.

SCORPIO
Traveller – I am the Smith who forges the sword which conquers, I am too the fire of its formation and the water of its tempering.
Yet am I also the dragon which the sword slays, the snake who awakens Eden from its sleep of ignorance and the Eagle who is the messenger of the sun between the Gods and Men.

Take as my gift the poisoned cup of bitter experience and drink it to the dregs. Yet even as Thor could not drink dry the encircling oceans, even so will my cup never be emptied. Yet must you drink your fill and more, for the cup contains in reality the waters of life. Then must you be the alchemist and the transformer within the vessel of your own being and bring it forth anew, distilled by self-discipline into the perfect liquor of golden soul.

THE TRAVELLER
Lord of Sagittarius give me of your wisdom.

SAGITTARIUS
Traveller – I am your Teacher and your way shower. Even as the harvest of autumn stores up the fruits of the Earth to sustain you in the dark days of winter; even so will I garner with you the riches of your experience and open to you the hidden places where Wisdom dwells.

I am the swift steed which you ride as you go forth to the battles of Earth, and I am too the Unicorn which greets you in your Victory. Aim true in your quest and seek always the highest goal – then will I be the arrows of your direction and the course of your pathway.

The symbol I give you is the flaming torch of enthusiasm that your heart may be strong and your feet sure upon the rainbow bridge which leads to your destiny.

THE TRAVELLER
Lady of Capricorn give me of your wisdom.

CAPRICORN
Traveller – I am the ancient of days and the dark of the year. If you seek me you must seek in the dark and the cold of winter. The days are short in which you may find the Light when you enter my time.

I am age and the fullness of wisdom; if you would seek the fruits of my long years, look in the harsh realities of physical life. Taste deep of Earth, its joys and sorrows, freedom and servitude.

I give you a symbol to remind you of this, look at the spiral and know that as you circle it you must also progress. In solitude find companionship, in grief find joy, in having be able to relinquish, in happiness know there is always the sorrow of tomorrow. But in this knowing feel no grief, for each turn of the spiral reveals a new life from a death, a success from a failure and freedom from the bonds of experience.

THE TRAVELLER
Lord of Aquarius give me of your wisdom.

AQUARIUS
Traveller – I am the Ageless Teacher of the Wise, I am freedom from the ties of the past and the initiator of the new. I will lead you from the ways of the known and guide you upon the pathways of the future.

I am the first warmth which melts the ice caverns of winter, I am the promise of spring and the rebirth of life. My Priestess is the queen of heaven, by whom you are replenished and refreshed from the benevolence and compassion which pours forth from her being. My Priest is the Lord of the skies, by whom you are sustained from the waters of knowledge and insight which flow forth from his jar of inspiration.

Take as my gift the chalice of life, fill it with your knowledge, experience and wisdom, that every man and woman may drink of it in equality and peace.

THE TRAVELLER
Lady of Pisces give me of your wisdom.

PISCES
Traveller – I am the dreamer of dreams and the liberator of the spirit. I am the deep sea of Being in which swim the dual aspects of yourself. For you are both male and female, mind and spirit, body and soul, the inner and the outer.

I am the sea which seeks nowhere yet is everywhere, I contain great treasures yet am empty, I have great knowledge and yet know nothing.

Oh wanderer, empty yourself of what you know, unlearn all you have been taught. Become an empty vessel to be filled. Thus will you begin to be illumined by your own inner Light and no longer by the reflected light of the Sun.

The symbol I give you is the celestial girdle which binds together the twin fishes of my sign. Remember their unity, which symbolises the balance within you and the oneness of your Self within the kingdom of the oceans of your inner world.

THE TRAVELLER
(Complete the circle and stand in front of Sun in the West)
Great One of Light, the spirits of the stars have given to me of their wisdom. Yet would I seek further. Again I say - you who are the end and the beginning of my journey, tell me its purpose.

SUN
Traveller, mine is the power that draws you hence, yet am I not the Initiator of your journey. Even as my place and power are set and defined by a greater One – so too is the vast circle of your journey drawn by an unseen hand upon the pathways of the heavens.

Seek the wisdom of the one who is the pivot of the sky, who neither moves nor travels but holds firm the pillar of the Universe, the unchanging one about whom all turn. Poised in that eternal stillness, it may be Polaris has observed the path you travel and can tell you of its purpose.

POLARIS
(Rise and face North)

THE TRAVELLER
(Circle the Temple and stand in front of Polaris)
Holder of the still centre of the turning wheel of the heavens, tell me, have <u>you</u> seen and understood the purpose of my journey?

POLARIS
Traveller, know that my place as pivot of the heavens is but an illusion. Only for those on Earth do I appear to uphold the circles of the stars, for I too am part of their eternal journeys.

In the vast aeons of time all moves and changes, even so, as the wheels of space turn, another will come to stand in my place.

Know that there is no star, no sun, no planet, yea even the smallest speck of dust in the vast Cosmos which remains forever unmoved and unchanged.

THE TRAVELLER
Is there then no end to my journey, no resting-place, no purpose?

POLARIS
There is an end to all journeys and a completion to all becomings, yet are they everywhere on the seamless circle of Time.

Traveller – know that we are part of the unfolding of Creation, its purpose is our purpose and its becoming is our becoming.

Know that you have already arrived at the end of your journey for you are the very spirit of movement.

Know also that you have already achieved your purpose for you are here and now and ARE.

SPACE
(Rise, and stand at the right hand of the Traveller)
Traveller, within my realm have been set the shining stars

of heaven and they have given to you of their wisdom.

The Children of the Sun have been set in their appointed course to give to you their influences and powers.

You have passed through my emptiness and known my vastness, you have touched my boundaries which are but the doorways of my beginning.

Traveller – you who have seen the vast panorama of the heavens, have you learnt nothing of your purpose?

TIME
(Rise and stand at the left hand of the Traveller)

Traveller, majestic and wondrous are the patterns I weave; a day, a year, an age, a thousand million years I measure by the slow turning of the skies. Mine is the hand that turns the page which never can return, yet too does my finger trace the passing of the aeons between infinity and eternity.

Traveller – you who have known both the fleeting moment and the eternity of cosmic time, have you learnt nothing of your purpose?

THE TRAVELLER

Wise Rulers of Space and of Time, neither the Sun nor Polaris could tell me of my purpose and my destiny – do you then know the answer?

SPACE

Traveller – you are the Observer who carries the light of understanding within you. Know that you are the seed of knowledge within the Cosmos.

TIME

Traveller – you are the Thinker who carries within you the ability to change the patterns of nature. Know that you are a directing intelligence within the Cosmos.

POLARIS

Traveller – you are the Lover who cares for and nurtures all creatures of Creation. Know that you are emotion and devoted tenderness within the Cosmos.

TIME, THE TRAVELLER AND SPACE
(Circle to stand in front of Moon.)

MOON
Traveller – you are the Mystic who understands the Mysteries and bridges space and time with thought.

TIME, THE TRAVELLER AND SPACE
(Circle to stand in front of Sun.)

SUN
Traveller – you are the Philosopher and Sage who brings the light of consciousness into the realm of matter.

You are a spark of that Eternal Spirit which is the Creator and Upholder within the Cosmos. You are the forerunner, the trail-blazer, the Seed Bearer of Light and the Conductor of Souls.

THE TRAVELLER
Great Sun you have spoken true. Polaris has seen the vastness of my journeying and understood that the nature of all things is motion, change and love.

Space has seen that without an Observer there is none to stand in wonder before the marvels of Creation.

Time has seen that without a Thinker there is none to build with and use the elements of Creation.

Lady Moon has seen that conscious spirit dwells within the outer form.

And you Great Sun have seen that without that spark of Eternal Spirit all is but dead matter, unthinking, unknowing and unknown.

To you was given the task of nurturing these Sparks of Spirit, who have represented the spirits of the macrocosm within this microcosm, that they too might also grow to be Travellers in their turn.

Your task is well done for I have heard much wisdom spoken here and seen the Light of Spirit shine brightly within your realm.

So does the Great Plan behind Creation unfold and evolve according to Law. Even so do these Sparks of Spirit gathered here follow their own specific plan, they too work within the

Law ordained for their Universe that the objectives of the Light may be manifest in Earth. It is well that this is so.

I will take back this knowledge of their progress to the Great One who sets all our courses and leave you with my blessing.

THE TRAVELLER, SPACE AND TIME
(With Space at the right hand of the Traveller and Time at the left hand of the Traveller, the three process around the Temple.

Traveller gives a blessing to each person, this may be done by placing one hand on their head, looking into their eyes, saying something to them, holding a hand or in any way which seems appropriate.)

MUSICIAN
(Start music after the blessing is completed (except for Polaris, Space and Time) for exit of Traveller. River Track 12)

THE TRAVELLER, SPACE AND TIME
(When the Blessing is complete the three complete a full circle together around the Temple, Space and Time return to their places. The Traveller gives the blessing last to Polaris, Space and Time at their stations.

The Traveller completes a single circle alone and exits)

MUSICIAN
(Turn off music)

TIME
So is our work completed and it is time to return this microcosm of the heavens to the macrocosm.

SPACE
The stars and the planets have brought their influences and wisdom to our Temple. Let us now give thanks for their eternal presence in our skies and in our lives and for their assistance in our work.

(Rise and move to the East. Then follow the circle sun-wise, marking each Zodiac station by facing the Officer and pointing in their direction with arm held straight out)

Our thanks to the constellation of Aries for your presence

as you return to outer space.

Our thanks to the constellation of Taurus for your presence as you return to outer space.

Our thanks to the constellation of Gemini for your presence as you return to outer space.

Our thanks to the constellation of Cancer for your presence as you return to outer space.

Our thanks to the constellation of Leo for your presence as you return to outer space.

Our thanks to the constellation of Virgo for your presence as you return to outer space.

Our thanks to the constellation of Libra for your presence as you return to outer space.

Our thanks to the constellation of Scorpio for your presence as you return to outer space.

Our thanks to the constellation of Sagittarius for your presence as you return to outer space.

Our thanks to the constellation of Capricorn for your presence as you return to outer space.

Our thanks to the constellation of Aquarius for your presence as you return to outer space.

Our thanks to the constellation of Pisces for your presence as you return to outer space.

(Return to centre and face Polaris)

Polaris we thank you for having assisted us in our work, return now to your place at the hub of the northern skies and so remain our guiding star.

SPACE
(Return to station and sit)

POLARIS
(Rise, extinguish candle, circle the Temple and exit unaccompanied)

TIME
(Rise, circle Temple to stand in front of Moon in the East)

The Eastern horizon glows and the night draws to its close. Return now to rest and with our thanks veil your bright beauty with the day.

MOON AND TIME
(Moon rises, Time take Moon's hand and circle the Temple together to the West, facing Sun)

TIME
Great Sun, Lord of the sky of day, now are the heavens yours to rule. Illumine the Earth once more with your life giving rays and close with us the mysteries of the night.

MUSICIAN
(Gradually increase the light as Sun and Time circle the Temple so the light is fully up when the Sun is back in the East)

SUN
(Sun rise, Moon take seat, Sun circle Temple to original station in the East with Time following just behind. Sun face west. Time return to station and sits)

I am the dawn in the East and the returning daylight. Only the Moon, who shares my light, may also share my sky. All others now I place at rest.

(Circle the Temple slowly facing outwards from the circle at each place of a Planet, extending the arm and pointing upwards)

(Between Sun and Aries)

I give our thanks to Mercury and veil his light with day.

(Between Taurus and Gemini)

I give our thanks to Venus and veil her light with day.

(Between Cancer and Leo)

I give our thanks to Mars and veil his light with day.

(Between Virgo and Moon)

I give our thanks to Jupiter and veil his light with day.

(Directly facing Moon)

I give our thanks to Moon and veil her light with day.

(Between Moon and Libra)

I give our thanks to Saturn and veil his light with day.

(Between Scorpio and Sagittarius)

I give our thanks to Uranus and veil his light with day.

(Between Capricorn and Aquarius)

I give our thanks to Neptune and veil his light with day.

(Between Pisces and Sun)

I give our thanks to Pluto and veil his light with day.

(Return to station and face West)

Thus are the wonders of the night concealed and the day's work begins.

TIME
(Rise)
So is our Work completed and our theatre of the macrocosm closed.
(Be seated)

SPACE
(Circle the Temple until facing the Watcher of the West.

Extend one arm fully forwards, finger pointing above the Watcher)

Oriel, we thank you for your protection of the western sphere of space. Return now to the Void by the Light of your star Antares and leave with us your blessing.

(Lower arm so finger points at the Watcher of the West.)

Watcher of the West, by the Light of Antares and with the strength of Oriel you watched well. The heavens behind us were in your care.

How do you report?

WATCHER OF THE WEST
I guarded well and all is at peace in the heavens behind us.

(Extinguish candle.)

SPACE
(Circle the Temple until facing the Watcher of the South.

Extend one arm fully forwards, finger pointing above the Watcher.)

Gabriel, we thank you for your protection of the southern sphere of space. Return now to the Void by the Light of your star Formalhaut and leave with us your blessing.

(Lower arm so finger points at the Watcher of the South.)

Watcher of the South, by the Light of Formalhaut and with the strength of Gabriel you watched well. The heavens beneath us were in your care.

How do you report?

WATCHER OF THE SOUTH
I guarded well and all is at peace in the heavens beneath us.

(Extinguish candle)

SPACE

(Rise, circle the Temple until facing the Watcher of the East.

Extend one arm fully forwards, finger pointing above the Watcher)

Michael, we thank you for your protection of the eastern sphere of space. Return now to the Void by the Light of your star Aldebaran and leave with us your blessing.

(Lower arm so finger points at the Watcher of the East.)

Watcher of the East, by the Light of Aldebaran and with the strength of Michael you watched well. The heavens before us were in your care.

How do you report?

WATCHER OF THE EAST

I guarded well and all is at peace in the heavens before us.

(Extinguish candle)

SPACE

(Circle the Temple until facing the Watcher of the North.

Extend one arm fully forwards, finger pointing above the Watcher)

Raphael, we thank you for your protection of the northern sphere of space. Return now to the Void by the Light of your star Regulus and leave with us your blessing.

(Lower arm so finger points at the Watcher of the North.)

Watcher of the North, by the Light of Regulus and with the strength of Raphael you watched well. The heavens above us were in your care.

How do you report?

WATCHER OF THE NORTH

I guarded well and all is at peace in the heavens above us.

(Extinguish candle)

MUSICIAN

(Start music for exit
On Earth as it is in Heaven Track 1)

SPACE
(Return to station)
Everyone please rise.

SPACE AND TIME
(Together circle the Temple and exit)

MOON
(Moon leads the exit from the Temple, everyone completing the circle sun-wise.)

THE FOUR WATCHERS
(Exit the Temple in order North, East, South and West)

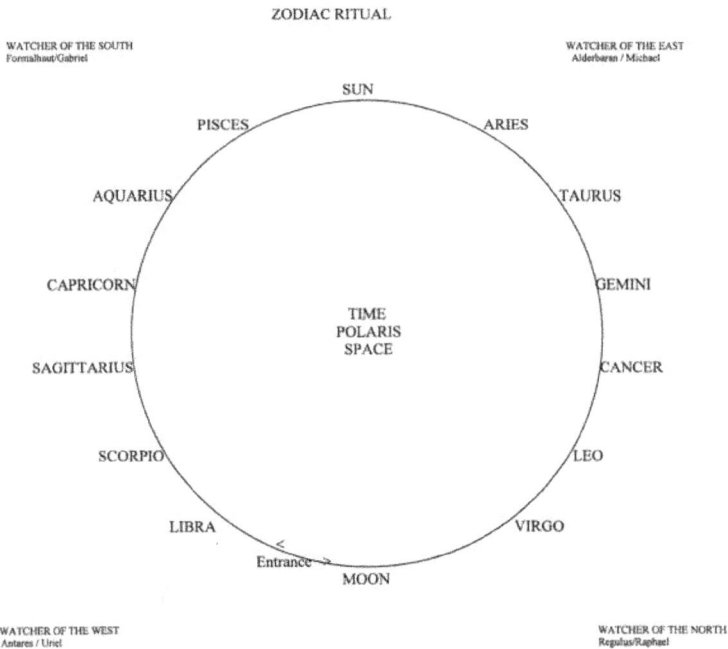

ZODIAC RITUAL

WATCHER OF THE SOUTH
Formalhaut/Gabriel

WATCHER OF THE EAST
Alderbaran / Michael

SUN

PISCES

ARIES

AQUARIUS

TAURUS

CAPRICORN

GEMINI

TIME
POLARIS
SPACE

SAGITTARIUS

CANCER

SCORPIO

LEO

LIBRA

VIRGO

Entrance

MOON

WATCHER OF THE WEST
Antares / Uriel

WATCHER OF THE NORTH
Regulus/Raphael

THE TRAVELLER   / A COMET

Morning Ceremony

There is a central altar, seats are arranged in a circle. Seat in East for Officer.
On the altar are sufficient <u>unlit</u> candles, one for each person attending.
The Sword is at the Eastern Station.
All enter and are seated.
Officer enters carrying the Sacred Light.

OFFICER
Companions, please rise in honour of the Light.
(Places Sacred Light on centre of Altar and proceeds to Station in the East.)
Please be seated.
Blessed is the returning light of day which banishes the dread shadows of the night.
(pause)
Blessed is the life giving sun in its rising, bringing renewed life and vitality to all.
(pause)
Companions let us attune with the spiritual sun behind the sun that its influence may fill and enrich our day.
(Officer goes to the Altar and lights one candle. Each person in turn goes to altar and lights one candle.)

OFFICER
(Gives INVOCATION and PATHWORKING)
(Music for meditation if desired)
(At close of meditation Officer takes the Sword and goes to the first person to their left and holding the Sword, hilt towards the person before them, says the Dedication. Each gives the Dedication to the next person and hands on the Sword)
(Dedication)
Serve and defend the Light throughout the day.
(At the close of the Dedication the Officer returns the Sword to the Eastern Station and says)
So is the invisible returned to the visible. All Light is one.
(Officer exits. Each exits in their own time.)
(Officer returns and ensures all lights are safe or extinguished)

Invocation

EHEHIEH - EHEHIEH - EHEHIEH

Omnipotent Power, the stars of the heavens are but as jewels in Thy crown.

Metatron, Lord of Illumination, radiate the Divine Light within me and about me.

JEHOVAH - JEHOVAH - JEHOVAH

Omnipresent Wisdom teach me to be wise in all things.

Ratziel, Archangel of the Creative Forces, empower the life force within me that I may be strong in body, mind and spirit.

JEHOVAH ELOHIM - JEHOVAH ELOHIM - JEHOVAH ELOHIM

Omniscient Understanding of all creation, teach me to understand with humility.

Tzaphkiel, Lord of the Temple of the Divine, sanctify my body and mind that within me may be a true temple of the Most High.

EL - EL - EL

Source of all mercy, look kindly upon all my faults.

Tzadkiel, Archangel of Benevolence and Certainty, help me to be calm in the midst of life's turbulence.

ELOHIM GEBOR - ELOHIM GEBOR - ELOHIM GEBOR

Holder of the scales of justice, weigh my heart with compassion.

Khamael, the Avenging Angel and the protector, hold thy sword before me.

JEHOVAH ALOAH VA DAATH - JEHOVAH ALOAH VA DAATH - JEHOVAH ALOAH VA DAATH

God of love and harmony, touch me with thy grace.

Raphael Lord of Healing keep me in health and strength.

JEHOVAH TZABAOTH - JEHOVAH TZABAOTH - JEHOVAH TZABAOTH

Lord of the Hosts of Heaven, grant me victory over darkness.

Haniel Archangel of Beauty, open my spirit to the splendours of earth.

ELOHIM TZABAOTH - ELOHIM TZABAOTH - ELOHIM TZABAOTH

God of the Hosts of Heaven, lead me in the ways of Truth

and Honour.

Michael, Archangel of Magic and Holder of the Gates of Worlds, open the Pathways of Light before me.

SHADDAI EL CHAI - SHADDAI EL CHAI - SHADDAI EL CHAI

Thou art the Mighty Living God, the Foundation of all manifestation.

Gabriel, Lord of Dreams, teach me to dream true by night and by day.

ADONAI HA ARETZ - ADONAI HA ARETZ - ADONAI HA ARETZ

Thine is the Kingdom, the Power and the Glory.

Sandalphon, Lord of Air, Fire, Water and Earth

Enfold me in Thine Arms. AMEN AMEN AMEN

Evening Ceremony

There is a central Altar with seats arranged in a circle about it.

The Sacred Light is on the Altar and sufficient lit candles, one for each person attending.

There is a Chalice containing Water on the Altar.

(Officer is seated in the West)

All enter and are seated.

OFFICER

Companions. Please rise in honour of the presence of the Light.

Please be seated.

Blessed is the quiet of evening and the approaching hours of sleep and rest.

(pause)

Blessed are the dreams and spirit journeys of the night which teach and nourish our deeper selves.

(pause)

Companions, let us attune with the silver light of the guardian Moon, that we may rest in peace and safety until the dawn.

Let us meditate.

OFFICER

(Gives PATHWORKING if required. Music for meditation if desired.

At close of meditation Officer goes to Altar and blesses the Chalice and then gives the blessing to first person on their left by touching them with the water on the centre of the forehead and saying the blessing, then hands them the Chalice. Each blesses the next person and hands on the Chalice)

(Blessing)

Rest in peace and safety through the night.

(When the Chalice returns to the Officer, replace it on the Altar. Extinguish one candle. Each person then extinguishes one candle in turn and hand on the snuffer)

OFFICER

(When all have returned to their place Officer says)

So is the visible returned to the invisible. All Light is one.

(Officer exits. Each exits in their own time. Officer returns and ensures all lights are safe or extinguished.)

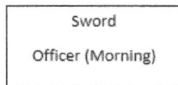

Dedication to the Light Ritual[1]

OFFICERS
Priest of the East
Priestess of the West
Guardian of the Lights
Guardian of the Sacred Fire
Guardian of the Doorway

TEMPLE ARRANGEMENTS
Chairs for stations at East, West, South, North and Doorway
Three candles on table behind station of the East
Three candles on table behind station of the West
Three candles on central altar in triangle base to west
Sacred flame at station in the north
Incense burner at station in the south
Bell and striker at doorway
Guardian of the Lights has sacred light, taper, candle snuffer and matches at station in the North
Guardian of the Sacred Fire has the incense burner at station in the South
Guardian of the Doorway has bell and striker at doorway station.

ENTRY INTO THE TEMPLE
Guardian of the Doorway admits all attending who are then seated.
When all is in readiness the officers enter as follows
Guardian of the Lights and Guardian of the Sacred Fire enter, Guardian of the Sacred Fire leading, proceed to stations and remain standing.
Priestess of the West and Priest of the East enter, Priestess of the West leading, proceed to their stations and remain standing.

Ritual

PRIEST OF THE EAST
(Gives THREE KNOCKS)

---

[1] An Opening and Closing Ritual Modified from the Rothley Ritual

GUARDIAN OF THE DOORWAY
(Responds with THREE STROKES ON BELL)

PRIEST OF THE EAST
Guardian of the Doorway - whom have you admitted?

GUARDIAN OF THE DOORWAY
(Rises)
The Priest of the East, the Priestess of the West and the servants of the light.

PRIEST OF THE EAST
From what do you guard us?

GUARDIAN OF THE DOORWAY
From the intrusion of the profane, disturbance of the Temple and from those who fear the light.

PRIEST OF THE EAST
Priestess of the West - who opens the Temple?

PRIESTESS OF THE WEST
The Priest of the East. The Priestess of the West, the Guardian of the Lights and the Guardian of the Sacred Fire.

PRIEST OF THE EAST
Guardian of the Sacred Fire - help us to prepare this Temple. Everyone please rise.

GUARDIAN OF THE SACRED FIRE
(Censing Ceremony)
> The Guardian of the Sacred Fire proceeds with Incense Burner to the East via the West and North, taking the Censer to the Priest of the East who makes the sign of blessing.
> The Guardian of the Sacred Fire then censes the East with three swings to the right, three to the left and three forwards. The Guardian of the Sacred Fire then censes each quarter in the same manner. Then returns to Station of South)

PRIEST OF THE EAST
Priestess of the West - what is the dedication of the Temple?

PRIESTESS OF THE WEST
To the Light.

PRIEST OF THE EAST
Who mediates the Light for the Temple?

PRIESTESS OF THE WEST
Three are the mediators of the Light. The Lords of Flame, the Lords of Mind and the Lords of Form.

PRIEST OF THE EAST
What are the gates of the Temple?

PRIESTESS OF THE WEST
Three are the gates of the Temple.
Illumination, intuition and consciousness.

PRIEST OF THE EAST
What are the keys of the gates?

PRIESTESS OF THE WEST
Three are the keys of the gates.
The inner mind, the intellect and the senses.

PRIEST OF THE EAST
What are the lights of the Temple?

PRIESTESS OF THE WEST
Three are the lights of the Temple.
The light invisible, the light visible, and symbolic light.

PRIEST OF THE EAST
Let the light of the Temple be revealed

PRIESTESS OF THE WEST
Guardian of the Lights - assist us to bring light to this Temple.

GUARDIAN OF THE LIGHTS
(Lights taper from Sacred Flame then proceeds to the East via the North.)

PRIEST OF THE EAST
(Waits until Guardian of the Lights reaches position at Lights in the East.)

PRIEST OF THE EAST
How then is the Temple illumined?

GUARDIAN OF THE LIGHTS
(As each group of attributes is named the Guardian of the Lights lights in turn the three candles of the East from right to left)

PRIESTESS OF THE WEST
By sight and sound and touch *(light candle)*
By reason, knowledge and thought.*(light candle)*
By limitless light, the inner light and the light of the sun. *(light candle)*

GUARDIAN OF THE LIGHTS
(The Guardian of the Lights goes to the West of the Central Altar via the South to light the three Altar candles. She lights first the single candle nearest the East, then the right hand candle nearest the West and finally the left hand candle nearest the West. Guardian of the Lights then continues to the West via South.

As each group of three attributes is named the Guardian of the Lights lights in turn the three candles of the West from right to left.)

PRIEST OF THE EAST
By inner vision, intuition and emotion *(light candle)*
By love, compassion and wisdom *(light candle)*
The teaching of dreams, the inner pathways and the light of the moon *(light candle)*

GUARDIAN OF THE LIGHTS
(Returns to station in the North)

PRIESTESS OF THE WEST
In dedication to the service of the Light and by the aid of these mediators, I turn the keys and open the gates of this Temple that all may receive illumination and serve the Light.

PRIEST OF THE EAST
I proclaim this Temple duly dedicated, opened and prepared for working.
(Gives THREE KNOCKS)
Please be seated.

Closing Ceremony

PRIEST OF THE EAST
(Gives THREE KNOCKS)
Everyone please rise.

PRIEST OF THE EAST
Priestess of the West - is the work of the day accomplished?

PRIESTESS OF THE WEST
The day's work is done.

PRIEST OF THE EAST
Then let the Temple be sealed and the light veiled.
Guardian of the Lights assist us to close this working of the Temple.

GUARDIAN OF THE LIGHTS
(Guardian of the Lights takes snuffer and goes, via the East, to the lights in the West)

PRIEST OF THE EAST
May the gates of the moon be closed and the pathways of the mind be sealed.

GUARDIAN OF THE LIGHTS
(Guardian of the Lights extinguishes the three lights of the West slowly.
Proceeds via the North to the West of the Central Altar to extinguish three candles, first left hand candle nearest West, then right hand candle nearest West and finally the single candle nearest the East. Continues to the East via the North)

PRIESTESS OF THE WEST
May the gates of the sun be closed and the pathways of consciousness sealed.

GUARDIAN OF THE LIGHTS
(Guardian of the Lights extinguishes the three lights of the East slowly and returns to station via South.)

PRIESTESS OF THE WEST
In dedication to the service of the Light and with gratitude to our mediators, I turn the keys and close the gates of this Temple that all may depart in peace.

PRIEST OF THE EAST
So be it veiled and sealed.
(Gives THREE KNOCKS.)

GUARDIAN OF THE DOORWAY
(Gives three STRIKES ON BELL.)

PRIEST OF THE EAST
Guardian of the Doorway. All may now depart in peace.

GUARDIAN OF THE DOORWAY
(Opens the door and sees all exit correctly)
Officers leave the temple in the following order.
Priest of the East exits by way of the South.
Priestess of the West exits via the North, East, South and West.
The Guardian of the Lights exits via the East, South and West.
The Guardian of the Sacred Fire exits via the South and West.
Guardian of the Doorway then sees all leave the Temple.

Altar of the East
✦ ✦ ✦

Priest of the East

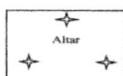

☆
Guardian
of the
Lights

✦
Altar
✦ ✦

Guardian
of the
Sacred
Fire
Incense
△

Priestess of the West

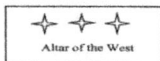

✦ ✦ ✦
Altar of the West

Guardian
Gong

The Presence of the Light Ritual

OFFICERS

Officer of the West
Officer of the East
Guardian
(It is preferable that the Officer of the East and the Officer of the West should be man and woman. It is not important which Officer takes a particular office)

REQUIREMENTS

The Temple has two rows of seats facing each other.
There is a seat in the West and one in the East for the Officers.
A central Altar, cubical if possible, covered with a dark blue cloth.
A single unlit candle on the centre Altar.
A single unlit candle at West and East.
Matches.
A taper in the East.
A candle snuffer at the East.
A tape recorder for music and tapes.
The Temple may be censed prior to the ceremony.
The Temple lighting should be as low as practicable to permit reading.

Ritual

The Officers of the West and East are seated in their places.
>*Soft music may be played for the entry.*
>*The Guardian admits all who wish to be present. All circle the Temple deosil and are seated.*
>*The music is turned off and the Guardian ensures there is total silence.*

OFFICER OF THE EAST

In the beginning naught was. Out of silence and space movement was born.
>*(Lights candle. Carrying candle in front at eye level, the Officer circles the Temple, returns and is seated.)*

OFFICER OF THE WEST
From movement was created energy. The nature of energy became an endless flowing around the circle of opposites and thus was polarity established.

(Lights candle. Carrying candle in front at eye level, the Officer circles the Temple, returns and is seated.)

OFFICER OF THE EAST
The mighty forces of the cosmos revolved in an endless spinning and creation came into being.

(Both Officers circle the Temple with lighted candles, they start together so that when the Officer of the East is in the South the Officer of the West is in the North, then they return and are seated. Timing so that both arrive back at their stations at the same time is important.)

OFFICER OF THE EAST
Being is ever luminous in the radiation of its energy, therefore the nature of creation is light.

Light is eternally becoming. From the depths of its radiance creation created the creator, who abides at the centre.

At the heart of the universe is the logos, the Holy One, whose law is omnipotent and whose Presence is Light.

(Takes light from candle with taper and proceeds to central Altar and lights the Sacred Flame. Extinguishes taper)

This flame is the declaration and establishment of the presence of Divine Light within this Temple.

(Raises both hands and holds them one either side of the Sacred Flame.)

May the Holy One who is our source and our sustainer abide with us. All light is one.

(Officer returns to the East and is seated.)

OFFICER OF THE EAST
Imaged in form in the mind of the infinite, reflections unborn, of the great cosmic dance, sparks of the light sent forth from the morning, to evolve from the darkness, to unite with the light.

Let us now join in meditation and attune with the presence of the Light.

(Appropriate music is played for at least five minutes. Turn off music)

Those who so wish may approach the altar and in silence

make their salutation and private communion with the light, standing in the west facing the east.

While they are doing so let us focus our thoughts on the Presence of the Light at our altar so that we may give and they receive.

(Music is played for this salutation. The Officer of the East sets the example. When all who wish have been to the Altar, discontinue music)

OFFICER OF THE WEST

To rise upon the planes of manifestation of our universe is not to change one's place in space - it is to change the focus of one's awareness. For all the planes exist in the same space but after another manner.

When we transfer our consciousness to the plane of mind and emotion we exist upon that plane and we become aware of its particular realities.

OFFICER OF THE EAST

At the heart of consciousness is our everlasting spirit, the spark of the divine which is the essence of our true self, the eternal traveller through all the planes of the universe and the cosmos.

We are creations of the cosmos and children of the logos.

We are one with it, and it with us, unto the completion of the universe.

By raising our consciousness from the material to the spiritual planes we become aware of the logos - and it becomes aware of us.

By silently using the mantra "I am" concentrate your consciousness into the silence and create an inner space in which you may know the touch of the Holy One.

Let us now enter the peace and the silence of meditation.

(Allow five to ten minutes for meditation in total silence)

OFFICER OF THE WEST

May the Light Eternal abide with you always.

(Short pause)

Bring your awareness slowly back to the material plane by focusing your attention on your physical body.

(Few minutes of soft music)

OFFICER OF THE EAST
(Proceeds to central Altar with candle snuffer.)

As the sun sinks in the west to close our day, so do we return this symbol of Divine Light to the greater and close this Temple.

(Extinguishes sacred flame).

The light visible is at rest, the light eternal dwells within us. All light is one.

(Returns to East)

OFFICER OF THE WEST
(Takes candle and circles the Temple deosil)

OFFICER OF THE EAST
(Takes candle and circles Temple deosil)

OFFICER OF THE WEST AND OFFICER OF THE EAST
(Both Officers circle the Temple deosil arriving in the North and South respectively at the same time. Both Officers exit on reaching the West)

GUARDIAN
(See that all depart in silence in their own time.)

Officer of
the East

ALTAR

Officer of the
West

The Children of Gaia Ritual

The Ritual is designed to invoke healing and blessing for Gaia and her children.

TEMPLE FORMAT.
The Temple plan is the Caduceus with the top in the East
The Watchers of the Heavens are at the four Cross Quarters

OFFICERS.
Four Officers of the Cross Quarters. The Watchers of the Heavens.
North East	*Aldebaran*
South East	*Regulus*
North West	*Fomalhaut*
South West	*Arcturus*

Six Star Lords.
North (East to West)
Moon
Jupiter
Venus
South (East to West)
Sun
Saturn
Mars
Two Teachers, Two Adepts, Two Illumined Ones at the Cross Points of the Caduceus
One pair at each cross point
One man, one woman at each point
Men on Pathway from the North
Women on Pathway from the South
Son of Gaia and Daughter of Gaia at the beginning of the Path of the Caduceus
Officer in the East
Hermes
Officers in the West
The Cup Bearer
Chiron
Officer of the Door
Guardian
Musician

TEMPLE ARRANGEMENTS

Stations of the Cross Quarters
Large White Candle at each Station
Stations of the Star Lords
Appropriate Planetary Candle at each Station
Stations at the Cross Points of the Caduceus
Children of Gaia
Stations at the beginning of the Caduceus
Son of Gaia (North) Daughter of Gaia (South)
Station of the East
Large White Candle
Globe candle for The Light
Station of the West
Cup for Cup Bearer
Large White Candle placed near Cup Bearer
Seating for
Hermes
The Watchers of the Heavens
The Star Lords
The Cup Bearer
The Guardian of the Door
Tables at each Station for Candles.
Caduceus for Hermes
Wand for Chiron
Gong, CD player and music for Musician
Small non-drip candles, or electric, for each participant at the West.
All the Children of Gaia and Chiron are standing.

Ritual

GUARDIAN OF THE DOOR
(Enters Temple and stands at Station.)

WATCHERS OF THE HEAVENS
(Enter Temple and are seated at Stations in the Cross Quarters.)

HERMES
(Enters and Opens the Temple. Lights the Candles of the East and West.

Lights the Candles of the Watchers of the Heavens. Lights the Candles of the Star Lords.

Is seated at Station)

MUSICIAN
(Starts music for Entry.)

GUARDIAN OF THE DOOR
(Admits all except the Officers.
All are seated North or South behind the Stations of the Watchers of the Heavens)

THE STAR LORDS
Enter in pairs
(Right)
Sun
Saturn
Mars
(Left)
Moon
Jupiter
Venus

CHILDREN OF GAIA
(Enter in pairs and walk the Path of the Caduceus each pair stopping in turn at their Station.
> *The Two Illumined Ones*
> *The Two Adepts*
> *The Two Teachers*
> *The Son and Daughter of Gaia)*

CHIRON
(Enters carrying Wand and stands at Station)

CUP BEARER
(Enters carrying Cup and sits at Station.)

MUSICIAN
(Stops music.
Strikes Gong three times.)

CHIRON
(Rises)

I, Chiron, stand Mediator for the Children of Gaia. I am

their link between the worlds, known and unknown, upper and lower, inner and outer. I am their teacher and their counsellor, the voice which speaks in the stillness of their souls. I am the voice of their inspiration and their learning.

Listen to my words, Children of Gaia, for I ask of you an account of your stewardship of earth.

Into your hands was placed power over the creatures and treasures of earth. But this was not for dominion over them. To you was given the gift of consciousness of self, the ability to reach up in mind towards the Great Light. With this gift was given a responsibility, for you are the way-showers of evolution and all the Earth treads also in your footsteps.

How say you - is all well with earth?

SON OF GAIA
Great one – I hear your voice. Much have we learnt of Earth, the land is fruitful at our bidding and we have found treasures of great worth for our use and enjoyment.

Great are our cities and the works of our hands and of our minds. We have harnessed the energies of Earth which serve us at our command and to our will all creatures are subject.

DAUGHTER OF GAIA
Great one - I hear your voice. Mighty indeed are the works of men and women. We have learnt to conquer sickness and the mortal ills of humankind. Life comes at our command and death stays its hand at our will.

CHIRON
Great indeed are your achievements - but I ask again - is all well with Earth?

SON OF GAIA
To all things there is a price. From Earth we have taken such as we needed and now we are learning that these things are not limitless. But the ingenuity of our technology will provide as we require.

CHIRON
These things are of your material world, you speak not of the

spirit and the soul - therefore I ask again - is all well with Earth?

DAUGHTER OF GAIA
Great one - the soul of mankind sleeps and only the few are awake in the night. Ignorance and prejudice rule in the land and the Teachers of men walk no longer in our midst. We would seek that knowledge which is a Light in the darkness but know not where it may be found. Great one - we ask it from you.

CHIRON
Children of Gaia - I have spoken to your sages in the silence of meditation, I have inspired your poets and your song-makers. Through the voice of religion have I reached out to you and in the sanctuary of your hearts have I walked.
Yet is my voice as a whisper upon the wind and only the faintest echo from your hearts returns to me.

SON OF GAIA
Great one - we have heard your voice and followed your precepts, yet would we seek further and follow the quest for the attainment of higher consciousness that we too may become of your stature.

DAUGHTER OF GAIA
Great one- from rock to plant, from animal to man, the creatures of Earth have sought long for their destiny. We as their representatives plead for your aid and your guidance, that we may find the way and lift all of earth into the higher realms of spirit. Show us the way that we may no longer dwell in the darkness, open the pathways before us that we may enter the Kingdom of Light.

CHIRON
My children, that which you ask is not mine to give. My teaching have I given to you and the Light which I carry have I shone upon you. More than this you must seek from those who are to me as I am to you.

SON OF GAIA
Great One - we know not these Mighty Ones, neither do we

know the pathways which approach their realms. It is to you that we look to show us the way.

DAUGHTER OF GAIA
Together we plead for your assistance. Will you be our mediator and take our request to the Mighty Ones?

CHIRON
(Pauses as if to consider the request.)
This I will do. I will approach the Mighty Ones and ask their help for the Children of Gaia.

CHIRON
(Makes the Journey to the Mighty Ones, going first to Fomalhaut, then Aldebaran, next Regulus and finally Arcturus.)

CHIRON
(Facing Fomalhaut)
Mighty One - I bring greetings from the Children of Gaia.

Much have they learnt of Earth and many are their accomplishments in mastering their environment. But now they would seek further and wish to find the way to higher consciousness. They would lift all that is Gaia to the next plane of manifestation. Mighty One, I come bearing the request of the Children of Gaia for your aid in their quest.

FOMALHAUT
Brother - I, Fomalhaut, stand Watcher of the Heavens.

My task is to ensure the inheritance of the generations and the continuity of all things.

I cannot give you that which you seek - you must go elsewhere.

CHIRON
(Facing Aldebaran)
Mighty One - I bring greetings from the Children of Gaia. I come from our brother Fomalhaut seeking your aid for the Children of Gaia in their sacred quest, will you aid them?

ALDEBARAN
Brother - I, Aldebaran, stand Watcher of the Heavens.
My task is to energise the Universe and to watch over the cycles of being.

I cannot give you that which you seek, you must journey further.

CHIRON
(Facing Regulus)

Mighty One - I bring greetings from the Children of Gaia.
I come from our brother Aldebaran seeking your aid for the Children of Gaia in their sacred quest. Will you aid them?

REGULUS
Brother - I, Regulus, stand Watcher of the Heavens.

My task is to govern the pathways of the Cosmos. Mine are the forces of change and of fortune. I cannot give you that which you seek - you must go onward.

CHIRON
(Facing Arcturus)

Mighty One - I bring greetings from the Children of Gaia.

I come from our brother Regulus seeking your aid for the Children of Gaia in their sacred quest. Will you aid them?

ARCTURUS
Brother - I, Arcturus, stand Watcher of the Heavens.

My task is to see that all functions in order and honour. I cannot give you that which you seek - ask it of the Star Lords for they influence the destiny of humankind.

CHIRON
(Returns to the West then makes the Journey to the Star Lords in the following order: Venus, Jupiter, Moon, Sun, Saturn, and Mars.)

CHIRON
(Facing Venus)

Sister Venus - I come as messenger for the Children of Gaia. Long have they laboured to master the lessons of Earth and in this they have achieved much. Now would they learn also the lessons of the spirit and in the learning lift themselves and all Earth nearer to the Source of all Being. All that I know I have taught them but this is not adequate to their need. From the Watchers of the Heavens I have sought guidance but they could not give me what I sought.

Lady, I come to you seeking your aid for the Children of Gaia in their sacred quest. Will you aid them?

VENUS

The Children of Gaia have drunk long of my cup. The lessons of the senses have I taught them and under my influence have they learnt the pleasures of the arts and of beauty. With me they have known the warmth of companionship and the passion of lovers. In giving them of pleasure, luxury and contentment I have brought them all of which I know - that which you now seek I cannot give to you - ask it of my brother Jupiter.

CHIRON
(Facing Jupiter)

Brother Jupiter - I come to you from our sister Venus seeking your aid for the Children of Gaia in their sacred quest. Will you aid them?

JUPITER

I have brought growth and stability to the Children of Gaia. Under my influence they have learnt the power to create and build their reality. I have taught them the strengths of philosophy, religion and idealism. If these do not fulfil their need there is nothing more I can give to them - ask it of my sister the Moon.

CHIRON
(Facing the Moon)

Sister Moon - I come from our brother Jupiter seeking your aid for the Children of Gaia in their sacred quest. Will you aid them?

MOON

Mine is the gateway to the inner mind and along my pathways have the Children of Gaia found the well-spring of their quest.

Through memory and instinct have I taught them and in the depths of their beings I have awakened their sensitivity and receptivity. Through the swirling images of imagination and vision have I led them to the doorway of the inner worlds.

These things have they learnt of me and there is nothing more I can give to them, if they need still more, ask it of my brother the Sun.

CHIRON
(Facing the Sun)

Brother Sun - I come from our sister the Moon seeking your aid for the Children of Gaia in their sacred quest. Will you aid them?

SUN

From my substance were Gaia and all of her children created. I pour forth the life energy which sustains them and by my will their growth and fertility endures.

In my light have they found their dignity and nobility and their souls have seen me as a mirror of the gods. My power I give them forever and my warmth and vitality shines upon all. I have lit the path of their childhood and their maturity - if they now need more I cannot give it - ask it of my brother Saturn.

CHIRON
(Facing Saturn)

Brother Saturn - I come from our brother the Sun seeking your aid for the Children of Gaia in their sacred quest. Will you aid them?

SATURN

Under my influence the Children of Gaia have learnt patience and caution, they have understood the virtues of order, steadfastness and discipline.

I have shown them the consequences of their actions and they have come to accept these as their own responsibility. My power is severe and my justice impartial. I have taught them the meaning of hardship and they have found the strength which grows from its endurance. With my teaching they have accepted their own sovereignty and walked free of the limitations imposed upon them by outgrown authority. I have prepared them, but what they seek now I cannot give them - ask it of my brother Mars.

CHIRON
(*Facing Mars*)
    Brother Mars - I come from our brother Saturn seeking your aid for the Children of Gaia in their sacred quest. Will you aid them?

MARS
The desire of the Children of Gaia to move and to change springs from my influence upon them. I have awoken their assertiveness and fired them with my energy and strength. They have learnt my lessons well and now reach out to further achievement. They know the essence of driving action and with bold and ardent spirit demand now our response and our aid. Yet have I given them all that I have and so must answer you - they need to look higher for that which they seek.

CHIRON
(*Returns to the West*)

CHIRON
Children of Gaia - I have sought long and far to aid you in your quest. From the Watchers of the Heavens and the Lords of the Stars have I asked aid for your cause. These mighty ones have given of their wisdom and their knowledge to the utmost of their power, yet do I bring you nothing from my journey. I cannot aid you further. In this quest you must follow your own wisdom and seek your own answers from on high.

CHIRON
(*Takes Cup from the Cup Bearer and takes it to the Son and Daughter of Gaia giving it to the Son of Gaia.*)
    Take this cup, the symbol of the receptive mind and seek those among you who can walk closest to the Light. Ask of them that they will aid your quest.
    (*Returns to West*)

THE CHILDREN OF GAIA
(Walk the Path of the Caduceus to the Two Teachers.)

SON OF GAIA
Speaking to the Teacher (Man)

Wise One - you have shown us the way of the sages and taught us the thoughts of the philosophers. We have studied the ancient traditions and read deeply of the writings of the wise ones. We have followed the dogma of religion and sought in great temples for the truth. Yet are our hearts empty - fill our cup that we may drink of the waters of higher knowledge.

TEACHER (Man)

All that we know of the adepts we have taught you. We have spoken to you of tradition and all the recorded knowledge of mankind. If this still leaves an emptiness in your soul we cannot give you what you seek - you must go higher.

SON OF GAIA
(Turns to Daughter of Gaia and gives her the Cup.)

The ways of the intellect no longer fulfil our need, I give to you this cup that you may ask for that which we seek with the voice of intuition.

DAUGHTER OF GAIA
(Takes Cup and gives it to the Teacher (Woman)

Wise One - I give this cup into your keeping and ask that you will journey further with it and seek the source from whence it may be filled.

TEACHER (Woman)
(Takes Cup and both Teachers walk the Path of the Caduceus to the Two Adepts. The Son and Daughter of Gaia remaining in the place of the Teachers.)

TEACHER (Woman)
(Speaks to the Adept (Woman)

Holy One - we have taught the Children of Gaia all that we know and the pupils have become as knowledgeable as the teachers. We would go higher together and seek that knowing which brings the flowering of higher consciousness. I bring this cup as the symbol of our quest and would ask you to fill it from your wisdom that we may partake of your enlightenment.

ADEPT (Woman)

All that we know of the Illumined Ones we have taught you. The ways of the inner worlds have we made plain to you and given into your hands the tools of imagination and meditation.

We have lived among you as hermits and holy ones and taught you by our example. Nothing more remains that we can teach you, if you seek more - you must go higher.

TEACHER (Woman)

(Turns to Teacher (Man) and gives him the Cup)

The ways of the wise no longer fulfil our need. I give you this cup that you may ask for that which we seek with the voice of the spirit.

TEACHER (Man)

(Takes Cup and gives it to the Adept (Man)

Holy one - the Children of Gaia and their teachers seek to go higher than your knowledge, will you take this cup and seek the answers to our need?

ADEPT (Man)

(Takes the Cup and both Adepts walk the Path of the Caduceus to the two Illumined Ones. The Two Teachers remaining in the place of the Adepts.)

(Speaks to the Illumined One (Man)

Blessed One - we have taught the Children of Gaia and their Teachers all that we know of wisdom. We come now as their representatives asking that you will share with us your vision and fill this cup that we too may come to the end of our quest and drink of the shining draught of Illumination.

ILLUMINED ONE (Man)

Our Brothers and Sisters - all that you need for your quest you already know. The pathways of Illumination are open before you and the keys of the doors are in your hands. If then you are still unable to penetrate the veil of understanding we cannot further assist you - you must go onward.

ADEPT (Man)
(Turns to Adept (Woman) and gives her the Cup.)
The ways of the Illumined Ones remain closed before us. I give you this cup that you may ask for that which we seek with the voice of the soul.

ADEPT (Woman)
(Takes Cup and hands it to the Illumined One (Woman).)
Blessed One - into your hands we entrust this cup. The Children of Gaia, their Teachers and Adepts ask that you seek the last key which they still lack and open the realms of the Shining Ones before them.

ILLUMINED ONE (Woman)
(Takes Cup and the two Illumined Ones complete the Path of the Caduceus and stand before Hermes.)

ILLUMINED ONE (Woman)
(Facing Hermes)
Sacred One - hear our plea from your place in the realms of Light. The Watchers of the Heavens and the Lords of the Stars bade us seek the pathways of our quest within ourselves. This we have done and still our quest is not ended. Now do we as the representatives of the Sons and Daughters of Gaia, their Teachers, Adepts and Illumined Ones come to thee seeking thine aid.

Hear our plea, fill our cup from the starry wisdom and light our way with the Fire of Heaven.

ILLUMINED ONE (Women)
(Gives the Cup to Hermes)

HERMES
I am Son of the Sun and Messenger of the Gods.
I am the Communicator and the Initiator.
If it is your will to know of the Mysteries then must I fulfil my function and bring to you the Light of the Most High.
Say then what do you seek?

ILLUMINED ONE (Man)
We seek the way to higher consciousness for all of Earth.

HERMES
How do you seek this?

ILLUMINED ONE (Woman)
By working on ourselves, by learning the lessons of Earth and understanding that all experiences do but teach. Thus do we gain our freedom from the pain and disappointments of life, knowing that these are but chains which bind us only by our will.

HERMES
Where then do you seek the way?

ILLUMINED ONE (Man)
We seek it in all life and in the centre of ourselves.

HERMES
When do you seek?

ILLUMINED ONE (Woman)
From the past, though the present and into the future which are all in the ever-moving now.

HERMES
Why do you seek?

ILLUMINED ONE (Man)
Because we have discovered the existence of our true selves. We have seen the peace which sleeps in our depths and heard an echo of wisdom from on high. We have walked in the shadow of the Great Ones and a ray of the Great Light which shines at the heart of all has shone upon our souls.

HERMES
How then do you seek?

ILLUMINED ONE (Woman)
By dedicating ourselves to the quest.

HERMES
My children you have spoken well.
By this knowledge you have placed your feet upon the pathways to higher consciousness.

ILLUMINED ONE (Man)
Sacred One - we come to you seeking the key which will open the doorways before us.

HERMES
My children - the name of the key is love and emblazoned upon the doorway is service.

Above all, it is by caring and dedication to each other that you grow.

Go forward in company, be to each other a support and a solace. Share your lives in tolerance and understanding. Claim your freedom and your victory and in so doing become as guardians and as guides to those who are the younger Children of Gaia.

Know my children that you are Gaia and Gaia is you. You create Gaia even as you are created of her. You are the little creation within the greater creation and your little will is but a part and a reflection of the greater Will of Gaia.

Seek not for your individual progress but blend with and become part of the evolution of all.

Know this in your hearts, for to accept this truth, to live it and become part of it, is to love with a sacred and holy love that is a singing in the heart and a celebration of life.

My gift to you is - that you need none - for you already possess all. Your love is the love of the Most High and your light is the Light Eternal. Let them shine forth, for this is the way, the quest and the grail.

I, as messenger of the Most High, give unto you the blessing, the healing and the love of the Eternal.

Go forth and carry this Light for humanity and for Gaia.
(*Lights the globe candle which becomes THE LIGHT.*)
So let it begin.

MUSICIAN
(Starts music.)

HERMES
(Pauses until music has played for a few moments, then lifts THE LIGHT and comes forward in front of Station.)

ALL CHILDREN OF GAIA
(The Illumined Ones, the Adepts, the Teachers and the Children of Gaia step apart to leave a space for Hermes to walk down between them.)

HERMES
(Carries THE LIGHT, held high, forward down the centre between the Two Illumined Ones. He passes between the Two Adepts then the Two Teachers and the Son and Daughter of Gaia

Reaching the Cup Bearer, Hermes hands THE LIGHT to her, bows and then turns and walks back between the four pairs behind him and is seated at his Station.)

CUP BEARER AND CHIRON
(When Hermes has returned to his place the Cup Bearer and Chiron take THE LIGHT to each person. The Cup Bearer carrying THE LIGHT and Chiron the small candles. Each person lights their candle from THE LIGHT. They take their LIGHT in the following order;
Children of Gaia
Teachers
Adepts
Illumined Ones
Star Lords starting at the Sun and ending at the Moon
The Watchers of the Heavens starting at Regulus and ending at Aldebaran.
All others participating. Ending in the East in front of Hermes.
The Cup Bearer and Chiron return to the West between the Children of Gaia and lead the procession out.)

THE CHILDREN OF GAIA
(When the Cup Bearer and Chiron reach the West the Children of Gaia, the Teachers, the Adepts and the Illumined Ones form the procession behind them.)

THE STAR LORDS
(The Star Lords pass in front of Hermes and join the procession in pairs)

THE WATCHERS OF THE HEAVENS
(The Watchers of the Heavens pass in front of Hermes and join the procession)

ALL
(All others come from the North and South East to meet in front of Hermes and join the procession)

MUSICIAN AND GUARDIAN
Join the procession as the last person passes)

CUP BEARER
(THE LIGHT is carried to some appropriate place where the candles can be placed safely and remain burning)

HERMES
(Remains in the Temple to close and extinguish the Candles then depart.)

The Children of Gaia Ritual Plan

The Path up the Caduceus

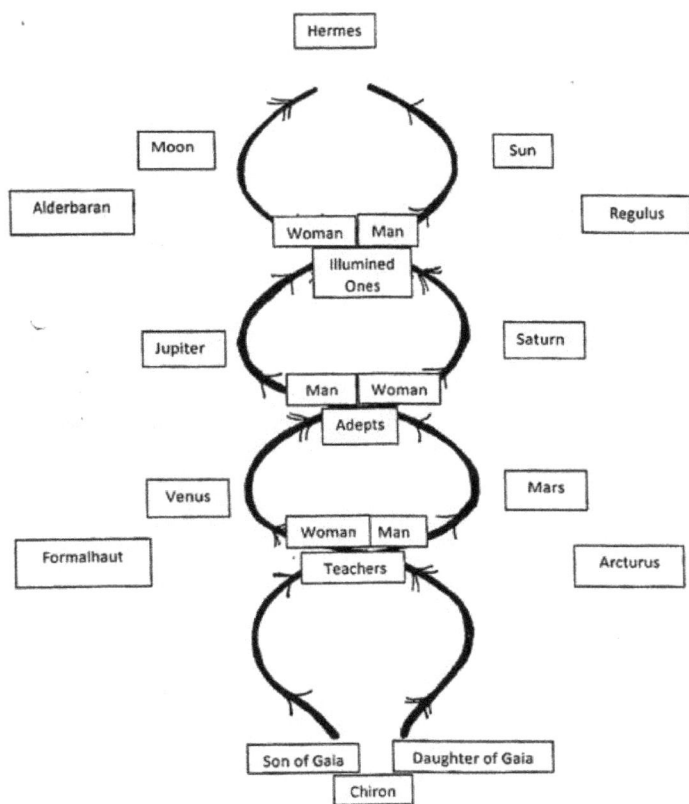

Hermes

Moon

Sun

Alderbaran

Regulus

Woman | Man

Illumined
Ones

Jupiter

Saturn

Man | Woman

Adepts

Venus

Mars

Woman | Man

Formalhaut

Teachers

Arcturus

Son of Gaia

Daughter of Gaia

Chiron

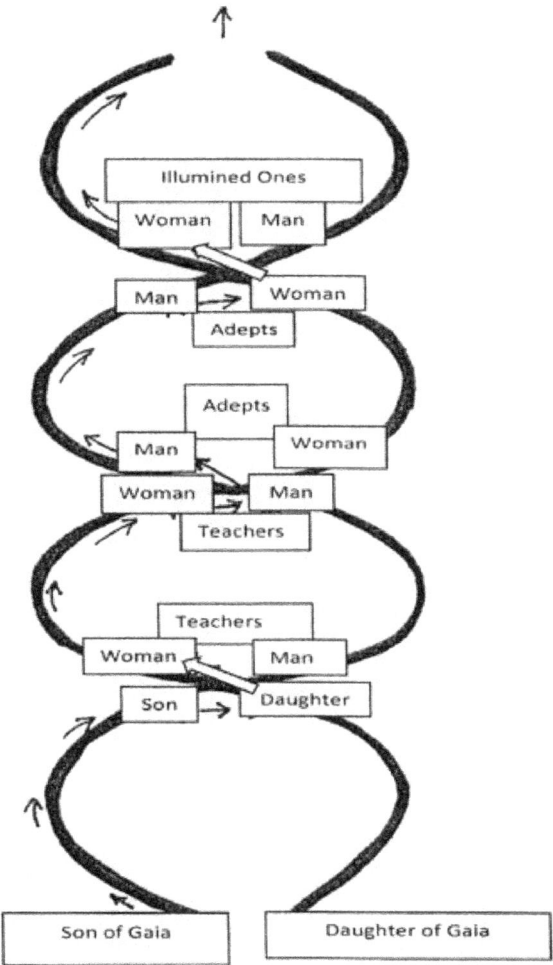

The Children of Gia

Plan for the Passing of the Cup

Illumined Ones
Woman | Man

Man | Woman
Adepts

Adepts
Man | Woman

Woman | Man
Teachers

Teachers
Woman | Man

Son | Daughter

Son of Gaia | Daughter of Gaia

The Cosmic Parents Ritual

<u>OFFICERS</u>
All Father
All Mother
Orator

Sun	*Gold*	*Male*
Mercury	*Yellow/Gold*	*Neutral*
Venus	*Green*	*Female*
Earth	*Deep Pink*	*Female*
Moon	*Pearly Pink*	*Female*
Mars	*Red*	*Male*
Asteroids		*Male/Female*
Jupiter	*Deep Blue*	*Male*
Saturn	*Blue Pearl*	*Male*
Uranus	*Purple*	*Male*
Neptune	*Deep Green*	*Male*
Pluto	*Black*	*Male*

Musician
Guardian
Each Planet has a Voice who speaks on their behalf.

<u>REQUIREMENTS</u>
Screen with translucent curtain before All Father and All Mother
Kneeling cushion
Stands and hanging lights, blue candles for these
Veils for all the Officers of the Planets in appropriate colours
Gong
Sword
Mirror (approximately 10inch diameter round)
Staff
Two matching jugs or Trident
Pomegranate
Music and player
Music: The Armed Man. A Mass for Peace by Karl Jenkins.

Entry	*The Armed Man*
Blessing	*Agnus Dei*
	Sanctus
Exit	*Benedictus*

Ritual

(Temple lights are low. Seats for the All Father and All Mother are behind translucent screen, before them is a kneeling cushion. On either side of them are hanging lights.

The translucent screen is either open or can be parted in the centre so everyone passes between them)

GUARDIAN
(Enters and takes station just inside doorway)

MUSICIAN
(Enters and turns on music for entry)

ALL FATHER AND ALL MOTHER
(Enter together, circle the Temple, and proceed to their places and are seated.

They sit back to East facing West, All Mother at the left hand of the All Father)

PLANETS AND ASTEROIDS
(Enter in order; each circles the Temple and is seated. Each waits for the previous Officer to be seated before entering; except for the Asteroids, who enter together.

Order of entry is Sun, Mercury, Venus, Earth, Moon, Mars, Asteroids, Jupiter, Saturn, Uranus, Neptune, Pluto.

All the Planets are veiled.)

(NOTE. The Voices of the Planets sit among the Asteroids and move with them.)

ORATOR
(Enters last, circles the Temple and is seated)

MUSICIAN
(Allow the music to play for a few minutes after all are in place to allow the Temple to settle and quieten then turn off music)

ORATOR
Behold. I am the Voice of the One.

I was, am and will be. I am Chaos and Order.

I dwell in the Un-manifest, from whence I stretch forth my hand to create.

I bring forth form from the formless and inscribe My Will upon the vast canvas of space.

I am Mind; my thoughts and my memory are the Laws of Life and of Form.

My right hand is the All Father and my left hand is the All Mother.

They are the two powers of the circle of becoming.

They are the instruments of My Will and the parents of My Creation.

ALL FATHER
I am the right hand of the One, I hold the reins of the positive potential within the Un-manifest.

ALL MOTHER
I am the left hand of the One, I hold the reins of the negative potential within the Un-manifest.

ALL FATHER
I am Power – Let us create manifestation.

ALL MOTHER
I am Love – Let us create manifestation.

MUSICIAN
(Loud and long roll on the gong)

ORATOR
Behold, the Children of my Children. They dance in the spinning spirals of the galaxies.

VOICE OF THE SUN and SUN OFFICER
(When the Voice of the Sun speaks The Sun Officer rises, raises hands to level of eyes, both palms facing outwards in gesture of blessing. Stays at Station but slowly rotates as if radiating power to all)

I am the Voice of the Sun.

I am the first born of the first born, the source and the sustainer of the created.

I am the fluid Fire of becoming and the frozen particles of space.

All things are of my essence and come forth from me, as it was in the beginning and shall be unto the end.

I am the Eternal Lord of the Heavens and the God of a thousand names.

I have been called by the name of Amun, of Osiris, Ptha and Ra. I was Adonis, Apollo and Adonai. Also Brahma, Mithras and Bel. I am Sol Invictus.

I am born as the Child of the Morning, blaze in glory as Lord of the Noon, I descend in the west and pass to my rest in the deep dark halls of Annwn.

I am winged as the Lion of the East, wield the sword that is raised for the right, I am glory and power and the day-time star and the God of all things of the Light.

(Officer of the Sun is seated)

VOICE OF MERCURY and OFFICER OF MERCURY

(When the Voice of Mercury speaks the Officer of Mercury rises, raises hand to side of mouth, palm outwards in gesture of speaking and circles round the Sun Officer as if speaking a message to all)

I am the Voice of Mercury.

I am the swift traveller of the Universe. I cling close to my source and hasten ever to return to my beginning.

I am both male and female and also the eternal child.

Mine are the powers of intercession and intelligence. I mediate between the above and the below.

My wings are upon the feet of all messengers and communicators.

My powers are also of the trinity, formed with Sulphur and Salt, which is that of the creative essences concealed within the mantle of manifestation. I speak of the hidden mysteries in all things.

Harken to my message for I am the bearer of the secrets of my Parents.

(Officer of Mercury is seated)

VOICE OF VENUS AND OFFICER OF VENUS

(When the Voice of Venus speaks the Officer of Venus rises, holds out arms, hands towards each other as in a gesture of embracing all and

circles round the Officer of the Sun and Officer of Mercury)

I am the Voice of Venus.

I am the Star of the Morning and of the Evening, I accompany the rising and the setting of my Lord the Sun.

I am Aphrodite, Ishtar and Isis. Yet am I also Lucifer and Quetzalcoatl, for I am the lover <u>and</u> the beloved.

As Goddess I arose from the foam of the sea and I am as a guiding star and a beacon to those who sail upon the deep.

I tie the sweet knots of love which both bind and set free – for the lessons of life are learnt by my joys and the deep cutting thrust of my knife.

Embrace me even as I embrace you.

VOICE OF EARTH AND OFFICER OF EARTH.

(When the Voice of Earth speaks the Officer of Earth rises, points upwards with the right hand and downwards with the left hand and circles round the Officers of Sun, Mercury and Venus)

I am the Voice of Earth.

I am the womb and the cradle of Life. Upon my breast all living things are nourished and thrive.

I am Gaia, the blue jewel floating in the dark sea of space.

I am love and beauty and grief,

I am gentle and violent and cruel.

I am the mystery of mysteries for I am fertile in the midst of a barren waste.

Mine are the seas and sky, the mountains, valleys and plains. Mine are the flowers and the trees and all creatures great and small.

My children are the vehicles and the teachers of Consciousness for I am the seed ground of the Gods.

(Officer of Earth is seated)

VOICE OF THE MOON AND OFFICER OF THE MOON

(When the Voice of The Moon speaks the Officer of The Moon rises, holds aloft the circular mirror in one hand and circles round the Officers of Sun, Mercury, Venus and Earth)

I am the Voice of The Moon.

I am the Mistress of Time and of Tides, my face is the mirror of the Sun by which he illumines the deep shadows of Earth.

My light waxes, blossoms and wanes, I am the three aspects of the Mother; Maiden, Mother and Crone. I am Artemis, Selene and Hecate also Diana, Herah and Danaa.

Mine are the rhythms of growth and fertility and the depths of emotions, instincts and the dark side of the sub-conscious.

Yet too is mighty Thoth under my influence and the words and shapes of your minds.

I am sleep and the dreams of the night, yet too when my face is veiled by day, I bring waking dreams also and the wisdom which flashes in intuitions spark.

I am the subtle powers of nature's life and you ebb and flow to my will.

(Officer of the Moon is seated)

VOICE OF MARS AND OFFICER OF MARS

(When the Voice of Mars speaks the Officer of Mars rises, holds at carry the sword in one hand and circles round the Officers of Sun, Mercury, Venus, Earth and Moon)

I am the Voice of Mars. I am the Warrior and I wield the sword of the Mighty Ones.

I am fire and blood and conflict – my way is fierce and brutal and dangerous.

Yet I also defend and protect.

I am the Lord of will-power, passion and courage.

My ways are those of discipline and organisation. Though I destroy yet do I also create.

I protect the weak, defend the right and my sword is before all who tread the long Path of the Light.

(Officer of Mars is seated)

ALL VOICES AND VOICES OF THE ASTEROIDS

We are the Voices of the Asteroids.

We are neither suns nor planets but fragments of the one that was.

We are as you are, separate and individual yet together forming a body of the One.

We know your separation and your aloneness. Yet do we also know your company and your unity. As you form the body of humanity on Earth so do we form the Belt of the Asteroids, eternally circling in company within the confines of our orbit.

We are numerous as the tongues and races of men, we too are large and small, bright and dark, important and insignificant.

We bear the names of the great ones of fable, myth and legend, we are the small mirrors of your history and also the potential for your destruction.

VOICE OF JUPITER AND OFFICER OF JUPITER

(When the Voice of Jupiter speaks the Officer of Jupiter rises, making gestures as of giving to right and left in royal manner circles round the Officers of Sun, Mercury, Venus, Earth, Moon and Mars)

I am the Voice of Jupiter.

I am the Mighty One of the Mighty Ones, the Great One of the Heavens.

Noble, stately and slow is my progress through the mansions of the stars. I am the Year Star for I reside long in my passing and return to my beginning only at the twelfth re-birth of the Sun.

I am Father of the Father Gods for I was ancient before I was Marduk and Zeus.

I am the fire of Earth and of heaven, mine is the fire and the roar of the thunderbolt.

I bring expansion, generosity and warmth to the nature of humanity. My influences are jovial, self-confident and generous.

I am the Law Give and the Regulator.

I am Judgement and Power – I am Deus Optimus Maximus.

(Officer of Jupiter is seated)

VOICE OF SATURN AND OFFICER OF SATURN

(When the Voice of Saturn speaks the Officer of Saturn rises and, leaning on staff, circles round the Officers of Sun, Mercury, Venus, Earth, Moon, Mars and Jupiter.)

I am the Voice of Saturn.

I am the Lord of Time and of Fate.

I turn the slow wheels of the heavens and mark the brief span of your life.

I toss the dark dice, form the patterns of life and spin the chance wheel of your fate.

I am darkness and winter and endings, I am Death and the

ceasing to be.

I am bondage and limits and binding, yet the cut of my scythe sets you free.

In the darkness and depth of the winter, my feast is abandoned and wild.

Rejoice, celebrate, eat drink and be wild, for the sun is re-born as a child.

I am Death and the great winged Dragon, who is guard of the door between worlds.

I stand at the gate where eternity waits, when you pass beyond space and time.

(Officer of Saturn is seated)

VOICE OF URANUS AND OFFICER OF URANUS

(When the Voice of Uranus speaks the Officer of Uranus rises, holds one hand as if to hide his face and circles round the Officers of Sun, Mercury, Venus, Earth, Moon, Mars, Jupiter and Saturn.)

I am the Voice of Uranus.

I am the concealed one who walks in the dark depths of space, eccentric and long is the path of my journey. I am the ancestor of the gods and Lord of the Primordial Sky. I came forth from Gaia the Earth Goddess and with her I created the giants of a hundred hands, Cyclops of the single eye and the mighty Titans.

My children found not favour in my heart and into the depths of the underworld I thrust them, all but Cronus who then most cruelly wounded me.

I am the Lord of the twists and turns of fate, my ways are eccentric, mobile and impulsive. Yet do I also govern the independence and inventiveness of humanity.

Remember me for I was there in the beginning and will be even unto the end.

(Officer of Uranus is seated)

VOICE OF NEPTUNE AND OFFICER OF NEPTUNE

(When the Voice of Neptune speaks the Officer of Neptune rises and holding the two jugs or Trident circles round the Officers of Sun, Mercury, Venus, Earth, Moon, Mars, Jupiter, Saturn and Uranus)

I am the Voice of Neptune.

I rule all realms of water, I govern the rivers, lakes and

seas.

Mine is dominion over the vast oceans and I hold the reins of the tides and build the mountains and troughs of the waves.

I am the Earth-shaker and also Poseidon, I was sire to the winged horse Pegasus, I ride on the storm tossed surf and gallop my white horses on the crest of the foam topped sea.

I am storm and the silver mirror of the ripple-less sea when becalmed.

I am shallows and depths of the oceans floor and the calm of the peaceful lagoon.

I am vapour that rises as cloud, I am rain and sweet streams and the deep hidden spring of the life giving waters of wells.

I am the Lord of the Deep for I dwell in the dark depths of outer and inner space. Mine are the worlds of dreams, I bring delusion, illusion and knowledge. I am the Way-shower into psychic reality and higher perception. I am the steed of the soul – ride me.

(Officer of Neptune is seated)

VOICE OF PLUTO AND OFFICER OF PLUTO

(When the Voice of Pluto speaks the Officer of Pluto rises and holding a Pomegranate, circles round the Officers of Sun, Mercury, Venus, Earth, Moon, Mars, Jupiter, Saturn, Uranus and Neptune)

I am the Voice of Pluto.

I am the hidden one, for no eye may see me directly, nor glimpse my face, for I wear the mask of invisibility.

I am Lord of the Underworld, King of Hades and ruler of the Land of the Dead.

If you will – seek for the entrance to my realm in the dying light of the West – enter my dark halls through the clefts and caverns of Earth.

Few come willingly to my domain for all must pass the great dog Cerberus who guards my gate and pay Charon the ferrymen to cross the river Styx.

Some who come I banish to dark Tarterus and some may pass to the blessed realms of Elysian's fields.

On which path shall I send you?

(Officer of Pluto is seated)

ORATOR

Let us relax and allow our minds to dream.

Look at your body, feel it from the inside, be IN it. Feel the space from your feet to the top of your head.

This is your Earth vehicle, your space ship which enables you to live on this planet.

Your eyes are the windows of the ship, your arms and legs the tools it works with, your brain the computer that governs its workings.

But we want to look at the energies behind the physical vehicle, the subtle laws and forces that underlie our bodies and the creation of the world.

Feel these energies and patterns within you. Feel the beat of your heart, which keeps the life giving blood circulating, the in drawn breath and exhalation that fills you with the forces of life.

Think about all those hidden automatic activities, which go on day after day keeping you fit, healthy and active. Think of the powers, which make these things happen.

Now expand your awareness to the room in which you sit – the landscape in which this room is situated – the country you are living in, where it is on the Earth's surface – then to the sphere of the Earth itself. Try to feel the energies which keep all of this working and in its place.

Now expand your awareness to the solar system of which Earth is a part. Look down on it and see the Sun shining in the centre, slowly turning on its own axis. See the planets orbiting the Sun, each of its own colour, in its own position and place in the pattern, think about the energies of these planets and the influences they have on each other. Watch this mighty pattern and see the small blue jewel of the heavens that is our home.

Now expand your awareness to the galaxy of which we are a part, see the vast swirling disc of stars and planets. Draw back your viewpoint so that you can see other galaxies of all patterns and shapes, each one composed of immense numbers of stars and planets, perhaps having some which are similar to our own solar system.

Now expand your awareness to the Limitless Space in which these galaxies are suspended, feel the hidden energies which hold them in their places. Let your mind's eye look deeper and deeper into this limitless space, finding no end but expanding endlessly into eternity.

Now find the point within your own consciousness, which is observing this immensity, and within that point seek that which knows and recognises your own essence and where it belongs. Seek your energy source in the vastness of space. Know where you belong and allow yourself to resonate with it, this is the place you have always known of, it is the home you have always felt exiled from and to which you long someday to return. This is the energy source we instinctively KNOW exists, this is the energy we personify as Gods.

This energy is our All Father and All Mother. Allow yourself to feel their presence enfolding and surrounding you.

(pause)

Slowly become aware of your connection with your physical vehicle and gradually bring your consciousness back into it. You may remain aware of your contact with your Cosmic Parents, however when you feel a touch on your physical vehicle be ready to come back into the Temple and continue our ceremony.

MUSICIAN
(Turns on the music for The Blessing)

ORATOR AND GUARDIAN
(Orator and Guardian now act as conductors, gently touching each person and making sure they are centred before asking them to rise, then taking each person in turn to the All Father and All Mother for their blessing and returning them to their place.
Orator goes for the last blessing)

ALL FATHER AND ALL MOTHER
(When each person approaches, indicate they should, if possible, kneel before you.

All Father and All Mother join hands and with their other hand, each holds the hand of the person in front of them so that a triangle is formed.

All Father and All Mother speak two lines each, alternating who begins, to each person, they should look into each person's eyes as they do so)

Behold, we are the Eternal Trinity.

You are a cell in the Mind of God, immortal, eternal and radiant.

Know this and carry our Light into the world.

With this touch receive our blessing.

(Conductor comes forward and indicates recipient should rise and returns them to their place. This is continued until all have received the blessing)

MUSICIAN
(When Orator and Guardian have returned to their places, and Orator indicates, turn off the music)

ORATOR
So have we touched and felt the presence of our Cosmic Parents. Know that they dwell ever within you and you abide in their Love.

Now it is time for us to enfold our knowledge of our Divine Source once more within us and draw across our consciousness the veil of protection which shields our earthly being from too much knowledge and too much Light.

Bring the focus of your consciousness back to the earth sphere, then downwards into your physical body on the earth plane. Awaken and open your eyes.

OFFICER OF PLUTO
(Rises and removes veil)
I am Pluto, I give you my blessing of Immortality.

OFFICER OF NEPTUNE
(Rises and removes veil)
I am Neptune, I give you my blessing of Inner Vision.

OFFICER OF URANUS
(Rises and removes veil)
I am Uranus, I give you my blessing of freedom in the Inner Places.

OFFICER OF SATURN
(Rises and removes veil)
I am Saturn, I give you my blessing of long life.

OFFICER OF JUPITER
(Rises and removes veil)
I am Jupiter, I give you my blessing of expansion and power.

OFFICER OF MARS
(Rises and removes veil)
I am Mars, I give you my blessing of my protecting sword.

OFFICER OF MOON
(Rises and removes veil)
I am Moon, I give you my blessing of true dreams.

OFFICER OF EARTH
(Rises and removes veil)
I am Earth, I give you my blessing of the Mystery of Life.

OFFICER OF VENUS
(Rises and removes veil)
I am Venus, I give you my blessing of earthly love.

OFFICER OF MERCURY
(Rises and removes veil)
I am Mercury, I give you my blessing of the unravelling of my Secret.

OFFICER OF SUN
(Rises and removes veil)
I am Sun, I give you my blessing and my Light.

MUSICIAN
(Turn on Exit music)

ALL MOTHER AND ALL FATHER.
(Rise and come forward in front of the screen, pause hand in hand)

ALL
(Rise as the Cosmic Parents appear in front of screen and remain standing.

Officers of the Planets turn and face the Asteroids in the South when the Cosmic Parents begin their process.

As the Cosmic Parents pass each Officer of the Planets in the centre the Officer turns and faces the Asteroids on the other side of the Temple so they are always facing the Cosmic Parents who pass between them and the Asteroids)

ALL MOTHER
I am the All Mother, I give you my blessing and my Love.

ALL FATHER
I am the All Father, I give you my blessing and my Love.

ALL MOTHER AND ALL FATHER
(Both walk forward together between the two lines, starting in South, they pass between the Asteroids and Officers of the Planets, they smile and gesture their blessings as they pass, they circle the Temple one and half times then exit)

EXIT
(Orator leads out the Officers of the Planets followed by the Asteroids. The Musician and Guardian exit)

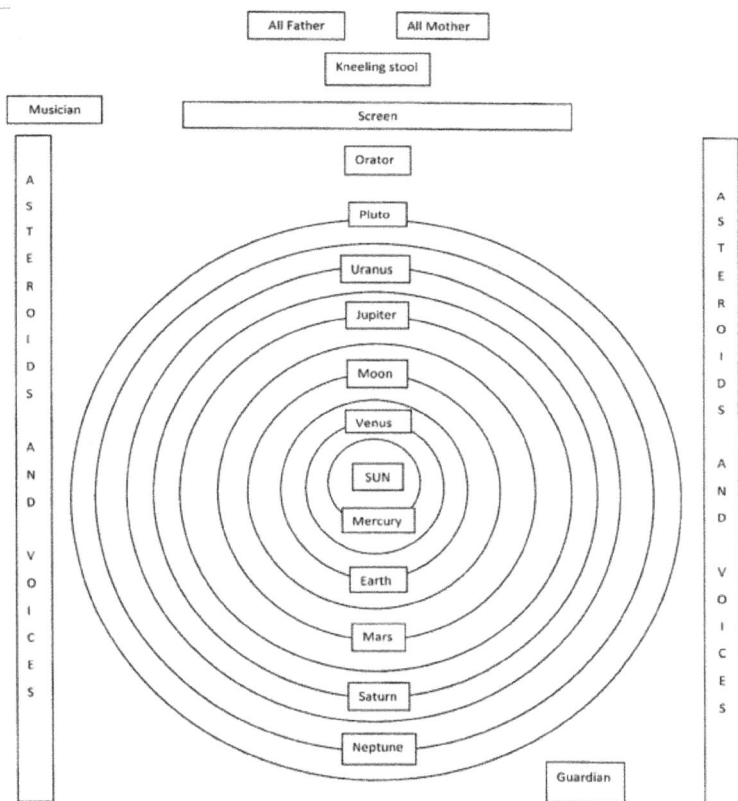

All Father   All Mother

Kneeling stool

Musician   Screen

Orator

Pluto

Uranus

Jupiter

Moon

Venus

SUN

Mercury

Earth

Mars

Saturn

Neptune

Guardian

ASTEROIDS AND VOICES

ASTEROIDS AND VOICES

Doorways of the Mind Ritual

OFFICERS
Keeper of the Door of the Temple
Keeper of the Door of the Sanctuary
Keeper of the Door of the Mind
Keeper of the Door of the Spirit
Keeper of the Door of the Soul
Musician

REQUIREMENTS
Banner for behind the Keeper of the Door of the Soul
Sword for Keeper of the Door of the Temple
Sword for Keeper of the Door of the Sanctuary
Book for Keeper of the Door of the Mind
Chalice and scented oil for Keeper of the Door of the Spirit
Lighted lamp for Keeper of the Door of the Soul. Also night lights, one for each Traveller and taper
Small table in front of each Officer of the Doors
Candles and holders, matches and snuffers for each Officer of the Doors.
Tape recorder
Music

Ritual

KEEPER OF THE DOOR OF THE TEMPLE
Enters, having seen all participants are ready prior to entering the Temple and instructed them on their entry.

Switch on music. Sanctum Sanctorum Track One

Stands in front of chair facing doorway sword held at carry, it may be placed on the small table when necessary.

Officers enter in order, Keepers of Doors of Sanctuary, Mind, Spirit, Soul carrying their sword, book, cup and lamp respectively and are seated, placing their emblems on the small table.

(Lights station candle)

Will the first traveller please approach the door of the Temple.

(Travellers come forward one at a time and stand in front of the

Keeper of the Door of the Temple

Ask questions when they are standing in front of him/her. Each must answer the following questions.)

Who are you who comes to this Holy Temple?

What do you bring with you?

Will you travel to the end of the journey?

(When satisfactory answers are given)

It is good, the password to gain access through the Door of the Sanctuary is – *(whispers password in ear)* – proceed now upon your journey.

(Travellers take any seat in north or south side.

Entry is continued until all have been admitted.

Switch off music.

Seals the Temple doorway)

Keeper of the Door of the Sanctuary, all have been admitted and the Temple is secure.

KEEPER OF THE DOOR OF THE SANCTUARY

It is well. This sacred Sanctuary must also be safely guarded so that all may proceed in peace.

(Rises.

Lights station candle.

Faces East.)

In the East I ask the protection of mighty Raphael, may he spread his wings about us and make our memory clear.

(Faces South)

In the South I ask the protection of mighty Michael, may he spread his wings about us and his sword be our defence.

(Faces West)

In the West I ask the protection of mighty Gabriel, may he spread his wings about us and awaken our intuition.

(Faces North)

In the North I ask the protection of mighty Auriel, may he spread his wings about us and keep us strong in our resolve.

(Faces West, points upwards)

Above us I ask the protection of mighty Metatron, may he spread his wings about us and bring us the Grace of the Most High.

(Points downwards)

Below us I ask the protection of mighty Sandalphon, may he spread his wings about us and keep safe the gates of our bodies.

(Is seated)

Our Sanctuary is now sealed and we may work in safety within.

This is our secure space within the physical realm, here we may allow our bodies to rest and our minds to enter the deeper inner realms of consciousness.

I ask you now to relax and allow your thoughts to quieten and look inwards.

You see an inner image of this sanctuary and become aware of the presence of the Keeper of the Door of the Mind. If you would travel deeper you must pass this Keeper. In your mind see yourself rise and go before the Keeper of the Door of the Mind who looks up at you enquiringly. You are asked to give the password you were given by the Keeper of the Door of the Temple, you lean forward and whisper it in the ear of the Keeper who looks down at the book, checks against your name then nods his/her acceptance of the correctness of the password. You move forward towards the door behind the Keeper of the Door of the Mind and as you do so it swings open and you pass through.

KEEPER OF THE DOOR OF THE MIND
(Rises. Lights station candle and is seated)

Welcome Traveller in the realm of mind. This hall, which you see about you, represents your thinking intelligence and I am the Keeper of the Door of the Mind. I will be your guide until you find that which you seek.

See, within this hall there are many doors. Here there is one that leads to the room of learning, if you enter here you may explore all the practical knowledge that has been accumulated on earth. Here is the store of what is known in science, in medicine, in architecture, in building and all the many skills, which are required in the outer world. Is this the doorway you would choose?

Come, walk a little further, here is another door, this one leads to the knowledge of the arts, of painting, sculpture and all the manner of ways in which humanity can beautify and enrich the world. If you enter here you can become skilful in these things, if not in this lifetime in some future life because of the choice you make to enter this door now.

The next door leads to the healing arts, the skills of doctors, surgeons, nurses and those who minister to the many ills of the human body.

All around this hall are many more doors, each leading to a different path through life, to different skills and vocations.

There are too, doors which lead to illusions, dead ends and false pathways. Their doors appear enticing and full of promise of sensual delights, but the sweetness grows sour and the fruits are bitter upon the tongue. Avoid these doors if you are wise.

Some doors lead to gratification of self and inflation of the ego, while others lead to selfless service; look well at the symbols upon the doors, they will assist you in your choice. Choose now which door you will enter, go within and explore what lies beyond.

(Several minutes of music. Sanctum Sanctorum Track Two)

It is time now to come back into my hall. Finish anything you may be doing, remember what you have seen and the choices you have made within the room you entered. I will meet you in the hall when you are ready.

(Pause)

I ask each of you now to come before me in your mind and tell me which door you chose, I will record your choice in my book as you record it in your memory.

(Pause)

The doors of this hall lead to many experiences, some of which we look back on with sorrow or regret. Yet all experiences are but lessons upon the way and it is not good that you should carry burdens once the lessons are learned. Allow me to assist you in leaving those burdens behind, think for a moment what it is you carry in sorrow or regret, then if you will, lay your burden down in my keeping, go free of it, and walk on to the hall of spirit.

(Pause)

Come now, the Keeper of the Door of Spirit awaits you, I bid you farewell, may your choices always bring you rich experiences.

Now you approach the Keeper of the Door of Spirit.

KEEPER OF THE DOOR OF SPIRIT

(Rises Lights station candle and is seated)

Welcome Travellers to my hall, this is the place of awareness of the worlds of the spirit. From here you may awaken to inner experiences and learn how to use the techniques of the subtle realms.

Around this hall are many doors, come, let us explore before you choose.

Here is a door named Seers, if you choose this door you will learn how to use far sight and know of things far distant from you in time and space. You may become a guardian of the Temple who watches on the inner planes, or a messenger for those who cannot travel of their own will.

See, this door here is named Priest and Priestess, within this door you may learn the ways of ritual and how to bring through power to some stated purpose. This door leads to the place where Shamans and Magicians learn their skills, perhaps it was here that Merlin trained or tribal Wise Woman or Medicine Man learnt to walk the pathways of the dreamtime or to climb the ladders whose rungs are knives.

Another door leads into the school where mediums and those who work in trance are trained to provide a voice for intelligences who have no physical form. This is a path fraught with dangers and one that requires a very skilful teacher. Perhaps you would prefer to learn of dowsing, to be able to find water, minerals or other things not visible to mortal eyes; or the skills of psychometry or accessing to learn how to find hidden knowledge of the history of objects or places. All these things and more you may learn of from this hall. Make your choices and you will set your course towards learning these things. Yet it may be you have already learnt of all these things and are ready in your turn to open the door upon which is written the one word: Teacher. Entering this door will commit you to many, many other learning experiences, it will demand every last drop of your energy, time, knowledge, experience and dedication. Think well before you enter here for in doing so you offer up in service your present and your future lives.

Look well at the names upon the doors, then having made your choice go within and explore what lies beyond. But remember, knowing is not always joyful, it can be painful, frustrating and dangerous. Be sure you are willing to pay the price before you travel further, there is no disgrace in discretion and self- knowledge, if you are not yet ready pause a while in my hall, for be sure the time will come when you will find yourself once more before the doors.

(Several minutes of music. Sanctum Sanctorum Track Three)

It is time now to come back into my hall. Finish anything you may be doing, remember what you have seen and the choices you have made within the room you entered. I will meet you in the hall when you are ready.

(Pause)

I ask each of you now to come before me in your mind and tell me which door you chose. Then drink from my cup that your memory may be blessed and clear. These doors are the means of access to those skills which material men think do not exist, learning mastery of these hidden abilities will not always be a blessing or a joy. There will come times when you know, when it is painful or dangerous to know, when another's destiny is clear before your eyes, yet there is nothing you can do to turn away the sword of fate; but there will come times too when your heart will sing because of the Light you have learnt to shine upon another's path.

Come now the Keeper of the Door of Soul awaits you. I bid you farewell, may you always be blessed in the path you choose. Now you approach the Keeper of the Door of Soul.

KEEPER OF THE DOOR OF SOUL
(Rises, Lights station candle and is seated)

Welcome Travellers to my hall. This is the place of awareness of the soul. Here you may touch the deepest part of yourself, that immortal self which is a spark of the Divine. This spark is what you are, it is what remains when mortal bodies return unto the Earth from which they sprang

Your soul is where your consciousness dwells, it carries your memory from life to life and links you to your source within the depths of inner space. There are many doors within my hall, each one leads to a different path, a different technique by which the soul can grow. Beyond the doors of my hall you can find teachers, guides and inner contacts who have no form on earth but dwell within the inner Light. Theirs are the ways of inner teaching, by dreams and visions, intuition and the whispers of that small inner voice which speaks to us in the silence of the mind.

Upon the doors are written, mystic, magician, devotee and many more, each one marked by the colour of its ray. The paths beyond the doors may be solitary or you may walk the way in company. They may follow well marked paths along the ways of religion and established schools, you may meet an inner plane teacher who takes you within their care, or you may venture forth alone into the unknown, treading your own path of discovery and exploration. Having come this far you will know the choice which suits you best but remember, we can change our path, retrace our steps and explore a different way, but in the end each one will arrive at the same destination, the knowledge of ourselves and the full flowering of our inner rose. Choose now your door, pass through and spend some time learning a little of what lies ahead.

(Several minutes of music Sanctum Sanctorum Track Five)

It is time now to come back into my hall, slowly withdraw from your own experience and come back to join me once more.

(Pause)

As we gather here in the Hall of Soul a subtle change begins to occur, the walls about us look less solid, they begin to softly glow as if illuminated from behind and then their outlines shimmer and blend. Behind each wall there slowly emerges a shining figure, then in all their splendour and majesty, about us stand the Winged Man, the Winged Lion, the mighty Eagle and the Winged Bull. They guard the entrance to the Realms of Light, their wings reach upwards, touch and form a shining circle beyond which shines a greater Light. Slowly we move upwards and pass through the circle, about us is only Light, in our consciousness is a great knowledge of our oneness with the Light, each other and all creation.

(Several minutes of music Sanctum Sanctorum Track Six)

Begin to feel the presence of the Hall of Light drawing you back down from the realm of Light, slowly you descend, the Holy Living Creatures once more about you, then they too fade and the walls of the hall become solid once more.

Let the memory of your visit to these high realms return with you into your material worldly existence. Allow the memory to sustain and nourish your inner life and know that you have briefly touched the realm of your true home. Beyond the ties of time and space, beyond the hold of form and force, beyond the span from birth to death, beyond the world of joy and grief, your soul's eternal journey brings you back to dwell once more within the hollow of your Creators hand.

(Pause)

Now is the time for your return back into the outer realms, allow yourself to centre back in the Hall of Souls, come before me in your mind that I may give you my blessing, then walk through the doors, back into the Hall of Spirit and see the doors of my hall gently close behind you.

(Extinguish station candle)

KEEPER OF THE DOOR OF SPIRIT

Welcome back Travellers to my hall. Your journey is nearing its completion, come now before me that I may give you my blessing, then walk through the doors, back into the Hall of Mind and see the doors of my hall gently close behind you.

(Extinguish station candle)

KEEPER OF THE DOOR OF MIND

Welcome back Travellers to my hall. Lock the memory of your journey securely where you may return to it any time you choose. Now come before me that I may give you my blessing, then walk through the doors, back into the Sanctuary and see the doors of my hall gently close behind you.

(Extinguish station candle)

KEEPER OF THE DOOR OF THE SANCTUARY

Welcome back Travellers to the Sanctuary. You have journeyed deep into the inner realms, may its blessing remain with you. Come now before me that I may give you my blessing to take with you back into your life in the world. The journey is over, let us seal our Sanctuary in peace and safety.

(Rises.

Faces East)

In the East I thank mighty Raphael for his protection and gift of clarity of memory, may he fold his wings and seal our Sanctuary.

(Faces South)

In the South I thank mighty Michael for his protection and his sword held in our defence, may he fold his wings and seal our Sanctuary.

(Faces West)

In the West I thank mighty Gabriel for his protection and the gift of intuition, may he fold his wings and seal our Sanctuary.

(Faces North)

In the North I thank mighty Auriel for his protection and for giving us strength, may he fold his wings and seal our Sanctuary.

(Faces West, points upwards)

Above us I thank mighty Metatron for his protection and for bringing us the Grace of the Most High, may he fold his wings and seal our Sanctuary.

(Points downwards)

Below us I thank mighty Sandalphon for guarding the gates of our bodies, may he fold his wings and seal our Sanctuary.

Our Sanctuary is now closed and sealed. Keeper of the Door of the Temple, unseal the doorway that all may depart in peace.

(Extinguish station candle)

KEEPER OF THE DOOR OF THE TEMPLE

(Unseals the door of the Temple)

Keeper of the Door of the Sanctuary the door is unsealed, all may now receive their blessings and depart into the outer world.

(Extinguish station candle)

(Start music. Novus Magnificat Track One

Beginning with the Traveller nearest the north-east, everyone goes to each of the Keepers of the Doors to receive their blessing and then exits the Sanctuary. After the last from the north side has left the Keeper of the Door of Soul the south side begin with the Traveller nearest the south-east.)

Blessings of the Keepers of the Doors are;

KEEPER OF THE DOOR OF SOUL, *gives lighted night light to each*

KEEPER OF THE DOOR OF SPIRIT, *blesses each on forehead with scented oil.*

KEEPER OF THE DOOR OF MIND, *touches finger to lips with sign of silence and bows to Traveller.*

KEEPER OF THE DOOR OF THE SANCTUARY, *touches each lightly on head with tip of sword.*

KEEPER OF THE DOOR OF THE TEMPLE, *stands at door, sword at carry, and bows to each Traveller as they leave.*

When all Travellers have departed the Officers leave in order Keeper of Doors of Soul, Spirit, Mind, Sanctuary and Temple.

Keeper of the Door of the Temple ensures all candles and lights are safely extinguished.

Doorway of the Mind Ritual Plan

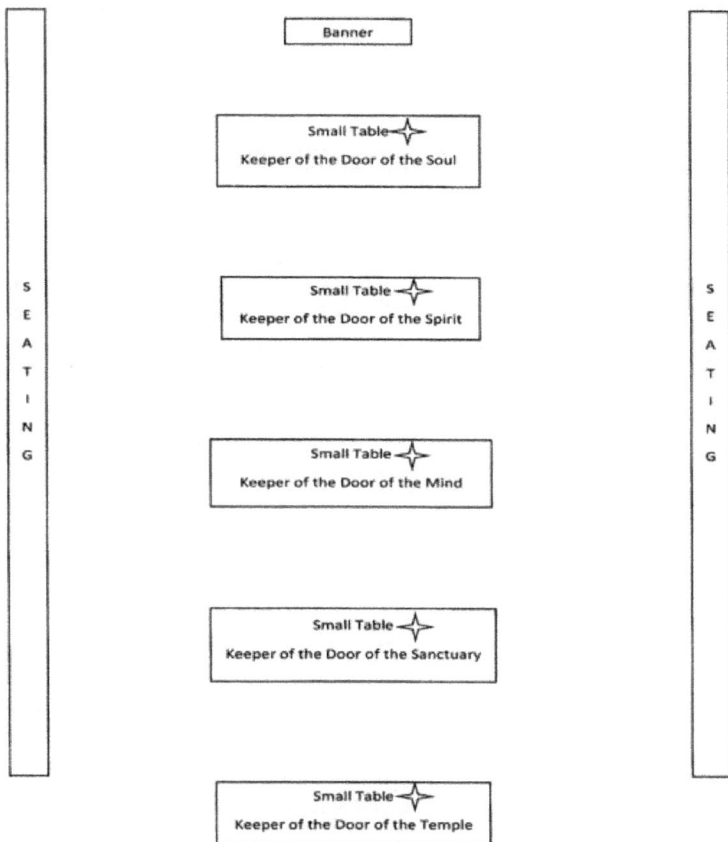

Banner

Small Table

Keeper of the Door of the Soul

Small Table

Keeper of the Door of the Spirit

Small Table

Keeper of the Door of the Mind

Small Table

Keeper of the Door of the Sanctuary

Small Table

Keeper of the Door of the Temple

S
E
A
T
I
N
G

S
E
A
T
I
N
G

Dream Ritual

OFFICERS

West: Lady of the Night, black veil, female
East: The Transformer, yellow veil, male
South: The Life giver, green veil, female
North: The Wise Man, black veil male
South west: Lady Venus, blue veil, female
North west: The Protector, red veil, male
North east: Lady Moon, silver veil, female
South east: Sirius, white veil, male
Guardian

TEMPLE ARRANGEMENT

There is a central altar with eight white candles arranged in an eight sided star pattern, point to the east, around a silver star with small sacred light in centre.
There is a taper and candle snuffer on altar.
The appointed officer has a pack of tarot cards.
The room is as dark as possible to commence.
All officers except the guardian are veiled in the colour of their station.
All officers are seated at their stations.
There is soft haunting music playing.

Ritual

All Officers are veiled and seated at their Stations.
> *Soft, haunting music is playing.*
> *Light is as low as possible.*

GUARDIAN

(Admits all others participating and remains at station near door throughout.
> *Music is allowed to continue until the atmosphere is quiet and still.*
> *When music stops all Officers rise at a signal from Officer in the West. They move forward to central Altar. Starting with the Officer in the West they light the eight candles in turn in a clockwise manner. When the candles are lit they all turn together and return to their*

119

stations, pausing until all are ready they are seated at the same time.
All Officers remain seated and do not stand when speaking)

LADY OF THE NIGHT
From the point in the West of the fading day, from the first deep shadows of night, I call forth the light of the moon and the stars and the arch of the Milky Way.

THE TRANSFORMER
From the point in the East of approaching night, where the darkness is velvet and deep, I call forth the rest of the end of the day and the folds of the mantle of sleep.

THE LIFE GIVER
From the point in the South of the highest arch, on the path of the wandering stars, I call forth the threads that destiny weaves with the force of the planets' powers.

THE WISE MAN
From the point in the North of the polar star, the hub of the heavens wheel, I call forth the strength of the northern Bear to guard, to guide and to seal.

LADY VENUS
From the South West point of the evening star, the beacon of love and of hope, I call forth the Queen of the twelve star crown who rules the way of the heart.

THE PROTECTOR
From the North West point of the Eagle's star, from the depths of unchanging space, I call forth the Lords who guard in the night to turn their eyes to this place.

LADY MOON
From the North East point of the rising moon, the silver queen of the night, I call forth the depths of the hidden mind and the visions of inner sight.

SIRIUS
From the South East point of the radiant one, great star of

wisdom and light, I call forth the keys which open the gates to the realms of dream and of night.

APPOINTED OFFICER
(The Officer now says that the purpose of this ritual is to bring a waking dream that will be uplifting and instructional in whatever way each person needs or desires. As a key to the dream a Tarot card may be used. The Officer takes a card at random from the pack. This card is then named and described in detail to set the scene for the Dream. Music may be played or silence maintained for a period not longer than fifteen minutes.

At the close of the Dream period the Officer recalls everyone to the Temple, everyone is then invited to share the content of their dream and to state what they have learned.

Music may be played for a short time)

SIRIUS
From the South East point of the mystic star, which shines on the door of dream, I take back the keys and fasten the gates of the inner lands we have seen.

THE LIFE GIVER
From the point in the South on the planets' path, when the zenith of night is passed, I draw forth the veil of the wakening day and the lights of the darkness are masked.

LADY VENUS
From the South West point in the shining ring, of the zodiac's blazing stars, I ask that love's power will abide with us still through the coming daylight hours.

LADY OF THE NIGHT
From the point in the West where the shadows fly and the last of the night will fade, I prepare the place of eternal rest where the old and the past are laid.

THE PROTECTOR
From the North West point of the Eagle's star, as the heavens fade to sleep, I thank the Lords of the watch of the night and bid them depart in peace.

THE WISE MAN
From the point in the North of the guarding bear where the night and the day are as one, I bid him return to his ancient ways with our thanks for his service done.

LADY MOON
From the North East point where the night hours end and the mind begins to wake, I seal the depths of the moon's domain and bid you all awake.

THE TRANSFORMER
From the point in the East of the dawning day, in the rising splendour of light, I close the night paths of the deep inner mind and open the way of the day.

(All Officers rise together and go to central Altar. Starting with Sirius they extinguish the eight lights in turn, leaving the centre Sacred Light burning. All turn together and return to their stations. The Lady of the Night exits and all follow her, circling the Temple to do so.)

GUARDIAN
(Sees all exit quietly in their own time.)

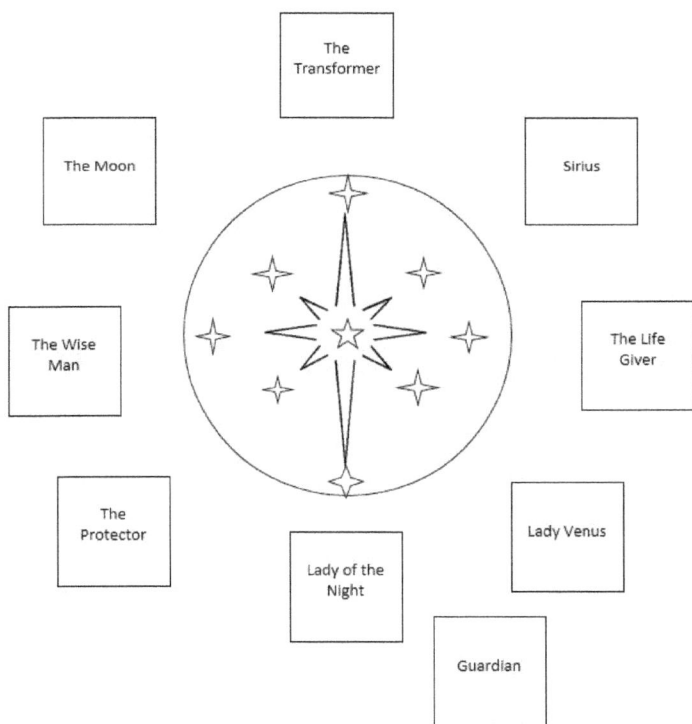

The Transformer

The Moon

Sirius

The Wise Man

The Life Giver

The Protector

Lady Venus

Lady of the Night

Guardian

The Galactic Ritual

The Temple is arranged as per the attached plan.
Room lighting should be as low as possible consistent with being able to
read the scripts.

<u>OFFICERS</u>
Musician
Time
Space
Earth
Sun
Moon
Mercury
Venus
Mars
Jupiter
Saturn
Uranus
Neptune
Pluto
Milky way
Sirius
Formalhaut
Vega
Arcturus
Aldebaran
Regulus
Antares
Betelgeux
Andromeda
Triangular galaxy
Small Megallanic cloud galaxy
Large Megallanic cloud galaxy
The Superclusters   gold veil
The Great Walls   gold veil
The Great Attractor   black veil

REQUIREMENTS
CD player
CD music
Gong
Two gold veils
One black veil
Dark blue screen, or curtains, behind the Great Attractor
Tripod lights for either side of The Great Attractor
Small tables for Sun and Milky Way
Two large candles, one each for Sun and Milky Way
Ten smaller candles also on Sun table
Twelve smaller candles also on Milky Way table
Shoulder capes for EARTH, MOON, THE SUN AND MILKY WAY
Two Candle snuffers, one on Sun table one on Milky Way table
Singing bowl or bell.

Ritual

MUSICIAN
(Enters and lights the two lights on either side of the Great Attractor and The Sun and Milky Way large candles. Switch on music)
TIME *and* SPACE *enter and stand either side of the doorway.*
THE GREAT ATTRACTOR *enters and is seated.*
The two side columns enter in twos, order as follows;

SUPERCLUSTER	*THE GREAT WALLS*
SMALL MEGALLANIC CLOUD	*LARGE MEGALLANIC CLOUD*
ANDROMEDA GALAXY	*TRIANGULAR GALAXY*
ANTARES	*BETELGEUX*
ALDEBARAN	*REGULUS*
VEGA	*ARCTURUS*
SIRIUS	*FORMALHAUT*
NEPTUNE	*PLUTO*
SATURN	*URANUS*
MARS	*JUPITER*
MERCURY	*VENUS*

(The centre column enter in order)
MILKY WAY
THE SUN
MOON
EARTH

(All except the Great Attractor remain standing until everyone is in the Temple, taking their lead from Earth everyone is then seated)

NOTE. Everyone remains seated when speaking, only rising to light the candles.

(If there are more attending than the number of Officers, the remainder join with the Galaxies or Megallanic Clouds, they speak the parts together)

MUSICIAN
(Allow the music to play for a few minutes to let the Temple settle then switch off music.)

TIME
(Strikes gong loudly and slowly twelve times)

I am the holder of the Gates of Time. I measure the minutes, hours, days and years of your life. I count the eternal journeys of your planet Earth as it spins through the heavens and follow its yearly path around your Sun. I am the recorder of your history and the brief span of humanities existence upon Earth.

Know that I am the creation of your perception, for your days and your nights exist only at the place where you stand. For to the Sun it is always day upon Earth and from the depths of space it is eternal night. I am an illusion beyond the little span of your lives, know this and I will set you free of my bonds, for behold your consciousness is unbounded and unlimited and your thought may journey to the outermost reaches of the Universe. A thought has no speed of travel, it is thought and it is known – yea even to the outermost galaxy in the heavens.

(Strikes gong loudly and slowly twelve times)

SPACE
I am the holder of the Gates of Space. I give you height and depth and length, I build for you the three dimensions of Earth. I mark the separations between you and define your measurements of your world. I am those places that you think empty and which appear to separate your Earth from all other heavenly bodies. I am the distance between two hands reaching out to each other in love and friendship, and I am also the vast dark secret depths of the sky into which you gaze, seeking

companionship in your aloneness.

Mine is the barrier which limits your explorations of the physical Cosmos, yet are my pathways open to the seeking of your spirit.

EARTH

I am Planet Earth, I am your Home and your parent. You are born of my substance and sustained by my abundance. I am your vehicle, which carries you as travellers through the cycles of the solar system.

I nurture you and provide for you. Everything in your life and your existence is a part of me, you are my children and my pupils. For in my school I teach the great lessons of life: your joys and your sorrows, your successes and your failures, are but stages and necessities for your growth. Treasure and respect me as I treasure and respect you, and wake and sleep in my embrace.

SUN

I am the Sun, the Parent of your Parent. I am the pivot of your celestial journey, I hold the thread which binds you and holds you to your place in the heavens. Your day is marked by my coming and your night is the dark which follows my going. I am warmth and light and life. I determine your times and your seasons and I am the arbiter of your destiny.

About me circle your Brothers and Sisters who are also my children and my light and power sustains them even as it sustains you.

I have been worshipped as your God and honoured as the Logos who guides your spirit. I am the great Radiator of Light but I am not the God of all Gods.

My Light illuminates all within its radiance, yet too my beams travel ever onward towards the depths of the Cosmos and an alien eye on an unknown world.

Come, let us build a vessel of thought that you may go forth and seek another mind that knows, another world wherein a spirit dwells, another soul who reaches out to seek and touch and know, that in the vastness of what Creation is, they do not live alone.

I give you my sunbeams to travel on, the hidden powers of

my spiritual energies to expand your awareness and the love which binds us to be a beacon to guide you back home.

(Rises and lights one candle on Sun table and returns to place)

MOON

I am Moon, child of Sun and of Earth. I turn my face ever towards you that the light of my Father may yet shine in your darkness when the night falls upon you.

I am the regulator of the concealed tides of your world, I govern the plants growth and the cycles of your lives. I draw the deep waters towards me and govern the ebbs and flows of your seas.

Mine are the things of mystery and the deep pools and wells of the mind. I bring you intuition and insight and access to the subtle worlds of the soul.

I give you light in the dark for your journey and the knowing that knows without thought, I watch at the gate which guards vision and fate and welcomes you home at the dawn.

(Rises and lights one candle on Sun table and returns to place)

MERCURY

I am Planet Mercury, sibling of Moon and Earth. I spin the closest to our parent Sun and I am known as the swift one of the heavens. I am the Messenger of the Gods so I give to you for your journey the power of communication, the ability to remember and to record for others those things you will see and learn.

(Rises and lights one candle on Sun table and returns to place)

VENUS

I am Planet Venus, sibling of Mercury and Earth. My path is the closest to my sister Earth in whose sky I am the Morning and the Evening Star. At all times and in all places have I been the bringer of hope and of love, for I am the Lover and the Beloved. I am the star which shines eternal in the heavens, the symbol of the sure victory of the human spirit.

I give you for your journey the love that binds and strengthens, so that my love may shine brightly between you and be as a guiding star within your heart.

(Rises and lights one candle on Sun table and returns to place)

MARS

I am Planet Mars, sibling of Venus and Earth. I am the first of the planets beyond my sister Earth and the most like her in family resemblance. I am known as the Red Planet for I shine with that hue in your skies. I have been known as the Bringer of War and am the associate of all who fight and who follow the Path of the Warrior.

Yet do I give you for your journey not strife but the sword of protection and the fearless heart of the warrior to wield it should you have need.

(Rises and lights one candle on Sun table and returns to place)

JUPITER

I am Planet Jupiter, sibling of Mars and Earth. I am the largest planet of our family so it is fitting that I have been called the Father of the Gods. I am Lord of the thunderbolt and wielder of heavenly fire, they who walk in my realm need a strong mind, arm and heart. I also rule the faculties of the abstract mind and the expansion of understanding, therefore I give you for your journey wisdom to understand what you see and hear and the courage to go into the unknown.

(Rises and lights one candle on Sun table and returns to place)

SATURN

I am Planet Saturn, sibling of Jupiter and Earth. I turn the wheel, which governs your fate and sift through the sands of time. My scythe gathers in the harvest of years and I bind you with age and the weight of the years.

Though the cycles of time turn beauty to age and everything crumbles to dust, yet my circles still grace the form of my face as I turn at my own slow pace.

I give you for your journey patience to persist in it.

(Rises and lights one candle on Sun table and returns to place)

URANUS

I am Planet Uranus, sibling of Saturn and Earth. I am the ancestor of the gods and Lord of the Primordial Sky. Deep and dark and mysterious are my ways, I govern the twists and turns of your fate and the impulsive ways in which you move and act and live.

I give you for your journey the independence of spirit which prompts you to make it.

(Rises and lights one candle on Sun table and returns to place)

NEPTUNE

I am Planet Neptune, sibling to Uranus and Earth. Mine are all the moistures of Earth, the seas, the lakes, rivers and streams. I am rain and the fresh morning dew. I am the moisture in air and the prism of the rainbow.

I am in all of the cells of your body, I am your life blood and all your fluids, without me no life can exist, know this and respect me. I am the blessing of Earth that is given to no other of our sibling planets, keep me pure and clear. I am too the Way-shower into psychic reality and higher perception so I give you for your journey access to my pathways.

(Rises and lights one candle on Sun table and returns to place)

PLUTO

I am Planet Pluto, sibling to Uranus and Earth. I rule in the dark places of Earth, mine are the caverns and caves, the realms of those who know not the light, yet I know too of the strange beauty that lies hidden within those depths.

I dwell in the remote cold dark regions of space, far away from the warmth of our parent Sun, yet the key to the blessed realms of the Elysian Fields is in my keeping. Take my key upon your journey and open with it the doors you seek that the unknown may become the known.

(Rises and lights one candle on Sun table and returns to place)

MILKY WAY

I am the Milky Way, the galaxy which is the Parent of your Parents' Parents. I am the vast spiral of stars and planets and dust of which your Sun family is an eternal part. You travel the Cosmos in my company, I spread my arms wide and embrace two thousand thousand million stars, together we spin a mighty dance about our dark mysterious centre whose power hold us to our place.

I am the soft glow which arcs across Earth's dark night sky, I am your vast extended family, I am the nursery of your past, your present and your future.

Look to the siblings of your Sun, the bright stars of my family and ask their blessings upon your journey.

SIRIUS

I am the Star Sirius, sibling of your Sun, you see me in the constellation of Canis Major.

So vast is our galaxy that though I am your nearest neighbour, my light travels eight and a half light years to reach your Sun. Since the time before the before time I have graced your skies. My rising heralded the coming of the life giving waters to the fields of ancient Kem. My light was sacred to the Lady Isis and kissed the feet of the gods in the hidden depths of sacred temples.

For your journey I place you in the care of my Lord Anubis, he who knew me when the world was young.

(Rises and lights one candle on Milky Way table and returns to place)

FORMALHAUT

I am the Star Formalhaut, sibling to your Sun. You see me in the constellation of Pisces Australis, the great Fish of the southern skies.

My light travels twenty-two light years to reach your Sun. I am one of the four ancient Royal Stars and have been placed as one of the Watchers of the Heavens.

I will keep watch upon your journey and light your way.

(Rises and lights one candle on Milky Way table and returns to place)

VEGA

I am the Star Vega, sibling to your Sun. You see me in the constellation of Lyra which is named for the great lyre which Apollo gave to Orpheus long ago.

My light travels twenty-six light years to reach your Sun.

I am named for the swooping eagle who dives through the sky with swept back wings and comes as a messenger from other realms.

I will accompany you upon your journey and guard you with my keen far sight.

(Rises, lights one candle on Milky Way table, returns to place)

ARCTURUS

I am the Star Arcturus, sibling to your Sun. You see me in the constellation of Bootes, the herdsman.

My light travels thirty-six light years to reach your Sun.

I have been seen as a star of ill omen and the bringer of storms by those who sail the seas of Earth. But you journey not on Earth but in the vast deeps of space where no tides flow nor storm winds blow.

I am also the bringer of honour and wealth so I give to you the opportunity of finding both upon your journey.

(Rises and lights one candle on Milky Way table and returns to place)

ALDEBARAN

I am the Star Aldebaran, sibling to your Sun. You see me in the constellation of Taurus the great Bull of the heavens.

My light travels sixty-eight light years to reach your Sun. I have been the representation in the heavens of the Great Bull of Osiris, the Apis Bull and Serapis. I have inspired with courage the followers of Mithras and graced the sacred Temples of the warrior race. I have shone with favour on those who wield power and wealth and riches in the world.

I am one of the four Royal Stars and set as a Watcher of the Heavens, as my gift for your journey I give you the courage to persist in it.

(Rises and lights one candle on Milky Way table and returns to place)

REGULUS

I am the Star Regulus, sibling to your Sun. You see me in the constellation of Leo, the Little King and Lion's Heart of Heaven.

My light travels eighty-five light years to reach your Sun.

I have been called Domicilis Solis, the dwelling place of the Sun, for it was in my sign that the Sun rose on the day of creation.

I am Regulus the King. I am first of the ancient Royal Stars and have been set as the first of the Watchers of the Heavens.

I will keep watch upon your journey and keep you safe for none will dare challenge my authority and power.

(Rises, lights one candle on Milky Way table, returns to place)

ANTARES

I am the Star Antares, sibling to your Sun. You see me in the constellation of Scorpio, slayer of the great hunter Orion.

My light travels one hundred and seventy light years to reach your Sun.

I am the gate to the Great Mysteries and holder of the Light-Fire of the Gods.

I am one of the ancient Royal Stars and one of the four Watchers of the Heavens.

I will keep watch upon your journey and open the Gates of the Mystery before you.

(Rises and lights one candle on Milky Way table and returns to place)

BETELGEUX

I am the Star Betelgeux, sibling to your Sun. You see me in the constellation of Orion the great hunter.

My light travels four hundred and twenty-five light years to reach your Sun.

My light shines as a beacon of hope for I signify the one who was slain and revived, I remind you that death is but the doorway, which leads to rebirth.

I give you as my gift upon your journey the knowledge that you already have everlasting life.

(Rises and lights one candle on Milky Way table and returns to place)

MILKY WAY

Now you are known to my children, the siblings of your Sun. Turn now and look beyond your home galaxy. We are not alone but part of a larger family called the Local Group, these are other galaxies which accompany us on our great journey. So vast is our family that even at the speed of light the journey from edge to edge would take six million years.

Pause now and look back, see my great spiral as if you were looking down upon it, a swirling spiral of light against the dark background of space. See the siblings of your Sun twinkle and shine across my surface. Then look for your own Sun out on one of the far arms, focus in as if looking down on it from above and see your home Sun encircled by its planets, there, see, a small blue sphere which is your home planet Earth. But we are not returning just yet, return to your viewpoint of my galaxy, then turn and look out into the darkness.

See those faint spots of light? They are my sibling galaxies.

ANDROMEDA
I am the Andromeda Galaxy, sibling to the Milky Way. I am linked to your Milky Way and we move through space in company.

You see me as a large hazy cloud in the skies of Earth for light from my huge company of stars travels two and a half million light years to reach your Sun.

(Rises and lights one candle on Milky Way table and returns to place)

TRIANGULAR GALAXY
I am the Triangular Galaxy, sibling to the Milky Way. I too am linked to your galaxy and travel in your company.

You see me as a faint glow in your skies for light from my galaxy of stars travels three million light years to reach your Sun.

(Rises and lights one candle on Milky Way table and returns to place)

SMALL MEGALLANIC CLOUD
I am known as the Small Megallanic Cloud Galaxy, sibling to the Milky Way. I am both sibling and satellite to your Milky Way for I orbit round your galaxy, though only once in every one and a half billon years.

(Rises and lights one candle on Milky Way table and returns to place)

LARGE MEGALLANIC CLOUD
I am known as the Large Megallanic Cloud, sibling to the Milky Way, I too slowly orbit your galaxy and travel in your company.
(Rises and lights one candle on Milky Way table and returns to place)

MILKY WAY
Now you know the vast cosmic family to which you belong. But the Suns and Planets, star systems and galaxies appear to you as

barren empty worlds, devoid it seems of that great gift called life that flourishes upon Earth.

Yet every star may shield within its light an unknown world where others dwell, who also feel and think and know. Another world where those who are your kin look up and see the heavens filled with different stars and also reach out in thought to touch with mind to mind.

Behind you lies the Earth that you call home, before you lies the vast dark space of cosmic void. Extend your mind and reach before, behind, above, below and then on either hand. Go seek a living soul who dwells upon some other world and in your mind touch theirs and know you walk in company.

(Approximately five minutes silent meditation. Milky Way signals end of the meditation period with singing bowl or bell)

SUPERCLUSTERS
Far in the unimaginable distance within the void are other galaxies, other families far greater than your own, we are known as superclusters. Perhaps upon some little world sheltered in the wings of distant stars, a mind looks up and seeks the patterns of different stars. Another Sun illuminates the day but the same spirit soul lives within that mind.

Know that the family of your Milky Way is very small against the families which exist within the clusters of my galaxies.

My light reaches out across the void and joins with yours in cosmic company.

THE GREAT WALLS
Great as are the superclusters greater still are the Great Walls, they form when blending one into another. Behind the northern and the southern skies, beyond the galaxies and superclusters we are as bulwarks defending heaven. Seven hundred and fifty million light years long we stand sentinel at the gates of the vast Unknown.

THE GREAT ATTRACTOR
I am the Great Attractor, the great pivot of your long journey through space. I draw you and your family of galaxies and superclusters ever onwards towards me. I am the deep dark

mystery for none knows of my nature nor my purpose.

I am the concealed of the concealed for my nature is not of light as you know it. I am the centre of your future and know the answers to the riddles of Creation.

I call you to me and though your brief span on Earth is too short for you, as you now are, to be there at the journeys end, yet is your spirit more enduring than the greatest star, your soul's life span longer than the vast distances of space and the spark of light and life within you of the nature of the God of Gods.

I call you to me as a Mother calls her children home, not just from little Earth but from the thousand thousand Earths where spirits dwell.

Come my children, welcome my embrace and listen while I whisper deep truths for you to treasure in your hearts.

MUSICIAN
(Plays music for meditation)

THE GREAT ATTRACTOR
(The Great Attractor gives any message that may have been received)

And now my children, it is time for you to return to Earth. Treasure those things you have heard and learnt within your heart and take them back home to enrich and empower your life journey.

Go now with my blessing upon you.

MILKY WAY
Children of Earth, I bid you now return, withdraw from the far reaches of the Great Walls and Superclusters, come back across the deep cosmic void, come back past the great galaxies to the Local Group, come back to me and see the shining spirals of my arms spread out below you and sink within my sea of stars.

SUN
Children of Earth, your Parents' Parent calls you home. Find me in my own especial place, come down from the high stars and once more feel the warmth and light I shine upon you. Come home to your own familiar stars and skies.

MOON

Children of Earth your parents' sibling calls you home, pause on my silver lands and look down upon your planet home. Watch as the deep blue of the seas and the browns and greens of the continents turn below you. Watch day turn into night and the lights of men shine forth even as the stars of the galaxies shone in your visions.

EARTH

Children of Earth I call you home, come back and find your own especial place where your physical body waits for you. Slip gently back and feel its familiar shape around you. Come back and open your eyes in full consciousness, here and now in this Temple.

(pause)

If Moon or Sun or Milky Way have any thoughts they wish to share with us, please do so now.

(When Moon, Sun and/or Milky Way have given their messages)

Now must we return within the dominion of Space and Time.

SPACE

Far have you journeyed within my realms, now I bring you back into the world of Earth and fix my earthly limits about you once more.

TIME

(Strikes gong loudly and slowly twelve times.

TIME takes candle snuffer and extinguishes all the candles first on the Milky Way table and then all on the Sun table. The two lights of the Great Attractor are left burning)

The twelve hours of the night are passed and a veil of light is drawn across the sky. The deeps of space and all the stars are now concealed and you must return to the full life and light of Earth.

(Strikes gong loudly and slowly twelve times)

Come now, our gate is open and all may now depart.

MUSICIAN
(Starts exit music.

TIME *and* SPACE *stand either side of the door and supervise the exit. The two side columns exit in pairs, beginning from the West they go to the East, bow to Great Attractor, turn and return down the same side and exit.*
The centre column go to the East via the North, in order EARTH, MOON, SUN, MILKY WAY *each bows to the Great Attractor and exit via the South. The Superclusters and Great Walls, remove their veils, bow to* THE GREAT ATTRACTOR *and exit north and south respectively and finally* THE GREAT ATTRACTOR *exits followed by* TIME *and* SPACE)

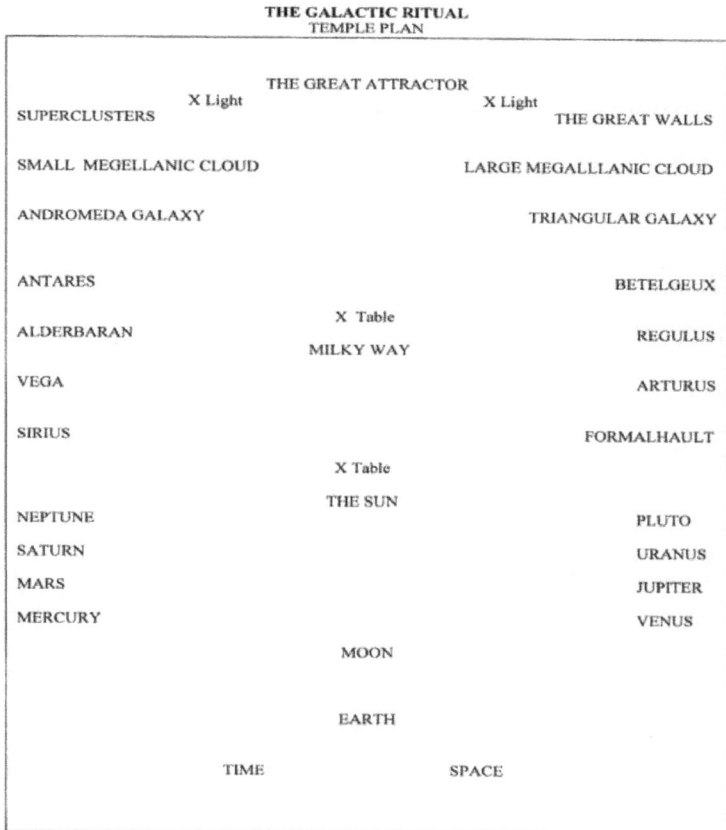

THE GALACTIC RITUAL
TEMPLE PLAN

	THE GREAT ATTRACTOR	
X Light		X Light
SUPERCLUSTERS		THE GREAT WALLS
SMALL MEGELLANIC CLOUD		LARGE MEGALLLANIC CLOUD
ANDROMEDA GALAXY		TRIANGULAR GALAXY
ANTARES		BETELGEUX
	X Table	
ALDERBARAN		REGULUS
	MILKY WAY	
VEGA		ARTURUS
SIRIUS		FORMALHAULT
	X Table	
	THE SUN	
NEPTUNE		PLUTO
SATURN		URANUS
MARS		JUPITER
MERCURY		VENUS
	MOON	
	EARTH	
TIME		SPACE

Creation Ritual

REQUIREMENTS
Four small feathers
Small bowl of water
Candle for Fire Officer
Small bowl of sand
Candle at each Quarter
Tree for the centre of the Temple
Large bowl of water or mirror for the well
Large ball of thread, string or rolls of ribbon for Web
Pair of Scissors
Gifts for the building of Earth. One for each participant. Flowers, fruits, crystals, Animal or human figures etc.
Tape Recorder
Music
Shoulder capes of appropriate colours for Elements Officers
Black Robes for Daughters of Night.

OFFICERS
ELEMENT OF AIR	*(woman)*
ELEMENT OF WATER	*(woman)*
ELEMENT OF FIRE	*(man)*
ELEMENT OF EARTH	*(man)*
THREE DAUGHTERS OF NIGHT	
PAST	*(woman)*
PRESENT	*(woman)*
FUTURE	*(woman)*
GUARDIAN / MUSICIAN	*(man)*

TEMPLE PREPARATION
Guardian / Musician is at the door
Seats arranged in a circle with entry spaces at East and West
Four chairs, one in each quarter, reserved for the Elements Officers
Seven chairs in the East, outside the circle, for the Officers

Ritual

(Guardian is at the West
All the Officers are seated in the East outside the circle, hoods up,
facing east so they are as invisible as possible from the Temple)

MUSICIAN
(Admits all participants, except Officers from West)

AIR
(Enters from the East, carrying four small feathers. Proceeds to the
centre of the Temple and faces East.
    Intones OM *prolonging the sound as long as possible)*
I am the first breath of the Element of Air. Out of the
nothingness of the un-manifest was I formed from the outbreath
of the Holy One - the Creator of all.

I am the bearer of the Word, the foundation and Law of
the Universe.

I am the breath of your life and the words of your mouth.

Use me with wisdom and caution and accept my gift.

(Air goes to the East and blows a feather off the hand towards the
Quarter. Repeats this at South, West and North and is seated in the
East)

WATER
(Enters from the East carry a small bowl of water, blue if possible.
Proceeds to the centre of the Temple and faces West)
I am the moisture on the breath of Air and the Element of
Water. My body is the oceans of the deep and my tears are the
raindrops of heaven.

The rivers and lakes are my children and all flowing
things are their inheritance.

I am your life blood and your sustainer.

Preserve me in purity, neither shed nor defile me and
accept my gift.

(Water goes to the West, dips fingers in the water and sprinkles
a few drops towards the Quarter. Repeats at North, East and South and
is seated in the West)

FIRE
(Enters from the East carrying a lighted candle and proceeds to centre, faces South)

I am energy, the life power of the Most High. I am Light and the Element of Fire.

I am the Illuminator of the darkness and the fire of vitality and life.

I am your day star and your night star. Warmth and light are the essence of my being.

I am the sight of your eye and the pulse of your heart.

Live in my light and accept my gift.

(Fire goes to South and lights the candle, proceeds to West, North and East lighting the candle at each and is seated in the South)

EARTH
(Enters from East carrying small bowl of sand, proceeds to centre and faces North)

I am the creation of the Creator, the visible form of the Unseen, the Element of Earth.

My body is the atoms of manifestation. I am the hills and the valleys, the high places and the low.

The rocks are my bones and growing things my flesh.

Your body is my body.

I am all living things and the Body Temple of the Most High.

Live in me in reference and sanctity and accept my gift.

(Earth goes to North and sprinkles a few grains of sand. Repeats at East, South and West and is seated in the North.

The four Officers of the Elements rise together and go forward to the centre, standing facing each other in a square they link hands by holding each other's wrists to form a square)

AIR
The powers of the air and the winds are formed.

WATER
The powers of the water and seas are formed.

FIRE
The powers of the Sun and fire are formed.

EARTH
The powers of the Earth and life are formed.

ALL
Fiat, Fiat, Fiat.
(The four Officers raise their clasped hands then bring them quickly down and break the hold.
The four Officers raise their right arm and point upwards between them)

AIR
The Creator formed the height and sealed it with the dome of heaven.

ALL
(The four Officers lower their right arm and point to the floor between them)

EARTH
The Creator formed the depth and sealed it with the molten core of Earth.

ALL
(The four Officers turn to face the East and point to the East, arm straight out)

AIR
The Creator formed the East and sealed it with the rising Sun.

ALL
(The four Officers turn to face the West and point to the West, arm straight out)

WATER
The Creator formed the West and sealed it with the setting Sun.

ALL
(The four Officers turn to face the South and point to the South, arm straight out)

FIRE
The Creator formed the South and sealed it with the noonday Sun.

ALL
(The four Officers turn to face the North and point to the North, arm straight out)

EARTH
The Creator formed the North and sealed it with the Polar Star.

ALL
(Each Officer turns to face their own Quarter)

ALL
Fiat Lux.

ALL
(The Officers return to their own Quarter and are seated)

MUSICIAN
(Turns on music. The Three Daughters of Night now enter, first FUTURE carrying the Well, second PRESENT carrying the Tree, third PAST carrying the Thread and the scissors. They circle the Temple clockwise three times gradually approaching the centre and stand facing each other)

MUSICIAN
(Turns off the music)

PRESENT
From the Air and Water, Fire brought forth the Mist of Creation.

Out of the Mist we came; Daughters of the Night of Chaos.

Into the light of the manifest we bring the gifts of life and being.

Weavers of the Threads of Time, we spin with the pulse of the time of the now, and the life of the past which was then, the Web which will be in the time yet to come, when the Tree of the World is in flower.

(Places the Tree in the centre)

As the Present and what is now, I plant the World Tree, its

roots and branches spread out over the whole Earth. In its protection the plants and animals flourish.

Its roots reach down into the land and bring forth strength; its branches reach up into the vast heavens and bring forth wisdom.

It is the Guardian of the Earth and the link between the worlds, seen and unseen.

FUTURE
(Places the Well beside the Tree)

As the Future and what will be, I place at the foot of the Tree the Well of Fate whose waters nourish and sustain the Tree.

In its shining surface are reflected the ever changing patterns and movements of the Web of Life.

From its waters flow the causes and effects which weave the destinies of man and nature.

Look in the Well and see the future which your present and your past create.

PAST
We are the Daughters of Time, the givers of birth and of death.

We spin the threads of the Web that you weave.

With the weft of the now through the warp of the past, the shuttle of time weaves the Web that will be.

As the Past which has been I am memory's Grail, drink deep of my cup or cut the ties which are chains.

PRESENT
In this time of the now, from the memory of the patterns of the past, let us build the world of the future, with beauty, with knowledge and with love.

Let each bring their gift for the world which is to be.

MUSICIAN
(Turns on the music.
Each person in turn comes forward and places their gift about the Tree)

MUSICIAN
(Turns off the music when all have returned to their seats)

FUTURE
Now shall we weave our Web of Time, hold the threads of the past in your left hand and the threads of the future in your right

hand.

MUSICIAN
(Turns on the music for the building of the Web as Future and Present begin to weave the Web)

FUTURE AND PRESENT
(FUTURE holds the threads and PRESENT goes to each person at random and builds the Web using different colours for past and future, making sure that the threads are long enough to lie on the floor. The past is woven for everyone first, followed by the future.

The threads for the past are held in the left hand and the threads for the future in the right hand)

MUSICIAN
(Turns off the music when the Web is complete and Past and Future return to centre)

PAST
The past may be sweet or bitter, you may desire memory or freedom from the ties of the past. Remember and choose.

(PAST then goes to each individual and asks them if they wish the thread of the past to be cut and acts accordingly)

PRESENT
That which is done is over and forgotten, that which IS binds and links us, that which will be is yours to design.

Now place your Web about the Tree of Life and the Well of Fate.

We, the Daughters of Night and weavers of the threads, will guard it well.

(All come forward gathering the threads of the Web and place them in a circle about the Daughters of Night then return to their places)

FIRE
(Rises)

The Sun is long past noon and the evening of this day approaches.

(Extinguish candle)

WATER
(Rises)

> The Sun descends to rest in the West and life sleeps.
> *(Extinguish candle)*

EARTH
(Rises)

> The night enfolds us and we rest in dream.
> *(Extinguish candle)*

AIR
(Rises)

> The Sun sets and the Sun rises. Light is eternal.
> *(Takes the candle and places it beside the Well and returns to*
seat)

FUTURE
So is the day of creation ended.

In its ending is the beginning, for the past, present and future are one.

In the pattern of the Web of Creation your life is a star.

You too build a pattern in the Web of your life, weave it well and remember, every new direction you take is but a different thread which adds to, but does not change, the integrity of the pattern of your life so far.

Only at your life's end is the pattern complete.

Come, look in the Well of Fate and see the rich colours and designs of the Web you weave.

MUSICIAN
(Turns on the music

> *Each person comes forward, starting from the West, looks in the Well (mirror) for as long as they wish and then departs the Temple.*
>
> *When all except the Officers have left the Temple the four ELEMENTS leave, looking in the Well as they do so. In order, Air, Water, Fire, Earth. Finally, the Daughters of Night extinguish the candle, circle the Temple three times and depart)*

MUSICIAN
Turns off the music and leaves the Temple)

CREATION RITUAL PLAN

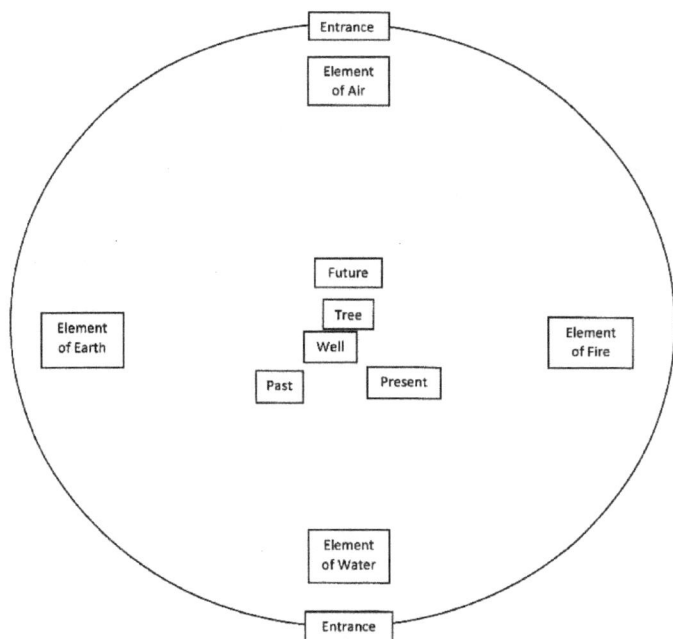

○ ○ ○ ⬭Chairs⬭ ○ ○ ○

Entrance

Element
of Air

Future

Tree

Well

Element
of Earth

Past

Present

Element
of Fire

Element
of Water

Entrance

Guardian/Musician

Form and Force Ritual

OFFICERS
Monad
Duad
Triad
Tetrad
Pentad
Hexad
Heptad
Ogdoad
Ennead
Decad
Guardian
Musician

REQUIREMENTS
Round Central altar
Altar cover
Central light holder and candle
Ten candle holders
Ten candles
Tapers
Snuffers
Matches
CD player and Music CD
(A central light is lit and placed on the altar in the Temple by Monad
before the ritual begins)

MUSICIAN
(Switch on entry music. Track One 'Nature's Chants')

GUARDIAN
(Admits the Officers who enter in order 9,7,5,3,1,2,4,6,8,10 and go to
their places and are seated. Admits all other participants who are then
seated)

MUSICIAN
(Switch off music)

GUARDIAN
(Seals the doorway three, four and five.)
Ruler of the Monad, all have been admitted in due form, the Temple is sealed and secure and I am guarding the inner and outer portals.

MONAD
It is well. Stand vigilant that our work may proceed in security and peace.

GUARDIAN
I will obey your command, the Temple is safe and secure in my keeping.

MONAD
(Rises and goes to altar)
Companions of Light, assist me to open this Temple.

Behold the single flame, *(points to central light)* this represents the Light that was before light began, the eternal energy which had no existence yet dwelt in the Mind of the Divine, waiting, all potential and potent. The Light which was, is and ever will be.

From the depths of the is not, into the is and the will be, I call forth the Light of the Divine from the unknown into the known, from the un-manifest into the manifest.

I bid you be still that the ever shining Light may dwell within this place.

By the power of our sincere intent, I call forth the powers of the Monad, the One Light, which radiates from no beginning, which shines without shadow or reflection. The inner light eternal which illumines the soul and empowers the spirit.

May the One Light which is the source of all Light and Being make manifest in this place the Light of creation.

(Lights candle one from the first light with taper then extinguishes taper. Remains standing at altar)

DUAD
(Rises and goes to altar)
While all is One, nought is. From the depths of the Creative Light came the Word and there was darkness within

the light. Then were created all the polarities of manifestation.

By the power of our sincere intent, I call forth the powers of the Duad, the polarities of being. Positive and negative, male and female, wealth and poverty, life and death, dominion and slavery, peace and war, beauty and ugliness, wisdom and foolishness.

Make manifest the balance of the Duad within our Temple.

(Lights candle two from the first light with taper then extinguishes taper. Remains standing at altar)

TRIAD

(Rises and goes to altar)

While there are two all is in balance, but also all is static. Nothing increases, nothing grows. Then one blends with two, the polarities meet and fuse and behold there are three.

By the power of our sincere intent, I call forth the powers of manifestation of the Triad. The child who is born of man and woman, the physical world which is born of idea and thought, the soul which develops within matter and spirit.

Make manifest in this Temple the Triad which is ever the result of the joining of the Duad.

(Lights candle three from the first light with taper then extinguishes taper. Remains standing at altar)

TETRAD

(Rises and goes to altar)

With the establishment of the Tetrad creation is manifest. For the creative fire burns, the life giving air blows, the flowing water nourishes and the earth sustains.

By the power of our sincere intent I call forth the manifest powers of the tetrad. From the east comes Raphael bearing the wand of power, from the south comes Michael bearing the sword of justice, from the west comes Gabriel bearing the cup of wisdom and from the north comes Auriel bearing the platter of earth.

Make manifest in this Temple the Tetrad and the powers of the directions and their qualities.

(Lights candle four from the first light with taper then extinguishes taper. Remains standing at altar)

PENTAD
(Rises and goes to altar)

The four Elements of Air, Fire, Water and Earth make manifest the created world; then enters in the Fifth Element, Spirit, the Quintessence and behold there is Life. Life manifests in humankind and every living plant or creature of air, sea or land. The Pentad has ever been the symbol of perfect humanity.

By the power of our sincere intent I call forth the living powers of the Pentad. Bringing into this Temple the strength of the personality, intelligence and consciousness of humanity.

From the morning and the evening come forth the loving influences of the ancient star goddesses, Ishtar, Inanna and Isis, bringing love, compassion and fertility to life. From the sun at noon and the dark of midnight come forth the strong influences of the ancient sun gods, Helios, Mars and Sol, bringing the masculine body strength, fearlessness and courage.

Make manifest in this Temple the powers of humanity, the compassion of the feminine, and the strength of the masculine.

(Lights candle five from the first light with taper then extinguishes taper. Remains standing at altar)

HEXAD
(Rises and goes to altar)

The earth based triangle of manifestation interlaces with the spirit based triangle in the hexagram, revealing the perfect balance of creation. One is a reflection of the other but after another manner. As above, so below.

By the power of our sincere intent I call forth the living powers of the Hexad, bringing the energies of the above and the below to this Temple.

From the east flows healing, from the south protection; from the west flows wisdom, from the north elemental powers; from the above flows spiritual love and strength from the below.

Make manifest in this Temple the energies of the directions and balance within us the heavenly and the terrestrial.

(Lights candle six from the first light with taper then extinguishes taper. Remains standing at altar)

HEPTAD
(Rises and goes to altar)

Now we have the Triad, representing the soul of humanity, joining with the Tetrad, representing the earth of the body. So manifests the Heptad, the sacred number of the spirituality of humanity.

By the power of our sincere intent I call forth the living powers of the Heptad. Allow the spiritual power of the Light to flow down and into you; from the crown of your head *(pause)*, to the area of the third eye *(pause)*, down to the throat *(pause)*, allow it to descend to and grow in your heart *(pause)*, descending again to your solar plexus *(pause)* then again to just below your navel area *(pause)* and finally resting at the base of your spine, allow it to shine.

Make manifest in this Temple the power of the soul and the spirit that the Inner Light may shine within us.

(Lights candle seven from the first light with taper then extinguishes taper. Remains standing at altar)

OGDOAD
(Rises and goes to altar)

All the influences of the Ogdoad now flow down into our being. Open yourself to the life force of the Sun *(pause)* the emotional strength of the Moon *(pause)* the intelligence of Mercury *(pause)* the love of Venus *(pause)* the energy of Mars *(pause)* the prosperity of Jupiter *(pause)* the generosity of Saturn *(pause)* and the Divine influence of the realm of the celestial stars.

By the power of our sincere intent I call forth the living powers of the Ogdoad. The influences of the planets and the stars flow down and awaken within us. From the Earth flow forth the energies of the eight spoked wheel of the seasons, the summer and winter solstices, the spring and autumn equinoxes and the energies of the four fire festivals.

Make manifest in this Temple the powers and the forces of the natural world and the cosmos within which we live.

(Lights candle eight from the first light with taper then extinguishes taper. Remains standing at altar)

ENNEAD
(Rises and goes to altar)

We have now reached the Ennead, the number of perfection. Here we are enfolded in the emanations of the triple trinity, the three divine manifestations in the three planes of being, the worlds of spirit, soul and matter.

By the power of our sincere intent I call forth the living powers of the Ennead. The creative power of the spirit which flows from the Nothing, through the Infinite Light and the Limitless Light. The consciousness of the soul which brings knowledge, love and will. And the attributes of the body which manifest as the senses, emotions and appetites.

Make manifest in this Temple the touch of the Divine spirit, the perfection of humanity and the harmony of our fellowship.

(Lights candle nine from the first light with taper then extinguishes taper. Remains standing at altar)

DECAD
(Rises and goes to altar)

As it is said in the Sepher Yetzirah, the book of The Formation of the World;

'Ten are the Sephiroth out of nothing, and not the number nine; ten and not eleven. Comprehend this great wisdom, understand this knowledge, inquire into it and ponder on it, render it evident and lead the Creator back to His throne again.

The Ten Sephiroth out of nothing are infinite in ten ways: The beginning infinite. The end infinite. The good infinite. The evil infinite. The height infinite. The depth infinite. The East infinite. The West infinite The North infinite. The South infinite, and the only Lord God, the faithful King, rules over all from His holy habitation for ever and ever.'

By the power of our sincere intent I call forth the infinite powers represented by the Sephiroth and Paths of the Tree of Life. May they inspire and teach us all the days of our lives.

(Lights candle ten from the first light with taper then extinguishes taper. Remains standing at altar)

ALL TEN OFFICERS
(Join hands and silently invoke the energies into the Temple)

MONAD
Our Temple is open, let the Light shine.

(All officers release hands, together bow to the altar, turn and

return to their places, circling the altar and led by 9).

MONAD
Relax and close your eyes. Be in the place most sacred to you, it can be a physical place or an inner place. Allow the atmosphere to manifest. Feel the peace and holiness of this place, allow the Light to manifest. Listen, look and be receptive to however the Inner chooses to manifest and reveal itself to you. Be still and receive.

MUSICIAN
(Turn on music. Track Eight 'Nature's Chants' by Global Journey. Play to the end of the track.)

MONAD
Our work is complete, give thanks for your experience, return to our outer Temple and open your eyes.
    Does anyone wish to share any insights or experiences?
    (Allow time for discussion)
    Companions of the Light, assist me to close this Temple.

DECAD
(Rises and goes to altar)
    With our thanks I return the powers of the Decad to rest.
    (Extinguishes tenth candle and remains standing at altar)

ENNEAD
(Rises and goes to altar)
    With our thanks I return the powers of the Ennead to rest.
    (Extinguishes ninth candle and remains standing at altar)

OGDOAD
(Rises and goes to altar)
    With our thanks I return the powers of the Ogdoad to rest.
    (Extinguishes eighth candle and remains standing at altar)

HEPTAD
(Rises and goes to altar)
    With our thanks I return the powers of the Heptad to rest.
    (Extinguishes seventh candle and remains standing at altar)

HEXAD
(Rises and goes to altar)
>With our thanks I return the powers of the Hexad to rest.
>*(Extinguishes sixth candle and remains standing at altar)*

PENTAD
(Rises and goes to altar)
>With our thanks I return the powers of the Pentad to rest.
>*(Extinguishes fifth candle and remains standing at altar)*

TETRAD
(Rises and goes to altar)
>With our thanks I return the powers of the Tetrad to rest.
>*(Extinguishes fourth candle and remains standing at altar)*

TRIAD
(Rises and goes to altar)
>With our thanks I return the powers of the Triad to rest.
>*(Extinguishes third candle and remains standing at altar)*

DUAD
(Rises and goes to altar)
>With our thanks I return the powers of the Duad to rest.
>*(Extinguishes second candle and remains standing at altar)*

MONAD
(Rises and goes to altar)
>With our thanks I return the powers of the Monad to rest.
>*(Extinguishes first candle and remains standing at altar)*

ALL OFFICERS
(Join hands and silently absorb any remaining energy)

MONAD
The light is at rest. Our Temple is closed.
>*(Officers break hands and Monad takes up the centre light)*
>Behold the one Light, this Light shines eternally.

Guardian, our work is complete, please unseal the Temple that all may depart in peace.

<u>GUARDIAN</u>
(Unseals the Temple and opens the doors)

Ruler of the Monad, the doorway is open and all may now depart.

<u>MUSICIAN</u>
(Turns on exit music. Track Five of Natures Chant)

<u>ALL OFFICERS</u>
(Pentad leads the Officers, who circle the altar, from the Temple.)

<u>GUARDIAN</u>
(Sees that all exit in due order)

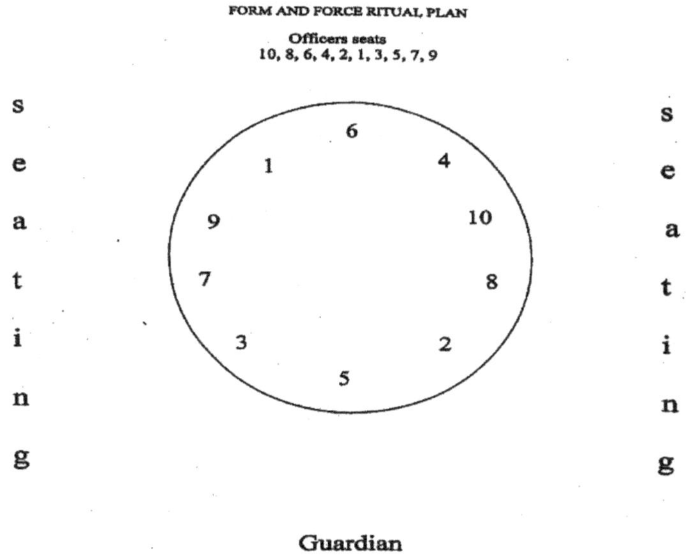
FORM AND FORCE RITUAL PLAN
Officers seats
10, 8, 6, 4, 2, 1, 3, 5, 7, 9
seating
6
1
4
9
10
7
8
3
2
5
seating
Guardian

Mobius Ritual

OFFICERS

Office of the Past	*Male*
Officer of the Future	*Female*
Officer of Time	*Male*
Officer of Space	*Female*

REPRESENTATIVES: PAST

Creation
Solar Systems
Geological Ages
Life
Humanity
Tribes
Civilisation
Empires
Warfare
Peace
The Gods
Space Exploration
Spiritual Teachers
Dreamtime

REPRESENTATIVES: FUTURE

Birth
Tomorrow
The Natural World
Health
Equality
Social order
Medicine
Technology
Freedom
Knowledge
Myths
Intergalactic communication
Expansion of consciousness
Cosmic consciousness

PREPARATION OF TEMPLE

Seats are set in two circles as per plan, one for each representative.
One seat in the centre of each circle, for Past and Future.
Two seats facing each other at crossing point for Time and Space.
Small table in centre of each circle.
Large candle on each altar.
Small candle (night light) one for each Representative on altar of their circle plus one on each for Time and Space. (Sixteen on each)
Matches, tapers and snuffers on altars.
Gong, or Tibetan bowl, at the station of Past.
Music.
Music player.

Ritual

Music for Entry
> *(Past and Future ensure music is switched on before entering.*
> *One of the Representatives should be responsible for switching off the music when all have entered and then for switching on for the Infinity Walk and again for exit)*

PAST AND FUTURE

(Enter together, each turns, FUTURE to right, PAST to left, and proceed to outside of circles, they turn at the crossing point, walk forward together then enter their respective circle at the crossing point and go to their station.
> *NOTE. All are seated on entry then rise when speaking)*

TIME and SPACE

(Admit all Representatives, those of Past circle first followed by those of Future Circle.
> *The Past Circle enter via the south, entering at the crossing point then circling clockwise*
> *In order;*
> *Dreamtime, Spiritual Teachers, Space Exploration, The Gods, Peace, Warfare, Empires, Civilisation, Tribes, Humanity, Life, Geological Ages, Star Systems, Creation.*
> *The Future Circle enter via the south, entering at the crossing point then circling anticlockwise.*
> *In order:*
> *Cosmic Consciousness, Expansion of Consciousness, Myths,*

Knowledge, Freedom, Technology, Medicine, Social Order, Equality, Health, The Natural World, Tomorrow, Birth.

TIME and SPACE enter together TIME from South, SPACE from north, meeting at crossing point of circles, TIME goes to right and circles, PAST circles clockwise to station, SPACE goes to right and circles, FUTURE circles anticlockwise to station.
(Switch off music)

TIME
(Faces east and points with right hand to east, brings hand over head in large circle at each turn)

From sunrise *(faces and points to west)* to sunset *(faces and points to south)* from noon tide *(faces and points to north)* to midnight. *(points upwards)* from then *(points downwards)* until now *(crosses arms over chest)* from beginning to end *(facing east spreads both arms out sideways)* I call upon the Lords of Time who rule the span of life on Earth, to seal this time within the present moment and be with us in this place.

SPACE
(Faces east and points with right hand to east, brings hand over head in large circle at each turn.)

From the east *(faces and points to west)* to the west *(faces and points to south)* from the south *(faces and points to north)* to the north *(points upwards)* from zenith *(points downwards)* to nadir *(crosses arms over chest)* from the infinite to the finite *(facing west spreads arms out sideways)* I call upon the Lords of Space who rule the measures of the realm of Earth, to seal this Temple in the bonds of place and be with us in this space.

PAST
(Faces east and points with right hand to east brings hand over head in large circle at each turn.)

From beginning *(faces and points to west)* to ending *(faces and points to south)* from the was *(faces and points to north)* to the is *(points upwards)* from the birth *(points downwards)* to the present (*crosses arms over chest)* from has been to now *(spreads arms out sideways facing north)* I call upon the Lords of all things Past to open wide the gates of memory, to fill this Temple with the garnered harvest of our time on Earth and be with us in this place.

(Lights candle)

FUTURE

(Faces East and points with right hand to East brings hand over head in large circle at each turn.)

From the now *(faces and points to west)* to the will be *(faces and points to south)* from the dream *(faces and points to north)* to the fact *(points upwards)* from the hope *(points downwards)* to the real *(crosses arms over chest)* from the now to the then *(spreads arms out sideways facing south)* I call upon the Lords of Future Times, to lift the veil which hides the things to be, and in this Temple show a glimpse of what will be and dwell awhile with us within this place.

(Lights candle)

PAST

(Sounds gong three times allowing sound to fade between each.)

SPACE

In the Beginning I was alone for I am Space. Nothing existed to fill my aloneness, I was without limit or substance. Boundless was I, an empty theatre in which the play of creation was yet to be.

(Enters circle of Future, circles anti-clockwise, pausing to light small candle from centre candle and returns to station)

TIME

The Beginning moved on into the Then and I was, for I am Time. I am the distance between the first and the last, the pause between birth and death, which marks the beginning and ending of all things and all lives. I am the measure of existence, the duration of the ages of creation and the pause between the in-breath and the out-breath.

(Enters circle of Past, circles clockwise, pausing to light small candle from centre candle and returns to station)

SPACE and TIME

We are the parents of the Future and the children of the Past. Where we meet and blend is only NOW.

PAST

I stand at the point between the Now and the Beginning for I am the Past, I am all things which have been. I am all those things that are held in the well of memory, I am all things which are the roots and the seeds of the Now.

(Lights small candle from centre candle in own circle, circles clockwise and returns to station)

FUTURE

I stand at the point between the Now and the Will Be for I am the Future, I am all things in potential, I am fluid and contain all possibilities.

(Lights small candle from centre candle in own circle, circles anti-clockwise and returns to station)

PAST AND FUTURE

We are the long story of the formation of the Earth, we are the history of humanity and the chapters yet to be written.

PAST

(Sounds the gong six times, allowing each to fade between strikes.)

CREATION

I am Creation, I was there in the beginning and responded to the sounding of the Word. I gathered the first matter from the chaos of space and moulded it into manifestation according to the dictate of the One. I stretched forth my hand and behold there was light, I turned and behold there was darkness also.

(Lights small candle from centre candle, circles clockwise and returns to station)

STAR SYSTEMS

I am the vast family of stars and planets which make up the Star Systems of our Universe.

I am galaxies beyond galaxies within the infinity of space. We are the children of Creation and the fruits of the womb of the Most High. We are born and live and die in the endless cycles of the heavens. We are the Father of your Sun and the Mother of your Earth, we are their parents and their sustainer. Upon my right hand spin your brother and sister stars, I turn and they are upon my left hand also, ever unto the limitless bounds of space.

(Lights small candle from centre candle, circles clockwise and returns to station)

GEOLOGICAL AGES

I am the slow processes of the evolution of Earth. I am the lava flows of the primordial land and the tides of the ancient seas. I am the uplifting of the mountain ranges and the slow wearing away of the land masses. Fire and wind, water and ice are the tools I wield to carve and shape the Earth. My ages were ancient as the ancient of days ere the stage of Earth was set.

(Lights small candle, circles clockwise and returns to station)

LIFE

I am the first stirring of the miracle of Life, I am the first cells in which the pulse stirred, the unity from which sprang the infinite diversity, which is the outer face of the manifestation of the One Life on Earth.

I am the microbes and viruses, the trees and plants, the fish in the seas, the insects and birds and all animals great and small.

(Lights small candle from centre candle, circles clockwise and returns to station)

HUMANITY

I am the first ancestor of Homo Sapiens, I am the one who awakened and knew 'I AM'. I am the one who stirred in the long sleep of animal life and awoke to the possibilities of the world around me. I used the first tool and lit the first fire. I began the long journey to control and improve my environment. My genes live in you who are my heirs and the progenitors of the future.

(Lights small candle from centre candle, circles clockwise and returns to station)

TRIBES

I am the first Tribe who learned the strength of community. I am the builder of the first shelters from the elements and the emergence from cave dwelling. I am the planter of the first corn and the gatherer of the first harvest. I am the first who learned to place the food pot upon the fire and to cleanse water by heat. I stretched forth my hand to my brother, and turned, and my sister was beside me also – and we dwelt together.

(Lights small candle from centre candle, circles clockwise and returns to station)

CIVILISATION

I am civilisation. Mine was the hand which drew the first paintings upon the walls of my dwelling and learnt the uses of herbs in healing. I gathered together the Tribes and together we learned to build our society and develop laws, ethics and culture. I am the parent of your great cities, your parliaments and confederations, I am organised society and a secure way of living.

(Lights small candle from centre candle, circles clockwise and returns to station)

EMPIRES

I am the founder of the great Empires. As Alexander the Great of Macedonia I conquered Syria, Egypt, Babylonia, Persia and northern India. As Caesar I conquered for, ruled and organised the mighty empire of Rome. I swept across the plains of Asia to the very borders of the European world as Genghis Khan. I won, ruled and integrated the mighty empire of China. I rose from humble roots as Napoleon to take the throne of France. I spread the power and influence of England across the globe; for a time, an empire on which the sun was said to never set.

(Lights small candle from centre candle, circles clockwise and returns to station)

WARFARE

I am Warfare; the conflict which arises between nations when ambition, greed and aggression rule the hearts of men. I am slaughter and bloodshed, grief and pain and destruction. I am the destroyer of the creations of civilisation, I am death in a thousand guises; yet too are valour, heroism and bravery learnt in my refining fire.

(Lights small candle from centre candle, circles clockwise and returns to station)

PEACE

I am Peace, the calm which follows the tumult of war. I am quiet and stillness and time for reflection. I am an ordered way in which the child may grow to maturity and the old end their days in quiet. I am opportunity for growth and the development of culture. I am fragile as glass and precious as diamonds, I must be sought with care and preserved with love.

(Lights small candle from centre candle, circles clockwise and returns to station)

THE GODS

I represent the Gods, those faces with which humanity endows the Divine. They are the unseen forces which lie within and behind the manifestations of Earth, they are the projections of the deepest levels of the mind of mankind, seen as in a mirror darkly. They are those powers we cannot tame or name yet which we know are arbiters of our fate.

(Lights small candle from centre candle, circles clockwise and returns to station)

SPACE EXPLORATION

I am that restless, seeking spirit in humanity which ever desires to explore the unknown. I am that spirit which took climbers to the top of the highest mountains, explorers to the coldest polar caps, pilots to the speed of sound and divers to the deepest depths. I am the desire to know which drives the bravest to do and dare and go. I am the spirit of adventure which made humanity lift its gaze unto the stars and turn its mind and heart and skills to conquest of the mysteries of space.

(Lights small candle from centre candle, circles clockwise and returns to station)

SPIRITUAL TEACHERS

I am of the Teachers, those who have seen beyond the boundaries of the material world. I have glimpsed the real behind the illusion, I have touched the essence of the worlds of Light. I know the truth that human spirits may walk free of the bonds of Earth and know and think and BE in realms unseen except to inner sight. I have touched an echo of the great Divine and seen the splendour which is Life in Light, and knowing this, have turned and held out my hand to yours.

(Lights small candle from centre candle, circles clockwise and returns to station)

DREAMTIME

I am that time outside time, I am the past which lives in the now, the now which exists in the future. I was the before time when Earth was formed and shaped and made. I am the now time when all is known and seen and understood. I am the realm of far vision and the Shaman's journey. I am the world of your imagination where you plan and hope and dream, it is from here that you walk forward into the Future.

(Lights small candle from centre candle, circles clockwise and returns to station)

TIME

We have travelled the circle of the Past, let us all celebrate this point in our journey.

(All in the Past circle rise, join hands and led by Time walk round the circle back to their places chanting as they go)

ALL

Let us celebrate the Circle of the Past.

BIRTH

I am the coming into being, the birth, the beginning. Nothing exists on Earth that did not have a beginning. Every atom was born of Space out of the Sun. Every cell of life was born of parents of its kind. Every soul and spirit is a child of the Divine.

(Lights small candle from centre candle, circles anti-clockwise and returns to station)

TOMORROW

I am Tomorrow, the time which never comes, I am dreams of what will be, I am plans and wishes which may or may not come true. I am ambitions well planned and illusions that entice the mind from the real. I am promise and a will o' the wisp, always just ahead but never reached. If you are to die tomorrow you will live forever!

(Lights small candle from centre candle, circles anti-clockwise and returns to station)

THE NATURAL WORLD

I speak for the Natural World, the plant and animal life of Earth. You think you live in a stable world where the land and sea, the climate and atmosphere are unchanging and dependable – but this is illusion, everything in my world is constantly in motion, mighty ebbs and flows in the energies of Earth cause seas to flood and mountains to rise, temperatures to increase and decrease and species to be born and die. The future of Earth emerges from its past, learn its rhythms and how to live within its instability.

(Lights small candle from centre candle, circles anti-clockwise and returns to station)

HEALTH

I am Health, both of humanity and nature. There are no boundaries, for you are part of nature, what affects the Earth affects you likewise. Your body obeys the same laws, responds to the same causes and thrives or perishes according to the same well-being or otherwise of its environment. Every cause has its effect and what you set in motion reacts upon you and all about you.

You cannot maintain human health if you do not maintain the health of all the natural world about you.

(Lights small candle from centre candle, circles anti-clockwise and returns to station)

EQUALITY

Everything in nature is balance. Equality is not in each creature being or having the same, equality is in each having the opportunity to fulfil its full potential. Life lives upon life, predators become victims in the great circle of the species. In human life each person is not equal in what they receive from life but the victory and the balance lies in what we each make of it.

(Lights small candle from centre candle, circles anti-clockwise and returns to station)

SOCIAL ORDER

When all humanity learns to respect the rights of others, then will theft and deceit be exiled from society. When the strong no longer seek to impose their will on the weaker, then will force and unjust domination no longer be part of human life. When countries are truly ruled by principles of truth and justice, then will governments no longer be corrupt. When ideals are lived in every day affairs, then will humanity truly live in harmony.

(Lights small candle from centre candle, circles anti-clockwise and returns to station)

MEDICINE

The healing of the ills of life has ever been a sacred vocation. From tribal Wise Ones to the skills required to interchange a human heart, there have always been those who dedicated their lives to the art of healing. I see a time when Healers will understand the causes of ill health and will cure or cancel them before they manifest, rather than having to strive to remove their effects from bodies in distress.

(Lights small candle from centre candle, circles anti-clockwise and returns to station)

TECHNOLOGY

In but a few short years the technology now known and used in human society has changed the way of life and learning more swiftly than the spirit's growth. I see a time when what we know now will seem as little as the skills of stone age man, when from the seeds of this our time, will grow a world of seeming miracles. Then will all nature be at our command and all the tasks of mundane life be but a memory of manual toil. Yet too I see this future world as fraught with danger and despair if wisdom and understanding do not also grow.

(Lights small candle from centre candle, circles anti-clockwise and returns to station)

FREEDOM

I see a time when humanity shall truly know what freedom is, when it is understood that personal freedom is not the following of personal will or desire, neither is it the bending to another's will to gain a false security. True freedom is in full knowledge of the laws which lie behind the working of the world, in knowing the true limits which nature imposes upon us and the consequences of their infringement. It is in recognising our place within the vast scheme of the Universe, in accepting that unpleasant results do but warn us of boundaries crossed. True freedom is in living, moving, growing, thinking and reaching our full potential within the limits set by life on Earth.

(Lights small candle from centre candle, circles anti-clockwise and returns to station)

KNOWLEDGE

Knowledge is a double edged sword, it can be used for good or ill, progress or destruction. Yet to deny knowledge is to close the gate before progress and growth. It is the choice of humanity how its knowledge will be used, to take our species forward and to use our knowledge for the benefit of all life on the planet, – or to allow it to be misused to our destruction.

(Lights small candle from centre candle, circles anti-clockwise and returns to station)

MYTHS

Myths are the stories which transmit our history, they conceal great truths and tell us of ancient thoughts and beliefs. We are living the myths of tomorrow, tales will be told of ancient folk who lived before the wonders of scientific invention became the commonplace and necessities of modern life. Our stories will tell of a different world, a time and place long gone when they are told. Our heroes will live on and take their place among the great ones who once walked the Earth and left their golden footsteps in the sands of time.

(Lights small candle from centre candle, circles anti-clockwise and returns to station)

INTERGALACTIC COMMUNICATION

I look into the glass of future times and hear the sound of voices yet unheard, the touch of minds which never lived on human Earth but had their birth in some far distant galaxy yet unknown. I see a time when the bonds of isolation will be untied and we will know that other minds exist and think and know. We will be able to reach out across the stars and know our kin who also dwell within the families of deepest space.

(Lights small candle from centre candle, circles anti-clockwise and returns to station)

EXPANSION OF CONSCIOUSNESS

I see a future time when humanity shall learn to know the many worlds of consciousness existing in the Universe, shall see the familiar material world for what it is, but one layer in the many levels within the Cosmic Mind. When seeking inward we shall come to know the many worlds unseen, which have no form to mortal eye yet are as real to mind as the material world to body senses. I see a time when those with inner sight are valued for the Light they bring to dispel the dark clouds of long held ignorance.

(Lights small candle from centre candle, circles anti-clockwise and returns to station)

COSMIC CONSCIOUSNESS

I know that in the fullness of timeless time not one small spark of spirit shall remain unlit, unloved within the lands of Earth. That every soul shall reach the sacred realms of Light and having learnt and grown in Earth's hard school will take the Path which leads onwards towards its destiny. Then will the rich harvest of the Light Bearers be gathered in and the purpose of this Earth at last shall be fulfilled.

(Lights small candle from centre candle, circles anti-clockwise and returns to station)

SPACE

We have travelled the circle of the Future, let us all celebrate this point in our journey.

(All in the Future circle rise, join hands and led by Cosmic Consciousness walk anti-clockwise round the circle back to their places chanting as they go)

ALL

Let us celebrate the Circle of the Future.

PAST

(When all have returned to their places and are seated)
Now is our purpose accomplished.

FUTURE

And the seeds of the future are set.

TIME

Let us celebrate the Oneness of Being.

SPACE

By walking the Infinite Path.

(Turn on music for the walk.

All in the Past circle, and Space, turn to their left, all in the Future circle turn to their right. TIME leads by walking into the Future circle towards BIRTH, COSMIC CONSCIOUSNESS passes behind TIME into the Past circle. All then walk the two circles crossing each other alternately where the circles meet, thus walking the form of the symbol of Infinity. When the path has been walked three times TIME stops and all stop at their original station and are seated)

PAST

(Sounds the gong nine times slowly allowing the sound to fade between each strike.)

TIME

(Faces east and points with right hand to east, brings hand over head in large circle at each turn)

From sunrise *(faces and points to west)* to sunset *(faces and points to south)* from noon tide *(faces and points to north)* to midnight. *(points upwards)* from then *(points downwards)* until now *(crosses arms over chest)* from beginning to end *(spreads both arms out sideways facing north)* I thank the Lords of Time for being with us in this place and close this Temple time.

(Brings hands together. Enters circle of Future and extinguishes all small candles)

SPACE

(Faces east and points with right hand to east brings hand over head in large circle at each turn.)

From the east *(faces and points to west)* to the west *(faces and points to south)* from the south *(faces and points to north)* to the north *(points upwards)* from zenith *(points downwards)* to nadir *(crosses arms over chest)* from the infinite to the finite *(spreads arms out sideways facing south)* I thank the Lords of Space for being with us in this place and close this Temple space.

(Brings hands together. Enters circle of Past and extinguishes all the small candles.)

PAST

(Faces east and points with right hand to east brings hand over head in large circle at each turn.)

From beginning *(faces and points to west)* to ending *(faces and points to south)* from the was *(faces and points to north)* to the is *(points upwards)* from the birth *(points downwards)* to the present *(crosses arms over chest)* from has been to now *(spreads arms out sideways facing north)* I thank the Lords of all things Past for being with us in the place and close this Temple.

(Brings hands together and then extinguishes candle)

FUTURE

(Faces East and points with right hand to East brings hand over head in large circle at each turn.)

From the now *(faces and points to west)* to the will be *(faces and points to south)* from the dream *(faces and points to north)* to the fact *(points upwards)* from the hope *(points downwards)* to the real *(crosses arms over chest)* from the now to the then *(spreads arms out sideways facing south)* I thank the Lords of Future times for being with us in this place and close this Temple.

(Brings hands together and then extinguishes candle)

PAST

(Sounds gong twelve times allowing sound to fade between each.)

FUTURE

Everyone please rise and leave the Temple.
(Switch on music for exit.)

TIME

(Leads out all in the Past circle, PAST following after CREATION, going straight out behind circle of Future to south.)

SPACE

(Leads out all in the Future circle, COSMIC CONSCIOUSNESS first, FUTURE following after BIRTH, going straight out behind circle of Future to north)

THE GODS

SPACE EXPLORATION

SPIRITUAL TEACHERS

PEACE

DREAMTIME

EXPANSION OF CONSCIOUSNESS

INTERGALACTIC COMMMUNICATION

MYTHS

COSMIC CONSCIOUSNESS

TIME

KNOWLEDGE

WARFARE

PAST

FREEDOM

ALTAR

TECHNOLOGY

EMPIRES

ALTAR

MEDICINE

CIVILISATION

SOCIAL ORDER

FUTURE

TRIBES

SPACE

HUMANITY   LIFE   GEOLOGICAL AGES

CREATION

STAR SYSTEMS

BIRTH

TOMORROW

EQUALITY

HEALTH

THE NATURAL WORLD

Mobius Ritual Plan

The Sirius Star Ritual

(An Opening and Closing Ritual designed to allow a central space for optional workings)

TEMPLE ARRANGEMENTS
Temple plan is as an eight pointed star with Officers at the Four Quarters and the Four Cross Quarters. The Officers form two equal armed crosses.
The Magus is in the centre of the Temple.
Magus has Censer with lighted incense.
Large Candle at East.
Guardian at Doorway. Guardian has Gong.
Sacred Light between East and West.
There should be chairs for each Officer to use during the work directed by the Magus.

OFFICERS
East.	*VEGA*
South	*ARCTURUS*
West	*SIRIUS*
North	*ALTAIR*
North East	*MAN*
North West	*BULL*
South West	*LION*
South East	*EAGLE*
Centre	*MAGUS*
Doorway	*GUARDIAN*

Ritual Opening

ENTRY OF OFFICERS.
Magus enters first at West, followed immediately by the other Officers, circles Temple clock-wise then goes to centre from the West.

Officers enter at West in order – Sirius, Lion, Arcturus, Eagle, Vega, Man, Altair, and Bull. Sirius circles the Temple going via North to East and stopping at West. Each Officer stops as they reach their Station.

GUARDIAN
(Strikes Gong four times)

MAGUS
Everyone please rise.
(Censes Temple circling it as does so)
On the centre I declare the presence of the Light Eternal radiating from the invisible.

Let the Temple of the Macrocosm be reflected in this mirror within the microcosm so that this place becomes a true Temple of the Light.

So mote it be.

ALL
So mote it be.

MAGUS
Please be seated
Officers only please rise.
(Moves to East via West and North and faces East)
In the East I greet thee, Ra, Lord of the Morning rising in splendour to open the new day.
(Moves to South and faces South)
In the South I greet thee, Horus, Lord of the Noonday. On thy wings are wisdom, glory and power.
(Returns to Centre via the West)

SIRIUS
I stand in the light of Sirius, bright star of Love and Wisdom, which shines eternal in the heavens and upon the doorway of the Temple of Initiation.

From the West I look into the darkness of winter and the longest night, and perceive the rising of the new born sun.

The light recedes and the light returns from aeon to aeon unto the end of the Universe.

VEGA
(Lights Station Candle)

ALL
(All Officers move to the next Station on their left clockwise so that the Lion is now in the West)

LION
I stand in the sign of Leo and see the powers of Air in the form of Archetypal Man, body temple of The Divine, ruling the powers of the light in Aquarius.

Now is the cleansing of winter accomplished and all stirs to change.

Life dies and life is re-born. Now is the time of the invocation of the life-force.

ALL
(All Officers move to the next station on their left)

ARCTURUS
I stand in the light of Arcturus, star of fortune and honour. From the west I see the rising of the herald of spring, the opener of the new year, the Sun at the spring equinox.

Even as the sunrise and the sunset balance upon the scales of time at noon-day, so too are day and night twin halves of the circle of light at the time of new awakening.

ALL
(All Officers move to the next station on their left)

EAGLE
I stand in the sign of Scorpio and see the powers of earth in the form of the Bull, symbol and representative of the creative power in nature, ruling the powers of the light in Taurus.

Now is the time for the sowing of seed, of fertilisation and new kindling. All life awakens from winters sleep and the energy of creation floods through man and nature.

ALL
(All Officers move to the next station on their left)

VEGA
I stand in the light of Vega, star of enterprise and leadership.

From the west I look into the brightness of Midsummers day and see that now all things have achieved their full potential.

I see the light poised in mid-heavens at noon-day, shining in its full maturity and glory.

As the lesser light illumines the day, so let the Light Eternal shine in this Temple.

MAGUS
Please be seated.
(The work of the day is now presented by the Magus. This may be a Pathworking, address, talk, meditation or any suitable item.

The Magus indicates the end of the work as appropriate or by saying)
So mote it be.

Closing

MAGUS
Officers only please rise.

ALL
(All Officers move to the next station on their left)

MAN
I stand in the sign of Aquarius and see the powers of fire in the form of the Lion, symbol and representative of strength and vigour, the guardian and the ruler of the powers of the light in Leo.

Now is the time of ripening and fruition. All things come to the peak of their growth and the seeds of their future are set.

ALL
(All Officers move to the next station on their left)

ALTAIR
I stand in the light of Altair, star of confidence, diplomacy and courage.

From the west I see the waxing night encroach on summer's day to stand as its balanced reflection on autumn's equinox.

This is the time of harvesting and rich abundance when earth gives of her bounty and all creatures give praise and thanksgiving.

ALL
(All Officers move to the next station on their left)

BULL
I stand in the sign of Taurus and see the powers of water in the form of the Eagle, symbol of courage and transmutation, ruling the powers of the light in Scorpio.

Now is the time of sleep and of dying when all things withdraw and turn inwards.

The outworn and old pass away in winter's cleansing and the hidden seeds of the new, slumber in secrecy.

ALL
(All Officers move to the next station on their left)

VEGA
I stand in the East and watch the setting of the waning sun.

Now are all things accomplished, the cycle of life completed and the day done.

The darkness of night enfolds us and in our nights dreaming the memory of our journey empowers us for the new day.

All things are at rest.
(Extinguishes station candle)

MAGUS
(Moves to and faces West)

In the West I greet thee Isis, Mother of the Eternal. Embrace us in thy safe keeping.

(Moves to and faces North)

In the North I greet thee, Nephthys, Lady of the Night. Commend us to thy son Anubis, Walker between the Worlds and Opener of the Ways.

(Returns to Centre via East and South)
(On the Centre facing East)

In the evening I greet thee, Osiris, Lord of the Underworld.

Bear us safely in thy barque of millions of years to a new dawn and a new day.

So is the Visible returned to the Invisible. All Light is one.

GUARDIAN
(Strikes gong four times.)

ORDER OF EXIT
The Magus exits Temple via the West. Sirius follows immediately behind the Magus followed in order by the Lion, Arcturus, the Eagle, Vega, the Man, Altair and finally the Bull; the Officers circling the Temple as appropriate from their station to the West. The Guardian sees all others exit by circling the Temple.

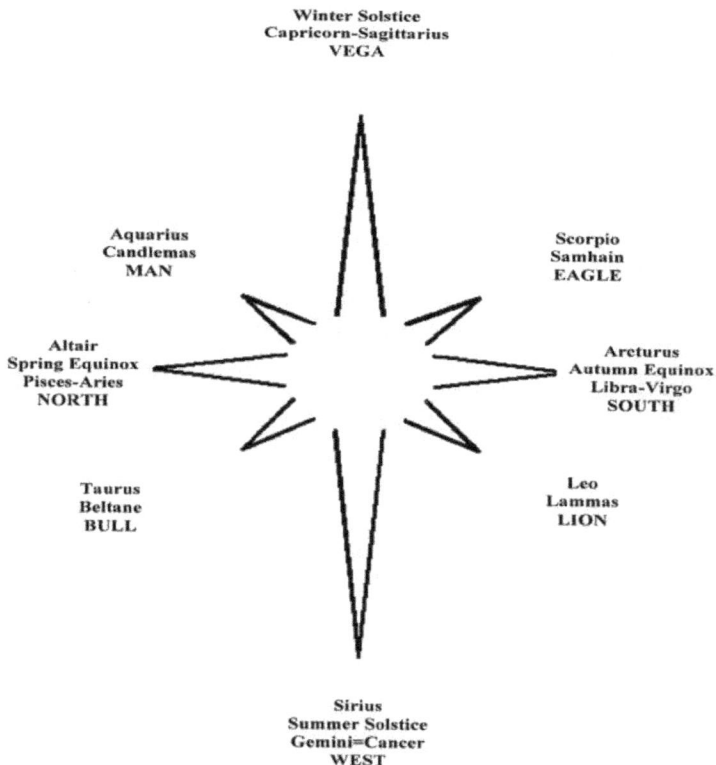

Winter Solstice
Capricorn-Sagittarius
VEGA

Aquarius
Candlemas
MAN

Scorpio
Samhain
EAGLE

Altair
Spring Equinox
Pisces-Aries
NORTH

Arcturus
Autumn Equinox
Libra-Virgo
SOUTH

Taurus
Beltane
BULL

Leo
Lammas
LION

Sirius
Summer Solstice
Gemini=Cancer
WEST

Pentagram Ritual

OFFICERS
GUARDIAN
SPIRIT
EARTH
WATER
AIR
FIRE

The duties of the GUARDIAN are to see that all enter and leave the Temple in order and to secure the privacy of the Temple.
Officers are placed in the shape of the Pentagram as on attached plan. SPIRIT Officer has lighted candle in holder suitable for carrying. The candle is placed behind the Spirit Officer except when being carried.

Ritual

SPIRIT
I stand in the place of the head in the figure of the human in the Microcosm. Mine is the place of the intellect, the directing powers of the brain and the focus of consciousness.

EARTH
I stand in the place of the right lower limb in the figure of humanity in the Microcosm. I maintain balance and mobility together with my partner the left lower limb. By our powers the body vehicle has independent movement and stability in the world.

WATER
I stand in the place of the left upper limb in the figure of humanity in the Microcosm. I am the mirror image of my partner the right upper limb and together we make possible the embrace of the lover and the protection of the young.

AIR
I stand in the place of the right upper limb in the figure of

humanity in the Microcosm. I am the instrument of action and creativity, mine is the function of control over the material world. Together with my partner the left upper limb I make possible all skills and practical actions.

FIRE
I stand in the place of the left lower limb in the figure of humanity in the Microcosm. I maintain balance and mobility together with my partner the right lower limb. Together we establish our place upon the Earth and walk free upon the highlands and lowlands.

SPIRIT
Together we enclose, protect and make functional, the body of humanity in the Microcosm.
(Each Officer calls their own Element in an invoking manner following each other in sequence)

EARTH
Earth

WATER
Water

AIR
Air

FIRE
Fire

SPIRIT
Spirit

SPIRIT
I am the ruling power of intelligence in the vehicle of humanity in the Microcosm. I direct all action, motivate the formation of society and underpin the complexity of human activity in the world.

EARTH
I wield the powers of the Element of Earth in the Microcosm. My Element is the sustainer of all growth and fecundity, the womb of humanity and of all seeds. I am the Mother of Life in all its forms.

WATER
I wield the powers of the Element of Water in the Microcosm. The waters of the Earth, seas, rivers and lakes are under my dominion. I am the life blood which flows in the veins of life and I nurture all nature with dew and rain. Mine is the power of storm and of flood and the gentle drift of the winter's snow.

AIR
I wield the powers of the Element of Air in the Microcosm. I am the first and the last breath, which measures a life's span. I pass through all living things and the lung of the world breathes to my rhythm. I am the storm wind and the summer breeze, I destroy and I sustain yet I pass unseen through the world.

FIRE
I am the powers of the Element of Fire in the Microcosm. I am the warmth that awakens the seed from the slumber of winter, I am the heat of summer and the glow of a winter's blaze. I animate and preserve life, yet I am too the destroyer and the great cleanser which makes all things renew.

SPIRIT
By our functions do we make possible life within the Macrocosm.
By our actions is the Earth a living, breathing, conscious, entity in space.

(Each Officer calls their own quality in an invoking manner following each other in sequence)

EARTH
Ground.

WATER
Moisture

AIR
Wind

FIRE
Warmth

SPIRIT
Life

SPIRIT
I stand in the place of the great luminaries of the heavens. I, and the natural world about me, are empowered with life from the beneficent rays of the Sun. When the Sun sleeps the Moon enlightens my darkness both of body and of spirit.

EARTH
I stand in the place of the spring constellations of Aries, Pisces and Aquarius which bring the powers of this quarter of the heavens into the Microcosm. In our skies are the ruling planets of Jupiter and Uranus bringing meaning to form and giving solutions and endings in the Microcosm.

WATER
I stand in the place of the summer constellations of Cancer, Gemini and Taurus which bring the powers of this quarter of the heavens into the Microcosm. In our skies are the ruling planets of the Moon, Mercury and Venus bringing intuition, thought and life into the Microcosm.

AIR
I stand in the place of the autumn constellations of Libra, Virgo and Leo which bring the powers of this quarter of the heavens into the Microcosm of humanity. In our skies are the ruling energies of Venus, Mercury and the Sun bringing protection, manifestation and expansion out of the Macrocosm into the Microcosm.

FIRE
I stand in the place of the winter constellations of Capricorn, Sagittarius and Scorpio which bring the powers of this quarter of

the heavens into the Microcosm. In our skies are the ruling planets of Saturn, Jupiter and Mars bringing meaning, movement and reflection into the Microcosm.

SPIRIT
Together we are the celestial panorama above and represent the powers of the heavens which radiate down upon the Microcosm. *(Each Officer calls their own sphere in an invoking manner following each other in sequence)*

EARTH
Earth

WATER
Planets

AIR
Constellations

FIRE
Universe

SPIRIT
Cosmos

SPIRIT
I stand in the shadow of the Great Ones of the Macrocosm. The representatives of the unseen power which draws the patterns and turns the wheels of Creation.

EARTH
I stand in the shadow of Uriel, Archangel of Earth and mediator between the Macrocosm and the Microcosm. His are the ways of truth and teaching for he is the bringer of knowledge from the Divine. In his care is the sphere of Earth, held as a precious jewel in the palm of his hand.

WATER
I stand in the shadow of Gabriel, Archangel of Water and mediator between the Macrocosm and the Microcosm. His are

the ways of vision and magic and he is the bearer of revelations from on high. He is the angel of mercy, resurrection and hope.

AIR
I stand in the shadow of Raphael, Archangel of Air and mediator between the Macrocosm and the Microcosm. His are the ways of beauty and life. His touch is of beauty and balance. He is the angel of healing who brings the blessing of the Most High to the afflicted.

FIRE
I stand in the shadow of Michael, Archangel of Fire and mediator between the Macrocosm and the Microcosm. He is the 'Disperser of Darkness' and wields the mighty sword of justice in the service of the Most High. His touch is wisdom, knowledge and power.

SPIRIT
We are enfolded within the wings of the Great Ones.
(Each Officer calls their own Archangel in an invoking manner following each other in sequence)

EARTH
Uriel

WATER
Gabriel

AIR
Raphael

FIRE
Michael

SPIRIT
The Ancient and Shining Ones

SPIRIT
Oh raise your hearts and minds to the realm of Light beyond light.

EARTH
For there is a Lord of the Earth who is greater than the greatest, who is the One in whom all live and move and have their being.

WATER
The One who is the God of Hosts, to whom all Angelic Powers bow in reverence and awe.

AIR
The One who is the Almighty Living God, who has existed from the beginning of eternity which has no beginning and no end.

FIRE
The One who is limitless power, absolute harmony and eternal duration.

SPIRIT
Let us enter the Mystery in silence and peace.
(Each Officer calls their own letter in an invoking manner following each other in sequence)

EARTH
Yod

WATER
He

AIR
Vav

FIRE
He

SPIRIT
Shin
(The Officers now walk the Pentagram with the light. Beginning with SPIRIT who walks to Earth and hands him/her the light. Spirit remains in the place of Earth, Earth takes the light to WATER, who then takes the light to AIR, who takes the light to FIRE, who takes it to the place of Spirit. The Officers keep changing places and exchanging the light until each Officer has returned to their original station.

When SPIRIT is again in his/her place and has the light, he/she leaves the Pentagram and circles the Temple slowly and in silence five times then returns to his/he place)
ALLOW A FEW MINUTES OF SILENCE

SPIRIT
So have we received, let us now seal the secrets of the Mystery in our hearts and withdraw once more into the Microcosm. I bid you remember.
(Each Officer calls their own letter in an invoking manner following each other in sequence)

EARTH
Yod

WATER
He

AIR
Vav

FIRE
He

SPIRIT
Shin

SPIRIT
May the blessings and the protection of the Great Ones remain with you. I bid you remember.
(Each Officer calls their own Archangel in an invoking manner following each other in sequence)

EARTH
Uriel

WATER
Gabriel

AIR
Raphael

FIRE
Michael

SPIRIT
The Ancient and Shining Ones

SPIRIT
See about you the great luminaries of the heavens and seek your own planet and place within the Universe. I bid you remember.
(Each Officer calls their own sphere in an invoking manner following each other in sequence)

EARTH
Earth

WATER
Planets

AIR
Constellations

FIRE
Universe

SPIRIT
Cosmos

SPIRIT
Descend now into the Microcosm and know yourself once more within the sphere of Earth. I bid you remember.
(Each Officer calls their own quality in an invoking manner following each other in sequence)

EARTH
Ground.

WATER
Moisture

AIR
Wind

FIRE
Warmth

SPIRIT
Life

SPIRIT
Now feel yourself once more within your physical body, a Microcosm within the mighty Macrocosm, a living part of the Great Mystery of Life. I bid you remember.

(Each Officer calls their own Element in an invoking manner following each other in sequence)

EARTH
Earth

WATER
Water

AIR
Air

FIRE
Fire

SPIRIT
Spirit

SPIRIT
Our work is accomplished, all may now depart in Peace.

GUARDIAN
Sees that all participating depart, the Officers leaving last.

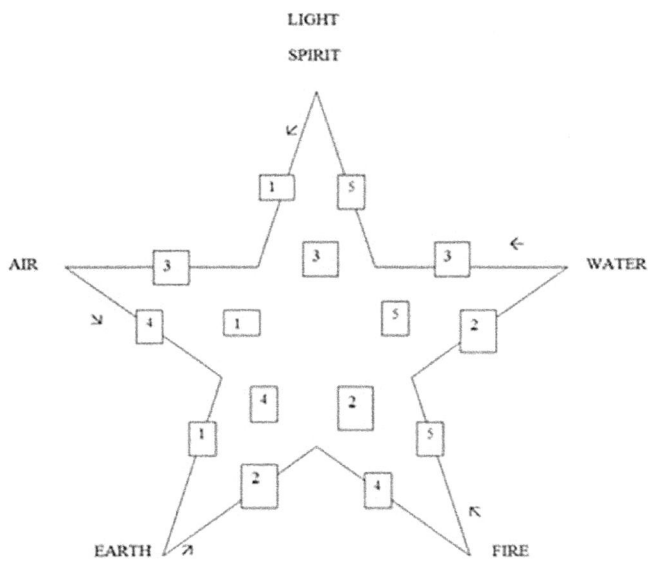

LIGHT

SPIRIT

AIR

WATER

EARTH

FIRE

189

Hexagram Ritual

OFFICERS
Officers One, Two and Three wear White Robes and are male.
Officers Four, Five and Six wear Black Robes and are female.
Officer Seven wears gold robe and gold mask.
Guardian.

REQUIREMENTS
Six Chairs arranged in two triangles as per plan.
A small low altar in centre between the Officers.
Altar cloth with Hexagram drawn upon it.
Candle in centre of Hexagram on small Altar.
Gong for Guardian.
Eight officers, three male, three female.
Officer Eight can be male or female.
Recorder player and music.

Ritual

GUARDIAN
(Sees that the Temple is correctly prepared. Lights the candle.
Admits all except the Officers. When all is prepared the six Officers of
the triangles enter, Officer Seven enters later in the ceremony. The
Guardian is then seated near the doorway.

OFFICER ONE, TWO AND THREE.
(Officer One enters first, Officer Two and Three following behind, they
go to their places in this triangular formation and are seated)

OFFICERS FOUR, FIVE AND SIX.

Officers Four and Five enter together followed by Officer Six, they go to their places in this Triangular formation and are seated.

Each Officer rises to speak and remains standing until returning to their seat after forming the Hexagram when all are seated together.

The Hexagram is formed by the Officers of each triangle joining hands, over the arm of the Officer to their left and under the arm of the Officer on their right.

GUARDIAN
(Sounds the gong six times slowly)

OFFICER ONE
I stand at the first point of the triangle of Divinity, I represent the Divine Light which is the source of all, the Infinite and Limitless Light which has no source nor form and whose existence is conceived only as Power within the Un-manifest.

OFFICER TWO
I stand at the second point of the triangle of Divinity, I represent the Omnipotent and Omnipresent Power of Divinity which governs and directs all that is created.

OFFICER THREE
I stand at the third point of the triangle of Divinity. I represent the Consciousness of the Creator which designs, controls and directs everything within the created Universe.

OFFICER SIX
I stand at the first point of the triangle of manifestation, I represent all that is form in the manifest Universe, the stars of the heavens, the earth, sea and sky of Earth and all the manifold vehicles of Life therein.

OFFICER FIVE
I stand at the second point of the triangle of manifestation, I represent the intellectual life of humanity, all the stored knowledge acquired through the centuries and the applications of science, medicine and art.

OFFICER FOUR

I stand at the third point of the triangle of manifestation, I represent the aspirations of humanity, its perpetual desire to expand, its search for new realms to conquer and improve and to enrich the lives of all living on Earth.

OFFICERS ONE, TWO AND THREE

(Move forward to stand at the three points of the white triangle)

OFFICERS FOUR, FIVE AND SIX

(Move forward to stand at the three points of the black triangle)
(The six officers then join hands to form the interlaced triangles of the Hexagram)

OFFICERS ONE, TWO AND THREE

(Say together in intoning fashion)
        Macrocosm.

OFFICERS FOUR, FIVE AND SIX

(Say together in intoning fashion)
        Microcosm.
        (The six Officers break the Hexagram simultaneously and emphatically and return to their stations)

OFFICER ONE

I stand at the first point of the white triangle of the Planetary Powers. I represent the influence of planet Saturn within Creation. I guard the gateway between Eternity and the realm of Time and Space. I bring order, discipline and self-knowledge into manifestation. I rule Time and draw the limits of life and existence.

OFFICER TWO

I stand at the second point of the white triangle of the Planetary Powers. I represent the influence of the planet Mercury within Creation. I am the Cosmic Messenger communicating between the Above and the Below. I bring intelligence, wisdom and reason into manifestation. I rule memory and am the storehouse of garnered wisdom.

OFFICER THREE

I stand at the third point of the white triangle of the Planetary Powers. I represent the influence of the planet Venus within Creation. I am the great Mediator who brings harmony and balance between the diverse opposites within manifestation. I rule love, balance and integrity and am the bringer of beauty and the laws of proportion.

OFFICER SIX

I stand at the first point of the black triangle of the Planetary Powers. I represent the influence of the planet Moon within Creation. I am the reflector of knowledge from the sub-conscious to the conscious. Mine are the powers of intuition and sensitivity. I rule the tides and cycles of Earth, I am the overseer of fertility, growth and instinct.

OFFICER FIVE

I stand at the second point of the black triangle of the Planetary Powers. I represent the influence of the planet Jupiter within Creation. I am the great dispenser of harmony and justice. Mine are the powers of benevolence, generosity and compassion. I rule the warmth and life in nature, I am the bringer of mercy and the giver of joy.

OFFICER FOUR

I stand at the third point of the black triangle of the Planetary Powers. I represent the influence of the planet Mars within Creation. I am the warrior who defends and destroys, bringing necessary change to the forms of manifestation. I rule courage, determination and passion, I am the defender of right and the sword of will.

OFFICERS ONE, TWO AND THREE

(Move forward to stand at the three points of the white triangle)

OFFICERS FOUR, FIVE AND SIX

(Move forward to stand at the three points of the black triangle)
(The six officers then join hands to form the interlaced triangles of the Hexagram.)

OFFICERS ONE, TWO AND THREE
(Say together in intoning fashion)
> Heaven.

OFFICERS FOUR, FIVE AND SIX
(Say together in intoning fashion)
> Earth.

(The six Officers break the Hexagram simultaneously and emphatically and return to their stations)

OFFICER ONE
I stand at the first point of the white triangle of the Directions. I represent the Above, the place from whence all descends. I am the quintessence of the Elements, the unifying source of all elemental energy, the matrix that allows energy to emerge from the four material elements.

OFFICER TWO
I stand at the second point of the white triangle of the Directions. I represent the East from whence flows the power of the Almighty Living God. I am the bearer of the magical wand with which I direct the flow of power of the Element of Air into manifestation.

OFFICER THREE
I stand at the third point of the white triangle of the Directions. I represent the South from whence flows the power of the Lord of Hosts. I am the bearer of the sword, which is the defender of the right and the conductor of the authority of Initiation. Through this sword is directed the flow of power of the Element of Fire into manifestation.

OFFICER SIX
I stand at the first point of the black triangle of the Directions. I represent the Below where all manifests and from whence the power of the Lord of the Earth flows back in return to its source. This is the theatre of all manifestation, action and material being, yet here also is the doorway to the Underworld and the deep dark hidden places.

OFFICER FIVE

I stand at the second point of the black triangle of the Directions. I represent the North from whence flows the power of the Lord of Earth. I am the bearer of the Platter of Plenty which nourishes and sustains all who partake of its abundance and receive the power of the Element of Earth.

OFFICER FOUR

I stand at the third point of the black triangle of the Directions. I represent the West from whence flows the power of the God of Hosts. I am the bearer of the Cup, which is ever full and overflows with the wine of intuition and wisdom. From this Cup all may drink of the waters of vision and the power of the Element of Water.

OFFICERS ONE, TWO AND THREE

(Move forward to stand at the three points of the white triangle)

OFFICERS FOUR, FIVE AND SIX

(Move forward to stand at the three points of the black triangle)
(The six officers then join hands to form the interlaced triangles of the Hexagram)

OFFICERS ONE, TWO AND THREE

(Say together in intoning fashion)
North, South, East, West, Above, Below

OFFICERS FOUR, FIVE AND SIX

Say together in intoning fashion)
Air, Fire, Water, Earth, Quintessence
(The six Officers break the Hexagram simultaneously and emphatically and return to their stations)

OFFICER ONE

I stand at the first point of the triangle of the incarnating spirit. I represent the Divine nature in humanity. I am that spark of the Divine that descends from on high into the realm of experience to grow in knowledge and wisdom. I am the silver thread which ever binds the child to the parent, the soul to the source and humanity to its God.

OFFICER TWO

I stand at the second point of the triangle of the incarnating spirit. I represent the soul nature in humanity. I am that essence of the Divine, which illuminates and guides the evolving spirit. I am the unknown knowledge which silently speaks of the Light from which the spirit emerged.

OFFICER THREE

I stand at the third point of the triangle of the incarnating spirit. I represent the higher self of humanity. I am their link with the higher, I am the small still voice of conscience and the infallible communicator who guides and directs through the forest of errors of the manifest world.

OFFICER SIX

I stand at the first point of the triangle of bodily existence. I am the physical vehicle by and through which knowledge of the world is gained. I am the teacher in the hard school of experience. I teach control and discipline, respect and care for the physical body.

OFFICER FIVE

I stand at the second point of the triangle of bodily existence. I am the emotional nature of humanity, it is thorough my forces that the spirit learns to love and to deal with hate. I am the motivating power which drives ambition and striving, my restless energy empowers the seeking spirit ever onward on its path.

OFFICER FOUR

I stand at the third point of the triangle of bodily existence. I am the mental faculties of humanity. I am intelligence and intellect, mine are the stores of knowledge acquired through the ages, the beauties of art and of music, the skills of science and medicine and the abilities of learning and wisdom.

OFFICERS ONE, TWO AND THREE

(Move forward to stand at the three points of the white triangle)

OFFICERS FOUR, FIVE AND SIX
(Move forward to stand at the three points of the black triangle)
(The six officers then join hands to form the interlaced triangles of the Hexagram)

OFFICERS ONE, TWO AND THREE
(Say together in intoning fashion)
The Soul

OFFICERS FOUR, FIVE AND SIX
(Say together in intoning fashion)
The Human Vehicle
(The six Officers break the Hexagram simultaneously and emphatically and return to their stations)

OFFICER ONE
I stand at the first point of the triangle of spiritual consciousness. I represent the first syllable of the name of Wisdom. I am SOL the eternal Light, which is the source of all illumination both material and spiritual.

OFFICER TWO
I stand at the second point of the triangle of spiritual consciousness. I represent the second syllable of the name of Wisdom. I am OM the glory of that which knows the emanations of the Most High.

OFFICER THREE
I stand at the third point of the triangle of spiritual consciousness. I represent the third syllable of the name of Wisdom. I am ON, for I am the truth within the created and all that is.

OFFICER SIX
I stand at the first point of the triangle of mundane consciousness. I represent the living vehicle of the family of humanity. I am the functions by which life is sustained and reproduced. I am the body which is formed from the substance of the Material Sun and vitalised by it.

OFFICER FIVE

I stand at the second point of the triangle of mundane consciousness. I represent the spirit of the family of humanity. I am the heart from which all emotions spring. I am feeling, compassion and hope. I am the Intellectual Sun which is redeemed by the true light of grace.

OFFICER FOUR

I stand at the third point of the triangle of mundane consciousness. I represent the soul of the family of humanity. I am the body's brain and all the functions it governs and directs. I am thought and word and action. I am the power of the Spiritual Sun, the source of all, the Divine Spirit working within the world.

OFFICERS ONE, TWO AND THREE

(Move forward to stand at the three points of the white triangle)

OFFICERS FOUR, FIVE AND SIX

(Move forward to stand at the three points of the black triangle)
        (The six officers then join hands to form the interlaced triangles of the Hexagram)

OFFICERS ONE, TWO AND THREE

(Say together in intoning fashion)
        Solomon.

OFFICERS FOUR, FIVE AND SIX

(Say together in intoning fashion)
        Adam and Eve.
        (The six Officers break the Hexagram simultaneously and emphatically and return to their stations)

OFFICER ONE

I stand at the first point of the triangle of eternal consciousness. I represent the first of the great trinity of symbols which embody the Divine Light. For I am the first of the Three Great Lights. I am the Spiritual Sun which manifests the power of God the Creator, the Eternal Father, the Source of all, the Divine Spirit within the sphere of causation.

OFFICER TWO

I stand at the second point of the triangle of eternal consciousness. I represent the second of the great trinity of symbols which embody the Divine Light. For I am the second of the Three Great Lights. I am the Intellectual Sun which radiates the life of God the Son, of Christ the Mediator and Lucifer the Light Bearer within the sphere of mediation.

OFFICER THREE

I stand at the third point of the triangle of eternal consciousness. I represent the third of the great trinity of symbols which embody the Divine Light. For I am the third of the Three Great Lights. I am the Material Sun which is the Holy Spirit that pervades manifestation. I am the Sun of energy and a storehouse of power in the sphere of effects, I am the reflector of the Light, Life and Truth of the Divine Source.

OFFICER SIX.

I stand at the first point of the triangle of awakened consciousness. I represent the material nature of the incarnating spirit. I am the Body which partakes of the animal nature of Earth, I am the reflector in Earth of the Light of the three fold Divinity and bear witness to it in the physical world.

OFFICER FIVE

I stand at the second point of the triangle of awakened consciousness. I represent the intellectual nature of the incarnating spirit. For I am the Spirit force within humanity which is redeemed by the true light of grace, the transmission of the spiritual Light to the intellectual mind by virtue of the Mediator, the personified higher intellect and soul nature.

OFFICER FOUR

I stand at the third point of the triangle of awakened consciousness. I represent the spiritual nature of the incarnating spirit. I am the Soul which is illuminated by the spiritual sun and ever remains in contact with its Higher Self, its Soul Nature which dwells in the superior worlds and partakes of the Divine Eternal Nature.

OFFICERS ONE, TWO AND THREE
(Move forward to stand at the three points of the white triangle)

OFFICERS FOUR, FIVE AND SIX
(Move forward to stand at the three points of the black triangle)
(The six officers then join hands to form the interlaced triangles of the Hexagram)

OFFICERS ONE, TWO AND THREE
(Say together in intoning fashion)
Divinity

OFFICERS FOUR, FIVE AND SIX
(Say together in intoning fashion)
Illumination

OFFICER ONE
Thus is our Hexagram formed and understood.
(The six Officers break the Hexagram simultaneously and emphatically and return to their stations)

OFFICER SIX
Let us now contemplate the meaning and purpose of our Hexagram. Please relax and close your eyes and enter into contemplation of this sacred symbol which is a key of entry into the Inner Worlds.

GUARDIAN.
(Turns on music for the meditation period. While this is playing he/she quietly removes the central altar and candle, this may be placed somewhere outside the Hexagram area and left alight)

OFFICER SEVEN
(Enters the Temple while the music is playing and stands in the centre of the Hexagram. When all is ready the SIX OFFICERS form the Hexagram around Officer Seven)

GUARDIAN
(Turns off the music)

OFFICER SIX
Our contemplation is now accomplished. Please return to full consciousness of the Temple and open your eyes.

GUARDIAN
(Sounds the gong seven times)

OFFICER SEVEN
I stand at the seventh point of the Hexagram, about me are the two triangles symbolising the spiritual and material Universes linked together in the nature of yourself, as a human being, who partakes of both Earthly Nature and Heavenly Divinity. I represent the Spirit of the Hexagram, its Sun of Potency, together we are the sum of the symbol, we represent the Eternal ONE, the Unity of Divinity.

Within each of us and every living thing, there is a centre of Life and Light that may grow to be a Sun. When the heart of humanity is vitalised and aware of its true nature, the Divine Power grows into a source of Light, which regenerates the body, illuminates the mind and radiates through the spirit. Then will your Sun shine forth into the worlds, illuminating all with whom it comes in contact. Then will you have found the Elixir of Life, be in possession of the Philosophers Stone, be worthy to stand in the centre of the Hexagram of Existence and indeed have reached the completion of the Great Work.

(The six Officers break the Hexagram simultaneously and emphatically and return to their stations and are seated)

OFFICER SEVEN
Let us now blend our light and turn the key of the Hexagram within us.

(Officer Seven now goes to each person beginning with Officer One then each Officer in turn, then to each participant. He/She bonds with each person by placing a hand on their head, holding their hand or meeting their eyes or as feels appropriate to each.

When Officer Seven has completed the bonding he/she exits the Temple).

GUARDIAN
(Allows a time of silence then sounds the gong seven times)

OFFICER ONE

I stand at the point of Wisdom within the triangles of the Hexagram. I represent all that the soul learns in its long journey. I am all Wisdom within the Mind of the Most High. May the blessing of Eternal Wisdom by upon you, grow to maturity within you and assist you in your quest.

OFFICER TWO

I stand at the point of Strength within the triangles of the Hexagram. I represent the strength which the soul gains from persistence in its long journey. I am the courage, potency and power needed to achieve the goals of the spirit. May the blessing of Strength be always within you and assist you in your quest.

OFFICER THREE

I stand at the point of Beauty within the triangles of the Hexagram. I represent the beauty revealed within every aspect of Creation. I am the splendour of the starry heavens and the magnificence revealed in humanity and nature. May the blessing of beauty sustain and comfort you and assist you in your quest.

OFFICER FOUR

I stand at the point of Glory within the triangles of the Hexagram. I represent the brilliance of the Everlasting Light, which supports and sustains every aspect of Creation. I am the light that illuminates your world and the Light which is of the nature of the Eternal. May the blessing of Glory and Light shine upon you and assist you in your quest.

OFFICER FIVE

I stand at the point of Power within the triangles of the Hexagram. I represent the energy of the Unmanifest flowing into Creation to build the Manifest. I am the force of focussed will, the director of destiny and the transformer of mundane humanity into the splendour of the illuminated. I am the power of the awakened and enlightened Ones. May their power flow through you and with you and assist you in your quest.

OFFICER SIX

I stand at the point of manifestation of the Kingdom. I represent the realm of the Most High who is the Lord of Earth. I am your today and your tomorrow, your future, present and past. I am your failures and your victories. I stand at the door that leads to the accomplishment of your purpose and I place in your hands the key which opens the gate to the completion of your quest.

OFFICERS ONE, TWO AND THREE
(Move forward to stand at the three points of the white triangle)

OFFICERS FOUR, FIVE AND SIX
(Move forward to stand at the three points of the black triangle)
(The six officers then join hands to form the interlaced triangles of the Hexagram).

OFFICERS ONE, TWO AND THREE
(Say together in intoning fashion)
Wisdom, Strength and Beauty

OFFICERS FOUR, FIVE AND SIX
(Say together in intoning fashion)
The Kingdom, the Power and the Glory

ALL OFFICERS TOGETHER
Forever and ever. Amen.

GUARDIAN
(Sounds the gong seven times.
The six Officers break the Hexagram simultaneously, all face the Temple entrance and leave, Officer Six leading, Officer Four and Five together, then Officer Two and Three together followed by Officer One)

GUARDIAN
(Starts exit music) Everyone, please rise and leave the Temple. *(Guardian leaves last ensuring the candle is extinguished)*

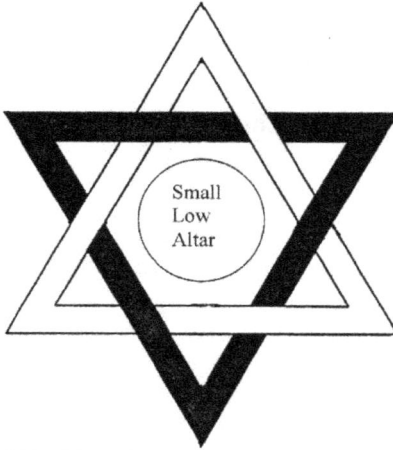

Chair
Officer One

Chair
Officer Two

Chair
Officer Three

Small
Low
Altar

Chair
Officer Four

Chair
Officer Five

Chair
Officer Six

Octagon Ritual

OFFICERS
ONE	*Male*
TWO	*Female*
THREE	*Female*
FOUR	*Female*
FIVE	*Female*
SIX	*Male*
SEVEN	*Male*
EIGHT	*Male*
GUARDIAN/ MUSICIAN	

There is a small round centre table covered with white or gold cloth.
Chairs for Officers in a circle round the table allowing several feet between chairs and table.
One large candle which Officer One carries in to the Temple.
All Officer wear white robes.
Gold cloth for centre table.
CD Player and music for entry and exit.

Ritual

GUARDIAN
(Admits all none Officer participants)

MUSICIAN
(Starts entry music.
   Om Hum So Hum from Tim Wheater Invisible Journeys.
   Officers enter in numerical order led by Officer One, they enter the circle from the East, circle around the centre table, rotating until Officer One is in the East)

OFFICER ONE
(Carries a lighted candle, which he/she places on small centre table. When Officer One returns to place all are seated)

MUSICIAN
(Fade out music gradually)

ALL
(All rise when they speak and remain standing until returning to their place after the salutations)

OFFICER ONE
One.

OFFICER TWO
Two.

OFFICER THREE
Three.

OFFICER FOUR
Four.

OFFICER FIVE
Five.

OFFICER SIX
Six.

OFFICER SEVEN
Seven.

OFFICER EIGHT
Eight.

OFFICER ONE
We are the eight spokes of the sacred wheel of the Sun, we spin eternally around the cycles of time and of space.

ALL OFFICERS
(The eight officers walk to the centre, join right hands, turn to left, stretch out left arm sideways and circle once. On completion of the circle they face centre, drop left hand to side and raise joined right hands high above candle and say)

ALL OFFICERS
Hail to the Mighty One, Sol Invictus Hail.
        (All drop hands, turn and return to their places and are seated)

OFFICER ONE

I am your Sun, the centre of your Universe, the bright day star of your existence. I am your parent, the source of your life and of your being. I bring light and warmth to the darkness of eternal space. I bring time to the turning of your home world. I give life and I take life, in my light are all things seen and revealed. I am the Logos of Light and of Life.

OFFICER TWO

I am Mercury, I am the smallest and swiftest of the children of the Sun, my path ever clings close to my parent whose brilliance dazzles the eye of those who would see me. The Ogdoadic star is my symbol in the systems of numbers and of magic. My influence upon humanity is upon the mind, reason and intelligence, I am the keeper of memory and the guardian of garnered wisdom. I am known as the messenger of the gods and the mediator between the above and the below.

OFFICER THREE

I am Venus, I am known as the morning and the evening star, whose rising and setting accompany the rising and the setting of our parent Sun. I trace the path of sacred geometry in the skies of Earth. I am the feminine influence of the planets and from time immemorial have been named for the Great Goddess. My influence upon humanity is through the emotions and the powers of love. I also hold balance in all things and wield the sword of justice.

OFFICER FOUR

I am Earth, your planet home. I am the jewel of the heavens, shining with the blue of the seas and blessed with the miracle of life. Alone among the children of the Sun I nurture and sustain the vessels of the life force. I am a miracle of creation, a cornucopia of beauty and a Temple in the service of the Most High.

OFFICER FIVE

I am Moon, daughter of Earth and grand-daughter of the Sun. I am the great reflector of the light, which illuminates the darkness of night upon Earth. I govern the ebb and flow of times and tides and the hidden forces of growth and fertility. My waxing and waning are a calendar and a clock to humanity. My influences are upon dream and the powers of the sub-conscious mind.

OFFICER SIX
I am Mars, the warrior of the skies. I am the masculine influence of the planets and from ancient times have been named for the gods of war. Yet my influence is not all conflict, I am energy and ambition and the tooth and claw of animal nature in all species. My colour is the red of life, blood, vitality and birth.

OFFICER SEVEN
I am Jupiter, the giant of the planet family. By my size I am the guardian of the solar system, drawing into myself comets, meteorites and cosmic debris. My title of Optimus Maximus defined me as the principal god of the ancient world. My influences are of generosity and fairness, benevolence, mercy and compassion.

OFFICER EIGHT
I am Saturn, the guardian between the material and the spiritual worlds. I guard the gateway between eternity and the realm of time and space. I am the Lord of Order, bringing self-knowledge, discipline and manifestation from the Unseen. I cut down the old, the useless and the unworthy but I raise up the persevering and endow them with wisdom.

OFFICER ONE
We are the eight solar bodies visible to the unaided eye, in eternal harmony we weave the threads of fate and destiny.

ALL OFFICERS
(The eight officers walk to the centre, join right hands, turn to left, stretch out left arm sideways and circle once. On completion of the circle they face centre, drop left hand to side and raise joined right hands high above candle and say)

ALL OFFICERS
Hail to the Mighty One, Sol Invictus Hail.

(All drop hands, turn and return to their places and are seated)

OFFICER ONE

Father and Mother to the Earth and all living things thereon, the Sun has, from the earliest times, been god and goddess to humanity in all times and all places.

I speak of Ra, the ancient and ever living one of Egypt. The eternal spirit who created himself and by his magic brought into being the four winds, the earth and the life giving waters of the inundation of the Two Lands. He spoke the word and by this he created all things. He sailed forever across the day sky in his Boat of Millions of years, his coming marked the dawning of the day and his going the darkening of evening.

OFFICER TWO

I speak of the one god of Akhenaten, Pharaoh of Egypt, the Aten whose living rays reached down to touch the Earth in nourishment and blessing.

How beautiful is your appearance on the horizon of Heaven,

O Living Aten who creates life.

When you rise on the eastern horizon

You fill every land with your beauty.

You are beautiful and great, gleaming high over every land.

Your rays they embrace the earth

To the furthest limits of what you have created.

From Akhenaten's Hymn

OFFICER THREE

I speak of Shamesh also called Utu, sun god of Babylonia and Sumer, the one who All Sees and who ruled truth, justice and right. He maintained law and order in society. He also brought clarity of vision to oracles and omens. He was the spirit and soul of the Law, he set the standards of truthful action and deeds in the world. He was worshipped in the Shining Houses of his temples for His was the will of the Ensouled Universe.

OFFICER FOUR

I speak of Helios, sun god of ancient Greece who also came to be called Apollo. He was seen as a supremely handsome man crowned with the shining aureole of the sun. In his chariot of the sun, drawn by four fiery solar steeds, each day he rode across the sky to sink into the ocean of the west at evening. Through the hours of night he drove through the world ocean, returning to the East each morning with the light of a new day. He was the bringer of light and the giver of sight. His myths are legion and his children numerous.

OFFICER FIVE
I speak of Surya and the sun gods of India who live on in the traditions of the Hindus and Buddhists of the modern world. Surya was seen as the store-house of inexhaustible power and radiance and his celestial body as the source and sustainer of all life on earth.

Throughout the lands of the East the Sun has been worshipped in many forms and under many names, having many powers and many attributes, but always remaining the Lord of the Sky and the giver of life.

OFFICER SIX
I speak of the ancient gods of the South American peoples, of Inti, sun god of the Inca people who also called him the Giver of Life. And of Tonatiuh, sun god of the Aztec and Mayan peoples. He was responsible for the sun moving across the sky, but in order for him to continue to do this he demanded human sacrifice on a fearsome scale.

OFFICER SEVEN
I speak of the Celtic gods of the sun, Taranis and Lugh. Taranis was an ancient sky god and also god of thunder. He carried the eight spoked wheel, the Celtic emblem of the Sun, its spokes representing the significant solar dates of the year.

Lugh was a god of light whose name means The Shining One. He was closely associated with harvest time and his festival was held at this season. He had many skills, he was a warrior, physician, druid, bard, smith, and brewer.

OFFICER EIGHT
I speak of Sol who was hailed in the Roman world as the

rising sun who dispelled the forces of evil, as the invincible conqueror of Rome's enemies, and as the companion and guardian deity of the emperor. Sol became identified with Mithras, the god of light who, by the slaying of a sacred bull, brought all into manifestation. In every Mithraic temple, the place of honour was occupied by a tauroctony, a representation of Mithras killing the sacred bull. Cautes and Cautopates, the celestial twins of light and darkness, were torch-bearers, standing on either side of Mithras, the Sun.

OFFICER ONE
So has veneration and worship of our Father/Mother Sun echoed down the centuries, it sounds still in the Mysteries and shines through the symbolism of all religions.

ALL OFFICERS
(The eight officers walk to the centre, join right hands, turn to left, stretch out left arm sideways and circle once. On completion of the circle they face centre, drop left hand to side and raise joined right hands high above candle and say)

ALL OFFICERS
Hail to the Mighty One, Sol Invictus Hail.
        (All drop hands, turn and return to their places and are seated)

OFFICER ONE
On the sacred wheel of time I stand at the point of the spring equinox when the light of day is equal to the dark of night and all life on Earth begins anew. The Sun rises in the cardinal sign of Aries whose element of Fire energises and warms the ground, seeds stir and vegetation and all creatures awake.

OFFICER TWO
On the sacred wheel of time I stand at the point of the first fire festival, the celebration of Beltane when the Sun God comes again to the Earth Maiden. The Sun rises in the fixed sign of Taurus whose element of Earth awakens fertility and brings forth new life in all nature.

OFFICER THREE

On the sacred wheel of time I stand at the point of the midsummer solstice when day is at its longest time. The Sun rises in the cardinal sign of Cancer whose element of Water refreshes the parched earth of summer bringing vigour and growth to all nature.

OFFICER FOUR

On the sacred wheel of time I stand at the point of the second of the fire festivals, the celebration of Lughnasadh when all things come to fruition. The Sun rises in the fixed sign of Leo whose element of Fire brings ripening of fruit and grain and all the land achieves maturity.

OFFICER FIVE

On the sacred wheel of time I stand at the point of the autumn equinox when day and night are once more equal and the fruits of nature's bounty are harvested. The sun rises in the cardinal sign of Libra whose element of Air brings the breath of life to all plants, animals and humans.

OFFICER SIX

On the sacred wheel of time I stand at the point of the third of the fire festivals, the celebration of Samhain when the veils between the worlds are thin and the gateway of winter opens. The Sun rises in the fixed sign of Scorpio whose element of Water cleanses and refreshes the land and the rivers, lakes and seas are renewed.

OFFICER SEVEN

On the sacred wheel of time I stand at the point of the winter solstice when night is at its longest time. The Sun rises in the cardinal sign of Capricorn whose element of Earth brings sleep and rest to all living things.

OFFICER EIGHT

On the sacred wheel of time I stand at the point of the fourth of the fire festival, the celebration of Imbolc when the first signs of winters end bring promise of Spring. The Sun rises in the fixed sign of Aquarius whose element of Air brings returning warmth in gentle breezes and gives voice to joy and praise.

OFFICER ONE
So has the wheel of the year turned from the beginning of time as the Earth follows her path around her parent Sun.

ALL OFFICERS
(The eight officers walk to the centre, join right hands, turn to left, stretch out left arm sideways and circle once. On completion of the circle they face centre, drop left hand to side and raise joined right hands high above candle and say

ALL OFFICERS
Hail to the Mighty One, Sol Invictus Hail.
　　　(All drop hands, turn and return to their places and are seated)

OFFICER ONE
The material visible Sun is the vehicle by and through which the powers of the Divine manifest on Earth. Yet is it but the outer face, for within the day light of the Sun are concealed the powers of the Sun behind the Sun, those fountains of life and immortal spirit whose presence ever shines forth. Even as the colours of the rainbow are concealed within the brilliance of white light, so are the worlds of the spirit concealed within the manifest.

OFFICER TWO
Red.

OFFICER THREE
Orange.

OFFICER FOUR
Yellow.

OFFICER FIVE
Green.

OFFICER SIX
Blue.

OFFICER SEVEN
Indigo.

OFFICER EIGHT
Violet.

OFFICER ONE
Even as colour is hidden within white, so too is the Inner Light concealed within the outer light.

ALL OFFICERS
(The eight officers walk to the centre, join right hands, turn to left, stretch out left arm sideways and circle once. On completion of the circle they face centre, drop left hand to side and raise joined right hands high above candle and say)

ALL OFFICERS
Hail to the Mighty One, Sol Invictus Hail.
  (All drop hands, turn and return to their places and are seated)
  (As they speak each Officer turns outwards so they are facing in the direction they are speaking of, at the close of their speech they turn back to face the centre of the circle)

OFFICER ONE
The intellectual or Soular Sun is the vehicle by and through which the powers of the subtle realms flow into the soul of life for it radiates the light of grace.

  I look to the East and face the rising Sun, the glory of the morning, reborn in the golden splendour of the dawn. Life, vitality and light shine once more upon the Earth and from the east Archangel Raphael sends down healing and strength.

OFFICER TWO
I look to the South-east from whence Regulus, Watcher of the Heavens, sends down the forces of change and fortune and governs the pathways of the Cosmos.

OFFICER THREE
I look to the South and face the mid-day Sun, the full heat of day shines forth in power and glory and from the south Archangel Michael sends down protection and balance.

OFFICER FOUR
I look to the South-west from whence Arcturus, Watcher of the Heavens, sends down the forces of stability and honour and governs the orderly function of Earth.

OFFICER FIVE
I look to the West and face the setting sun, the last glow of evening blazing in multi-hued glory and from the west Archangel Gabriel sends down the powers of vision and wisdom.

OFFICER SIX
I look to the North-west from whence Formalhaut, Watcher of the Heavens, sends down the forces which ensure the inheritance of the generations and the continuity of all things.

OFFICER SEVEN
I look to the North and face the darkness of perpetual night and from the north Archangel Uriel sends down the powers of teaching and knowledge.

OFFICER EIGHT
I look to the North-east from whence Aldebaran, Watcher of the Heavens sends down the powers which energise the Universe and watch over the cycles of being.

OFFICER ONE
(Facing the circle)
Thus do the servants of the Unseen watch over, protect and serve the Earth.

ALL OFFICERS
(The eight officers walk to the centre, join right hands, turn to left, stretch out left arm sideways and circle once. On completion of the circle they face centre, drop left hand to side and raise joined right hands high above candle and say)

ALL OFFICERS
Hail to the Mighty One, Sol Invictus Hail.
(All drop hands, turn and return to their places and are seated)

OFFICER ONE
The spiritual Sun is the vehicle by and through which soul and consciousness are emanated from the Divine Source.

The Chaioth-Ha-Qadesh, the Holy Living Creatures are the representatives of this Sun, they are mediators between the Divine and the material plane. They are set as Watchers in the four corners of Creation and represent the highest levels of the spiritual worlds to which humanity may aspire.

OFFICER TWO
I speak of the Winged Bull, he is an ancient emblem of the Primal Element of Earth. He represents the Lords of Form who serve evolution. The influences of the Winged Bull cause us to change, adapt and evolve, he is the urge TO BE. Spiritually he fosters the fertility of imagination and the creating of forms on the astral, he IS form in potential.

OFFICER THREE
Igne Natura Renovatur Integra - By fire nature is restored in purity; the inner fire of the spirit, the regeneration of nature by the influence of the sun symbolises the spiritual regeneration of mankind by the sacred fire which is truth and love.

OFFICER FOUR
I speak of the Winged Lion, he is an ancient emblem of the Primal Element of Fire. He represents the Lords of Flame who serve expansion of space in the creation of a cosmos. The influences of the Winged Lion cause us to develop the strength of courage and ruthlessness.

Spiritually he fosters creativity and inspiration, he inspires aspiration to Initiation.

OFFICER FIVE
Iaminim, Nour, Ruach, Iebschah – The four Primordial Elements of Water, Fire, Air and Earth, from which Creation is formed, both terrestrial and celestial.

OFFICER SIX
I speak of the Winged Eagle, he is an ancient emblem of the Primal Element of Water, he represents the Lords of Mind who serve the Teachers of Divine Wisdom. The influences of the Winged Eagle lead us to the great Mystery, the transmutation of the internal fire of life into the spiritual light-fire of the Gods.

Spiritually he leads us to the completion of the Great Work.

OFFICER SEVEN
INRI. I represents the active creative principle, N represents passive matter, the mould of all forms, R represents the union of the two principles and the perpetual transformation of created things, I represents the Divine principle and the creative strength which flows from it and returns to it everlastingly.

OFFICER EIGHT
I speak of the Winged Man, he is an ancient emblem of the Primal Element of Air, he represents the Lords of Humanity and Life who serve our spiritual nature and awaken us to our divine potential.
He leads us to knowledge of our spiritual body, which is the robe of our spiritual nature. It is the living Temple of the Living God.

OFFICER ONE
The Sun of our Universe shines without, the Light of the Divine shines within, the eternal and immortal Light of our Inner Sun shines from within to without.

INRI, Intra Nobos Regnum Dei,
The Kingdom of God is within us.

ALL OFFICERS
(The eight officers walk to the centre, join right hands, turn to left, stretch out left arm sideways and circle once. On completion of the circle they face centre, drop left hand to side and raise joined right hands high above candle and say)

ALL OFFICERS
Hail to the Mighty One, Holy One of Light, Hail.

(All drop hands and remain standing, as each speaks they turn and face outwards, each holds out a hand towards the participants as they make their blessing speech)

OFFICER ONE
May the blessing of our Parent Star ever shine upon you.

OFFICER TWO
May the blessings of the Planetary Spirits guide your destiny.

OFFICER THREE
May the Ancient Gods awaken from their sleep in time, guide you upon the paths of wisdom and give to you their blessing.

OFFICER FOUR
May the Wheel of Time give you long life and bless you with health and strength.

OFFICER FIVE
May you find all you seek at the rainbows end and walk under its multi coloured blessings all the days of your life.

OFFICE SIX
May the mighty Archangels and the Four Holy Creatures stand about you, guard and protect you and surround you with their blessings.

OFFICER SEVEN
May the spiritual forces of the Divine empower you, the Inner Light which radiates from the centre of Being shine through your Inner Sun and the blessing of the Most High be ever with you and about you.

OFFICER EIGHT
The blessing of the Light of the Sun, the blessing of the Light of the Spirit and the blessing of the true Light of the Eternal Mind and Soul of the Universe be with you and shine through you, now and always.

OFFICER ONE
With loving reverence we bow to the Inner Sun.

ALL OFFICERS
(All bow together towards the participants.
  All turn and face inwards.
  Together) Amen, Amen, Amen.
  (All officers face the centre candle and bow)

MUSICIAN
(Turn on music. (Gayatri from Tim Wheater, Invisible Journeys.)

  (Officers turn to their left and rotate until Officer One is in the West, then Officer One leads from the circle and others follow, all then go to the circle of participants, starting with first in northwest they circle clockwise. Standing before each one they bow and move on to next. When Officer One has completed the circle he/she leave the Temple followed by the other Officers as they complete their circle. If necessary, the Guardian indicates that participants should follow and exit after the last Officer has departed)

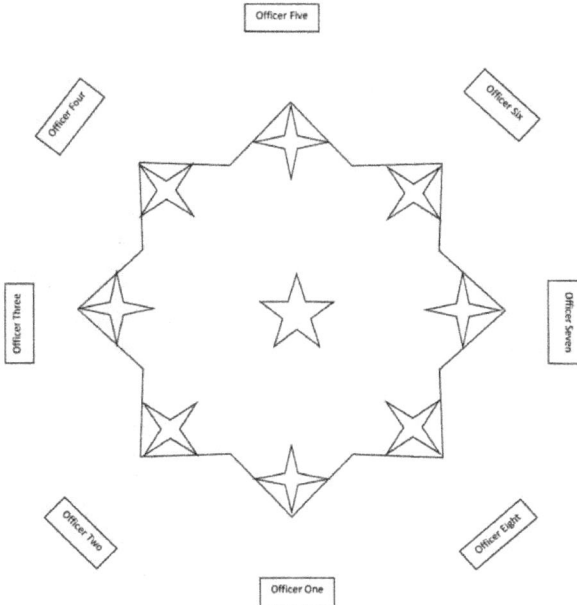

Water Ritual

OFFICERS
Officer of the East
Officer of the West
Officer of the South
Officer of the North
Guardian

REQUIREMENTS
Small altars at West, North, East and South.
On West, Chalice of water and candle.
On North, Chalice with water and candle.
On East, scented oil.
On South, taper and snuffer and candle.
The sacred light is lit on central altar.
There is an oil burner on central altar.
Soft music is playing. It is turned off when all are admitted.
All officers are seated at their stations.
The Guardian admits participants.

OFFICER OF WEST
(Rises and proceeds to the central alter facing west)
  Everyone, please rise and join me in making the Qabalistic Cross.
  Please be seated.
  (Returns to station and is seated.)

OFFICER OF THE EAST
(Rises and proceeds to central altar. Sprinkles scented oil on burner.)
  With the sweet scent of incense I cleanse this Temple. That it may be fresh and renewed as the drifting clouds in the heavens.
  (Returns to east and is seated.)

OFFICER OF THE SOUTH
(Rises and proceeds to central altar, lights taper from sacred flame)
  With the transmuting fire by whose power water becomes vapour I illumine this Temple.

(Proceeds to west and lights candle, then to north, east and south lighting each candle. Returns to place and is seated.)

OFFICER OF THE WEST
(Rises holding chalice and faces west.)

This temple we dedicate to the powers of water. From the west I call upon the Archangel Gabriel to seal and protect this temple, making of it a chalice into which may flow the waters of wisdom and of knowledge.

(Circles temple with chalice via north. Returns to station and is seated.)

OFFICER OF THE NORTH
(Rises holding chalice)

From the North I call upon Nixsa, King of the Elementals of Water. To bring the spirits of water to teach us in this Temple.

(Circles temple with chalice via east. Returns to station and is seated.)

OFFICER OF THE WEST

From the depths of the first logos have I come forth, out of the chaos of the primordial waters did I arise. For I am Mara, the great sea. Binah the eternal feminine and Isis the mother of all.

Come my children, immerse yourselves in the waters of creation, swim with me in the depths of the sea, ride on the rivers and streams and let me flow in your understanding.

Come my children, my Undines, my water elementals, from my throne in the western corner of creation let us travel as droplets on the west wind.

Higher and higher we rise, far below us shines the blue waters of the sea. Then something strange begins to happen. We look at each other and find we are becoming visible in a mass of white cloud. Faster and faster the wind takes us and we crowd ever closer together changing colour as we do so to a deep and ominous grey. Then suddenly we change - we are droplets of water falling, falling downwards through the air, then with an impact which scatters us in a thousand directions we hit the surface of the sea and plunge deep within it. Slowly we rise to the surface tossed and turned by the power of the turbulent waves which the storm winds now shape into great peaks and troughs.

For a long time we ride in the force of the storm, then slowly all becomes calm and we float gently and at peace in the warming sun.

Then as we watch the sun high above our heads, we become aware that we are moving gradually northwards, carried with a force we cannot resist as if within a river flowing within the sea.

OFFICER OF THE NORTH

Slowly the sun sinks into the western sea, but we are carried ever northwards through the descending darkness. We become aware of a change in temperature, we move less easily and more slowly.

A drowsy indolence makes us content to rest against each other. Then we realise a long time has gone by since we last were aware of any movement about us. Then slowly the sky lightens in the east and a white wonderland reveals itself about us. The reason for our immobility is immediately apparent for we are part of a vast expanse of ice which stretches as far as the eye can see. Pinnacles of ice reach upwards into the air and soft billowing snow drifts gently in the wind, forming ever changing patterns as it rolls and drifts across the surface of the ice. In the distance we can see high mountains with dark and barren sides lifting their white crowned heads into the violet coloured sky.

On the sides of the mountains broad glaciers slowly carve the rock into deep valleys which one day will know the rushing torrents our brothers and sisters form in the downward rush which follows on the thaw. But that is not yet. The winter winds bring still more of our kind and snow and ice grows fast above our heads. Slowly we sink deeper and deeper below the surface until we reach a place where we can move freely once again. Above our heads the light filters through the ice to give a gentle green coloured light to this new world.

We are surprised to realise this is no empty or lifeless place. Strange plants drift in the slow movement of the sea and fish such as warmer seas never bred dart here and there in search of smaller prey. We rest a while in this silent peaceful world. Yet without our realising it a slow current moves beneath the ice and we are part of it and needs must flow where it may take us.

After a long time of this gentle dreaming drifting we become aware of a subtle change in the light about us. The current takes us upwards with increasing speed, then suddenly we meet the air and bright shimmering sunlight warms every molecule.

OFFICER OF THE EAST

Higher and higher the sun climbs above us, brighter and brighter dances the light upon the surface of the water. We begin to feel uncomfortably hot and stretch to ease the discomfort, but we continue to expand and feel ourselves becoming lighter and lighter. Then we realise the sea is far below and we are travelling upwards with increasing speed. So thin and stretched have we become that we no longer feel to have any shape or form.

Far below we see the shining sea and as we are caught in the warm upward current of the air, the world below us blends into a kaleidoscope of swirling shape and colour.

In and out of alternating times of dark and light, we swing as the Earth's motion pulls us round and round. It seems we float for ever in this place of swirling clouds and rushing winds. Then we are caught within a cloud and once more feel ourselves falling back to earth. But now the pace is slowed as Earth swings into night, we hover, barely moving, just above the ground. Then suddenly we feel ourselves condense to dew and watch the grass blade bend beneath our sudden weight.

The first faint flush of dawn, then morning's brilliant light awakes the day and we, like diamonds, reflect its rainbow hue. Yet before the warmth of day can change our form the rain clouds gather and a summer shower sweeps us into a little brook. The pace is brisk and we enjoy our dancing leaping progress over rocks and falls.

Then from each side come other brooks and soon the stream has grown into a wide and stately river flowing with slow majesty between high walls of rock. On and on the river winds, through marsh and plain and cultivated land. Each mile brings new vistas into view and always the river grows in size as new streams come to join its swelling flow.

Then suddenly the pace is slowed and we find ourselves a part of a vast inland sea.

OFFICER OF THE SOUTH

Slowly we sink to the bottom of the lake. Here a strange new world of plant and fish awaits our discovery.

Slow seasons pass as we rest within the lake. It seems there is nothing here to cause our world to change. Yet a slow and subtle current is moving us along. Then with a sudden strong pull of movement we find ourselves in blackness, rushing madly headlong in the dark. Pushed this way and that by the force of our fall we constantly knock against the sides of the narrow channel through which we pass. Through many strange passages and chambers we are pushed and thrust, heated, cooled, strained and subjected to strange chemicals and processes.

Sometimes we escape from this whirling wheel of activity and find ourselves back in the quiet of the lake until once more the current takes us and we are off again through the cycle. Now the current catches us once again and we are off down another narrow tunnel, but this time the speed is so great we do not bump against the sides but are carried forward with a ferocious velocity, the force is irresistible and overwhelming. Then we are free and flying high into the air, but far below we see a sight such as we have never seen before. An inferno of fire rages on the ground, tongues of flame reach high into the sky and at its heart the fire shines white and it is as if we gazed into the sun. Then our momentum slows and we curve downwards, falling, falling, into the heart of the fire. A moment's exploding impact makes us reel, then we are free, rising as steam back into the sky.

OFFICER OF THE WEST

In due time we pass once more into the streams of earth, know the storms of sea and calm of lake. But then there comes the biggest change of all, for we have blended with the stream of life. Through stem of plant and tree we learn of the slow processes of vegetation. In fish and bird we learn of swim and flight. In animals and insects we feel the power of instinct drive us on. In vein and artery feel the pulse of life. In humankind we learn of mind and brain, of consciousness and independent thought and will. Slowly, slowly, do we thus evolve and in the fullness of time move on. Come my children, my undines. My water elementals. Rise with me into the blue vaults of heaven and know yourselves renewed within the cloud.

> I am the daughter of earth and water,
> And the nurseling of the sky;
> I pass through the pores of the oceans and shores:
> I change, but I cannot die.
> For after the rain when with never a stain
> The pavilion of heaven is bare.
> And the winds and sunbeams with their convex gleams
> Build up the blue dome of air,
> I silently laugh at my own cenotaph.
> And out of the caverns of rain
> Like a child from the womb, like a ghost from the tomb.
> I arise and upbuild it again.
> (*The Cloud,* by Percy Bysshe Shelley)

Such, my children, is the eternal cycle of your being. On you all living things depend. Plants and animals partake of your nature, in their veins you flow, the sustainer and vehicle of life. Without your presence all dies and at your coming all is resurrected, re-vitalised and blessed.

OFFICER OF THE NORTH
(Rises)
Our journey is over and we must return to our own form and place. Let us give thanks to Nixsa for allowing us to explore his realm and for the teaching we have received through the form of his Undines. In gratitude I close the north.

OFFICER OF THE WEST
(Rises)
Let this wisdom dwell in the vast seas of the mind that from these things which we have experienced may grow wisdom and compassion.

Let us give thanks to Gabriel for his protection of our Temple. In gratitude I close the west.

OFFICER OF THE SOUTH
(Rises)
May the transmuting power of fire and the illumination of

its light shine upon you and about you.

(Proceeds to West with snuffer and extinguishes candle, then to North and East extinguishing candles. Finally slowly extinguishes the candle of the South.)

In gratitude I close the South.

OFFICER OF THE EAST
(Rises)

May the work of this day remain with us to enlighten and expand our understanding of the realm of water. In gratitude I close the East.

Everyone please rise.

(Officers leave in order South, East, North, and West, Officers of the West and North leaving by way of the East)

(Guardian sees all exit and the central light extinguished)

```
              ┌──────────────┐
              │     East     │
              └──────────────┘




┌──────────┐                        ┌──────────┐
│  North   │         ( ✢ )          │  South   │
└──────────┘                        └──────────┘




              ┌──────────────┐
              │     West     │
              └──────────────┘
```

Ritual of Life

OFFICERS
GUARDIAN
MUSICIAN
THE NARRATOR
THE SUN
THE MOON
GAIA
THE CORN KING
YOUTH
MAIDEN
THE GREEN MAN
THE TREES

OAK
YEW
ELDER
WHITE POPLAR
ALDER
ROWAN
ASH
SPINDLE
BEECH
BLACKTHORN
HAWTHORN
BIRCH
HOLLY
HAZEL
APPLE
SCOTS PINE
ASPEN
WILLOW

THE BUSHES

BLACKBERRY
IVY
GORSE
HEATHER
HONEYSUCKLE
FERN

REQUIREMENTS
Large Candle for Sun
Matches or lighter for Sun
Small table in the West for Sun's candle and platter
Mask for Green Man
Mirror for Moon
Silver platter, Green Man face, grapes, fruit and greenery and cloth to cover until required
Two curtains in East to conceal the Green Man, arranged so he can enter between them
Mask for Green Man

Ritual

The intention of the ritual is the celebration of Life.
(The room is as dark as practical)

MUSICIAN
(Switches on music. Track One (Incantation. Tim Wheater. Track 5.)

GUARDIAN
(Admits all participants except Green Man, Maiden and Youth who are already in their place behind the curtains.
All are seated in a large circle)

MUSICIAN
(When all are settled, switch off music. Note. Do not allow to play beyond 2.30 minutes, where singing starts.)

NARRATOR
(Allow a few moments of silence.
   (Rises and goes to centre)

All was darkness and swirling energy, there was no form or light, only space and the intent of what was to be within the infinite Mind of the Creator.

In the depths of no time and no being, intent grew and behold, from the infinite Light of the most inner came forth a spark of the Divine and being became and the wheel of time turned for the first time.
   (Returns to centre and is seated)

SUN
(Rises and walks to centre of the circle carrying large candle)
Then the spark of the Divine expanded into heat and light, a body was formed of fire and light radiated out filling the darkness with light, and the swirling energy condensed into form.

Thus did I, the Sun, the first born of the Divine, come into existence, to be the parent in my turn of the manifest Universe in which I am the source of all heat and light and life.
(Lights candle)

GUARDIAN
(Switches on lights)

GAIA
(Rises and joins Sun in the centre, circling around Sun before speaking)
I am Earth, a daughter of the Sun. I was born of fire, nurtured by water and made fertile by air. Through millennia of time I was shaped by these mighty forces, sculptured by wind and weather, worn by glacier and flood and prepared to be the womb from which came the mystery of the birth of Life.

MOON
(Rises and joins Sun and Gaia in the centre, circling Gaia before speaking.

Carries a mirror with which she reflects the light of Sun's candle)
I am Moon, daughter of Gaia and grand-daughter of Sun. I too was born of fire but the powers of water and air were denied me. I walk in the shadow of my Mother and am but the mirror reflecting the light of the Sun in the darkness of her night.

My hidden influences are those of cycles and tides. I stir the seed from its slumber and bring forth fertility in due time and season.

SUN AND MOON
(Place their candle and mirror on the table in the West and return to their seats)

GAIA

From the hand of the Creator were scattered the seeds of all life, which germinated and sprang into being upon my breast. The mountains and valleys, the seas lakes and streams, the high places and the low places became filled with all manner of living things and there was no place left barren and empty.

(Fetches the silver platter of plenty and uncovers it.

Circles the Temple displaying the platter to all present. She then returns the platter to the West and is seated)

THE CORN KING

(Rises and goes to centre)

I am the Corn King, under my dominion are all growing things, the green grass and the fruits of the earth. My life is the cyclic time of the seasons, I am born with the sprouting of the corn, I rejoice in the fruitfulness of maturity and I die with the harvest. My progeny are the seeds that slumber beneath the winter's snow and I am resurrected with the returning warmth of spring. I am the willing sacrifice who dies to feed other life, I am immortality for I am born and die and am re-born in the eternal circle of life.

(Returns to place and is seated)

GREEN MAN

(Looks out from between the curtains, showing just his face, then steps fully into view)

I am the Green Man, the spirit of the woods. Under my protection are the trees, which give life to the creatures of the forest. I rule over the primeval forests still remaining from ancient times, the tropical and temperate woods and forests, which clothe our planet in green. Mine is the in breath and the out breath ever cleansing and renewing the air of Earth. My children do not wander restlessly about the Earth but stand sentinel with roots clinging ever to the nourishing breast of the Mother.

(As each tree and bush comes forward and speaks, The Green Man goes to meet him/her, conducts them to their appointed place and stands near them as they make their speech. He should try to convey a sense of overshadowing presence, moving about, looking over their shoulder and generally keeping attention on himself)

OAK
(Rises takes place on right side of the curtain opening)

I am the Oak Tree, the elder of the forest. I am the symbol of strength and endurance for my years are long and what is made of my wood is young when men are old and serves through the generations.

I have been regarded as sacred in many traditions, Herne the Hunter Lord of the Forest ran beneath my branches and Taranis shielded me from the forces of lightening and storm.

YEW
(Rises takes place on left side of the curtain opening)

I am the Yew Tree, the ancient one of the forest. I am the symbol of eternal life for my new growth springs from the old; and of eternal wisdom - for generations pass to generations yet do I endure. My wood is flexible and strong and served to defend this land.

ELDER
(Rises and takes place as in plan)

I am the Elder Tree, the symbol of sacrifice. The surrendering of something valued as an acknowledgement of the unseen, that there may be space for the things of the spirit. This is a giving which seeks nothing in return yet evokes a response from the Universe. I sacrifice to you my branches and twigs that they may protect you from dark forces.

WHITE POPLAR
(Rises and takes place as in plan)

I am the White Poplar the symbol of resurrection, the springing of new life from old. I represent the vital energy of the Universe that flows through all that lives. Life is a gift, loaned to the living for a space, which flows on at the death of its vehicle to animate another.

A white poplar stands on the threshold of the underworld, its roots reaching down into the waters of forgetfulness.

I give to you the scent of my leaves which rises in the smoke of incense in which is seen prophecy and vision.

ALDER
(Rises and takes place as in plan)

I am the Alder tree, I am the symbol of defence, sacred to Poseidon, god of the sea who guards all island realms.

I am sacred also to Chronos, god of time who guards us from the dangers and the sorrows of tomorrow.

In ancient times it was said that the first man was born of the Alder tree.

ROWAN
(Rises and takes place as in plan)

I am the Rowan, sacred to the Goddesses of the Sun. I give protection beneath the green of my branches and the red of my berries. I guard the homes and sacred places about which I am planted, for no evil may pass near to those within my protection.

In ancient times it was said that the first woman was born of the Rowan Tree.

ASH
(Rises and takes place as in plan)

I am the Ash tree, the symbol of the strength needed to survive in the face of great difficulties and to guard and protect our community, place and loved ones.

It was said that Yggdrasil the world tree was an Ash and that from its roots, deep within the ground, was drawn wisdom. The Ash has often been the choice for the Maypole Tree, representing the central pole supporting the Universe and the patterns formed by its turning, a reflection of the turning of the Earth and the stars, and our participation in their dance.

SPINDLE
(Rises and takes place as in plan)

I am the Spindle tree. From my wood is made the spindle upon which the thread of life is spun for the weaving of the web of destiny. I am the instrument of the three Fates, the Goddesses who weave and govern the vast tapestry underlying the immensity of creation. They weave the threads of the hidden worlds upon which the spirit walks.

BEECH
(Rises and takes place as in plan)

I am the Beech tree. I represent the doorways between life and death, the seen and the unseen, the hidden and the revealed. My gift is the learning, which comes in sleep vision and the words of the Oracle. Garner the wisdom that is gained from embracing life and treasure what experience teaches you. Grieve not for mistakes for they are often the keys which unlock learning.

BLACKTHORN
(Rises and takes place as in plan)

I am the Blackthorn tree. I am the symbol of the magic and miracle of life. I am the blood which flows through your veins, the heart which beats within your breast, the mystery of life which lies deep within you and links you to all other living life forms.

I am the eyes of the spirit that can see in the hidden places, that dreams the waking dreams of day and shows you your place in the immensity of the Universe.

HAWTHORN
(Rises and takes place as in plan)

I am the Hawthorn tree, I am the crown on the brow of the Maiden at Beltane. I bring fertility both to humans and to all growing things, I am the new growth which springs into renewed life with the spring.

I bring you a challenge that can inspire your character, its meeting and conquering can turn your fears into strength, your diffidence into courage and your inflexibility of thought into the adventure of vigour and new horizons.

BIRCH
(Rises and takes place as in plan)

I am the Birch tree, the Lady of the Woods. My branches are a sure aid against unfavourable influences and were used as a protection of land and place and child.

I rule beginnings; remember it is by listening to the voice of inspiration that we find a sure start and a successful conclusion to our endeavours.

HOLLY
(Rises and takes place as in plan)

I am the Holly tree, the symbol of energy and new beginnings. My fire is fierce, and also sacred, for it celebrates the winter solstice which is both an ending of the old and a beginning of the new. I decorate the door between the old year and the new.

Seize your opportunities with caution, for remember a fierce fire can burn with greater intensity. Follow your chosen purpose with steadfastness and strength and you will bear upon your head a crown of wisdom and success.

HAZEL
(Rises and takes place as in plan)

I am the Hazel tree, the symbol of ancient wisdom garnered down the ages and held within the memory of the ancestors. Seek intuitive knowledge in the depths of the memory of the mind of the Universe. Listen to the quiet still voice within.

But beware, for two of us side to side can be a doorway into the fairy realms from which you may return to other times and places than your own. Beware of illusion and the lure of fantasy.

APPLE
(Rises and takes place as in plan)

I am the Apple tree and I bring visions from beyond the illusion of our perceived reality. I will take you deep into the heart of Truth. I am the symbol of immortality and of the worlds that lie behind and beyond the material world; and I will teach you how to walk there.

For know that the fruits of the apple tree growing in the other-worlds were ever those of wisdom and knowledge.

SCOTS PINE
(Rises and takes place as in plan)

I am the Scots Pine tree, from my branches can be seen a clear and wide view of situations and problems in life. By climbing me, or a pole cut from my growth, do Shamans obtain this over-all viewpoint in order to assist those who seek their knowledge.

My foliage is evergreen and survives the cold of winter and the heat of summer, thus am I a symbol of resurrection and eternal life.

ASPEN
(Rises and takes place as in plan)

I am the Aspen tree, a crown of my leaves eases the transition at the end of life from this world to the other-world that lies beyond.

I am sacred to those who walk the paths of the subtle worlds, as Shamans, Priests or Mystics. I watch the paths of the inner worlds and guard them with my magic. All walkers of the worlds are protected by me, whether spirit helper, animal or magician.

WILLOW
(Rises and takes place as in plan)

I am the Willow tree, I represent the soul which flies in search of knowledge of the worlds which lie behind the visible, the traveller who seeks to know that consciousness which lies beyond the horizon of mortal life. I bring you inspiration which springs from the Divine spark within and leads you on to transformation and immortality.

BLACKBERRY
(Rises and speaks from place)

I am the Blackberry bush, I am symbolical of the difficulties and obstacles through which we must fight our way in life. Yet too I represent all that you value most, your skills, your relationships and your dreams. Understand that these are the true values of life, do not be deluded by material gains, these are necessary but not the key to happiness. Like my briers they can enmesh you in illusion and disappointment.

(Remains standing at place)

IVY
(Rises and speaks from place)

I am Ivy, I twist about the trees and bushes and clothe dead trees in new green. I am symbolic of the support that loved ones, family, community and country can give, for all are bound together even as I bind the trees together. Do not allow pride or over independence to become a barrier to accepting the help and support which others are ready and willing to give.

(Remains standing at place)

GORSE
(Rises and speaks from place)

I am the Gorse bush, the golden sun of my flowers brightens the day throughout the year. Even so am I symbolic of the fertility and power of the imagination that brightens your way. From imagination sprang every invention, achievement and idea of humanity. Use and train your imagination for it can bring you success in the world external and show you the doorway to the world within.

(Remains standing at place)

HEATHER
(Rises and speaks from place)

I am the Heather which brings a carpet of colour to woods and moor lands. When my flowers are white they bring luck and good fortune, when they are purple they clothe the mountains with beauty. I bring the insight which gives the strength to discard old ideas and illusions and build new opportunities in your life.

(Remains standing at place)

HONEYSUCKLE
(Rises and speaks from place)

I am the Honeysuckle, the sweet scent of my flowers brings fragrance to forest and wood. I represent the sweetness that flows from the teachings, practices and rituals of the Mysteries, the hidden knowledge whose finding brings meaning and purpose to life's journey. I grow beside the hidden path which leads to the centre where wisdom dwells.

(Remains standing at place)

FERN
(Rises and speaks from place)

I am the Ferns which grow upon the forest floor and I represent Truth in all you do and say. Keep faith with Truth both to the outer world and to yourself and you will gain the journey's end with honour.

MUSICIAN
(Switch on music. Track Two. (Incantation. Tim Wheater. Track 4.)

GREEN MAN
(Goes to stand in front of centre of curtains in East)

BLACKBERRY, IVY, GORSE, HEATHER, HONEYSUCKLE AND FERN
(All now leave their places and entering the circle from different directions weave a pattern between the Trees. As they meet they touch hands and move on passing by most of the Trees on their way. They stand still when Gaia speaks)

GAIA
(Rises, enters circle and walks between the Trees and bushes)

MUSICIAN
(Switch off music)

GAIA
Alas, although the land upon my breast is clothed in green, is fertile with plant and animal, is bright with Sun and washed by rain. Yet are there no eyes to behold this beauty, no ears to hear the call of birds, no senses to know the sweet fragrance of flowers upon the air, nor hands to gather harvest in nor tend the young.

GREEN MAN
(Comes forward to Gaia and takes her hands consolingly)
　　　Grieve not sweet Lady, for I have seen within my forest glade a maiden fair who has eyes to see and hands to touch, who looks upon the beauty of your world and is glad. I have seen too a youth who also rejoices in your world, with hands and mind to create and form new beauties from the bounty of your land and all that grows upon it.

GAIA

If this be so then bring them forth that I might greet them and rejoice.

MUSICIAN

(Switch on music Track 3. (Second Nature, Katherine Jenkins Track 9)

GREEN MAN

(Goes to curtains and draws them apart, the maiden comes forward, the Green man takes her hand and draws her into the Temple.

As the male singer is heard the Green man goes back and draws him too into the Temple. He brings the Maiden and Youth together who join hands looking into each other's eyes, then the Green Man leads then around the Temple between the Trees and the Bushes as if finding their way through the forest ending in front of Gaia)

Lady Gaia, I present to you this Maiden and this Youth, they represent the men and women of humanity who are come to walk upon your Earth, to know its beauty; to cultivate its plants, to tend and harvest its fruits and to care for all creatures who live thereon.

GAIA

It is with a joyous heart I greet you, tend the garden of Earth with care, assist the plants to grow, keep them free of weed and pest. Gather the fruits of the harvest and conserve them against the lean days of winter. Rejoice in the new life of spring and the splendour of summer's riches. Assist all creatures to live life to the full, keep pure the waters of earth and the air of the skies. In your care I place my trust, for you are the custodians of my garden. Use your gifts well.

(All the Trees, the Bushes, Gaia and the Green Man now join hands and form a circle around the Maiden and the Youth. They are in no particular order and speak their blessing from where they are in the circle. The Maiden and the Youth join hands and turn to each as they speak their blessing so they are moving about the circle)

THE GREEN MAN

I give you the gift of fertility.

OAK

I give you the gift of long life.

YEW
I give you the gift of wisdom.

ELDER
I give you the gift of unconditional love.

WHITE POPLAR
I give you the gift of sacred vision.

ALDER
I give you the gift of sons.

ROWAN
I give you the gift of daughters.

ASH
I give you the gift of strength.

SPINDLE
I give you the gift of destiny.

BEECH
I give you the gift of sleep vision.

BLACKTHORN
I give you the gift of good health.

HAWTHORN
I give you the gift of love.

BIRCH
I give you the gift of inspiration.

HOLLY
I give you the gift of steadfastness.

HAZEL
I give you the gift of memory.

APPLE
I give you the gift of truth.

SCOTS PINE
I give you the gift of far sight.

ASPEN
I give you the gift of walking in the subtle worlds.

WILLOW
I give you the gift of immortality.

BLACKBERRY
I give you the gift of happiness.

IVY
I give you the gift of loved companions.

GORSE
I give you the gift of imagination.

HEATHER.
I give you the gift of good luck.

HONEYSUCKLE
I give you the gift of knowledge of the Mysteries.

FERN
I give you the gift of finding the Elixir of life, the key to immortality.

GAIA
I give you the gift of LIFE.

NARRATOR
(Fetches the Maypole and hands it to the Green Man)

GREEN MAN
Come, let us celebrate with joy the life which is in us, the light which is above us and the love which binds us to each other.

MUSICIAN
(Switch on music Track 4 and Track 5 The Priests Track 8)
He holds up the Maypole and all take a ribbon and circle around the room joyously, drawing in those who are seated to join in)

RITUAL OF LIFE PLAN

MAN   WOMAN
              GREEN MAN
--------------CURTAIN----------------------

          OAK   YEW

     ELDER   WHITE POPLAR

                   ALDER

   ROWAN   ASH

              SPINDLE

  BEECH   BLACKTHORN

        HAWTHORN   BIRCH

              HOLLY

     HAZEL   APPLE

SCOTS PINE   ASPEN

           WILLOW

        Small table

The Four Worlds Ritual

OFFICERS
MALKUTH
YESOD
HOD
NETZACH
TIPHARETH
GEBURAH
CHESED
BINAH
CHOKMAH
KETHER
GUARDIAN
MUSICIAN

REQUIREMENTS
Tables and candles for each of the Ten Stations.
Table at position of Daath.
Symbol for Daath, Onyx crystal suggested.
Central Altar.
Six holders and candles on central altar.
Incense burner on central altar.
Charcoal.
Incense on North side of altar.
Small sacred light on central altar.
Matches.
Candle snuffers for Malkuth, Netzach and Hod.
Tapers for Malkuth, Hod and Netzach.
Shoulder capes of appropriate colours for Officers of the Stations.
Sword for Guardian.
Gong for Guardian.
Black Crystal at Daath.
Tape Recorder and Music for Musician.

Ritual

MUSICIAN
(Takes place in the Temple first
  Start entry music
  All acknowledge the Sacred Light on entry)

GUARDIAN
(Enters second. Check charcoal and Sacred Light are lit.
  Officers enter next in order, Malkuth, Yesod, Netzach, Chesed,
Chokmah, Kether, Binah, Geburah, Tiphareth and Hod; and are seated
  All others attending enter
  The Officers are seated as shown on plan. Yesod and Tiphareth
sit (and face) East and West of the Altar respectively)
  (NOTE Each Officer rises when speaking and is then seated)

MALKUTH
(When music ends)
  Guardian of the Doorway, do you affirm that the Temple is secure and that all within are present by free will and dedication to the Light?

GUARDIAN
By the right of my office, I do so affirm.

MALKUTH
This being so, I request that you seal the door of the Temple with the sign of protection.

GUARDIAN
(Seals the doorway with the sign of the Pentagram)

MALKUTH
Everyone please rise and assist me to sanctify this Temple by joining with me in making the salutation of the Qabalistic Cross.
  (After this is done)
  Please be seated.

GUARDIAN
(Sounds the gong ONCE)

Officers of this Temple in Earth, declare your station and function.

(Sounds the gong THREE times)

MALKUTH

My station is that of Malkuth, my symbol in the Temple of Earth is the sacred circle, by it I establish this Temple as a sacred space and define the limits thereof.

(Lights station candle, taking light from central altar. Takes the lighted candle and circles outer limits of the Temple with it, thus enclosing all within the circle)

This circle of light I declare to mark the boundary of our Temple, which none may pass who do not come in Light and Peace. So be it sealed.

YESOD

My station is that of Yesod, my symbol in the Temple of Earth is the sandals upon the feet of the servants of the Temple, which ensure that they walk in silence.

HOD

My station is that of Hod, my symbol in the Temple of Earth is the cubic stone, the altar in the centre of the sacred space, which is the manifestation of our intention and the focus of our dedication.

(Lights the central altar candles, taking the light from Sacred Light on altar. Returns to station and is seated)

NETZACH

My station is that of Netzach, my symbol in the Temple of Earth is the lamp, which is the way shower and the guide. I bring light to all that none shall walk in darkness and fear.

(Lights the station candles, taking the light from Malkuth, in order; Yesod, Hod, Geburah, Tiphareth, Binah, Kether, Chokmah, Chesed, and Netzach. Returns to station and is seated).

TIPHARETH

My station is that of Tiphareth, my symbol in the Temple of Earth is the Rose Cross. It is the hardships and trials of life, yet also the joy of the unfolding spirit which comes to full bloom at the heart of the equal armed cross.

GEBURAH
My station is that of Geburah, my symbol in the Temple of Earth is the holy sword of power, which is the destroyer of evil and the conductor of light. This sword gives power to the initiate and withholds it from the profane.

CHESED
My station is that of Chesed, my symbol in the Temple of Earth is the equalled armed cross of perfect balance. This cross is mercy and stability, compassion and power.

BINAH
My station is that of Binah, my symbol in the Temple of Earth is the chalice, held in the hands of the mother. It is the cup of sorrow which holds the golden liquid of joy. This chalice is the grail of the mysteries and communion with the Most High.

CHOKMAH
My station is that of Chokmah, my symbol in the Temple of Earth is a rock tablet on a sacred mountain top, upon which are carved the attributes of the Father, limitless power, absolute harmony, eternal duration.

KETHER
My station is that of Kether, my symbol in the Temple of Earth is the Divine Spark, the lightening flash of creation. This spark is the infinite uncreated Light at the heart of the finite.

MALKUTH
The powers of the Temple of Earth are now duly established, the Temple of Earth is prepared and functioning. The Temple of Mind may now be approached and entered.

MUSICIAN
(Start music and play for several minutes)
   NOTE (Officers remain seated when speaking until the return to the Temple of Earth)
   (When music ends)

YESOD

Officers of the Temple of Mind, call upon those guiding spirits, the holy angelic choirs, who are the guardians of the powers of Mind, to attune with us. That they may manifest their beneficent spirits and assist us to enter the Temple of Mind, and prepare us to approach the Temple of Creation.

(Yesod goes to central Altar and ignites incense. Starting in the North, Yesod makes the appropriate invoking sign of the Pentagram in each of the four Quarters. North, Earth; East, Air; South, Fire; West, Water; sealing the quarters with the Holy Names as follows:

North	ELOHIM
East	IESCHOUAH
South	ADONAI
West	YOD-HE-VAV-HE

(Returns to station and is seated)

YESOD

The Temple of Mind is thus sealed, guarded and protected.

GUARDIAN

(Sounds the gong SIX times)

MALKUTH

I stand in the sphere of Malkuth in the Temple of Mind. I call upon the angelic choir of the Ashim, the living flames of fire, which we see as a mighty wall of living flame surrounding our Temple. Come, be with us. Awaken within us our soul made perfect, that we may attune with the souls of the redeemed and, knowing our true potential, in our higher self experience the knowledge of the soul.

YESOD

I stand in the sphere of Yesod in the Temple of Mind. I call upon the angelic choir of the Kerubim, presidents of the elements, the living powers of the Holy Name, the souls of fire, who we see as mighty Lords ruling the fixed signs of the zodiac; the element of air in Aquarius, the element of fire in Leo, the element of earth in Taurus and the element of water in Scorpio; to come, empower and protect us in all aspects of the mind.

HOD

I stand in the sphere of Hod in the Temple of Mind. I call upon the angelic choir of the Beni Elohim, the mighty Sons of God who we see as great guardians about us, to come, inspire our hearts with wisdom and hold steady the scales of the balanced mind.

NETZACH

I stand in the sphere of Netzach in the Temple of Mind. I call upon the angelic choir of the Elohim, they who are both the feminine and the masculine of the divine, who we see as great graceful figures enfolding us in their beauty; to come, assist us to make manifest within us all virtues, goodness and excellence.

TIPHARETH

I stand in the sphere of Tiphareth in the Temple of Mind. I call upon the angelic choir of the Melekim, the principalities, the kings, who we see as mighty rulers standing about us in majesty; to come, instruct us that we may rule, with authority and power, the kingdom of the mind.

GEBURAH

I stand in the sphere of Geburah in the Temple of Mind. I call upon the angelic choir of the Seraphim, the powers, the fiery serpents, the great and flaming ones, who we see in awesome splendour climbing the heavens like the vast flames of the sun; to come, empower us with energy and strength of mind and will.

CHESED

I stand in the sphere of Chesed in the Temple of Mind. I call upon the angelic choir of the Chashmalim, Dominations, the bright shining ones, the brilliant ones, who we see about us as great columns of light; to come, help us to illumine with justice and truth the beacon of the mind.

BINAH

I stand in the sphere of Binah in the Temple of Mind. I call upon the angelic choir of the Aralim, the thrones, the chalices of the divine life energy, the seats of power and conveyors of the holy spirit, from whom we see the waters of life flowing all about us; to come, help us to immerse ourselves in the creative waters of Mara, the great sea.

CHOKMAH

I stand in the sphere of Chokmah in the Temple of Mind. I call upon the angelic choir of the Auphanim, wheels, the whirling forces, the encircling ones, who we see as the great lights of the galaxies revolving through space; to come, attune us with the celestial forces of the zodiac that every gate may be open and the zodiacal forces flow within our Temple of Mind.

KETHER

I stand in the sphere of Kether in the Temple of Mind. I call upon the angelic choir of the Chayoth-ha-Qadesh, the Holy Living Creatures, the seraphim, they who stand at the four corners of creation, who we see as the four great winged creatures. In the east the Man, in the south the Lion, in the west the Eagle and in the north the Bull; to come, that their influence may surround and encompass all who work in this Temple of Mind.

YESOD

The Choirs of Angels are present and presiding. The Temple of Mind is established and functioning. The Temple of Creation may now be approached and entered.

MUSICIAN

(Play music for few minutes)

TIPHARETH

(When music ends)

Officers of the Temple of Creation, call upon the Archangelic Beings whom we now ask to assist us to enter the Temple of Creation, and prepare us to approach the Temple of the Divine.

GUARDIAN

(Sounds gong nine times)

MALKUTH

I stand in the sphere of Malkuth in the Temple of Creation, I call upon the archangelic power of this sphere, to come and be present among us.

Before me I see Sandalphon, Archangel of Earth. He is tall, young, yet with the wisdom of the ages in his eyes. His dark curling hair falls to his shoulders, and in it are twined clusters of grapes and vine leaves which he wears like a crown. His long robes sweep about him in billowing folds and a medley of colours, russet red, gold and apple green, with here and there a flash of citrine and forest brown. In his hands he holds a pair of golden sandals, for he is the sandal bearer of the Gods. This is no ordinary footwear, for they are worn only by those who have learned to walk between the worlds and of their own right bear the title of Initiate.

Sandalphon, Lord of Earth, permit us to wear the sandals of the Initiate and enable us to enter into the sphere of Malkuth in the Temple of Creation.

YESOD

I stand in the sphere of Yesod in the Temple of Creation. I call upon the archangelic power of this sphere, to come and be present among us.

Before me stands Gabriel, the Strong One of God. Behind him is a great lake over which the moon rises against a dark indigo sky. His long blue robe is edged with silver and around his waist is a wide red girdle, on which is emblazoned his name in sacred letters. In his hands he carries a silver chalice which is filled to the brim with the waters of life, and above the water hovers an orange-yellow flame. He holds out the chalice towards us as if to invite us to drink.

Gabriel, Messenger of God, give us to drink from your Chalice and enable us to flow with the sphere of Yesod in the Temple of Creation.

HOD

I stand in the sphere of Hod in the Temple of Creation. I call upon the archangelic power of this sphere, to come and be present among us.

Before me stands Michael, the Perfect of God. He stands

upon a green hilltop and behind him a brilliant sunrise blazes across the sky in vivid shades of orange, yellow, gold and deepest red. His short robe of red and gold has a serviceable, almost military style. In his right hand he holds aloft a finely wrought sword, whose silver blade reflects the light of the rising sun, which ripples like flames of fire from tip to beautiful ornamental hilt. This is the supreme commander of the armies of Light, in his presence no thing of darkness can exist and all fears are put to flight.

Michael, Defender of God, protect us with thy sword that we may walk in safety in the sphere of Hod in the Temple of Creation.

NETZACH

I stand in the sphere of Netzach in the Temple of Creation. I call upon the archangelic power of this sphere, to come and be present among us. Before me stands Haniel, whose title is "I, the God". Fair and delicate of face and form, neither entirely masculine nor entirely feminine, but appearing rather a harmonious combination of the two, Haniel stands in a lush meadow with all the beauty of the natural world about him.

His emerald robe is brighter still than nature's colours can contrive, and tied about the waist is a scarlet girdle, the colour of bright poppies in a summer field. In his left hand he holds aloft a glowing lantern and in his right hand he bears a pair of scales. Behind him is a pale morning sky and rising low in the sky shines the silver light of Venus, the morning star.

Haniel, Instructor and Initiator, help us to maintain balance in our emotional nature, and thus learn within the sphere of Netzach in the Temple of Creation.

TIPHARETH

I stand in the sphere of Tiphareth in the Temple of Creation. I call upon the archangelic power of this sphere, to come and be present among us.

Before me stands Raphael, the Healer of God. Behind him is a clear blue sky, with the sun, at the height of its power, directly overhead. Tall, with golden hair, he wears a yellow robe which drifts slightly in a gentle breeze. Upon his feet are golden sandals which are winged and in his hand is a traveller's staff hewn from a hazel branch. Slung across his shoulder he carries a bow and arrows and from his waist is hung a crystal vial of golden yellow healing balm. His eyes draw ours irresistibly, they are golden amber and of remarkable depth and clarity, and as we gaze into them we know that he can see into our deepest self.

Raphael, wise Counsellor and Teacher, take our hand that we may grow in wisdom in the sphere of Tiphareth in the Temple of Creation.

GEBURAH

I stand in the sphere of Geburah in the Temple of Creation. I call upon the archangelic power of this sphere, to come and be present among us.

Before me is Khamael, the Burner of God. This is the Warrior of God and he is suitably garbed. His long scarlet cloak covers the armour beneath, but we can see his black gloved hands and here and there the gleam of shining chain-mail as he moves. His eyes are concealed behind the visor of a dark helm. In his right hand he holds aloft a very serviceable looking, great sword and his left hand rests on a large pair of scales, for he administers one half of the karmic law. About his waist is a large golden belt which bears his name in letters of pure flame.

Khamael, Administrator of Justice, judge us with compassion that we may safely pass through the sphere of Geburah in the Temple of Creation.

CHESED

I stand in the sphere of Chesed in the Temple of Creation. I call upon the archangelic power of this sphere, to come and be present among us.

Before me is Tzadkiel, the Righteous of God. He is tall and majestic and dressed in deep blue robes. His hair is shoulder length and golden and upon his feet he wears sandals of gold. In his right hand he holds a pastoral staff of office, surmounted by an equal armed cross, and his left hand too rests upon the scales for his is the loving balance to the severity of Khamael. His deep blue eyes, indeed his whole being, radiates his perfect understanding and merciful compassion.

Tzadkiel, who speaks through the inner voice, help us to listen when you speak and hear your wisdom through the sphere of Chesed in the Temple of Creation.

BINAH

I stand in the sphere of Binah in the Temple of Creation. I call upon the archangelic power of this sphere, to come and be present among us.

Before me is Tzaphkiel, the Watcher of God. Behind him is a vast dark sea and a stormy sky from which lightning flashes. He sits upon a mighty throne from where he fulfils his task of overseeing the karmic records. His jet black robes are relieved only by the lamen upon his breast which is a brilliantly coloured eye within the triangle. His is the watching Eye of God which sees and knows all. In his left hand he holds a black rod of office and in his right is a chalice, full to the brim with the fiery waters of life.

Tzaphkiel, who is the all-seeing of God, help us to open our own inner eye, that we may see true within the sphere of Binah in the Temple of Creation.

CHOKMAH

I stand in the sphere of Chokmah in the Temple of Creation. I call upon the archangelic power of this sphere, to come and be present among us.

Before me stands Ratziel, the Herald of God. Behind him is a great mountain peak which wears a crown of stars. His swirling grey robes are like misty vapour which conceal his face as clouds obscure the mountain top. In his right hand he holds a large book in which are contained the secrets of the universe which may only be read by divine inspiration.

Ratziel, holder of secrets of the Most High, give us knowledge that we may gain understanding through the sphere of Chokmah in the Temple of Creation.

KETHER

I stand in the sphere of Kether in the Temple of Creation. I call upon the archangelic power of this sphere, to come and be present among us.

Before me is Metatron, the archangel of the divine presence. The light behind him is so brilliant and his being so radiant, it is hardly possible to see his form. He is immensely tall and radiates great power. In his right hand he carries a sealed scroll which contains the divine plan.

As we look beyond him we can see nothing but a great light, which is not just illumination but a living moving presence which contains all colours, and yet is pure white brilliance.

Metatron, Archangel of the Divine Presence, shield our eyes that we may safely look into the sphere of Kether in the Temple of Creation.

As we turn and look back we see the ten Archangels. As we watch they each unfurl their wings and spreading them out towards each other, they form a mighty circle of power and protection about us which radiates with immense and sacred light. Then we know that they, who walk in the Greater Light, will permit us to be in the realms of Light in the Temple of Creation, and lead us to the doors of the Temple of Divinity.

TIPHARETH
The archangelic powers have been invoked. The Temple of Creation is accessed and functioning and we are prepared to enter the Temple of Divinity.

MUSICIAN
(Play music for few minutes)

KETHER
(When music ends)
Officers of the Temple of Divinity, lead us into the Temple of the Holy One that we may commune with the Most High.

GUARDIAN
(Sounds the gong twelve times)

MALKUTH
We stand in the yellow light of Malkuth in the Temple of Divinity.

About us are the Ashim and at our right hand is Sandalphon.

This is the Gate of the Kingdom, the doorway between Light and earth, death and life.

Here rules the Lord of Earth whose title is Adonai-ha-aretz.

Let us attune ourselves with this aspect of the Most High by intoning together, three times, this holy name.

Adonai-ha-Aretz

YESOD

We stand in the indigo light of Yesod in the Temple of Divinity.

About us are the Kerubim and at our right hand is Gabriel.

This is the treasure house of images, the foundation of the Kingdom of God.

Here rules the Almighty Living God whose title is Shaddai-el-chai.

Let us attune ourselves with this aspect of the Most High by intoning together, three times, this holy name.

Shaddai-el-Chai

HOD

We stand in the violet purple light of Hod in the Temple of Divinity. About us are the Beni Elohim and at our right hand is Michael. This sphere is the glory and the splendour of God.

Here rules the God of Hosts whose title is Elohim Tzabaoth.

Let us attune ourselves with this aspect of the most high by intoning together, three times, this holy name.

Elohim Tzabaoth

NETZACH

We stand in the amber light of Netzach in the Temple of Divinity. About us are the Elohim and at our right hand is Haniel. This sphere is the pinnacle of achievement and the celebration of victory.

Here rules the Lord of Hosts whose title is Jehovah Tzabaoth.

Let us attune ourselves with this aspect of the Most High by intoning together, three times, this holy name.

Jehovah Tzabaoth

TIPHARETH

We stand in the clear rose pink light of Tiphareth in the Temple of Divinity.

About us are the Melekim and at our right hand is Raphael. This sphere is the highest expression of beauty and harmony.

Here rules the Lord of Knowledge whose title is Jehovah Eloah va Da-ath.

Let us attune ourselves with this aspect of the Most High by intoning together, three times, this holy name.

Jehovah Eloah va Da-ath

GEBURAH

We stand in the orange light of Geburah in the Temple of Divinity.

About us are the Seraphim and at our right hand is Khamael. This sphere is governed by justice and strength.

Here rules the Almighty God whose title is Elohim Gibor.

Let us attune ourselves with this aspect of the Most High by intoning together, three times, this holy name.

Elohim Gibor

CHESED

We stand in the deep violet light of Chesed in the Temple of Divinity.

About us are the Chashmalim and at our right hand is Tzadkiel.

This sphere is the source of mercy and benevolence. Here rules the Majesty of God whose title is El.

Let us attune ourselves with this aspect of the Most High by intoning together, three times, this holy name.

El

BINAH

We stand in the crimson light of Binah in the Temple of Divinity.

About us are the Aralim and at our right hand is Tzaphkiel.

This sphere is the understanding of the Great Mother. Here rules the Lord God whose title is Jehovah Elohim.

Let us attune ourselves with this aspect of the Most High by intoning together, three times, this holy name.

Jehovah Elohim

CHOKMAH

We stand in the pure soft blue light of Chokmah in the Temple of Divinity.

About us are the Auphanim and at our right hand is Ratziel. This sphere is the wisdom of the supernal Father.

Here rules the Tetragrammaton, Yod, He, Vav, He, whose title is Jehovah. Let us attune ourselves with this aspect of the Most High by intoning together, three times, this holy name.

Jehovah

KETHER

We stand in the brilliance of the light of Kether in the Temple of Divinity.

About us are the Chaioth Ha Qadesh and at our right hand is Metatron.

This sphere is the crown, the concealed of the concealed. Here rules the "I am" whose title is Eheieh.

Let us attune ourselves with this aspect of the Most High by intoning together, three times, this holy name.

Eheieh

KETHER

We stand in the sacred Light of the highest world accessible to humanity. Let us, in silence, immerse ourselves in its sacred vibrations and take into ourselves the qualities of the spheres, that we may absorb them and take them back into our material world and our daily lives.

(Few minutes silence.)

KETHER

Holy, Holy, Holy, Great God of Galaxies
    Thou art the Unity concealed in polarity.
    In Wisdom Eternal Thy wonders are wrought
    From the darkness of life to the Light of the One.

MUSICIAN
(Play music for few minutes)

KETHER
(When music ends)

Officers of the Temple of Divinity, we will now withdraw from this sacred Temple. Each officer will individually express our gratitude to the Most High by intoning, three times, in turn, each of the sacred names as we depart.

Eheieh

CHOKMAH
Jehovah

BINAH
Jehovah Elohim

CHESED
El

GEBURAH
Elohim Gibor

TIPHARETH
Jehovah Eloah va Da-ath.

NETZACH
Jehovah Tzabaoth

HOD
Elohim Tzabaoth

YESOD
Shaddai-el-Chai

MALKUTH
Adonai-ha-eretz

GUARDIAN
(Sounds the gong twelve times.)

KETHER
We have now returned to the Temple of Creation under the

protection and direction of the Choirs of Angels and the Archangelic Beings.

Officer of the sphere of Tiphareth. Do you have anything to report from your observation of the un-manifest Sephirah of Knowledge?

TIPHARETH

I have / have not.

(Reports any vision, experience or message which may have been received. The Officer of Tiphareth may invite reports from those present if appropriate)

TIPHARETH

Officers of the Temple of Creation. Our communion with the Temple of Divinity is concluded and our work in the Temple of Creation accomplished.

Please lead us in thanking the Archangelic Beings for their support and assistance, as we depart the Temple of Creation and return to the Temple of Mind.

KETHER

Angel of the Divine Presence, Metatron, we thank you for opening the doors of the Temple and assisting us to enter therein.

We bid you farewell as we depart the Temple of Creation and return to the Temple of Mind.

CHOKMAH

Herald of God, Ratziel, we thank you for the knowledge we have been given.

We bid you farewell as we depart the Temple of Creation and return to the Temple of Mind.

BINAH

Watcher of God, Tzaphkiel, we thank you for opening our inner eye and permitting us to see.

We bid you farewell as we depart the Temple of Creation and return to the Temple of Mind.

CHESED
Righteous of God, Tzadkiel, we thank you for helping us to listen and hear the wisdom of the inner voice.

We bid you farewell as we depart the Temple of Creation and return to the Temple of Mind.

GEBURAH
Burner of God, Khamael, we thank you for your mercy and compassion which did not judge us unworthy.

We bid you farewell as we depart the Temple of Creation and return to the Temple of Mind.

TIPHARETH
Healer of God, Raphael, we thank you for your counsel and for the lessons we have been permitted to learn.

We bid you farewell as we depart the Temple of Creation and return to the Temple of Mind.

NETZACH
I, 'the God', Haniel, we thank you for helping us to maintain our emotional stability.

We bid you farewell as we depart the Temple of Creation and return to the Temple of Mind.

HOD
Perfect of God, Michael, we thank you for your protection and our safety.

We bid you farewell as we depart the Temple of Creation and return to the Temple of Mind.

YESOD
Strong one of God, Gabriel, we thank you for the message and inspiration we have received.

We bid you farewell as we depart the Temple of Creation and return to the Temple of Mind.

MALKUTH
Lord of Earth, Sandalphon, we thank you for permitting us to wear the sandals of the Initiate and return them into your safe keeping.

We bid you farewell as we depart the Temple of Creation and return to the Temple of Mind.

GUARDIAN
(Sounds the gong six times)

TIPHARETH
Officers of the Temple of Mind. The Temple of Creation is closed, we have taken leave of the Archangelic Beings and the doors are sealed.

Officer of the sphere of Yesod, have you any dedication of our work which you wish to make at this time?

YESOD
I have / have not.

(Officer of the Sphere of Yesod may make any dedication of the Light of the working as may be appropriate.)

YESOD
Officers of the Temple of Mind, our work in the Temple is completed.

Please lead us in thanking the Choirs of Angels for their presence and support as we return to the Temple of Earth.

KETHER
The Chayoth-ha-Qadesh, the Holy Living Creatures, we thank you for your influence and your watchfulness.

We bid you farewell as we depart the Temple of Mind and return to the Temple of Earth.

CHOKMAH
The Auphanim, the Whirling Forces, we thank you for opening the gates of the zodiacal powers.

We bid you farewell as we depart the Temple of Mind and return to the Temple of Earth.

BINAH
The Aralim, The Thrones, we thank you for allowing us to drink from your chalice of life force.

We bid you farewell as we depart the Temple of Mind and

return to the Temple of Earth.

CHESED
The Chashmalim, the Bright Shining Ones, we thank you for teaching us true and just rulership.

We bid you farewell as we depart the Temple of Mind and return to the Temple of Earth.

GEBURAH
The Seraphim, the Fiery Serpents, we thank you for strengthening us in mind and will.

We bid you farewell as we depart the Temple of Mind and return to the Temple of Earth.

TIPHARETH
The Melekim, the Kings, we thank you for helping us to act in goodness and excellence.

We bid you farewell as we depart the Temple of Mind and return to the Temple of Earth.

NETZACH
The Elohim, the Principalities, we thank you for helping us to wisely rule our kingdom of the mind.

We bid you farewell as we depart the Temple of Mind and return to the Temple of Earth.

HOD
The Beni Elohim, the Mighty Sons of God, we thank you for assisting us to hold steady the balance of our minds.

We bid you farewell as we depart the Temple of Mind and return to the Temple of Earth.

YESOD
The Kerubim, Rulers of the Elements, we thank you for empowering and protecting us.

We bid you farewell as we depart the Temple of Mind and return to the Temple of Earth.

MALKUTH

The Ashim, the Living Flames of Fire, we thank you for awakening within us our perfect soul and for this experience of our higher self.

We bid you farewell as we depart the Temple of Mind and return to the Temple of Earth.

GUARDIAN

(Sounds the gong three times)

YESOD

(Going to the North first, Yesod makes the appropriate banishing sign of the Pentagram in each of the four Quarters. North, Earth; East, Air; South, Fire; West, Water: sealing the quarters with the Holy Names as follows:

> *North* ELOHIM
> *East* IESCHOUAH
> *South;* ADONAI
> *West* YOD-HE-VAV-HE
> *(Returns to station and is seated)*

The Temple of Mind is closed and its purpose accomplished.

MALKUTH

Officers of the Temple of Earth, assist me to close this Temple that all may depart in peace.

(NOTE. Officers rise to speak and remain standing)

KETHER

My station of Kether is closed. The Divine Spark is eternal.

CHOKMAH

My station of Chokmah is closed. The power of the Father is infinite.

BINAH

My station of Binah is closed. The love of the Mother is limitless.

CHESED

My station of Chesed is closed. Life is the Perfect Cross.

GEBURAH
My station of Geburah is closed. Justice is immutable.

TIPHARETH
My station of Tiphareth is closed. The Rose opens in Light.

NETZACH
My station in Netzach is closed. The Lamp shines brightly.

(Extinguishes the station candles except Malkuth in order Yesod, Hod, Geburah, Tiphareth, Binah, Kether, Chokmah, Chesed and Netzach and returns to station.)

HOD
My station in Hod is closed. Earth is our altar.

(Extinguishes the altar candles except the Sacred Light. Returns to station)

YESOD
My station in Yesod is closed. Maintain the Silence.

MALKUTH
My station in Malkuth is closed. The sacred circle is dissolved.

(Extinguishes station candle.)

Officers of the Temple of Earth, your duties are done and the work ended. The Temple is closed.

Everyone please rise and join with me in making the salutation of the Qabalistic Cross.

(After this is done)

Guardian of the Doorway, unseal the doorway and permit all to depart in peace.

GUARDIAN
(Sounds the gong once)

MUSICIAN
(Play exit music)

GUARDIAN
(Unseals the doorway with the sign of the Pentagram and sees that all depart the Temple in order)

EXIT

All acknowledge the Sacred Light on exit.

Malkuth leads the exit followed by the Officers in order, Yesod, Netzach, Chesed, Chokmah, Kether, Binah, Geburah, Tiphareth and Hod.

All then exit together in a continuous clockwise direction starting from the South West. The Musician and Guardian exit last.

THE FOUR WORLDS RITUAL PLAN

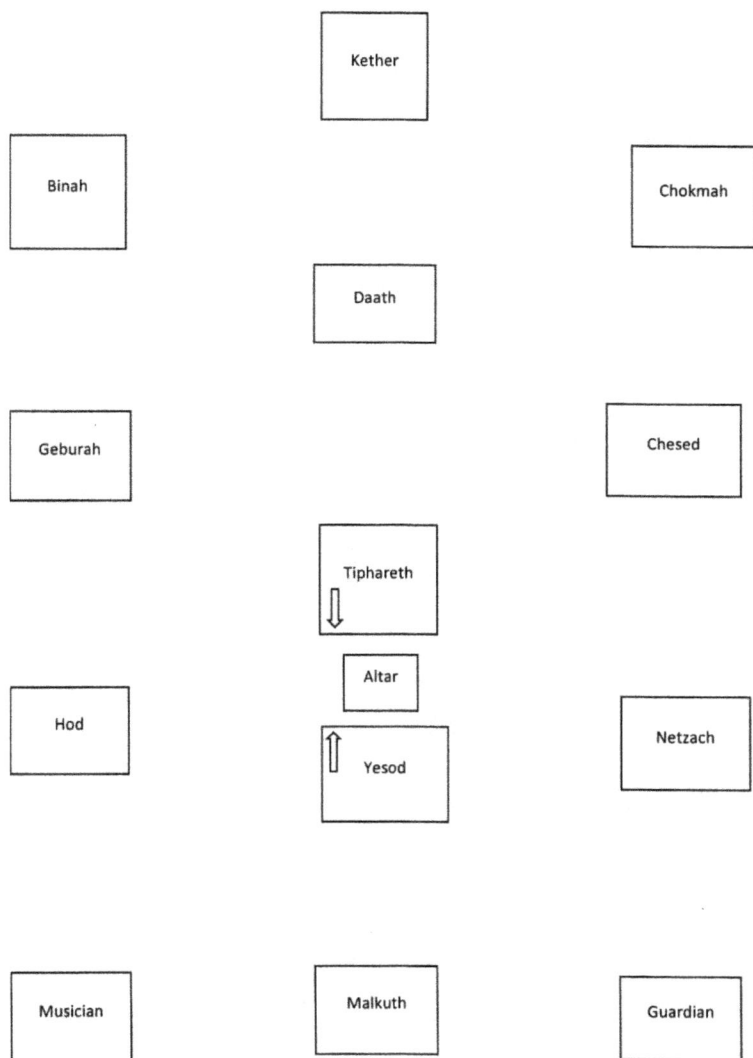

	Kether	
Binah		Chokmah
	Daath	
Geburah		Chesed
	Tiphareth ⇩	
	Altar	
Hod	⇧ Yesod	Netzach
Musician	Malkuth	Guardian

Rothley Ritual[2]

OFFICERS
Priest of the East
Priestess of the West
Guardian of the Lights
Guardian of the Sacred Fire
Guardian of the Doorway

OFFICERS OF THE SEPHIROTH
Chokmah
Binah
Chesed
Geburah
Netzach
Hod

TEMPLE ARRANGEMENTS
Chairs for stations at east, west, south, north and doorway.

Empty chair at right of Priest of the East for Unknown Guest.

Six chairs for officers of the Sephiroth arranged in form of two side pillars.

Chairs for non-officiating participants arranged in two rows facing each other across central aisle behind those of officers.

Central altar with six candles arranged in two interlacing triangles.

Charged chalice (water) in centre of central altar.

Nine candles on table behind station of the east, also station candle.

Nine candles on table behind station of the west, also station candle.

Sacred flame at station in the north.

Incense burner at station in the south.

Bell and striker at doorway.

Sephiroth stations. Small tables with appropriate coloured candles for six side pillar stations.

Chokmah   grey

---

[2] Written in collaboration with the Late John A.B. Fox

Binah	*black*
Chesed	*blue*
Geburah	*red*
Netzach	*green*
Hod	*orange*

Central pillar stations

Station candles at East and West.

Station candles at Daath and Yesod.

Daath	*grey*
Yesod	*indigo*

Priest of the East has the wand and the sword at station in the east.

Taper at station in east.

Candle snuffer at station in east.

Priestess of the West has the chalice and a taper at station in the west.

Guardian of the Lights has sacred light, taper, candle snuffer and matches at station in the north.

Earth symbol. (disc) at station in the north.

Guardian of the Sacred Fire has the incense burner at station in the south.

Guardian of the Doorway has bell and striker or gong at doorway station.

Guardian of the Doorway has the sheathed sword fixed to waist.

Tape recorder and music tapes.

The officers of the Sephiroth have staffs of the colours of their stations.

Chokmah	*grey*
Binah	*black*
Chesed	*blue*
Geburah	*red*
Netzach	*green*
Hod	*orange*

The Officers of the Sephiroth have shoulder capes of the colours of their stations.

ENTRY

Guardian of the doorway admits all none officers who are then seated.

When all is in readiness the officers enter as follows

Officers of the Sephiroth enter in pairs, proceed to their stations and remain standing.

Binah   Chokmah
Geburah   Chesed
Hod   Netzach

Guardian of the Lights and Guardian of the Sacred Fire enter together. Proceed to stations and remain standing.

Priestess of the West (first) and Priest of the East enter and proceed to their stations via the north.

The Priestess of the West carries the chalice.

The Priest of the East carries the wand.

Ritual

PRIEST OF THE EAST
(Gives three knocks)

OFFICERS OF THE SEPHIROTH
(Respond with three knocks with staffs in order;
*   Chokmah, Binah, Chesed, Geburah, Netzach, Hod.)*

GUARDIAN OF DOORWAY
(Responds with three strokes on bell)

PRIEST OF THE EAST
Guardian of the Doorway - whom have you admitted?

GUARDIAN OF THE DOORWAY
The Priest of the East, the Priestess of the West and the Servants of the Light.

PRIEST OF THE EAST
From what do you guard us?

GUARDIAN OF THE DOORWAY
From the intrusion of the profane, disturbance of the Temple and from those who fear the light.

PRIEST OF THE EAST
Priestess of the West - who opens the Temple?

PRIESTESS OF THE WEST
The Priest of the East. The Priestess of the West, the Guardian of the Lights and the Guardian of the Sacred Fire.

PRIEST OF THE EAST
Guardian of the Sacred Fire - help us to prepare this temple.
　　Everyone please rise.
　　(Censing Ceremony)

GUARDIAN OF THE SACRED FIRE
(The Guardian of the Sacred Fire proceeds with Incense Burner to the East via the West and North taking the Censer to the Priest of the East who makes the sign of blessing. The Guardian of the Sacred Fire then censes the East with three swings to the right, three to the left and three forwards. The Guardian of the Sacred Fire then censes the Stations of South, Guardian of the Doorway, West and North in the same manner.)

PRIEST OF THE EAST
Priestess of the West - what is the dedication of the Temple?

PRIESTESS OF THE WEST
To the Light.

PRIEST OF THE EAST
Who mediates the light for the Temple?

PRIESTESS OF THE WEST
Three are the mediators of the light. The Lords of Flame, the Lords of Mind and the Lords of Form.

PRIEST OF THE EAST
What are the gates of the Temple?

PRIESTESS OF THE WEST
Three are the gates of the Temple. Illumination, Intuition and Consciousness

PRIEST OF THE EAST
What are the keys of the gates?

PRIESTESS OF THE WEST
Three are the keys of the gates. The inner mind, the intellect and the senses.

PRIEST OF THE EAST
What are the lights of the Temple?

PRIESTESS OF THE WEST
Three are the lights of the Temple. The light invisible, the light visible, and symbolic light.

PRIEST OF THE EAST
Let the light of the Temple be revealed.

PRIESTESS OF THE WEST
Guardian of the Lights - assist us to bring light to this Temple

GUARDIAN OF THE LIGHTS
(Lights taper from Sacred Flame then proceeds to the East via the North)

PRIEST OF THE EAST
(Waits until Guardian of the Lights reaches position at lights in the East)

PRIEST OF THE EAST
How then is the Temple illumined?

GUARDIAN OF THE LIGHTS
(As each attribute is named the Guardian of the Lights lights in turn the nine candles of the East and then the West from left to right)

PRIESTESS OF THE WEST
By sight *(light candle)* and sound *(light candle)* and touch *(light candle)*
By reason *(light candle)* knowledge *(light candle)* and thought *(light candle)*
By limitless light *(light candle)* the inner light *(light candle)* and the light of the Sun. *(light candle)*
(The Guardian of the Lights goes to the west via the south.)

PRIEST OF THE EAST

By inner vision *(light candle)* intuition *(light candle)* and emotion. *(light candle)*

By love *(light candle)* compassion *(light candle)* and wisdom. *(light candle)*

The teaching of dreams *(light candle)* the inner pathways *(light candle)* and the light of the Moon. *(light candle)*.

PRIESTESS OF THE WEST

In dedication to the service of the light and by the aid of these mediators, I turn the keys and open the gates of this Temple that all may receive illumination and serve the light.

(The Guardian of the Lights returns to station via the north.)

PRIEST OF THE EAST

I proclaim this Temple duly dedicated, opened and prepared for higher working.

(Gives three knocks)

Please be seated.

PRIEST OF THE EAST

(Rises)

Officers of the Sephiroth, please rise and assist us to raise this Temple to the second plane of working.

PRIEST OF THE EAST

(Gives six knocks of wand)

OFFICERS OF THE SEPHIROTH

(Respond with six knocks each with Staffs in order; Chokmah, Binah, Chesed, Geburah, Netzach and Hod)

GUARDIAN OF THE DOORWAY

(Responds with six strikes on bell)

PRIEST OF THE EAST

(Lights station candle)

Everyone please rise.

In the name of Eheieh

I am the Priest of the Temple in Malkuth by me is the Temple established. I build the sphere of the powers of Kether in the middle pillar of the Temple. My mediator is Metatron, Lord of the Hidden Intelligence. My symbol is the crown, the concealed of the concealed. This sphere is the Lux Interna, the first principle which has no beginning and the experience of union with the most high.

Please be seated

GUARDIAN OF THE SACRED FIRE
(Charges the incense burner and delivers it to the Priest of the East via South, West and North then returns to Station and is seated.)

PRIEST OF THE EAST
(Priest of the East censes central altar.

Priest of the East makes the first circumambulation with lighted Censer, making the Sign of Nine when facing each of the four Quarter Stations)

The east I build from the Element of Air
The south I build from the Element of Fire
The west I build from the Element of Water
The north I build from the Element of Earth.

(Priest of the East makes the second circumambulation with the wand, pausing to face each quarter station in turn.)

I place in the east the sword of protection to guard and rule the working in this Temple.

I place in the south the wand of power to direct the forces of the unseen in this Temple

I place in the west the cup of compassion to bring strength and understanding into the working in this Temple.

I place in the north the platter of plenty to sustain and support the working in this Temple.

(Priest of the East makes the third circumambulation with the sword, pausing to face each quarter station in turn)

To the east I summon Raphael. Lord of Air and guardian of the pathways of spirit, to guide and direct the working in this Temple.

To the south I summon Michael, Lord of Fire and guardian of the pathways of power, to protect and guard the working in this Temple.

To the west I summon Gabriel, Lord of Water and guardian of the pathways of strength, to bring understanding and energy into the working in this Temple.

To the north I summon Auriel, Lord of Earth and guardian of the pathways of light, to bring wisdom into the working in this Temple

(Priest of the East returns to his Station, lights taper from station candle.)

OFFICER IN CHOKMAH
(Rises. Receives lighted taper from the Priest of the East. Lights station candle)

I build the sphere of the powers of Chokmah in the right hand pillar of the Temple and my mediator is Ratziel, Lord of the Illuminating Intelligence. My symbol is the uplifted rod of power, the conductor of the primary creative force. This sphere is the crown of creation, the splendour of unity, the supernal Father, the second glory and the vision of God face to face.

(Strikes floor with Staff -once)

OFFICER IN BINAH
(Rises. Receives lighted taper from the Officer in Chokmah lights station candle)

I build the sphere of the powers of Binah in the left hand pillar of the Temple and my mediator is Raphkiel, Lord of the Sanctifying Intelligence. My symbol is the chalice of life which is eternally receptive. This sphere is the supernal mother, the foundation of wisdom, it is Marah the great sea, it is silence and the vision of sorrow.

(Strikes floor with Staff - once)

OFFICER IN CHESED
(Rises. Receives lighted taper from the Officer in Binah. Lights station candle)

I build the sphere of the powers of Chesed in the right hand pillar of the Temple and my mediator is Tzadkiel, Lord of the Receptive Intelligence. My symbol is the orb, the ruling power which brings all into balanced harmony and stability. This sphere is the mighty king, the receptacle of the holy powers, which emanate all the spiritual virtues with the most exalted essences. It is obedience and the vision of love.

(Strikes floor with Staff - once)

OFFICER IN GEBURAH

(Rises. Receives lighted taper from the officer in Chesed. Lights station candle.)

I build the sphere of the powers of Geburah in the left hand pillar of the Temple and my mediator is Khamael, Lord of the Radical Intelligence. My symbol is the sword, the protector and the destroyer. This sphere is the lord of fear and severity, it is the defender of right and the administrator of justice. It is courage and the vision of power.

(Strikes floor with Staff - once)

OFFICER IN NETZACH

(Rises. Receives lighted taper from the Officer in Geburah. Lights station candle.)

I build the sphere of the powers of Netzach in the right hand pillar of the Temple and my mediator is Haniel, Lord of the Occult Intelligence. My symbol is the rose, the transmuting power of love and the realm of the emotions. This sphere is the beautiful lady, the lover and the loved, it is the balancing of the polarities and the vision of beauty triumphant.

(Strikes floor with Staff - once.)

OFFICER IN HOD

(Rises. Receives lighted taper from the Officer in Netzach. Lights station candle.)

I build the sphere of the powers of Hod in the left hand pillar of the Temple and my mediator is Michael, Lord of the Perfect Intelligence. My symbol is the apron of service of the Initiate of the lesser mysteries. This sphere is the hermaphrodite, the combining of opposite qualities, the maker of forms and the intellectual imagination. It is the realization of the glory of God manifesting in the created world and the vision of splendour.

(Strikes floor with Staff - once)

PRIESTESS OF THE WEST

(Rises. Receives lighted taper from the Officer in Hod. Lights station candle)

I am the Priestess of the Temple in Malkuth by me is the Temple opened.

I build the sphere of the powers of Malkuth in the middle

pillar of the Temple and my mediator is Sandalphon, Lord of the Resplendent Intelligence. My symbol is the magic circle, the plane of manifestation and completion. This sphere is the bride, the doorway between life and death, death and life. It is the place of fulfilment of spiritual forces on the plane of form it is the gate of the path of return and the vision of the holy higher self.

PRIESTESS OF THE WEST.
(Approaches the Yesod station with lighted taper and lights station candle)
I build the sphere of the powers of Yesod in the middle pillar of the temple and my mediator is Gabriel, Lord of Pure Intelligence. My symbol is the perfume which rises in the smoke of incense. This sphere is man in his body temple, the vehicle of the life forces and the treasure house of images. It is the realm of illusion, the sphere of the Moon and of magic and the vision of the working of the universe.
(Approaches the centre altar with lighted taper)

PRIEST OF THE EAST
(Approaches centre altar)

OFFICERS OF THE SEPHIROTH
(All raise their Staffs and hold them high, pointing towards the centre altar)

PRIESTESS OF THE WEST
(Lights the three outer triangle candles then the three inner triangle candles)

PRIEST OF THE EAST
We build the sphere of the powers of Tiphareth in the middle pillar of the Temple and our mediator is Raphael, Lord of the Mediating Intelligence. Our symbol is the rose cross, the rosa mundi with the thirty-two signs of the natural forces. This sphere is the majestic king and the sacred child. It is mystical illumination, the reflection of Kether, the sphere of sacrifice and the vision of the harmony of creation.

OFFICERS OF THE SEPHIROTH.
(All lower their Staffs as Priest of the East and Priestess of the West leave the Altar.)

PRIEST OF THE EAST AND PRIESTESS OF THE WEST
(Both return to their stations)

PRIEST OF THE EAST
(Lights Daath station candle as he returns to the East)

PRIESTESS OF THE WEST
I am the Priestess of the Temple in Yesod, by me is the Temple opened.

(Circumambulates the Temple and faces each station as she opens the Gateways.)

In the west I open the gateway of the mind, the portal between the outer and the inner worlds.

In the north I open the gateway of intuition that the channels may be free for the inflowing of knowledge.

In the east I open the gateway of meditation that in the calm stillness of our inner being we may drink from the spring of the waters of creation.

In the south I open the gateway of communication that we may know and receive from the source of all wisdom.

PRIEST OF THE EAST AND PRIESTESS OF THE WEST
(Both approach the altar and stand facing each other)

OFFICERS OF THE SEPHIROTH.
(All raise their Staffs and hold them high pointing towards the central altar.)

PRIEST OF THE EAST
I am the Priest of the Temple in Tiphareth by me is the temple opened.

PRIESTESS OF THE WEST
I am the Priestess of the Temple in Tiphareth by me are the pathways opened.

PRIEST OF THE EAST AND PRIESTESS OF THE WEST.
(Both return to their stations and all Officers are seated.)

PRIEST OF THE EAST
Let all focus the powers of the spheres upon the altar of the Temple in Tiphareth in service and dedication.

GUARDIAN OF THE DOORWAY
(Strikes the Gong ten times allowing the sound to fade away between each sounding.) Four minutes meditation.

GUARDIAN OF THE DOORWAY
(Sounds the Gong once)

PRIESTESS OF THE WEST
Let all approach in mind the grail of this altar of the Temple in Tiphareth that their needs may be filled from the source of all light, life and love.
Two minutes meditation.

GUARDIAN OF THE DOORWAY
(Sounds the Gong once)

PRIEST OF THE EAST
(Addresses the Priestess of the West and requests an offering from the Grail of Wisdom)

PRIESTESS OF THE WEST
(Gives address or other item followed by BENEDICTION.
Benediction. Priestess of the West goes to central altar, raises and blesses the chalice of water, then circumambulates the Temple, touching each person on the forehead in Blessing with the Water, returns the Chalice to the Altar and returns to her Station)

MUSICIAN
(Music is played during the Benediction. Music is discontinued when the Priestess returns to her station in the west)

PRIEST OF THE EAST AND PRIESTESS OF THE WEST
(Both go to the central altar, Priest of the East taking the candle snuffer)

PRIEST OF THE EAST
(Extinguishes the Daath station candle as he passes.)

PRIESTESS OF THE WEST
(Extinguishes the three candles of the inner triangle.)

PRIEST OF THE EAST
In praise and thanksgiving to the Most High we close the Temple in Tiphareth. By us are the pathways sealed.

PRIESTESS OF THE WEST.
(Extinguishes the three candles of the outer triangle)

PRIEST OF THE EAST
In honour and veneration of the powers of creation we lower the veils of the inner mind and close the Temple in Yesod.

PRIEST OF THE EAST AND PRIESTESS OF THE WEST
(Both return to their stations.)

PRIESTESS OF THE WEST
(Extinguishes Yesod station candle as she passes)
     (Extinguishes station candle)
     I close the sphere of Malkuth and give thanks to my mediator Sandalphon.

OFFICER IN HOD
(Extinguishes station candle)
     I close the sphere of Hod and give thanks to my mediator Michael.

OFFICER IN NETZACH.
(Extinguishes station candle)
     I close the sphere of Netzach and give thanks to my mediator Haniel.

OFFICER IN GEBURAH
(Extinguishes station candle)
     I close the sphere of Geburah and give thanks to my mediator Khamael.

OFFICER IN CHESED
(Extinguishes station candle)

I close the sphere of Chesed and give thanks to my mediator Tzadkiel.

OFFICER IN BINAH
(Extinguishes station candle)

I close the sphere of Binah and give thanks to my mediator Tzaphkiel.

OFFICER IN CHOKMAH
(Extinguishes station candle)

I close the sphere of Chokmah and give thanks to my mediator Ratziel.

PRIEST OF THE EAST
(Extinguishes station candle)

I close the sphere of Kether and give thanks to my mediator Metatron.

I am the Priest of the Temple in Malkuth by me is the Temple closed.

(Makes first reverse circumambulation with Wand, pausing to face each station in turn)

I offer our thanks to Auriel, Lord of Earth as he returns to his own realms.

I offer our thanks to Gabriel, Lord of Water as he returns to his own realms

I offer our thanks to Michael, Lord of Fire as he returns to his own realms.

I offer our thanks to Raphael, Lord of Air as he returns to his own realms.

(Makes second reverse circumambulation, pausing to face each station in turn)

I offer our thanks and return to rest the platter of plenty.

I offer our thanks and return to rest the cup of compassion.

I offer our thanks and return to rest the wand of power

I offer our thanks and return to rest the sword of protection

(Makes third reverse circumambulation, pausing to face each station in turn)

I offer our thanks and draw back into our beings the Element of Earth.

I offer our thanks and draw back into our beings the Element of Water.

I offer our thanks and draw back into our beings the Element of Fire.

I offer our thanks and draw back into our beings the Element of Air.

Everyone please rise.

In the name of Eheih. So mote it be.

PRIEST OF THE EAST

I now declare the work of this plane completed and the Temple returned to the first plane of working.

PRIEST OF THE EAST

(Gives six knocks)

OFFICERS OF THE SEPHIROTH

(Respond with six knocks of staffs in order; Chokmah, Binah, Chesed, Geburah, Netzach, Hod)

GUARDIAN OF THE DOORWAY

(Responds with six strikes on the bell)

PRIEST OF THE EAST

Priestess of the West - is the work of the day accomplished?

PRIESTESS OF THE WEST

The day's work is done.

PRIEST OF THE EAST

Then let the Temple be sealed and the light veiled.

Guardian of the Lights assist us to close this working of the Temple.

GUARDIAN OF THE LIGHTS

(Takes snuffer and goes to the lights in the West by way of the East and South)

PRIEST OF THE EAST
May the gates of the Moon be closed and the pathways of the mind be sealed.

GUARDIAN OF THE LIGHTS
(Extinguishes the nine lights of the West slowly then proceeds to the East via the North.)

PRIESTESS OF THE WEST
May the gates of the Sun be closed and the pathways of consciousness sealed.

GUARDIAN OF THE LIGHTS
(Extinguishes the nine lights of the East slowly and returns to station via South)

PRIESTESS OF THE WEST
In dedication to the service of the Light and with gratitude to our mediators, I turn the keys and close the gates of this Temple that all may depart in peace.

PRIEST OF THE EAST
So be it veiled and sealed.
        (Gives three knocks)

OFFICERS OF THE SEPHIROTH
(Respond with three knocks with staffs in order, Chokmah, Binah, Chesed, Geburah, Netzach, Hod)

GUARDIAN OF THE DOORWAY
(Gives three strikes on bell)

PRIEST OF THE EAST
Guardian of the Doorway. All may now depart in peace
        (Music is played for exit.
        Officers leave the Temple in the following order.
        Priest of the East exits by way of the South.
        Priestess of the West goes via the North followed by the Guardian of the Lights and the Guardian of the Sacred Fire and exits via the East and the South.
        The Officers of the Sephiroth exit in pairs in reverse order)

HOD *NETZACH*
GEBURAH *CHESED*
BINAH *CHOKMAH*

GUARDIAN OF THE DOORWAY
(See all leave the Temple correctly)

Message of the Priestess of the West Rothley Chapel

As students of mysticism and followers of a spiritual Path, we need to ask ourselves just what it is we are studying, why we are studying it and where the Path we follow is leading us. It is often somewhat difficult to put our answers to these questions, our inner most thoughts and deepest feelings, into words. But it is necessary to have some understanding of the goal in order to be clear about our means of achieving it. So we need to ask ourselves just what is the nature of the deep need we strive to fulfil by the way of life we follow.

The spiritual impulse exists in every human and has done so from the beginning of time, it manifests in the most primitive society and in the most complex and evolved civilisation. In one form or another, there have existed from the earliest times, Teachers and Schools who have taught the way of the spirit, its functions and techniques. From the Shaman who teaches his/her one apprentice to the Schools which have existed down the ages to guide large numbers of students.

The Mystery Schools have always taught reverence for the Divine, the right of each individual to their own concept of and approach to the Divine, personal responsibility, self-development, spiritual work and above all service, to the Light and humanity. The Mystery Schools teach mysticism and its techniques, they encourage their students to be independent in mind and spirit. They stress the responsibility of each individual to serve the community in which they live and the Schools of which they are a part. By their rituals and practices they provide the means by which the student may learn of the subtle worlds by their own experience and demand of them knowledge not belief. The student of the Mystery Schools practices their Teachings to the best of his or her ability. Living honestly and ethically in the world they work to develop themselves on all levels of their being and to perpetuate the Traditions and Work of their School.

The student of the Mysteries strives to gain Wisdom and to know Truth. There must be an ultimate and eternal Truth existing within the structure of the Universe both seen and unseen, Laws which underlie the whole way the Universe exists and operates. But what these may be is too vast and too immense to be encompassed within our truth. Humanity has discovered some of these Laws and has learnt how they can be directed to achieve specific results, but what has been discovered is only a brief glimpse behind the veil of the great unknown.

So Truth is, at best, ever only partial, we can never be sure that what we think is Truth is in fact true. Perhaps one of our greatest personal Truths is the recognition of this fact.

The scientific discoveries of the past hundred years depend on the truth of the facts which have been found to work, that effects are repeatable and consistent, that our physical universe works in accordance with stable Laws. For us these Laws are Truth. Whether they are immutable and unalterable we can never be sure, so even this Truth is relative to our present knowledge and state.

Just as the scientist has worked to discover these Laws of the physical Universe - so too have philosophers and mystics worked to discover the Truths of the none physical realms of the mind and the spirit. Within these subtle realms of being there are also things which work and things which do not - again we discover that the non-physical Universe too works in accordance with Laws.

How to judge what is spiritual Truth? Just as physical Laws are defined by their results, so too the Laws which govern the working of the mind and the spirit must also be judged by results. In the main humanity judges results in terms of what is beneficial and what is detrimental to its own life and comfort. The seeker for spiritual Truth usually applies the same criteria of good and bad results, what works and what does not, in determining what is their own Truth.

What is taken to be spiritual truth by one person or system may be very limited and untrue in the light of another's knowledge and experience. It is only by consistently testing and using the methods and teachings of spiritual systems that we slowly build our own personal Truth. What we KNOW from experience rather than what we believe from others teachings becomes the Truth on which we base our lives.

In all esoteric work the true Teacher works to assist others to attain to their own Knowledge and Truth and to defend their right to so seek.

To be able to pursue Truth in freedom we need to be able to live in a society which allows us to do so. One of the first ways of defending Truth is therefore to assist in the upholding of a free and open society by fulfilling our responsibilities as citizens.

Where the search for and defence of Truth is dangerous to our physical safety we need to be discreet in our activities. To try to defend Truth by physical force is to misunderstand the nature of Truth. To meet force with resistance most often results in defeat, for he who defends Truth with his life is no longer in manifestation to serve it.

In order for Truth to be available to everyone we need to ensure there is full access to the accumulated knowledge and wisdom of past societies and Teachers. We need to defend Truth by making knowledge as widely available as possible.

We need to offer our own Truth to others as and when they may seek it from us. We need to contribute our own efforts towards the perpetuation and availability of Truth.

We need to be ever vigilant to see evil where it manifests and to counter it with Truth and Light.

Above all we should be Silent, so that Truth is protected from the attacks of the ignorant, preserved for the seekers of the future and veiled from the mockery of the profane. The Light of Truth and Wisdom is hidden only by and from the ignorance and darkness of those who would attack it - to the wise it blazes as the beacon of hope and certainty which it is their duty and their privilege to defend and preserve.

Our physical plane Schools exist to teach and train those who follow the path of Light and strive to fulfil the purpose of their incarnation. But there exists too an unseen and non-physical School of the Light whose members recognise each other no matter what country, faith or time they may originate from; it is a fellowship of the spirit, a oneness of purpose, an intuition and a memory. Beyond all earthly Schools it is to this unseen School that we seek to belong and whose aims we seek to serve.

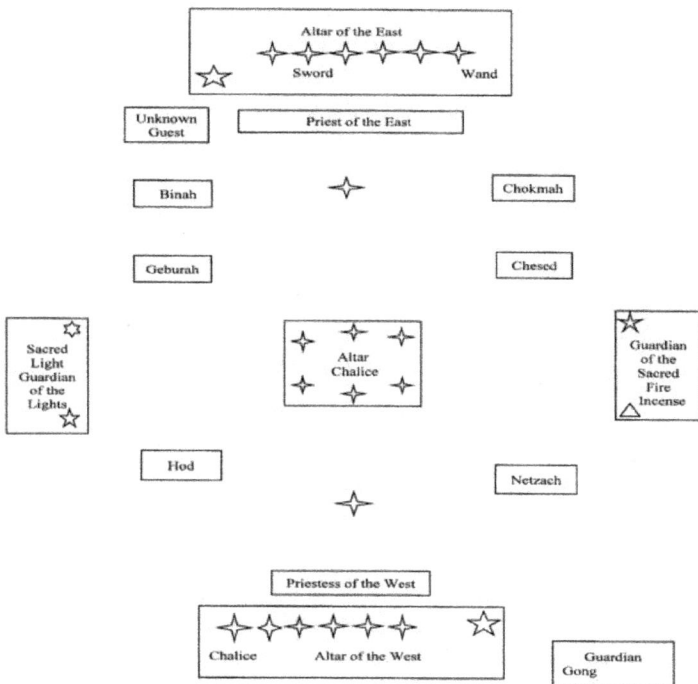

The Cross of the Elements Ritual

OFFICERS
PRIEST OF AIR
PRIESTESS OF WATER
PRIEST OF FIRE
PRIESTESS OF EARTH
WEAVER OF DREAMS OF AIR (WOMAN)
WEAVER OF DREAMS OF FIRE (WOMAN)
WEAVER OF DREAMS OF EARTH (MAN)
WEAVER OF DREAMS OF WATER (MAN)
GUARDIAN
MUSICIAN

REQUIREMENTS
There are EIGHT Officers plus the Guardian and Musician.
The four Priests and Priestesses sit with backs to the Altar as shown on plan.
The four Weavers of Dreams sit one at each corner of the Temple facing the Altar.
Central altar with single central LIGHT.
Small table in centre of East, South, West and North Triangles.
Station candle on each table in the Triangles in front of the Priests and Priestesses.
Scented Oil in East Triangle.
Candle for each participant in South Triangle.
Chalice of Water in West Triangle.
Bowl of Nuts in North Triangle.
Four candles, one at each corner of the Temple making a triangle with the Station candles.
Charcoal and Incense in South Triangle.
Seeds and Platter in North Triangle.
Tapers for Officers on Altar.
Matches.
Candle Snuffer on central Altar.
Shoulder capes for Officers in appropriate colours.
Tape recorder and music.
Four Eye of the Elements Cards.
Beasts of Albion Cards.

Ritual

MUSICIAN
(Enters Temple first. Lights central candle and starts music)

GUARDIAN
(Admits all none Officers)
        (Admits Officers in pairs in order as follows. They enter and are seated)
WEAVER OF DREAMS OF AIR
WEAVER OF DREAMS OF FIRE
WEAVER OF DREAMS OF EARTH
WEAVER OF DREAMS OF WATER
(In single file, the Priests and Priestesses enter and circle the Altar to their places and are seated in order as follows)

PRIESTESS OF WATER
PRIEST OF FIRE
PRIEST OF AIR
PRIESTESS OF EARTH.
(Note. All Officers rise when speaking)

GUARDIAN.
(Seals the doorway)

MUSICIAN
(Turns off music)

PRIEST OF AIR
(Rises and lights taper from central Light. Lights Station Candle)
        This Temple I dedicate to the work of the Light, may all within its portals serve in dedication under the protection and instruction of the Most High.
        (Lights candles at North East and South East)
        With this light I establish the triangle of the Element of Air, in this space I see the beauty of a summer sky and feel the fresh clean breezes of mountain air flowing about me.

PRIEST OF FIRE
(Rises and lights taper from central Light. Lights Station Candle. Places incense on the lighted charcoal)

With this fragrant smoke I establish the triangle of the Element of Fire. In this space I see the great burning orb of our Sun and the flames which spring from the heart of Earth through the volcanoe's fountains of fire.

PRIESTESS OF WATER
(Rises and lights taper from central Light. Lights Station Candle. Lights candles at South West and North West)

With this light I establish the triangle of the Element of Water. In this space I see the vast waters of the oceans, eternally renewed by lakes and streams. On my face I feel the gentle touch of a summer's mist and in my mouth the life giving waters of a sacred spring.

PRIESTESS OF EARTH
(Rises and lights taper from central Light, lights Station Candle. Sprinkles seeds on platter)

With these seeds I establish the Triangle of the Element of Earth. In this space I see the fertile fields and teeming life of earth and rejoice in the beauty of her mountains and plains.

PRIEST OF AIR
To the Triangle of Air I call Paralda, King of the Element of Air, and request him to bring his subjects the sylphs, zephyrs and fairies who inhabit the world of winds, breezes, and mountains. We ask his teaching and his blessing.

PRIESTESS OF WATER
To the Triangle of Water I call Nixsa, King of the Element of Water and request him to bring his subjects the undines and nymphs who live in the seas, lakes, and streams. We ask his teaching and his blessing.

PRIEST OF FIRE
To the Triangle of Fire I call Djin, King of the Element of Fire and request him to bring his subjects the salamanders and fire drakes who are the life and consciousness of flames. We ask his

teaching and his blessing.

PRIESTESS OF EARTH
To the Triangle of Earth I call Ghob, King of the Element of Earth and request him to bring his subjects the gnomes and dwarves who inhabit the interior of earth and guard her minerals and precious gems. We ask his teaching and his blessing.

WEAVER OF DREAMS OF AIR
(Has the cards of The Lion, The Dragon and The Unicorn)
To the Triangle of Air I call the Spirits of the Kingdoms.

I call the Lion who is the spirit of the Kingdom of Strength, the Dragon who is the spirit of the Kingdom of Wisdom, and the Unicorn who is the spirit of the Kingdom of Purity. We ask their guidance and the gift of the companionship of their animal helpers.

WEAVER OF DREAMS OF FIRE
(Has the cards of Mouse, Squirrel, Snake, Boar, Hound, Raven, Weasel, Fox, Wren, Bee, Horse and Spider)
To the Triangle of Fire I call the helpers of the Kingdom of Strength.

From them we seek help in meeting the challenges of life. That we may grow in knowledge and create within our lives the conditions which will enable us to become strong.

WEAVER OF DREAMS OF WATER
(Has the cards of Dolphin, Wolf, Redbreast, Otter, Cow, Pig, Hare, Swan, Eagle, Toad, Dove and Butterfly)
To the Triangle of Water I call the helpers of the Kingdom of Purity.

From them, we seek help in nurturing ourselves and others with compassion. That the voice of inspiration and intuition may speak to us and teach us to listen and grow.

WEAVER OF DREAMS OF EARTH
(Has the cards of Bear, Cockerel, Bat, Bull, Badger, Stag, hedgehog, Goose, Crane, Owl, Cat, and Salmon)
To the Triangle of Earth I call the helpers of the Kingdom of Wisdom.

From them we ask help in awakening and empowering our inner knowledge and their protection in our quest.

WEAVER OF DREAMS OF AIR

(Now requests all to come in turn and take one of the three cards which are held face down. According to which one is received they then go to the appropriate Weaver of Dreams who offers them the cards of the Kingdom, face down, from which to select one.

The card is noted and then returned. The Weaver of Dreams may assist with the meaning of the chosen card.

The Weaver of Dreams of Earth comes last and offers the cards to the Weaver of Dreams of Air to make his choice.

When all have a selected Helper there is a short meditation period)

MUSICIAN

(Plays music for a few minutes)

WEAVER OF DREAMS OF AIR

We are now prepared to enter the inner realms of the Elements and undergo their initiations.

You find yourself in a strange landscape, the colours are quite different to our usual physical world. Everything looks solid and real but if you touch it you find it is insubstantial and constantly changing as if it were but made of clouds which drift and shift in the ever moving air.

You are following a narrow path which is slowly climbing through a sunlit forest and accompanying you is your helper from one of the kingdoms

Speak to your helper and let them teach you how to understand what they say to you. They will be with you and guide you in the experiences ahead.

At last the trees thin and you come to the edge of the forest, the path goes on across a grassy hillside and begins to climb more and more steeply. You are feeling tired and begin to wonder if you have the strength to follow the path to the end. You breathe deeply of the clear mountain air and it invigorates and vitalises you.

At last you reach the summit of the mountain and your helper tells you that the Initiation of Air is now just ahead. You see that the mountain you have been climbing is in fact a twin and just ahead of you is a narrow path across the rocky ridge which connects the two. Your heart misses a beat at the realisation that your initiation is to be walking across this ridge path. Your helper whispers that you are in the inner worlds and that here you need not fear physical harm. While your mind understands this, your emotions find it of little help in conquering your fear.

But the only choice is either to go back and miss the initiation or to go forward. You dig deep into yourself to find the courage to go on, then step out onto the ridge. It is just wide enough for you to walk on, and on either side the mountain side drops steeply away, down and down to the forest far below. Step by cautious step you go forward, the wind buffeting you and making it even more difficult to keep your balance. Your helper is close by - how do they help you and what do they say? Listen well and remember.

Now you are half way across the ridge and your confidence grows as the knowledge blossoms inside you that you can make it to the other side. At last you step off the ridge onto the second mountain and with a sense of great relief start down the path which widens and winds down the now gentle slope of the hill.

WEAVER OF DREAMS OF FIRE

Now you have reached the trees of the forest once again and stroll along enjoying the fragrance of the trees and the glimpses of the animals and birds who live here. The peace is beautiful and you are in no hurry to leave the forest. But then there is a strange roaring noise and a smell which at first you cannot name. Suddenly you recognise it and alarm fills you - the forest is on fire.

Your instinct is to run as fast as possible to get clear of the trees and find safety. You begin to run faster and faster and a rising panic fills you as you begin to see smoke and flames springing up ahead of you. There is no escape from this initiation unless you retrace your steps and face the mountain ridge once again. Your helper whispers that the fire cannot harm you except in your imagination but the flames look no less dangerous for that.

Suddenly your helper gives a great cry of anguish and you stop dead in your headlong flight. Horror fills you as you see what has caused your helper's cry. Just ahead of you there is an island of trees, surrounded but not yet touched by the flames. Marooned on the island is your helper's mate, frozen into immobility with fear. Your helper now seems powerless in distress and begs you to do something to rescue their mate. Your compassion prompts you to go to the rescue but is not quite strong enough to overcome your fear, but then a small voice of pride taunts you into action and before you have time to think, you have rushed forward into the fire. The flames leap out to engulf you and you feel the charred forest floor scorching your feet, your skin burns and tightens in the intense heat. But you are committed now and there is no turning back. With a last leap you feel the cooler ground beneath your feet and reach out for your helper's mate. With your touch their paralysis is broken and they flee. You turn to watch as they reach safety and then you become aware once again of the perils of your own situation. You look for where the fire seems to be blazing the least fiercely, then with a final gathering of your courage you run forward through the flames. For some moments they roar about you, leaping several feet high, the heat sears your body and the hot air makes it almost impossible to breathe. Then you are clear and out of the fire, you feel the cool rush of the wind which is fanning the fire behind you but which now cools and refreshes you. Your helper is beside you again and expresses gratitude in the only way it knows.

WEAVER OF DREAMS OF WATER

Your path goes onward through the forest and as the trees thin somewhat you realise the ground is gently sloping downwards. At last you emerge from the forest to find yourself on a wide beach. There are patches of golden sands and large rocks strewn haphazardly about.

Before you are the deep blue waters of a vast sea with small gentle waves breaking on the shore. You walk down towards the water enjoying the clear fresh air which comes off the sea. Then you notice there is a small boat anchored just off shore which had been hidden from your view by a large rock. It is of strange design with a high carved prow and a small sail with a strange emblem worked upon it. Your helper indicates that you should board the boat and wading out through the shallow water you do so. It is easy to climb over the low side of the boat and once aboard you find it is larger than you at first thought. There are warm rugs and you also find supplies of food and water and other small necessities. While you have been engrossed in making these discoveries you have not noticed that the boat was moving, now when you look about you again the shore is distant, too far away for you to be able to swim back to it. You are adrift on this sea and unable to do anything about the situation. There are no oars and no engine, the wind fills the sail and carries you further and further out to sea.

There is nothing to be done but to enjoy the voyage. For a time it is pleasant and the gentle motion of the boat almost lulls you to sleep.

But then the temperature begins to drop, the sky darkens and the wind increases. You begin to feel decidedly uncomfortable and when it begins to rain your pleasure turns to increasing discomfort. You wrap yourself in the blankets and try to make yourself as comfortable as possible. Soon it is night and you sink into an uneasy sleep. With the first light of a stormy dawn you awake and find that there is no sight of land in any direction. Only the vast dark expanse of the restless sea. The wind increases and the rain lashes down and with every moment your anxiety grows. Then strangely you begin to feel the rhythm of the sea and something deep within begins to dance with its motion, you find the rain has collected in a can fastened to the boat's side and you gratefully drink the refreshing water. You pass the most fearful, strange, yet exciting day of your life, communing with the life of the sea. At last fatigue overcomes you and once more you sink into sleep. When you awaken the sea is calm, everywhere there is a pale grey mist through which the sun is just beginning to break, its beams filling your sight with dancing rainbows as it catches the moisture in the air.

Then the mist parts and you see a shore just within wading distance. You climb out of the boat and into the water which to your surprise is only knee deep and warm. In a few moments you have reached the land and feel the warm softness of the sands under your feet.

Waiting to welcome you is your helper and you realise with relief that you may be on a strange shore but you are neither alone nor lost.

WEAVER OF DREAMS OF EARTH

You look about you and realise you are standing in a small cove, before you are tall cliffs and on either side the sea washes against the rocks of the headlands. You begin to think it will not be so easy to leave this place without returning to the boat. But as you turn at this thought, you find that the boat has disappeared and you no longer have the option. You decide to look more closely at the cliffs to see if there is a pathway to the top. The idea makes you feel somewhat dizzy but you try hard to suppress your fear. But your apprehension was premature as you find on closer inspection there is no possible way the cliffs can be climbed without ropes and assistance. Your heart sinks, then just as you begin to feel despair creeping over you, a shadow behind a bush growing close to the cliff catches your eye. Pulling the foliage to one side you see a small opening in the rock face. Stooping down you find it is just high and wide enough for you to step through. Once inside you peer through the darkness ahead, trying to see whether there is a cave or passageway in front of you. You can see nothing. But there is little to lose so with considerable apprehension you step forward, feeling your way along by keeping contact with the rock wall. As you go on the passage takes a sharp turn and what faint light there was from the entrance disappears. Now the darkness is total, there are small noises about you and soft unidentifiable touches against your skin. The back of your neck tingles with fear. But you go on. Gradually the darkness seems to grow less dense and you realise there are small areas of phosphorescence which at least mark the boundaries of the passageway. The slope of the ground is gently upwards and you hope that this indicates that there will be a way out to the top of the cliffs. Then there is a glimmer of light before you and suddenly the passage takes a sharp turn and you emerge into the most beautiful cave you have ever seen. It is softly lit, but you cannot see the source of the light. The whole cave shimmers and gleams with every colour and type of crystal. Each magnifies the light and it is like being inside a rainbow. There are jewels of every kind here, the walls shine with the warm gleam of gold and diamonds, of a size you did not know was possible, glitter at every hand. There is wealth beyond imagination here. You have only to stretch out your hand and pick up the loose gems which are strewn across the floor. But these are the jewels and treasures of the earth and not yours to take. You let go of the possibility of riches and let the gems lie. The decision seems to open your eyes and you see another passageway on the far side of the cave. Your helper tells you that this is the way out and that you are now free to leave.

You hasten and enter the passage, it is dark, but not totally so and the going is now easier. You walk for a long time then at last there is a glimmer of light ahead and you know it is the end of your journey. Passing through the opening you emerge back into the room where your physical body is sitting. You stir and awaken from your dream journey back into full consciousness.

PRIEST OF AIR

You have experienced the initiations of Air, Fire, Water and Earth and been accompanied by your helpers on these journeys. Remember your helper and allow them to be your companions in your daily life experiences.

I will now give the gift of the Element of Air to all who wish to receive it. The gift is the scented oil which attracts the rulers and elementals of Air. May they assist you and bless you.

Please come to the East.

(All who wish to receive the gift come to the East and the Priest of Air touches their hands with the Scented Oil)

PRIEST OF FIRE

I will now give the gift of the Element of Fire to all who wish to receive it. The gift is the candle which gives heat and light and which attracts the rulers and elementals of Fire. May they assist and bless you.

Please come to the South.

(All who wish to receive the gift come to the South and the Priest of Fire gives them a lighted candle)

PRIESTESS OF WATER

I will now give the gift of the Element of Water to all who wish to receive it. The gift is clear water which sustains life and attracts the rulers and elementals of water. May they assist and bless you.

Please come to the West.

(All who wish to receive the gift come to the West and the Priestess of Water offers them the Chalice of Water to drink from)

PRIESTESS OF EARTH

I will now give the gift of the Element of Earth to all who wish to receive it. The gift is the fruits of the earth and attracts the rulers and elementals of Earth. May they assist and bless you.

Please come to the North.

(All who wish to receive the gift come to the North and the Priestess of Earth gives them nuts to eat. Note be aware of possible allergies)

PRIEST OF AIR

Now is the purpose of our ceremony concluded, let us give thanks to those who have assisted us in our work.

WEAVER OF DREAMS OF AIR

I give thanks to the spirits of the Kingdoms, the Lion, the Unicorn and the Dragon, for their presence and the assistance of their animal helpers and bid them return to their own place. May a blessing be upon them.

WEAVER OF DREAMS OF FIRE

I give thanks to the helpers of the Kingdom of Strength and bid them return to their own place. May a blessing be upon them.

WEAVER OF DREAMS OF WATER

I give thanks to the helpers of the Kingdom of Purity and bid them return to their own place. May a blessing be upon them.

WEAVER OF DREAMS OF EARTH

I give thanks to the helpers of the Kingdom of Wisdom and bid them return to their own place. May a blessing be upon them.

PRIEST OF AIR

I give thanks to Paralda, King of the Element of Air, and his subjects the sylphs, zephyrs and fairies who inhabit the world of winds, breezes, and mountains, and bid them return from whence they came. May peace be between us.

I see a great Eagle rise from the eastern triangle, upon his wings ride the Elementals and King of Air.

Seeker, if you would rise to the higher realms look to the Eagle that he may lend you his wings.

(Extinguishes the candles at North East and South East. Extinguishes Station Candle)

The triangle of Air is empty and our work done.

PRIEST OF FIRE

I give thanks to Djin, King of the Element of Fire and his subjects the salamanders and fire drakes who are the life and consciousness of flames and bid them return from whence they came. May peace be between us.

I see a great Spider weaving the web of the universe on the threads of which tread the Elementals and King of Fire.

Seeker if you would know of the hidden web, dance with the spider in its weaving.

(Extinguishes Station Candle)

The triangle of Fire is empty and our work done.

PRIESTESS OF WATER

I give thanks to Nixsa, King of the Element of Water and his subjects the undines and nymphs who live in the seas, lakes, and streams and bid them return from whence they came. May peace be between us.

I see seven Swans rising from the waters of a great lake and flying into the west, escorting the questing and departing spirits of humanity.

Seeker if you would know of the inner worlds of the West rise through the sunset with the swans.

(Extinguishes candles at South West and North West. Extinguishes Station Candle)

The triangle of the West is empty and our work done.

PRIESTESS OF EARTH

I give thanks to Ghob, King of the Element of Earth and his subjects the gnomes and dwarves who inhabit the interior of earth and guard her minerals and precious gems and bid them return from whence they came. May peace be between us.

I see a great Bear standing guard over the sleeping spirit of humanity.

Seeker if you would awake, walk with the bear.

(Extinguishes Station Candle)

The triangle of Earth is empty and our work done.

PRIEST OF AIR

(Turns to face Altar)

Companions, the One Light is our perpetual guide and guard.

Let us depart in peace.

MUSICIAN

(Starts music for exit)

GUARDIAN

(Unseals the doorway
Sees all exit correctly in order;
Priest of Air
Priest of Fire
Priestess of Water
Priestess of Earth
Weaver of Dreams of Air
Weaver of Dreams of Fire
Weaver of Dreams of Earth
Weaver of Dreams of Water
All others participating
Guardian
Musician)

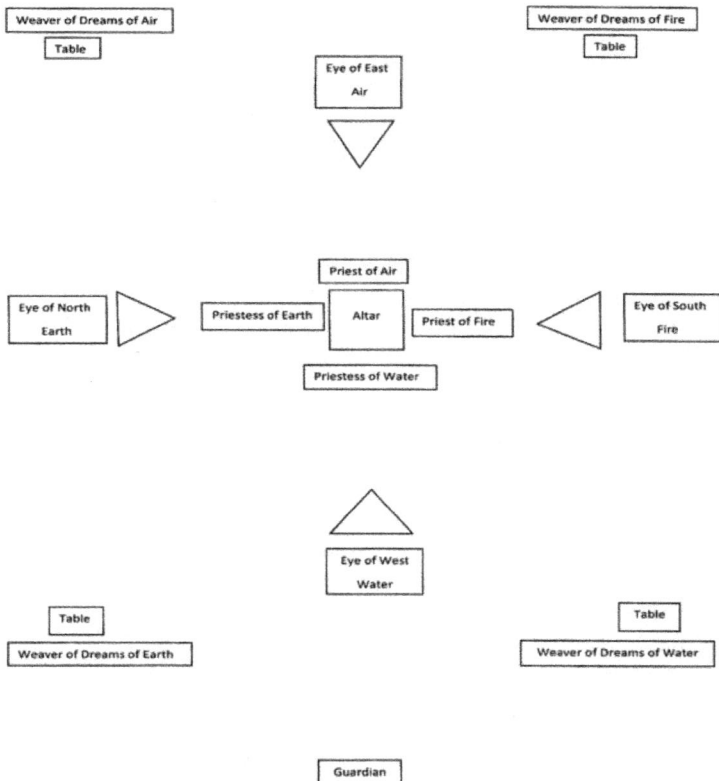

Sanctuary of Maat

(Note. The Questions of Maat and some of the text are taken from
Ancient Egyptian texts)

<u>OFFICERS</u>
Outer Guardian
Guardian One
Guardian Two
Musician
Priestess of Maat
Priestess of the Hours of the Day (White veil and robe)
Priestess of the Hours of the Night (Black veil and robe)

<u>REQUIREMENTS</u>
White Veil
Black Veil
White Robe
Black Robe
Three small tables or one large and one small
Two candles and snuffer
Chalice
Drinking Water
Bowl for hands
Two white feathers
Two red feathers
Ankh
Maat figure
Scented oil
Maat poster
Two stands and rod
Black curtain
Music and CD player

Ritual

The two Priestesses are standing in place. Priestess of the Hours of Day (white) and Priestess of the Hours of Nights (black) are veiled.
> *Priestess of Maat is seated facing west.*
> *The two candles are lit on altar.*
> *Guardian One and Guardian Two are in place facing West.*
> *Guardian One holds white feather*
> *Guardian Two holds red feather*
> *Very soft music is playing.*

MUSICIAN
(Turn on entry music. <u>Secret Garden. Dreamcatcher. Track 5)</u>

OUTER GUARD
(Ensures silence for some moments then admits participants.
> *Entry is to north and south. There is no circling.*
> *Outer Guard enters when all have been admitted.)*

MUSICIAN
(Turn off music at end of track)

TWO PRIESTESSES
(Are seated together)

PRIESTESS OF MAAT
(Rises, turns to face east)
One is Amun,
who keeps himself concealed from them,
who hides himself from the gods,
no one knowing his nature.
He is more remote than the sky,
He is deeper than the netherworld.
None of the gods knows his true form.
His image is not unfolded in the papyrus rolls.
Nothing certain is testified about him.
He is too secretive
for his Majesty to be revealed.
He is too great to be enquired after,
too powerful to be known.

(Turns to face west)
Content is Atum, father of the gods.
Content are Shu and Tefnut.
Content are Geb and Nut.
Content are Osiris and Isis.
Content are Seth and Neith.
Content are all the gods who are in the sky.
Content are all the gods who are on Earth,
who are in the flat-lands.
Content are all the southern and northern gods.
Content are all the western and eastern gods.
Content are all the gods of the nomes.
Content are all the gods of the towns.
(Turns to face east)
Hail, Maat. Lady of Balance and Justice.
Hail, Daughter of Ra, Lady of Truth.
Come forth from the realms of the Hidden Ones
Grace this place with your presence.
Hail Maat, Lady of Harmony and Order,
Be with us and bless us
Cleanse our hearts and touch us with grace
Enfold us with thy wings and breathe on us
The breath of eternal Life.
(Turns to face west)
Hail Maat, Lady of the Forty-Two Principles
May we be innocent of transgressing them.
Honestly admit when we have been guilty
And consign our errors to the fire of experience.
(Priestess of Maat slowly rotates as she asks the questions, appearing to direct them to the participants in turn)
I have not committed sin.
I have not committed robbery with violence.
I have not stolen.
I have not slain men and women.
I have not stolen grain.
I have not purloined offerings.
I have not stolen the property of the gods.
I have not uttered lies.
I have not carried away food.
I have not uttered curses.

I have not committed adultery.
I have made none to weep.
I have not grieved uselessly.
I have not attacked any man.
I am not a man of deceit.
I have not stolen cultivated land.
I have not been an eavesdropper.
I have slandered no other person.
I have not been angry without just cause.
I have not debauched another's wife or husband.
I have not abused my body.
I have terrorised none.
I have not transgressed the Law.
I have not been wroth.
I have not shut my ears to the words of truth.
I have not blasphemed.
I am not a man or woman of violence.
I am not a stirrer up of strife.
I have not acted or judged with undue haste.
I have not pried into matters.
I have not multiplied my words in speaking.
I have not worked witchcraft against others.
I have never stopped the flow of water.
I have never raised my voice arrogantly, or in anger.
I have not cursed God.
I have not acted with evil rage.
I have not stolen the bread of the gods.
I have not stolen from the spirits of the dead.
I have not snatched away the bread of a child.
I have nor treated with contempt the god of my city.
I have not slain the cattle belonging to the god.
I have wronged none, I have done no evil.
(Turns to face east)
Lady of Truth and Justice
Help us to mend the errors of our ways.
Balance the scales of all our deeds,
That the false may be balanced by the true
The thoughtless by the thoughtful
The unkind by the compassionate
And the indifferent by loving kindness.

Cleanse our hearts of all impurities
Open our inner eye to greater Truth.
Lead us in the ways of harmony and peace
Guide us in the paths of growth and Light.

(Goes to stand in front of the Priestess of the Hours of the Day who remains seated)

(Raises arm pointing upwards to draw down power, then lowers it to just above head of Priestess finally laying it on her head)

Maat – Maat - Maat

Make of your Priestess of the Hours of the Day a vessel of your power. Flow through her and bless those who come seeking your blessing.

(Goes to stand in front of the Priestess of the Hours of the Night who remains seated)

Raises arm pointing upwards to draw down power, then lowers it to just above head of Priestess finally laying it on her head)

Maat – Maat - Maat

Make of your Priestess of the Hours of the Night a vessel of your power. Flow through her and bless those who come seeking your blessing.

(Returns to place in the west)

All who so wish may now approach and seek the blessings of Maat from the Priestess of the Hours of the Day and the Priestess of the Hours of the Night.

MUSICIAN
(Turns on music, keeping volume soft. Yoga Liftstyle. Track 10 then from Track 1.)

PRIESTESSES OF THE HOURS OF THE DAY AND OF NIGHT
(Both rise for the blessings)

PRIESTESS OF MAAT
(Priestess of Maat now acts as guide seeing that entry is made between the two Guardians. No more than two Seekers at a time are admitted. She conducts them first to the bowl of water)

PRIESTESS OF MAAT
(Speaking to the Seeker, bidding them dip their fingers in the water)

Cleanse yourself of the world and of your past that you may approach Maat in purity and truth.

(Each seeker goes first to the Priestess of the Hours of the Day and then to the Priestess of the Hours of the Night. They then leave via the north and return to their places passing again between the Guardians)

PRIESTESS OF THE HOURS OF DAY

(May speak with each seeker as feels appropriate. Gives blessing by touching with feather. Then blessing by touching forehead with water saying;

Be blessed by the waters of Maat.

Finally holds hand up palm upwards and gently blows across it towards the seeker)

PRIESTESS OF THE HOURS OF THE NIGHT

(May speak with each seeker as feels appropriate. Gives blessing by touching with feather. Then blessing by touching forehead with oil saying)

Be blessed and live in Maat.

(Finally holds hand up palm upwards and gently blows across it towards the seeker.

When all who wish to do so have received the blessings all are seated. The three Guardians receive the blessing last)

MUSICIAN

(Turn off music)

PRIESTESS OF MAAT

(Rises, turns to face east)

Hail, Maat. Lady of Balance and Justice.

Hail, Daughter of Ra, Lady of Truth.

Who came forth from the realms of the Hidden Ones

We thank you for having graced this place with your presence.

Hail Maat, Lady of Harmony and Order,

Be with us and bless us, touch us with thy grace

Enfold us with thy wings and breathe on us

The breath of eternal Life.

(Turns to face west)

Content is Atum, father of the gods.

Content are Shu and Tefnut.

Content are Geb and Nut.

Content are Osiris and Isis.

Content are Seth and Neith.
Content are all the gods who are in the sky.
Content are all the gods who are on Earth, who are in the flat-lands.
Content are all the southern and northern gods.
Content are all the western and eastern gods.
Content are all the gods of the nomes.
Content are all the gods of the towns.
(Turns to face east)
One is Amun,
who keeps himself concealed from them,
who hides himself from the gods,
no one knowing his nature.
He is more remote than the sky,
He is deeper than the netherworld.
None of the gods knows his true form.
His image is not unfolded in the papyrus rolls.
Nothing certain is testified about him.
He is too secretive
for his Majesty to be revealed.
He is too great to be enquired after,
too powerful to be known.
The day's work is done.
All may depart in peace.
(Is seated)

MUSICIAN
(Turn on exit music. Secret Garden Dreamcatcher Track 16)

OUTER GUARDIAN
(Sees that all depart in silence. Exit is directly via south and north with no circling.

   The officers leave last.)

SANCTUARY OF MAAT
RITUAL PLAN

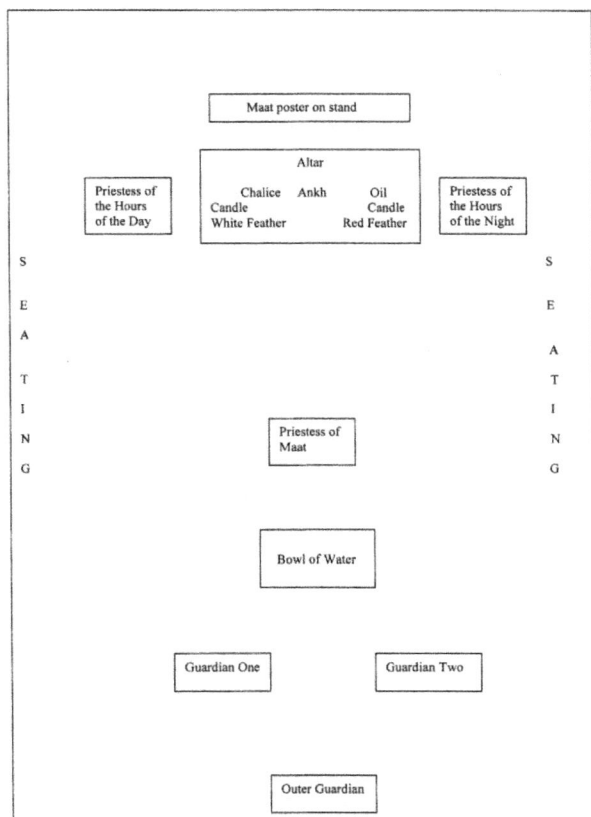

Maat poster on stand	

Altar

Priestess of the Hours of the Day	Chalice Ankh Oil Candle Candle White Feather Red Feather	Priestess of the Hours of the Night

S E A T I N G (left)

S E A T I N G (right)

Priestess of Maat

Bowl of Water

Guardian One		Guardian Two

Outer Guardian

The Sacred Temple Ritual

OFFICERS
East   *PRIEST OF ANUBIS*
South   *PRIEST OF MAAHES*
West   *PRIESTESS OF ISIS*
North   *PRIESTESS OF MAAT*
           GUARDIAN / MUSICIAN

TEMPLE ARRANGEMENTS.
Central altar
Central light
Four candles and holders
Four god form statues
Bowl of water with added salt and perfume
Feather
Dagger
Ankh
Matches
Snuffer
Four quarter altars
Black cloths
On southern altar, a sword
On northern altar, bowl with folded papers with one of the Blessings printed on each
On western altar, chalice of wine (two may be required) Also wipes for chalice
CD player and music
Gong

Ritual

MUSICIAN
Sees that light on central altar is lit.
     Starts music. Track One Sacred Treasures V (May need repeat for participants entry)

FOUR OFFICERS
Enter in procession, in order West, South, East, North, circle altar to

their places. Their chairs are facing the central altar. They take god form position. Officers should begin to make contact with their god forms.

NOTE. All officers rise to speak and then are seated again.

GUARDIAN
(Allow a little time for Officers to settle then admit all participants.)

MUSICIAN
(Turn off music.)

GUARDIAN
(Seals the Temple.
Strikes the gong six times.)

PRIEST OF ANUBIS
The Light of Ra rises, the East is illumined with His splendour.
He cometh to His Temple,
May the way be made sacred before Him.
Priestess of Isis, grace this place with blessings, sanctify and cleanse our Temple to receive Him.

PRIESTESS OF ISIS
(Takes bowl of water from altar. Circumambulates the Temple sprinkling water in several directions. She says the following several times as she does so.)
By salt and by water I cleanse this Temple. By perfume I make sweet the air, may its fragrance rise to welcome He who comes.
(Replaces bowl on altar, returns to place and is seated.)

PRIESTESS OF MAAT
Behold the Light of Ra shines in full splendour at High Noon. By His power He gives life and light to all. The Earth flourishes beneath His glory.
Priest of Maahes, devourer of the guilty and protector of the innocent, assume your duties as guardian of sacred places. From horizon to horizon make safe this place.

PRIEST OF MAAHES
(Takes dagger from altar. Circumambulates the Temple. He begins in

the south, facing each quarter as he comes to it and defining the boundaries of the Temple as he circles, he says several times)

From the darkness of ignorance and evil great Ra protect us.

(Replaces dagger on altar, returns to place and is seated)

PRIEST OF MAAHES

All truth and justice are revealed by the light of Ra. Be gone all creatures of darkness. The full light of day illumines the pure of heart.

Priestess of Maat, she who holds back chaos, holder of the scales of justice and keeper of balance and order; empower this Temple with your qualities.

PRIESTESS OF MAAT

(Takes feather from altar and circumambulates Temple, bestowing blessing with the feather as she does so saying several times)

The light of Ra shine upon you. The thoughts of your mind and heart be clothed in truth and understanding.

(Replaces feather on altar, returns to place and is seated)

PRIESTESS OF ISIS

Hidden are the pathways of the gods, concealed are the ways of the Shining Ones.

Silence and peace are the keys and purity of heart the gatekeeper.

Priest of Anubis, you who know the secret ways and walk between the worlds. Open the pathways before us and make wide the gates of Amenti.

PRIEST OF ANUBIS

(Takes ankh from altar and circumambulates Temple. Holding the ankh he directs this at each person as if using a key, saying as he does so)

Open the eyes of your spirit, walk in the halls of the mind, I will lead and you may follow; and remember that which you find.

(Places ankh on <u>eastern</u> altar, returns to place and is seated.)

PRIESTS AND PRIESTESSES

(All rise together and go to central altar. They then light the four candles as follows;)

311

PRIEST OF ANUBIS
Ra has risen. *(lights candle)*

PRIEST OF MAAHES
The gods guard. *(lights candle)*

PRIESTESS OF ISIS
Isis blesses. *(lights candle)*

PRIESTESS OF MAAT
Maat speaks. *(lights candle)*

PRIESTS AND PRIESTESSES
(Raise their right arm high, touching each other's hands in centre, place left hand on the shoulder of the officer to their left and say together)
Glory and honour to the first Creator.
(All drop their arms and say together)
Behold the light of Amun shines upon the night and upon the day, eternal is His watchfulness.
(Each picks up the candle in front of them, turning together they walk to the quarter altars and place the candles there, leaving room in front of them for the figures to stand. Then return to their places and are seated)

GUARDIAN
(Strikes the gong twelve times.)

PRIEST OF ANUBIS
(Rises, takes the Anubis figure from the altar, goes to eastern altar, raises the figure while saying the invocation facing east)
Hail Anubis, Lord in the land of Amenti, he who wears the Jackal mask – hail
Come to us
Speak to us
You who walk in the hidden ways show us where to place our feet.
Lead us
Guide us.
Hail Lord Anpu, Master of Wisdom, he who is mentor and Opener of the Ways – hail.
Teach us

Inspire us

In life and in death, Walker between the Worlds,

Be with us.

(Priest bows facing east. Then places figure in front of the candle. Turns and returns to place. He takes his chair and turns it to face east and is seated.)

PRIEST OF MAAHES

(Rises, takes the Maahes figure from the altar, goes to southern altar, raises the figure while saying the invocation facing south.)

Hail Maahes, son of mighty Sekhmet, he who is true beside her – hail.

Protect us

Defend us

You who nightly defend great Ra in his solar barque from the attacks of the serpent Apep;

Guard us from evil

Hail - Helper of the Wise Ones, who opens the mind to divination and insight

Keep clear our vision

You who guard all magical rites and are the protector of the initiates

Be with us.

(Priest bows facing south. Then places figure in front of the candle. Turns and returns to place. He takes his chair and turns it to face south and is seated.)

PRIESTESS OF ISIS

(Rises, takes the Isis figure from the altar, goes to western altar, raises the figure while saying the invocation facing west.)

Hail Isis, Lady of Magic. She who sits upon the throne of heaven;

Celestial Mother crowned with stars - hail.

Nurture us

Care for us

Lady of life and rebirth, she who is the healer of the wounds of Osiris;

In your compassion heal us.

Hail – Goddess of Wisdom, lady of the grain and of all natural fertility

Teach us
And succour us
By day and by night, in waking and in dreaming
Be with us.
(Priestess bows facing west. Then places figure in front of the candle. Turns and returns to place. She takes her chair and turns it to face west and is seated.)

PRIESTESS OF MAAT
(Rises, takes the Maat figure from the altar, goes to northern altar, raises the figure while saying the invocation facing north.)

Hail Maat, Lady of the Hall of Judgement, she whose names are Truth, Balance and Law – hail.

Guide us to truth

Lady of the Feather of Truth and holder of the Scales of Justice

Keep true our hearts.

Hail - Daughter of Ra, she who sustains the balance and harmony of the Cosmos

Sustain us in the Light of Ra.

That we may live by Maat, for Maat and in Maat

Be with us.

(Priestess bows facing north. Then places figure in front of the candle. Turns and returns to place. She takes her chair and turns it to face north and is seated)

MUSICIAN
(Starts music. Play for about four minutes. Attunement Track 2. Constance Demby
Stop music.)

PRIEST OF ANUBIS
Be still and be aware of the Presence of Anubis in the east, Maahes in the south, Isis in the west and Maat in the north.

As you look mentally in each direction you see each of them as a brilliant shining star, as you watch the stars appear to grow, their rays reaching out in all directions. Within the light of the star a form appears, this may be the form we associate with each figure or it may be something quite different, whatever it is this is FOR YOU. Reach out in your mind and approach the one which most attracts you. Acknowledge the Presence as a real inner plane Being.

You may communicate with this Being, bring your questions and concerns - and remember the answers you receive.

It does not matter how many of us associate with each Being, for they exist equally in every ray of light which emanates from them. Their consciousness is not limited as is ours but is like a hologram in which the same image exists in every particle of the one image.

Relax and allow your mind to touch the mind of one or more of the Beings.

MUSICIAN
(Start the music. Play to end of track Attunement Track 2. Constance Demby
Stop music.)

PRIEST OF ANUBIS
It is time now to give your thanks for what you have experienced and received. Do this, then fix the memory of your experience firmly in your conscious mind. Begin to withdraw your attention. See whatever forms you have been seeing slowly fade into the brilliance of the stars. Slowly the stars diminish in size until only a soft glow remains.

Return now to our outer Temple.

(Allow short period of silence to make sure everyone is returned.)

PRIEST OF ANUBIS
(Rises, approaches eastern altar, bows, takes ankh from the eastern altar, invokes power into it. Says facing east)

Hail Anubis, Walker between the Worlds.

I come before you to ask your blessing upon each person of this company.

Lord of the hidden ways, guide us. Take us by the hand and lead us from darkness to light.

May we hear when you whisper, see when you show us and feel your presence beside us.

Make of your Priest the instrument of your blessing.

(Priest of Anubis goes to each person, beginning to the south of

the eastern altar. He faces each person and touches them with the ankh. Returning to the eastern altar he replaces the ankh on the altar, bows to the east and returns to his seat.)

PRIEST OF MAAHES

(Rises, approaches southern altar, bows, takes sword from the southern altar, invokes power into the sword then holds it at carry. Says facing south)

Hail Maahes, son of mighty Sekhmet.

I come before you to ask your blessing upon each person of this company.

May we be strengthened by your strength and walk fearless in the dark places.

We ask your protection upon us as walkers of the ways of the Mysteries and workers in the Light.

Make of your Priest the instrument of your blessing.

(Priest of Maahes goes to each person, beginning to the west of the southern altar. He faces each person and touches them on the top of the head with the sword for a few seconds.

Returning to the southern altar he replaces the sword on the altar, bows to the south and returns to his seat.)

PRIESTESS OF ISIS

(Rises, approaches western altar, bows, takes chalice of wine from the western altar, invokes power into it. Says facing west)

Hail Isis, Celestial Mother crowned with stars.

I come before you to ask your blessing upon each person of this company.

Enfold us in your care, nurture and sustain us. Teach us to be wise in your wisdom and compassionate in your compassion.

Great Mother cradle us in your arms and empower the life force within us.

Make of your Priestess the instrument of your blessing.

(Priestess of Isis goes to each person, beginning to the north of the western altar. She faces each person and offers them the chalice of wine to drink. She should have a cloth to wipe the chalice. Returning to the western altar, she replaces the chalice on the altar, bows to the west and returns to her seat.)

PRIESTESS OF MAAT

(Rises, approaches northern altar, bows, takes bowl of papers from the

northern altar, invokes power into them. Says facing north)

Hail Maat, Lady of Truth and Justice.

I come before you to ask your blessing upon each person of this company.

May the words of our mouths and the actions of our hearts be guided always by your truth and balance.

Make clear our judgement and honest our intent, help us to so act and know ourselves that at the end our hearts balance true with your feather.

Make of your Priestess the instrument of your blessing.

Priestess of Maat goes to each person, beginning to the east of the northern altar. She faces each person offers them the bowl of folded papers. Each person should take one.

Returning to the northern altar she replaces the bowl on the altar, bows to the north and returns to her seat)

MUSICIAN
(Play a few minutes of music. Track One Sacred Treasures V)

GUARDIAN
(Strikes the gong six times)

PRIEST OF ANUBIS
The day's work is done.

The light of Ra sinks in the west and all prepare for rest.

PRIESTESS OF MAAT
(Rises and goes to northern altar, bows and says)

Hail Maat, Lady of Truth and Justice.

We do thank you for your presence in our Temple

We salute you

We honour you

We thank you for your blessing and your protection.

Speak to us when we call.

We part in peace and close the veils of the worlds.

Farewell.

(Bows to the north, takes the figure back to the central altar, returns to place. Turns chair to face central altar and is seated.)

PRIESTESS OF ISIS
(Rises and goes to western altar, faces west and says)

Hail, Isis. Celestial Mother of All
We do thank you for your presence in our Temple
We salute you
We honour you
We thank you for your blessing and your protection.
Nurture us when we call.
We part in peace and close the veils of the worlds.
Farewell.
(Bows to the west, takes the figure back to the central altar, returns to place. Turns chair to face central altar and is seated.)

PRIEST OF MAAHES

(Rises and goes to southern altar, faces south and says;
Hail, Maahes, son of mighty Sekhmet.
We do thank you for your presence in our Temple
We salute you
We honour you
We thank you for your blessing and your protection.
Guard us when we call.
We part in peace and close the veils of the worlds.
Farewell.
(Bows to the south, takes the figure back to the central altar, returns to place. Turns chair to face central altar and is seated.)

PRIEST OF ANUBIS

(Rises, goes to eastern altar and says)
Hail Anubis, Opener of the Ways,
We do thank you for your presence in our Temple
We salute you
We honour you
We thank you for your blessing and your protection.
Be with us when we call
We part in peace and close the veils of the worlds.
Farewell.
(Bows to the east, takes the figure back to the central altar, returns to place. Turns chair to face central altar and is seated.)

GUARDIAN

(Sounds the gong three times.)

FOUR PRIESTS AND PRIESTESSES

(All rise together, each goes to their quarter altar, raises candle and together return them to the central altar. They then extinguish the four candles as follows)

PRIESTESS OF MAAT

Maat spoke. *(Extinguishes candle)*

PRIESTESS OF ISIS

Isis blessed. *(Extinguishes candle)*

PRIEST OF MAAHES

The gods guarded. (Extinguishes candle)

PRIEST OF ANUBIS

Ra sinks in the west. *(Extinguishes candle)*

(Raise their right arm high, touching each other's hands in centre, place left hand on the shoulder of the officer to their left and say together)

Glory and honour to the first Creator.

(All drop their arms and say together)

Behold the light of Amun shines upon the night and upon the day, eternal is His watchfulness.

Let us depart in peace.

(Pause at altar while Temple is unsealed)

MUSICIAN

(Turns on exit music. Track 15 and 16 Sacred Treasures V)

GUARDIAN

(Unseals the Temple.)

(The Officers leave, in order, West, South, East, North. Guardian sees all participants exit.)

Maat's Blessings

Note. The Blessings are taken from many sources. My thanks to the authors of all of them.

Know! A person walks in life on a very narrow bridge. The

most important thing is not to be afraid.

Don't make the same mistake as all those people who give up trying to change because they feel stuck in their habits. If you truly want to, and are willing to work hard enough, you can overcome them.

Everything in the world- whatever is and whatever happens -is a test, designed to give You freedom of choice. Choose wisely.

You are wherever your thoughts are. Make sure your thoughts are where you want to be.

Is there something you really want or something you wish would happen? Focus every ounce of your concentration on that thing or event. Visualise it in fine detail. If your desire is strong enough and your concentration intense enough, you can make it come true.

Worldly desires are like sunbeams in a dark room. They seem solid until you try to grasp one.

Be forewarned: Man and money cannot remain together forever. Either the money is taken from the man, or the man is taken from the money.

Be like God and don't look for people's shortcomings and weak points. You will then be at peace with everyone.

It's easy to criticise others and make them feel unwanted. Anyone can do it. What takes effort and skill is picking them up and making them feel good.

The Architect of the world never does the same thing twice. Every day is an entirely new creation. Take as much as you can from what each new day has to offer.

Work on having only positive thoughts. It will do wonders for your mind.

Each day has its own set of thoughts, words and deeds, live in tune.

In the early stages of your spiritual journey, it may seem that Heaven is rejecting you and spurning all your efforts. Stay on course. Don't give up. In time, all barriers will disappear.

Growing spiritually can be like a roller coaster ride. Take comfort in the knowledge that the way down is only preparation for the way up.

Go carefully: Spiritual growth must proceed slowly and steadily. Too often we want to improve ourselves and our relationships so quickly that we make ourselves frustrated and confused.

Never insist that everything go exactly your way, even in matters spiritual.

Believe that none of the effort you put into coming closer to God is ever wasted - even if in the end you don't achieve what you are striving for.

Don't be frustrated by the obstacles you encounter on your spiritual journey- they are there by design, to increase your desire for the goal you seek. Because the greater your goal, the greater the yearning you'll need to achieve it.

Always remember: You are never given an obstacle you cannot overcome.

The light of the Infinite One is without form and only takes shape - for good or bad - in the recipient. Therefore, it is up to us. We have to do our best to shape God's light into blessing, not curse.

Take care, there is much power in a glance. If accompanied by a malicious thought, it can cause harm. This is what is known as the evil eye.

Have a good eye. Always see good in others. Spiritual awareness depends upon it. Spiritual awareness is lost when people dull their hearts with jealousy and develop an evil eye.

Seek the sacred within the ordinary. Seek the remarkable within the common place. Is not the Song of Songs at once a love song and the holiest of all sacred teachings?

Affirm your faith in yourself:

I believe that I am very important in God's eyes.

I believe that I can return, no matter how far I've strayed,

I believe that I have the inner strength to change.

I believe that I can become truly devoted and close to God.

Always wear a smile. The gift of life will then be yours to give.

Sometimes, people are terribly distressed but have no one to whom they can unburden themselves. If you come along with a happy face, you cheer them and give them new life.

We learn wisdom from failure much more than from success; we often discover what will do by finding out what will not do; and probably he who never made a mistake never made a discovery.

Never be afraid to tread the path alone. Know which is your path and follow it wherever it may lead you; do not feel you have to follow in someone else's footsteps.

Cease trying to work everything out with your minds, it will get you nowhere. Live by intuition and inspiration and let your whole life be a revelation.

Why destroy your present happiness by a distant misery which may never come at all? For every substantial grief has twenty shadows and most of the shadows are of our own making.

To be upset over what you don't have is to waste what you do have.

Life is like a wild tiger. You can either lie down and let it lay its paw on your head – or sit on its back and ride it.

We are members of a vast cosmic orchestra in which each living instrument is essential to the complementary and harmonious playing of the whole.

One may not reach the dawn save by the path of the night.

You are never asked to do more than you are able, without being given the strength and ability to do it.

Disillusionment with yourself must precede enlightenment.

We are injured and hurt emotionally – not so much by other people or what they say or do not say, but by our own attitude and our own response.

Each player must accept the cards life deals him or her. But once they are in hand he or she alone must decide how to play the cards in order to win the game.

It is important from time to time to slow down, to go away by yourself and simply BE.

Be very, very still and allow every new experience to take place in your life without any resistance whatsoever. You do not have to do anything, you simply have to be and let things happen.

Great spirits have always encountered violent opposition from mediocre minds.

Trials are but lessons that you failed to learn presented once again, so where you made a faulty choice before you can now make a better one, and thus escape all pain that what you chose before has brought to you.

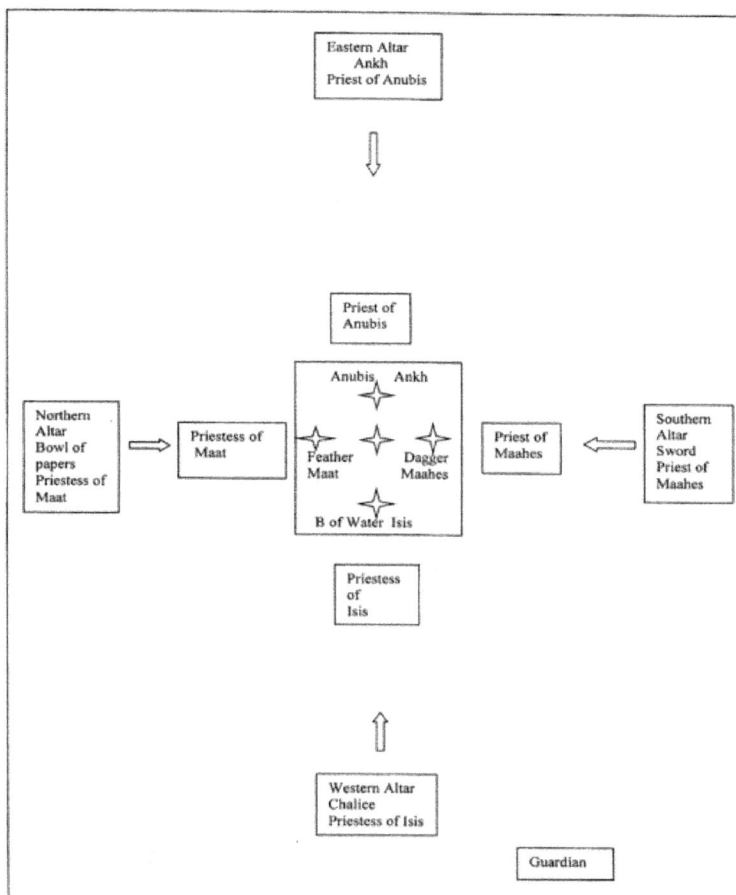

Eastern Altar
Ankh
Priest of Anubis

Priest of
Anubis

Anubis   Ankh

Northern
Altar
Bowl of
papers
Priestess of
Maat

Priestess of
Maat

Feather
Maat

Dagger
Maahes

Priest of
Maahes

Southern
Altar
Sword
Priest of
Maahes

B of Water Isis

Priestess
of
Isis

Western Altar
Chalice
Priestess of Isis

Guardian

The Altars of Light Ritual

REQUIREMENTS

Altar of Earth
Green cloth
Tarot cards
Earth chalice containing small crystals
Altar of Spirit
Red cloth
Bowl of salted water
Glass chalice containing lighted candle
Altar of Soul
Silver cloth
Essential oil
Chalice/bread and wine
Veil of Knowledge
White or gold veils
Altar of Divinity
Gold cloth
Two Gold masks
Roses
Glass chalice with water
Four small tables for the altars
Two candles on each altar
Matches and snuffer for each altar, or electric candles
Shoulder capes for Priests and Priestesses
Sword for Guardian of the West
Music CDs

OFFICERS

Guardian of the East
Guardian of the West
Priestess of Altar of Earth
Priest of Altar of Earth
Priestess of Altar of Spirit
Priest of Altar of Spirit
Priestess of Altar of Soul
Priest of Altar of Soul
Priestess of Veil of Knowledge

Priest of Veil of Knowledge
Priestess of Altar of Divinity
Priest of Altar of Divinity
Musician

PREPARATION
The altars are arranged as in plan. Cloths and candles are in place. The veil is arranged between the Altar of Soul and the Altar of Divinity Candles are lit on the Altar of Divinity.
All other items are carried in by the Priests and Priestesses.

Ritual

MUSICIAN
(Start music. Mozart. Laudate Dominum. Vespers and Litanies Track 5
NOTE. Allow to play to end of track.)

GUARDIAN
(Priest and Priestess of Divinity are seated in place prior to all entry.
Guardian of the West supervises entry of participants.
When all are in place and seated the Guardian admits all the other Officers
Guardian of the East enters, followed by Priestesses and Priests in pairs, in order, Veil of Knowledge, Soul, Spirit, Earth each going to the appropriate altar. Lastly Guardian of the West.

MUSICIAN
(Turn off music at end of track)

GUARDIAN OF THE EAST
(Rises)

Respected Guardian of the West, assume your duties and make safe our place of working. See that the Temple is secure from all intrusion and under your protection. Maintain your vigilance until the Temple is closed in peace.

GUARDIAN OF THE WEST
(Rises and faces west. Makes the sign of the Pentagram)

By the power of the Pentagram I seal this Temple on the

material level. With the strength of the sword will I protect its boundaries from intruders and the profane.

(Makes the sign of four and three.)

I stand vigilant for the duration of this working.

Respected Guardian of the East, the Temple is secure and guarded.

GUARDIAN OF THE EAST

(Rises and faces east. Makes the sign of the Pentagram)

By the power of the Pentagram I seal this Temple on the inner levels. With the strength of my will I will protect its boundaries from intruders and all wickedness.

(Makes the sign of four and three)

I stand vigilant for the duration of this working. This Temple is now sealed and guarded on the inner and the outer levels.

Everyone please rise.

(Opens the quarters, moving to each one as appropriate. Begins facing east.)

In the name of Ieschouah, I call upon Raphael, regent of the Divine, to empower the eastern quarter of this temple. The eastern quarter is now open.

(Facing south)

In the name of Adonai, I call upon Michael, regent of the Divine, to empower the southern quarter of this temple. The southern quarter is now open.

(Facing west)

In the name of Yod, He, Vau, He, I call upon Gabriel, regent of the Divine, to empower the western quarter of this temple. The western quarter is now open.

(Facing north)

In the name of the Elohim, I call upon Uriel, regent of the Divine, to empower the northern quarter of this temple. The northern quarter is now open.

(From the east, facing west)

In the name of INRI. Amen.

Please be seated.

PRIEST AND PRIESTESS OF EARTH

(Rise. Stand to west of altar facing east.)

PRIESTESS OF EARTH

I am the Priestess of the Altar of Earth. Here are celebrated the joys and sorrows of earthly life, the lessons which only life in a physical body can teach and the learning of skills and wisdom.

(Lights candle)

Everyone, *(pause)* see the energies build above the altar and flow down into the symbols I now lay upon it.

(Lays spread Tarot cards on altar and holds hand over them in blessing.)

I call upon the energies of the Kings and Powers of the Elements to empower this altar and to inspire the choices we will make.

(Pause for visualisation, then intoning in turn)

Air – Fire – Water – Earth.

PRIEST OF EARTH

I am the Priest of the Altar of Earth. Here are celebrated the emotions of earthly life. The love of man for woman and the path of the hearth fire.

Here are known the inspirations of great art and literature. Here too are learnt the qualities of leadership and selfless service.

(Lights candle)

Everyone, *(pause)* see the energies flow down as a stream of light into this chalice to inspire and teach.

(Places chalice on altar, holds hand over it in blessing)

I call upon the energies of the Angels, Archangels and Principalities which order the Universe, to empower this altar and show each one the best direction for their life experience.

(Pause for visualisation)

PRIEST AND PRIESTESS OF EARTH

(Both are seated together.)

PRIEST AND PRIESTESS OF SPIRIT

(Both rise and stand west of Altar of Spirit facing east)

PRIESTESS OF SPIRIT

I am the Priestess of the Altar of Spirit. Mine is the realm of the subconscious, of instinct, dreams, and intuition. Within my realms is the doorway into the inner worlds of the spirit and the pathways which lead to the realms of Light.

(Lights candle)

Everyone, *(pause)* see the energies flow down and transmute this salt and water into a cleansing balm of the spirit.

(Places bowl of salt and water on the altar. Holds hand over it in blessing)

I call upon the subtle energies of the planets, stars and cosmos to awaken the potential spirituality within us.

(Pause for visualisation)

PRIEST OF SPIRIT

I am the Priest of the Altar of Spirit. I am the keeper of the scrolls of memory, the artist who draws the images of the imagination. I am the opener of the inner eye whose vision reveals truth and reality.

(Lights candle)

Everyone, *(pause)* see the energies flow down and fill this chalice with the light of inspiration that it may illuminate our understanding.

(Places chalice on altar, holds hand over it in blessing)

I call upon the energies of the Powers, Virtues and Dominions which build the forces of creation and ask that they may assist us to see into the inner worlds.

(Pause for visualisation)

PRIEST AND PRIESTESS OF SPIRIT

(Both are seated together)

PRIEST AND PRIESTESS OF SOUL

(Both rise and stand west of the Altar of Soul facing east)

PRIESTESS OF SOUL

I am the Priestess of the Altar of Soul. Here we touch the energies of our Higher Self, that self which has always existed and is forever a spark of the Divine.

(Lights candle)

Everyone, *(pause)* reach inwards and upwards and feel the touch of your greater Self. Draw down the energies of love and power that we may blend with them and empower this altar.

(Places dish of oil on altar and holds hand over it in blessing)

I call upon the spiritual energies of the sun behind the sun to empower this altar and connect us with our Higher Self.

(Pause for visualisation)

PRIEST OF SOUL

I am the Priest of the Altar of Soul. Here we celebrate the oneness of our being, here we blend the material with the spiritual and awareness of the Divine awakes.

(Lights candle)

Everyone, *(pause)* open your hearts and minds and allow the sacred vibrations of soul to flow down and bless this bread and wine with grace.

I call upon the energies of the Thrones, Cherubim and Seraphim which surround the throne of the Divine to bless this altar as we join them in singing the Sanctus, Holy, Holy, Holy, Lord God of Hosts.

(Pause for visualisation)

PRIEST AND PRIESTESS OF SOUL

(Priest and Priestess of Soul are seated together)

PRIEST AND PRIESTESS OF VEIL OF KNOWLEDGE

(Priest and Priestess of Knowledge rise and stand either side of the central parting in the veil, facing each other)

PRIESTESS OF VEIL OF KNOWLEDGE

I am the Priestess of the Veil of Knowledge. I guard the left side of the portal of the sacred realms of the Divine. To pass through the veil of knowledge we must bring a pure heart and a worthy intent.

PRIEST OF VEIL OF KNOWLEDGE

I am the Priest of the Veil of Knowledge. I guard the right side of the portal of the sacred realms of the Divine. To pass through the veil of knowledge, remember the teachings of the Mysteries - ask, and it shall be given you; seek, and ye shall find; knock, and it shall be opened unto you.

PRIEST AND PRIESTESS OF VEIL OF KNOWLEDGE

(Both are seated together)

GUARDIAN OF THE EAST
Companions. All who wish to do so may now approach the Altars and receive the blessings of the Priests and Priestesses.

MUSICIAN
(Play music. Arvo Part. De Profundis

NOTE. This CD plays all through the blessings. It may be necessary to reduce the sound volume for a few of the louder tracks.

Play until Guardian of the West has returned from the Altar of Divinity)

GUARDIAN OF THE WEST
(Now directs the Companions to approach the Altar of Earth in turn. Each progresses to the next altar, through to the Altar of the Divine.)

PRIESTESS AND PRIEST OF EARTH
(Rise to greet Companion and remain standing until last companion has received the blessing.)

PRIESTESS OF EARTH
(The Tarot cards are face down. Priestess says to each Companion)

Receive the blessing of the Altar of Earth. Choose a card which will be your guide and help on the next stage of your journey.

PRIEST OF EARTH
(Priest says to each Companion)

Receive the blessing of the Altar of Earth. Take a stone to be a reminder of this step upon your journey.

(Companion moves on to next altar and next Companions comes to Altar of Earth.)

PRIESTESS AND PRIEST OF SPIRIT
(Rise to greet Companion and remain standing until last companion has received the blessing)

PRIESTESS OF SPIRIT
(Priestess says to each Companion)

Receive the blessing of the Altar of Spirit. Dip your fingers in this consecrated water and let it cleanse you of all past regrets and mistakes.

PRIEST OF SPIRIT
(Priest says to each Companion)
Receive the blessing of the Altar of Spirit. Pass your hand over the fire of this candle and be purified in body and spirit.
(Companion moves on to Altar of Soul)

PRIESTESS AND PRIEST OF SOUL
(Rise to greet Companion and remain standing until last companion has received the blessing)

PRIESTESS OF THE ALTAR OF SOUL
(Priestess says to each Companion)
Receive the blessing of the Altar of Soul. By this sign *(touches each palm with the scented oil)* you are acknowledged a seeker and the work of your hands is blessed.

PRIEST OF THE ALTAR OF SOUL
(Priest says to each Companion)
Receive the blessing of the Altar of Soul. *(offers a piece of bread which should be dipped in the wine and eaten)* By this sign you are acknowledged a speaker of Truth and the words of your tongue are blessed.
(Companion moves on to the Veil of Knowledge)

PRIESTESS AND PRIEST OF VEIL OF KNOWLEDGE
(Rise to greet Companion and remain standing, one each side of the central opening until last Companion has received the blessing)

PRIESTESS OF THE VEIL OF KNOWLEDGE
Companion what is your intent?

PRIEST OF THE VEIL OF KNOWLEDGE
Companion what do you seek?
(When answers have been received from the Companion the Priest and Priestess separate the veil in the centre and allow the Companion to pass through)

PRIESTESS AND PRIEST OF THE ALTAR OF DIVINITY
(When the Companion is at the Veil of Knowledge both rise and stand either side of the altar and remain standing until last Companion has been blessed.)

PRIESTESS OF THE ALTAR OF DIVINITY

I am the Priestess of the Altar of Divinity. I bid you welcome to this sanctuary of the Mysteries. You have proved yourself a true Seeker.

(Takes one of the roses and holds it briefly against the heart of the Companion.)

I give you this rose to symbolise the truths of the Mysteries which abide in your heart. Allow them to bloom and grow and be blessed.

PRIEST OF THE ALTAR OF DIVINITY

I am the Priest of the Altar of Divinity. *(touches centre of forehead with water)* Open your inner eye and see the truth of the Mystery. *(places hand on top of head)* Go onward and be blessed.

(Companion leaves the Altar of Divinity, they do not return through the Veil of Knowledge but exit to the side and return to their place and are seated.)

PRIEST AND PRIESTESS OF THE ALTAR OF SOUL

(When the last Companion is seated, both turn outwards and proceed to the Altar of Earth via the north and south respectively.

They then receive the blessing of the altar of Earth, pass to the Altar of Spirit and receive the blessing, then to their own Altar where they share the blessing then pass through the veil of Knowledge, finally returning to their stations)

PRIEST AND PRIESTESS OF THE ALTAR OF SPIRIT

(After the Priest and Priestess of Soul have passed, both turn outwards and proceed to the Altar of Earth via the north and south respectively. They then receive the blessing of the Altar of Earth, share the blessing at the Altar of Spirit, and pass to the Altar of Soul and through Veil of Knowledge, finally returning to their station.)

PRIEST AND PRIESTESS OF EARTH

(After the Priest and Priestess of Spirit have passed they share the blessing of the Altar of Earth, then proceed to the other Altars and through the Veil of Knowledge, finally returning to their place)

GUARDIAN OF THE EAST

(Proceeds to Altar of Earth and receives all the blessings. Returns to place)

GUARDIAN OF THE WEST
(Proceeds to Altar of Earth and receives all the blessings. Returns to place)

MUSICIAN
(Turns off music when Guardian of the West is seated.
All Priests and Priestesses are seated together)

GUARDIAN OF THE EAST
Priests and Priestesses in your several qualities, Companions in Light, our work for this ceremony is now accomplished.

Let us give thanks to the powers who have assisted us that we may depart in peace and grace.

(NOTE. Candles are left lit on the Altar of Divinity)

PRIEST AND PRIESTESS OF THE VEIL OF KNOWLEDGE
Rise and stand left and right of centre of Veil)

PRIESTESS OF THE VEIL OF KNOWLEDGE
The Companions of good intent have received the blessing of the Priest and Priestess of the Altar of the Divine. As Priestess of the Veil of Knowledge I now close and seal the left hand side of the veil.

(Closes left side of veil. Remains standing)

PRIEST OF THE VEIL OF KNOWLEDGE
The Companions go forward on their quest, blessed by the Priest and Priestess of the Altar of the Divine. As Priest of the Veil of Knowledge I now close and seal the right hand side of the veil.

(Closes right hand side of the veil. Remains standing)

PRIEST AND PRIESTESS OF THE ALTAR OF SOUL
(Both rise and stand in front of altar facing east)

PRIESTESS OF THE ALTAR OF SOUL
Let us give thanks to the spiritual energies of the sun behind the sun which have empowered this altar and connected us with our Higher Selves. May the powers of this altar now be closed and the blessings between us remain.

(Extinguishes candle. Remains standing)

PRIEST OF THE ALTAR OF SOUL

Let us give thanks to the spiritual energies of the Thrones, Cherubim and Seraphim which surround the throne of the Divine. May the powers of this altar now be closed and the song of the Sanctus, Holy, Holy, Holy, Lord God of Hosts remain in our hearts.

(Extinguishes candle. Remains standing)

PRIEST AND PRIESTESS OF THE ALTAR OF SPIRIT

(Both rise and stand in front of altar facing east)

PRIESTESS OF THE ALTAR OF SPIRIT

Let us give thanks to the subtle energies of the planets, stars and cosmos which awakened the potential spirituality within us. May the powers of this altar now be closed and the connection between us remain.

(Extinguishes candle. Remains standing)

PRIEST OF THE ALTAR OF SPIRIT

Let us give thanks to the energies of the Powers, Virtues and Dominions which build the forces of creation and assisted us to see into the inner worlds. May the powers of this altar now be closed and the powers of vision remain.

(Extinguishes candle. Remains standing)

PRIEST AND PRIESTESS OF THE ALTAR OF EARTH

(Both rise and stand in front of altar facing east)

PRIESTESS OF ALTAR OF EARTH

Let us give thanks to the energies of the Kings and Powers of the Elements which empowered this altar and inspired our choices. May the powers of this altar now be closed and the guidance of our choice remain.

(Extinguishes candle. Remains standing)

PRIEST OF THE ALTAR OF EARTH

Let us give thanks to the energies of the Angels, Archangels and Principalities which order the Universe and empowered this altar. May the powers of this altar now be closed and their influence remain to guide our life experience.

(Extinguishes candle. Remains standing)

GUARDIAN OF THE EAST
(Rises, facing west)

Everyone please rise.

(Closes the quarters, moving to each one as appropriate. Begins facing east)

In the name of Ieschouah, I give thanks to Raphael, regent of the Divine, for empowering the eastern quarter of this Temple.

May grace and peace abide between us.

The eastern quarter is now closed.

(Facing south)

In the name of Adonai, I give thanks to Michael, regent of the Divine, for empowering the southern quarter of this Temple.

May grace and peace abide between us.

The southern quarter is now closed.

(Facing west)

In the name of Yod, He, Vau, He, I give thanks to Gabriel, regent of the Divine, for empowering the western quarter of this Temple.

May grace and peace abide between us.

The western quarter is now closed.

(Facing north)

In the name of the Elohim, I give thanks to Uriel, regent of the Divine, for empowering the northern quarter of this Temple.

May peace and grace abide between us.

The northern quarter is now closed.

(From the east, facing west)

In the name of INRI. Amen.

(Makes the sign of the Pentagram)

By the power of the Pentagram I unseal this Temple on the inner levels.

Guardian of the West, please unseal the material Temple.

GUARDIAN OF THE WEST
(Unseals the Temple with the sign of the Pentagram and sign of four and three.)

By the power of the Pentagram I unseal this Temple on the material level.

Guardian of the East the Temple door is now open and all may depart in peace.

MUSICIAN
(Start exit music Classic FM. Smooth Classics Disc 3. Track 1)

GUARDIAN OF THE WEST
(Opens Temple doors.

Officers depart in order, Priest and Priestess of Altar of Earth, Priest and Priestess of Altar of Spirit, Priest and Priestess of Altar of Soul and Guardian of the East.

All Companions.

Priest and Priestess of Altar of Divinity.

Guardian of the West.)

The Altars of Light Ritual Plan

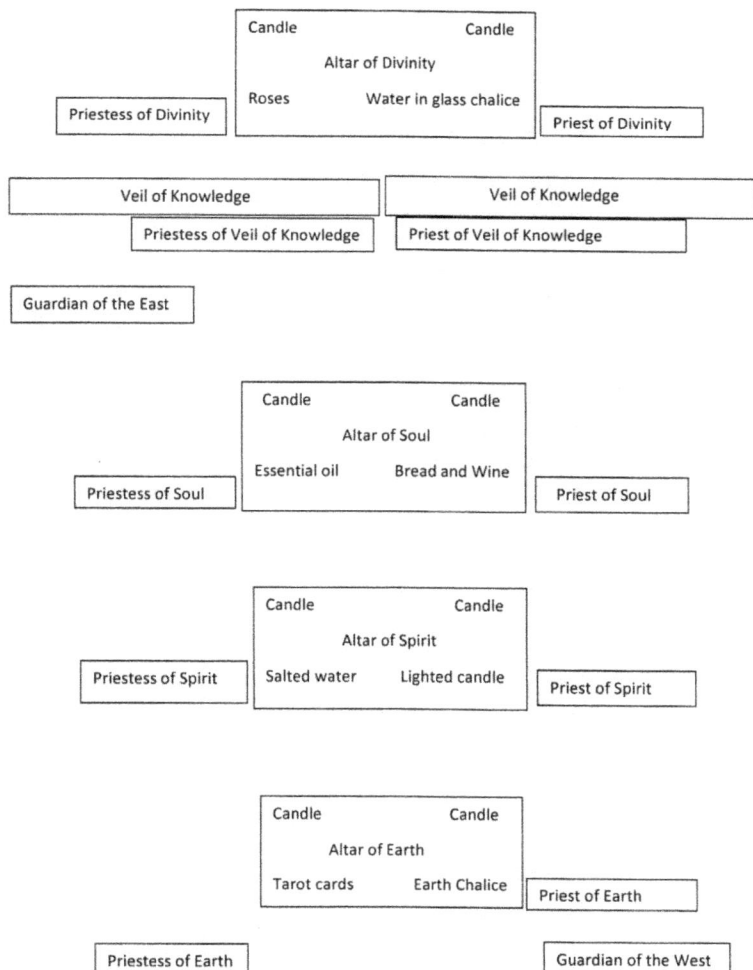

Candle	Candle
Altar of Divinity	
Roses	Water in glass chalice

Priestess of Divinity

Priest of Divinity

Veil of Knowledge	Veil of Knowledge

Priestess of Veil of Knowledge

Priest of Veil of Knowledge

Guardian of the East

Candle	Candle
Altar of Soul	
Essential oil	Bread and Wine

Priestess of Soul

Priest of Soul

Candle	Candle
Altar of Spirit	
Salted water	Lighted candle

Priestess of Spirit

Priest of Spirit

Candle	Candle
Altar of Earth	
Tarot cards	Earth Chalice

Priest of Earth

Priestess of Earth

Guardian of the West

The Holy Temple

OFFICERS
Priest
Oracle (Priestess)
Guardian One with sword
Guardian Two with sword
Conductor One
Escort
Musician

Format of the Temple as diagram
Two altars. One lower in the Temple area
One higher in the Chapel of Dedication.
Oracle is veiled and sits between the two screens, translucent silver in front, black behind her.
There are Sacred Lights on either side of the Oracle, she has a small table on which are bread and wine.

REQUIREMENTS
Two swords (matching if possible) for Guardians
Sword for Chapel of Dedication
Two tables
Small table
Platter
Chalice
Bread
Wine
Oil burner and Oils
Sacred Lights and Stands
Two large candles for Altars
Black cloth for screen
Silver translucent cloth for screen
Four stands to make screens
Kneeling stool
Large Veil
Gong
CD / Tape recorder
Music.

Inward Harmony. Constance Danby.
Elgar. Lux Aeterna for Exit.
Purpose is to attain a state of devotion, dedication and reverence.

Ritual

The Priest is in the Chapel of Dedication.
The Oracle is seated between the two screens.
The Two Guardians are standing just inside the entrance with raised swords.
The Conductor is outside with those awaiting admittance.
The Escort is within the Temple.
The Musician is in place west of the silver screen forward of the Oracle.
All candles are lit by the Priest before ritual commences.
All attending, except Officers wait IN SILENCE in the anteroom away from the Temple.

MUSICIAN
(Turns on music, playing softly)

CONDUCTOR
(Each person is brought to the entrance of the Temple individually by the Conductor.

They are told to enter an apparently open, unguarded doorway)

GUARDIAN ONE AND GUARDIAN TWO
(As each person comes through the doorway, bring the swords together in a cross before them, thus barring their entry.

Each question asked by the Guardians must be answered by each person entering or they are not allowed to do so. The acceptance of the answers is decided by the Guardians)

GUARDIAN ONE
Who approaches the Sanctuary?
(Answer required)

GUARDIAN TWO
By what Path have you travelled?
(Answer must state the name of a School, Tradition, Order etc. which they have worked within)

GUARDIAN ONE
What do you seek here?
(Answer required)

GUARDIAN TWO
Will you depart in Peace and Silence if you do not find it?
(Answer must be "yes, I will" or similar)

GUARDIAN ONE
Then enter and may your heart be pure.

GUARDIAN ONE AND GUARDIAN TWO.
(Lift swords to carry and allow entry by passing between them)

ESCORT
(Receives and conducts each person in turn to a seat in the Temple)

CONDUCTOR
(When all have been admitted enters Temple and is seated within in the North East)

GUARDIAN ONE AND GUARDIAN TWO
(After the Conductor has entered and is seated, turn and Guardian One seals the doorway and closes doors. Both then face each other, together placing swords at waist and are seated either side of the doorway)

MUSICIAN
*(Allow short period for everyone to settle then turn off music.
Sound gong seven times in format *******)*

PRIEST
(Enters Temple from the Chapel of Dedication, goes to the altar, takes burner, adds scented oil, then circles the Temple holding the burner, to cleanse the Temple then returns burner to Altar.

Goes slowly to East, South, West and North in turn, makes the Sign of the Pentagram and <u>silently</u> invokes the Presences.)

Returns to Altar and making sign of invocation, arms raised, palms uplifted)

(Conductor may assist by holding script)

Holy is the One who was, is and shall be, eternally and without end.

Holy is the One who created radiance from the ineffable essence of the Uncreated Light

Holy is the One who has walked beside thee and has brought thee to this place.

Holy is the One who is closer to thee than the voice of thine own heart.

Holy is the One who will teach and inspire thee if thy heart knowest how to desire it.

As Priest of this Temple, On the Centre, I invoke the Sacred Presence of the Divine.

(Returns to chair to East of Altar and is seated)

MUSICIAN

(Turn on music which should be loud enough to mask the conversations of the Oracle but not so loud as to be intrusive)

CONDUCTOR AND ESCORT

(Conductor goes to first person at the South East. Escort stands in South East ready to conduct each person from the Chapel of Dedication and back to their seat, but remaining outside the Chapel until required so each person has privacy)

(Quietly, to individual)

Do you wish to consult the Oracle?

(If the answer is yes, the person is conducted round the Temple and taken behind the translucent veil via the North East and instructed to be seated in front of the Oracle. The Conductor retires out of hearing but in a position to see when the Oracle has concluded)

ORACLE

(The content of the conversation with the Oracle is personal and conducted at the Oracle's discretion. When concluded the Oracle gives the blessing of bread and wine)

(Offers bread)

Partake of the gift of the Father and be blessed.

(Offers wine)

Partake of the gift of the Mother and be blessed.

You may now retire to the Chapel of Dedication.

CONDUCTOR

(Comes forward and conducts the person out via the North East and to the Chapel of Dedication where they are left alone until the next person arrives)

CONDUCTOR
(Goes to the next person in the South East and the process is repeated until everyone has had the opportunity of consulting the Oracle.

The last person to consult the Oracle is the Priest, on returning from the Chapel of Dedication he goes to the East of the Altar to close the Temple)

MUSICIAN
(Turns off music.)

PRIEST
(Goes slowly to East, South, West and North in turn, makes the Sign of the Pentagram and silently thanks and dismisses the Presences)

Holy is the One who was, is and shall be, eternally and without end.

As Priest of this Temple, On the Centre, I thank the Sacred Presence of the Divine and close this Temple.

So be it closed and sealed.

All may now depart in Peace and Love.
(Returns to station)

MUSICIAN
(Turns on exit music)

GUARDIAN ONE AND GUARDIAN TWO
(Rise and face each other, turn together to face doorway, Guardian Two unseals the doorway and opens the doors)

CONDUCTOR
(Proceeds to the West and directs the exit, from the South West first)

CONDUCTOR
(Follows last non Officer out)

ESCORT
(Follows the Conductor out)

PRIEST
(Exit)
MUSICIAN
(Exit)

GUARDIAN ONE AND GUARDIAN TWO
(Exit)

ORACLE
(Exits in own time)

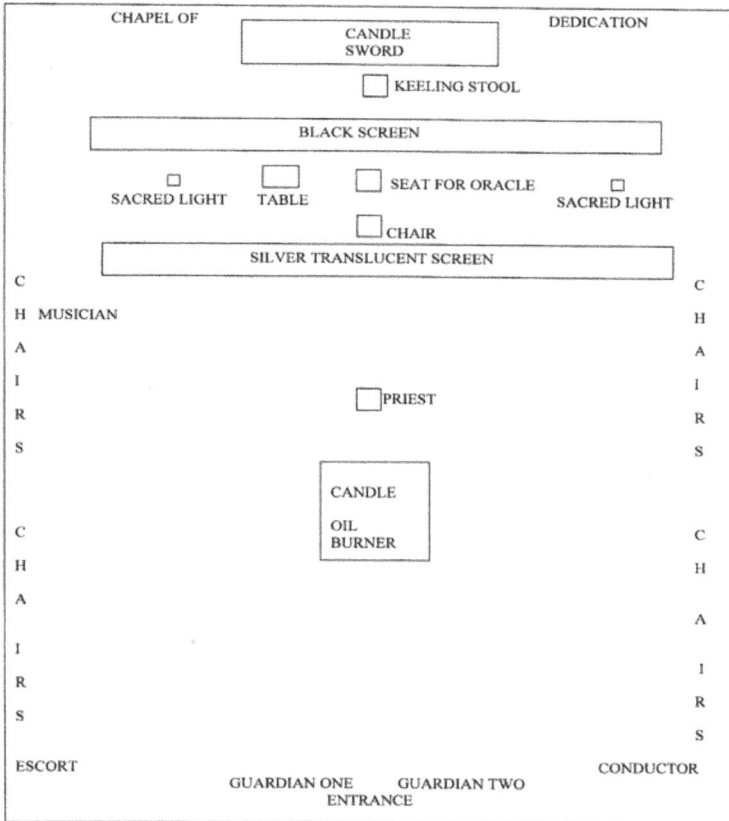

```
 _____
|   CHAPEL OF              ┌──────────────────┐   DEDICATION  |
|                          │    CANDLE        │               |
|                          │    SWORD         │               |
|                          └──────────────────┘               |
|                              □ KEELING STOOL                 |
|                                                              |
|   ┌──────────────────────────────────────────────────────┐  |
|   │                 BLACK SCREEN                          │  |
|   └──────────────────────────────────────────────────────┘  |
|                                                              |
|          □                □       □ SEAT FOR ORACLE    □     |
|     SACRED LIGHT       TABLE                      SACRED LIGHT|
|                              □ CHAIR                         |
|   ┌──────────────────────────────────────────────────────┐  |
|   │        SILVER TRANSLUCENT SCREEN                      │  |
| C └──────────────────────────────────────────────────────┘ C|
|                                                              |
| H  MUSICIAN                                                H |
|                                                              |
| A                                                          A |
|                                                              |
| I                            □ PRIEST                      I |
|                                                              |
| R                                                          R |
|                                                              |
| S                                                          S |
|                         ┌──────────────┐                     |
|                         │  CANDLE      │                     |
| C                       │  OIL         │                    C|
|                         │  BURNER      │                     |
| H                       └──────────────┘                    H|
|                                                              |
| A                                                          A |
|                                                              |
| I                                                          I |
|                                                              |
| R                                                          R |
|                                                              |
| S                                                          S |
|                                                              |
|  ESCORT                                      CONDUCTOR       |
|            GUARDIAN ONE      GUARDIAN TWO                     |
|                     ENTRANCE                                 |
|_____|
```

The Four Blessings Ritual

<u>OFFICERS.</u>
Bearer of the Sword
Bearer of the Wand
Bearer of the Chalice
Bearer of the Crystals
Guardian of the Temple

<u>FOUR BEARERS OF THE LIGHTS AT THE CROSS QUARTERS.</u>
Air-North-east
Fire-South-east
Water-South-west
Earth-North-west

<u>TEMPLE ARRANGEMENTS</u>
Four Bearers of the Lights at cross quarters as above.

East	*Bearer of the Sword*
South	*Bearer of the Wand*
West	*Bearer of the Chalice*
North	*Bearer of the Crystals*

Guardian at the doorway
Musician
Centre altar containing sacred flame in middle and twelve coloured lights of the zodiac surrounding it.
Four white candles at the cross quarters on centre table for the Bearers of the Lights.
Taper on table.
Four cross quarters. Small table at each station covered with cloth of the colour of the element it represents; East Blue, South Red, West Green, North Brown.
Musician to arrange music for entry of officers and as required in ritual.

Ritual

<u>ORDER OF ENTRY OF OFFICERS</u>
Guardian and Musician enter first and go to stations.
All none officers are admitted by the Guardian

The four Bearers of the Lights enter and go to stations.
The four quarter Officers enter in order
Bearer of the Chalice
Bearer of the Wand
Bearer of the Sword
Bearer of the Crystals
They process once round Temple then each stops at their station.

MUSICIAN
(Plays music for Entry of Officers)

BEARER OF SWORD.
(Censes Temple and Altar)

MUSICIAN
(Stops Music)

GUARDIAN
(Sounds Gong)

BEARER OF SWORD
Who stands guard over this Temple?

GUARDIAN
I stand guard over this Temple.

BEARER OF SWORD
Set seal upon the doorway that our work may proceed in peace and security.

GUARDIAN
(Sets seal on door with Sign of Pentagram)
    The seal is set and the Temple secure.

BEARER OF SWORD
(Takes sword, holds point upwards)
    I call upon the Lords of Light who rule the Element of Air, to breathe the breath of living Light into this place of working.
    (Holding sword before him circumambulates the Temple once going via South)

345

BEARER OF WAND
(Takes Wand, holding it upwards)

I call upon the Lords of Light who rule the Element of Fire, to light the vital flame of life and power within this place of working.

(Holding Wand before him circumambulates the Temple once going via West.)

BEARER OF CHALICE
(Takes the Chalice containing Water, holds it aloft)

I call upon the Lords of Light who rule the Element of Water, to direct the flow of the seas of consciousness within this place of working.

(Holding Chalice before her circumambulates the Temple once going via North)

BEARER OF CRYSTALS
(Takes bowl containing crystals, holds aloft)

I call upon the Lords of Light who rule the Element of Earth, to bring the strength of land and life into this place of working.

(Holding bowl of crystals before her circumambulates the Temple once going via East)

BEARER OF SWORD

I build the bridge of the eastern gate from the light of the rising Sun. Mine is the bridge from the dawn of the day to the height of the mid-day Sun.

BEARER OF WAND

I build the bridge of the noonday Sun which blesses with warmth and with life. Mine is the bridge of midsummer sun and the ripening beauty of earth.

BEARER OF CHALICE

I build the bridge of the setting sun to the time of sleep and of rest. Mine is the bridge that the Dreamers tread to the lands where the wise ones walk.

BEARER OF CRYSTALS

I build the bridge of the northern star to the deeps of the

moonless night. Mine is the bridge to all hidden things, to visions of space and of stars.

BEARER OF SWORD
Now let us build the rainbow bridge of the stars, the bridge which is the reflection of every facet that is man and woman.

(As each Bearer of the Lights is called, the Bearer lights the appropriate Zodiac lights on the centre Altar and returns to station taking the white candle from the centre table)

BEARER OF SWORD
I summon the bearer of the Lights of Air to build the foundation of the rainbow bridge.

The orange beam of Gemini to bring versatility, adaptability, and intelligence.

The emerald beam of Libra to bring companionship, sociability, and balance.

The violet beam of Aquarius to bring independence, tenacity, and friendship.

BEARER OF WAND
I summon the bearer of the Lights of Fire to bring life to our rainbow bridge

The red beam of Aries to bring energy, enthusiasm, and initiative.

The green/yellow beam of Leo to bring self-confidence, broadmindedness, and expansion

The blue beam of Sagittarius to bring honesty, idealism, and energy.

BEARER OF THE CHALICE
I summon the bearer of the Lights of Water to bring wisdom to our rainbow bridge.

The amber light of Cancer to bring diplomacy, sympathy, and emotion

The green/blue light of Scorpio to bring determination, persistence, and sense of purpose.

The crimson light of Pisces to bring sensitivity, sympathy, and warmth.

BEARER OF CRYSTAL

I summon the bearer of the Lights of Earth to bring stability to our rainbow bridge.

The red/orange light of Taurus to bring liberty, reliability, and security.

The yellow/green light of Virgo to bring exactitude, conscientiousness, and service.

The indigo light of Capricorn to bring prudence, caution, and discipline.

(When the Bearers of the Lights have their candles, music is played for the procession of the lights as they circle the Temple three times)

MUSICIAN
(Starts Music.)

BEARER OF SWORD

Let the Bearers of the Lights weave the circle of light around our central altar.

(Bearers of the Lights circle the Temple three times.

When the Bearers of the Lights have returned to their original place on the last circle they return their candles to the centre table and return to their stations)

BEARER OF SWORD

Everyone please rise.

Our rainbow constellation is now formed and shines out in the full splendour of light.

Let us join hands in token of our unity within the light, in expression of our love for each other and in celebration of the life we share.

(Pause while all join hands and stand in silence)
Please be seated.

MUSICIAN
(Stops Music)

BEARER OF SWORD
(Holds Sword at Carry)

As the reflection is the illusion of the reality, so too are we but reflections of our true self.

In memory of this truth I give you the gift of Air that you

may experience this and know that which you truly are.

(Circles Temple touching each on the top of the head with the Sword)

BEARER OF WAND
(Holds Wand at Carry)

As the Sun's rays are the living light which strikes forth the colours of the rainbow, so too is our vitality the reflection and the mirror of Cosmic Life. The flame of life burns bright if tended well. I give you the gift of fire that you may know and remember these things.

(Circles Temple touching each once on each shoulder with the Wand)

BEARER OF CHALICE
(Holds Chalice before her)

Even as the seas are the life blood of earth, so too is the raindrop the life form of the Rainbow. As we reflect the light so too do our colours become visible in the many hues of vibrant life.

The cup of life is bitter-sweet and deep yet every drop is vital to our need. I give you a gift of water in remembrance of these things.

(Circles Temple touching each on centre of forehead with water from Chalice)

BEARER OF CRYSTALS
(Holds Crystals before her.)

So have we formed a rainbow bridge which we each may cross to reach the heart of the other. Be we Man or Woman, of East or West, of whatever Tradition or School, our colours blend to form a healing rainbow that dances out around the World.

Each one of us is a reflecting drop, a tear of joy and sorrow in the eye of the Gods, an essential gleam in the great shimmering cosmic kaleidoscope of light.

I give to you a gift of earth that you may remember these things.

(Circles Temple giving each a gift)

GUARDIAN
The Rainbow Bridge is built and the gifts given, now do we all depart that we may start upon our journey.
(Sounds Gong)
(All Officers rise)
(Officers hold their symbols to front.)

BEARER OF CRYSTALS
I call upon the Lords of Light who rule the Element of Earth to seal the North in strength and life and with our thanks to close this Temple working.
(Circumambulates the Temple once going via West holding remaining crystals)

BEARER OF CHALICE
I call upon the Lords of Light who rule the Element of Water to seal the West in highest consciousness and with our thanks to close this Temple working.
(Circumambulates the Temple once going via South holding Chalice)

BEARER OF WAND
I call upon the Lords of Light who rule the Element of Fire to seal the South in love and power and with our thanks to close this Temple working.
(Circumambulates the Temple once going via East holding Wand)

BEARER OF SWORD
I call upon the Lords of Light who rule the Element of Air to seal the East with living light and with our thanks to close this Temple working.
(Circumambulates the Temple once going via north holding Sword.)

GUARDIAN
(Sounds Gong four times.)

GUARDIAN
Everyone please rise.
(Unseals door)

All may now depart in peace.

(Guardian quietly asks everyone, except the Officers, to leave the Temple starting with the South West and all following circling the Temple sun-wise.

Guardian exits and closes door, remaining outside to guard the door while the Officers close the Temple.

Officers extinguish the candles, close and seal the Temple before leaving)

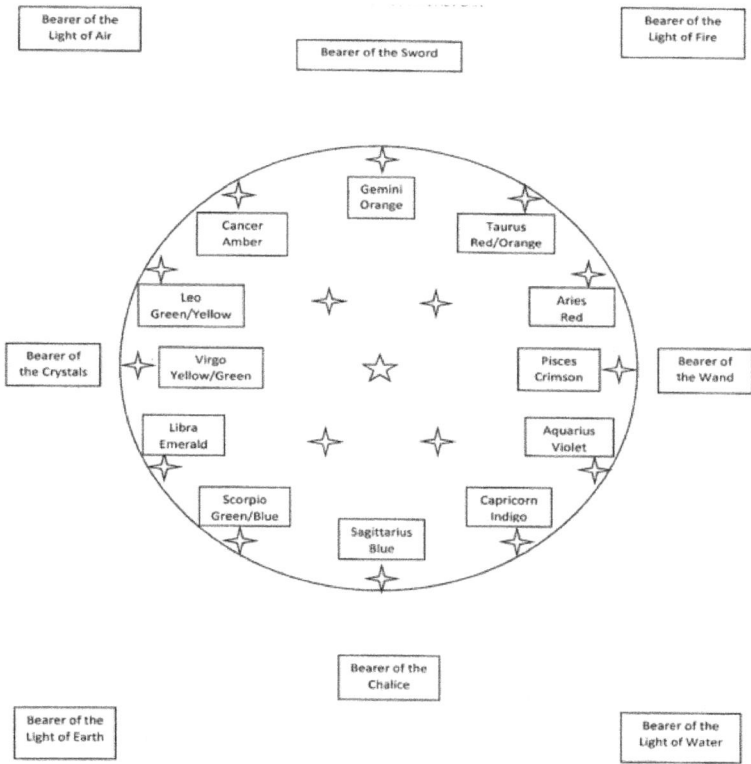

The Ladder Ritual

OFFICERS
Guardian
Narrator
13 Officers of the Steps
Lady of the Lights
Conductor on the Steps

REQUIREMENTS
13 Pieces to mark the steps. Small pieces of carpet are ideal
Altar
Gold cloth
Candles on Altar
CD player and music
Small electric tea lights, one for each participant
Tray for tea lights

Ritual

GUARDIAN
(Admits Narrator who is seated in the west,
    Admits all Companions. All are seated in any order.
    13 Officers of the Steps bring in the markers for the steps.
    Candles are lit on the altar before entry
    Lady of the Lights has tray with small candle for each
Companion)

NARRATOR
Respected Guardian, have all been admitted?

GUARDIAN
All have been admitted.

NARRATOR
Respected Guardian, please seal the door and remain vigilant of
our privacy and security.
    The Ladder as a tool and a symbol has existed in our
Western culture since time immemorial. The ladder has a place

in human history that dates back to the Mesolithic period, about 10,000 years ago. Cave paintings found in Valencia, Spain depict two people carrying baskets or bags. They are using a long ladder to access a wild honeybee nest and raid it for its precious content of honey. The ladder as we know it in modern times was developed by the ancient Egyptians and ancient Hebrews. Indeed the ladder figures in many of the ancient Egyptian paintings and writings. There is a very ancient Egyptian legend concerning Osiris and a so-called Ladder to Heaven. According to Egyptologist Wallis Budge, belief in a "ladder" as a means of reaching heaven is very old. A tradition carried down from pre-dynastic times stated that even Osiris himself was obliged to ascend into heaven by this Ladder: 'Ra stood on one side of it and Horus on the other, and they lifted Osiris up the Ladder step by step.' And in another text it is said 'Up-uat, who is Opener of the Ways, hath opened a way unto him; Shu the Sky Bearer hath lifted him up, the Gods of An make him ascend the Ladder and set him before the Firmament of the Heaven; Nut, the sky, extends her hand to him.'

In Egypt the ladder was worn as a protective talisman by both the living and the deceased. The amulet was believed to provide the deceased with the means of ascending from this world to the next. To the ancient Egyptians the Ladder symbolised a connection with the heavenly world and divine help in reaching the world of the Afterlife. Early Egyptian mythology placed the heavenly world above the earth, with its floor being the sky. To reach this a ladder was deemed necessary to reach the next world. The crystal floor of the next world rested upon four pillars which marked the cardinal points and it was the aim of every good Egyptian to go there after death. Indeed, the ladder appears in most ancient mythologies.

The concept that the sky is solid and connected to the earth by a ladder, rope or chain, is found mainly in the Niger bend, in Volta, and among the Yoruba in Nigeria. The Mamabolo of Rhodesian origin say that the sky god Modimo went up to heaven on a ladder, from which he removed the rungs. The sky-ladder myth is also found among the Rotse in Zambia, where their deity is said to have ascended along the thread of a cobweb...In addition the Tsonga and Zulu have a tradition concerning a ladder or rope leading up to the sky.

The ladder-to-heaven motif is also attested in Aboriginal Australia.

Probably the best known mythic story of the ladder comes from the Bible in Genesis 28:10-19: The story goes that Jacob left Beersheba, and went toward Haran. He came to the place and stayed there that night, because the sun had set. Taking one of the stones of the place, he put it under his head and lay down in that place to sleep. And he dreamed, and behold, there was a ladder set up on the earth, and the top of it reached to heaven; and behold, the angels of God were ascending and descending on it! And behold, the Lord stood beside him and said, "I am the Lord, the God of Abraham your father and the God of Isaac; the land on which you lie I will give to you and to your descendants; and your descendants shall be like the dust of the earth, and you shall spread abroad to the west and to the east and to the north and to the south; and by you and your descendants shall all the families of the earth bless themselves. Behold, I am with you and will keep you wherever you go, and will bring you back to this land; for I will not leave you until I have done that of which I have spoken to you." Then Jacob awoke from his sleep and said, "Surely the Lord is in this place; and I did not know it." And he was afraid, and said, "This is none other than the house of God, and this is the gate of heaven."

Another important book in Christian theology is 'The Ladder of Divine Ascent.' It is an ascetical treatise on avoiding vice and practicing virtue so that at the end, salvation can be obtained. Written by Saint John Climacus initially for monastics, it has become one of the most highly influential and important works used by the Church as far as guiding the faithful to a God-centred life, second only to Holy Scripture.

The ancient texts of Alchemy are rich in symbolism of the ladder, it is a common feature of alchemical symbolism, the rungs representing the seven metals, the operations of alchemy, both in the transmutation of metals and spirituality and the associated heavenly bodies.

Sometimes the ladder is twelve runged, corresponding to the twelve operations required for spiritual development.

In the alchemist and mystic Robert Fludd's (1574-1637) version of the ladder, the rungs are of inward levels, senses, imagination, reason, intellect, intelligence, and word.

Indeed we can say that the rungs of the Ladder of Alchemy are called John Dee 1527–1608, Heinrich Kunrath 1560-1605, Michael Maier 1568–1622, Robert Fludd 1574–1637, Elias Ashmole 1617-1692, Thomas Vaughan 1621-1666, and Isaac Newton 1642-1726.

The theme of the ladder also appears in literature and art. One of the most famous paintings of William Blake, poet, artist and visionary is of Jacob's Dream where the angels are seen ascending and descending along a ladder which curves up into heaven.

As Saint John Chrysostom writes: 'And so mounting as it were by steps, let us get to heaven by a Jacob's ladder. For the ladder seems to me to signify in a riddle by that vision the gradual ascent by means of virtue, by which it is possible for us to ascend from earth to heaven, not using material steps, but improvement and correction of manners.'

So in our personal journey, as we steadfastly ascend the rungs of The Ladder, we slowly raise ourselves, higher and higher, above the lower plane of the material and physical world. Upon reaching the higher rungs of The Ladder, we begin to touch the boundaries of Higher Consciousness. It is at these higher levels of consciousness that the mysteries of the Divine slowly begin to reveal their secrets to us. On reaching the topmost rung of The Ladder we enter the realm of highest consciousness. We have now left the frustrations, confusions and demands of the material world below us and are now finally able to enjoy the spiritual realms. Through our personal desire and effort we have achieved conscious entry into the infinite domain of enlightenment and our Higher Self.

NARRATOR
Companions, let us now build the Ladder.

VOICE OF FIRST STEP
(Rises and goes to place the first step in the appointed place)
I am the voice of the first step on the ladder of the Great Work. I come under the influence of Aries, whose symbol is the Ram representing determination and initiative. Mars is the ruling planet and Fire the Element of this step.

The work of this step is learning to be in control of our

own inner fires. We have to learn to be the master of our emotions and our ego. Here the lessons of life challenge our ability to admit our own defects. There is no place here for arrogance and our pride must be in our achievements not in our self-esteem. Now we must take responsibility for our own actions and their effects. *(Returns to place and is seated)*

VOICE OF SECOND STEP

(Rises and goes to place second step in the appointed place)

I am the voice of the second step on the ladder of the Great Work. I come under the influence of Taurus, whose symbol is the Bull representing virility and strength. Venus is the ruling planet and Earth the element of this step.

The work of this step is one of learning. It is now that we undertake disciplined courses of study. By training and practice we begin to gain understanding of the way the inner Universe works. Experiences brings knowledge, insights and personal knowledge of the Universe both physical and spiritual.

(Returns to place and is seated)

VOICE OF THIRD STEP

(Rises and goes to place third step in the appointed place)

I am the voice of the third step on the ladder of the Great Work. I come under the influence of Gemini, whose symbol is The Twins, representing the power of the intellect. Mercury is the ruling planet and Air the Element of this step.

The work of this step is the awakening of the twin sides of ourselves. To truly understand that we each have both a masculine and feminine sides to our personalities. These we must learn to integrate so we become our own true self. Listening to our own inner voice of intuition and inspiration becomes our guiding principle.

(Returns to place and is seated)

VOICE OF FOURTH STEP

(Rises and goes to place the fourth step in the appointed place)

I am the voice of the fourth step on the ladder of the Great Work. I come under the influence of Cancer, whose symbol is the Crab, representing hidden depths. The Moon is the ruling planet and Water the Element of this step.

The work of this step is on the heart and the emotions. Now control of the emotions is learned so that they become the energising fire of our inner work. The intellectual mind must become a partner not a dominator. We must learn to swim in the deep seas of the subconscious mind and to access its doorways into the unseen.

(Returns to place and is seated)

VOICE OF FIFTH STEP
(Rises and goes to place fifth step in the appointed place)

I am the voice of the fifth step on the ladder of the Great Work. I come under the influence of Leo, whose symbol is the Lion representing strength.

The Sun is the ruling planet and Fire the Element of this step.

The work of this step is to face and conquer the trials of daily life. To test our strength and determination in whatever life presents to us. Now what has been learnt in the first four stages must be put into practice, the direction of our lives must be examined and if necessary changes made. Every aspect of our inner and outer lives must be examined, the lessons of our mistakes absorbed and our successes acknowledge and celebrated.

(Returns to place and is seated)

VOICE OF SIXTH STEP
(Rises and goes to place sixth step in the appointed place)

I am the voice of the sixth step on the ladder of the Great Work. I come under the influence of Virgo, whose symbol is the Maiden, representing purity. Chiron is the ruling planet and Earth the Element of this step.

The work of this step is to become consciously aware of our unity with the spiritual forces of the Universe. In our outer and inner lives, it is now essential that our ethics are beyond reproach.

At this stage the student begins to train in order to contribute to the great work of helping others along the spiritual path.

(Returns to place and is seated)

VOICE OF SEVENTH STEP
(Rises and goes to place seventh step in the appointed place)

I am the voice of the seventh step on the ladder of the Great Work. I come under the influence of Libra whose symbol is The Scales of Justice representing balance and Divine Law. Venus is the ruling planet and Air the element of this step.

The work of this step starts with the inflow of spiritual power resulting from the work undertaken previously. New understanding dawns and the inner laws begin to reveal their workings. Here choices are often made between following the path of the mystic or that of the spiritual magician.

(Returns to place and is seated)

VOICE OF EIGHTH STEP
(Rises and goes to place eighth step in the appointed place)

I am the voice of the eighth step on the ladder of the Great Work. I come under the influence of Scorpio, whose symbol is the Scorpion, representing tenacity and emotion. Mars is the ruling planet and Water the Element of this step.

The work of this step is in being aware of what is really important in life. It is in not being afraid to fight for one's beliefs yet cautious in how we do so. It is understanding the temporary nature of life and knowing too the continuity of life and the renewal of all things.

(Returns to place and is seated)

VOICE OF NINTH STEP
(Rises and goes to place ninth step in the appointed place)

I am the voice of the ninth step on the ladder of the Great Work. I come under the influence of Sagittarius whose symbol is the Archer representing seekers of truth. Jupiter is the ruling planet and Fire the Element of this step.

The work of this step is the willingness to sacrifice personal interests and to work for the benefit of others. It is in giving up what hinders our effectiveness in spiritual work.

(Returns to place and is seated)

VOICE OF TENTH STEP
(Rises and goes to place tenth step in the appointed place)

I am the voice of the tenth step on the ladder of the Great

Work. I come under the influence of Capricorn, whose symbol is the Goat, representing persistence and strength. Saturn is the ruling planet and Earth the Element of this step.

The work of this step is a process of discarding what has been outgrown. It is too when tests of our sincerity, dependability and dedications come into our lives. The tests of doubt and loss of inner contacts create the dark night of the soul. Passed successfully the trials of this step lead to greater growth. It is now that one may indeed become an Initiate of the Mysteries.

(Returns to place and is seated)

VOICE OF ELEVENTH STEP
(Rises and goes to place eleventh step in the appointed place)

I am the voice of the eleventh step on the ladder of the Great Work. I come under the influence of Aquarius, whose symbol is the Water Bearer, representing progress. Uranus is the ruling planet and Air the Element of this step.

The work of this step is to offer our knowledge to others that they may drink of the waters of our experience. This step sees the flowering of the student into the teacher on one level and the entry into a higher degree of learning on another.

(Returns to place and is seated)

VOICE OF TWELFTH STEP
(Rises and goes to place twelfth step in the appointed place)

I am the voice of the twelfth step on the ladder of the Great Work. I come under the influence of Pisces, whose symbol is the Fish, representing spirituality. Neptune is the ruling planet and Water the Element of this step.

The work of this step is that of the Initiate. It is the ability to walk in full consciousness in and between the worlds, inner and outer.

(Returns to place and is seated)

VOICE OF THIRTEENTH STEP
(Rises and goes to place thirteenth step in the appointed place)

I am the voice of the thirteenth step, this step is the culmination of the Great Work. Upon the thirteenth step the soul reaches the source of itself and attains spiritual completion.

(Returns to place and is seated)

NARRATOR
Companions, let us now climb the ladder we have built.

MUSICIAN
(Start music. Classic FM. Smooth Classics Disc 3. Track 10. Play this track until all have passed the Thirteenth Step)

LADY OF THE LIGHTS AND CONDUCTOR ON THE STEPS.
(Both come forward and stand either side of the first step, Conductor on the north side, The Lady on the south side. Lady of the Lights has tray with sufficient small candles, one for each Companion. She gives one to each Companion which they carry as they climb the ladder.

The Conductor sees everyone climbs the steps safely, they should follow each other so there is a flow up the steps

When they have passed the thirteenth step they place their candle on the altar and remain standing around the altar)

NARRATOR
(When all Companions have reached the altar)
Respected Guardian, please unseal the doorway.

GUARDIAN
(Unseals the doorway)
The door is unsealed.

NARRATOR
(Takes light from Lady of the Lights and climbs the ladder. Followed by the Guardian, Conductor and finally Lady of the Lights)

NARRATOR
Companions, let us join hands and form a circle around the altar.

MUSICIAN
(Once all have reached the altar start music
Mozart Laudae Dominum. Vespers and Litanies
Disc One Track 16
When music ends

NARRATOR

Companions let us now depart in peace.
(All leave the Temple in any order)

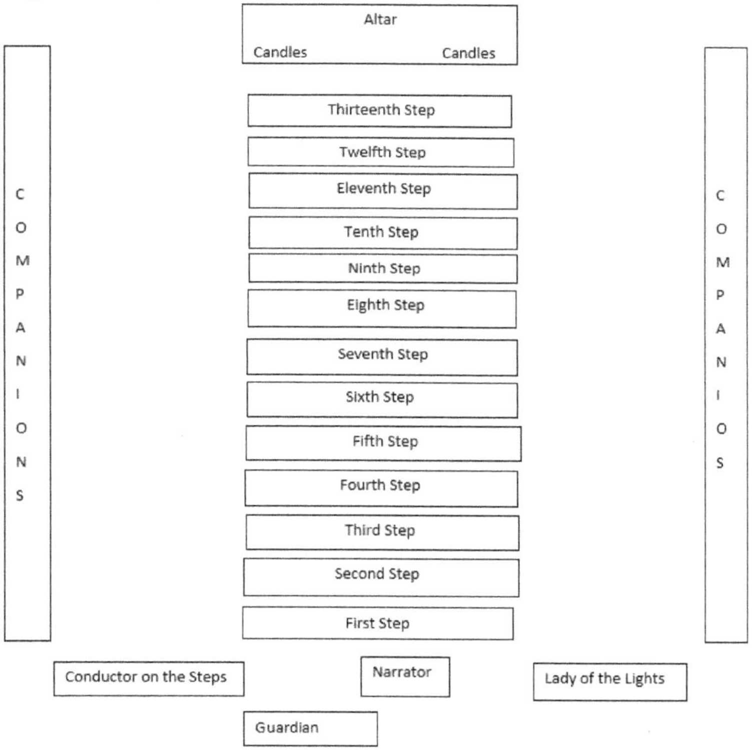
Altar
Candles
Candles
Thirteenth Step
Twelfth Step
Eleventh Step
Tenth Step
Ninth Step
Eighth Step
Seventh Step
Sixth Step
Fifth Step
Fourth Step
Third Step
Second Step
First Step
COMPANIONS
COMPANIOS
Conductor on the Steps
Narrator
Lady of the Lights
Guardian

The Temple of the Zodiac

OFFICERS
Guardian
Musician (Also rings bell)

The Void		*Black Scarf*
The Winged Man	*East*	*Cream Scarf*
The Winged Lion	*South*	*Red Scarf*
The Eagle	*West*	*Blue Scarf*
The Winged Bull	*North*	*Brown Scarf*
The Sun	*North East*	*Gold Sequin*
The Moon		*Silver Sequin*
Polaris		*Black/Silver Sequin*
Aries		*Red Cloak*
Taurus		*Orange Cloak*
Gemini		*Blue Cloak*
Cancer		*Green cloak*
Leo		*Yellow Scarf*
Virgo		*Green Scarf*
Libra		*Crimson Scarf*
Scorpio		*Black Cloak*
Sagittarius		*Yellow Scarf*
Capricorn		*Grey Cloak*
Aquarius		*Violet Scarf*
Pisces		*Blue Scarf*
Mercury		*Orange Scarf*
Venus		*Blue Sequin light*
Mars		*Red Sequin*
Jupiter		*Crimson Scarf*
Saturn		*Brown Scarf*
Uranus		*Green Scarf*
Neptune		*Blue Sequin dark*
Pluto		*Purple Scarf*

REQUIREMENTS
Central altar
Small tables at quarters with cloths
Three large candles
Coloured cloaks and scarfs

Electric candles, one for each participant
Music and CD player
Four Holy Creatures
Tibetan singing bowl or bell

Ritual

MUSICIAN
(Starts music for entry Sir John Tavener. Track 6. The Protecting Veil)
Supervises entry in order previously arranged.
Allow music to play to end of track. Switch off music when all settled)

GUARDIAN
(Seals the doorway)

THE VOID
(Goes to east of central altar, faces west, raises arms and looking upward says)
I am the voice of the void, from the depths of non being I call forth the word and creation awakens.
(Remains standing)

WINGED MAN
(Rises. faces East, raising arms says)
    I am the voice of the Winged Man. I call forth the powers of the world of Atziluth, the Divine Domain of Emanation.
    Manifest in this place the patterns and designs of the archetypes of creation.
(Turns to face west and remains standing)

THE EAGLE
(Rises, faces west, raising arms says)
    I am the voice of the Eagle, I call forth the powers of the world of Briah, the world of cosmic creation.
    Manifest in this place the powers of the Archangels who guide and direct the forces of creation.
(Turns to face east and remains standing)

WINGED LION
(Rises and faces south, raising arms says)

I am the voice of the Winged Lion, I call forth the powers of the world of Yetzirah, the formative world.

Manifest in this place the forms which clothe the energies of creation.

(Turns to face north and remains standing)

WINGED BULL
(Rises and faces north, raising arms says)

I am the voice of the Winged Bull, I call forth the powers of the world of Assiah, the manifest world.

Manifest in this place the shapes and forms of the material world.

(Turns to face south and remains standing)

WINGED MAN

I am the voice of the powers of the Element of Air. Manifest in this place your powers, energise us with the breath of life, the power of the mind, the force of intellect, inspiration and imagination.

THE EAGLE

I am the voice of the powers of the Element of Water. Manifest in this place your powers, awaken our emotion and subconscious powers, our intuition and psychic ability.

THE WINGED LION

I am the voice of the powers of the Element of Fire. Manifest in this place your powers, help us to accept change, to live with passion, creativity, motivation, will power, drive and dedication.

THE WINGED BULL

I am the voice of the powers of the Element of Earth. Manifest in this place your powers, bring us health and strength of the body, wisdom, knowledge, strength and prosperity.

(The Winged Man, The Eagle, The Winged Lion and the Winged Bull go to altar carrying the Holy Creatures which they place simultaneously on the altar at the appropriate quarter)

(Void goes to altar, standing in front of Winged Man)

THE VOID
(Draws large invoking pentagram above the altar, pausing at each point while the Officer speaks)
Spirit

THE WINGED BULL
Earth

THE EAGLE
Water

THE WINGED LION
Fire

THE WINGED MAN
Air

THE VOID
Manifest in this place the powers of body, mind and spirit.
(Lights three large candles. All return to their places and are seated)

POLARIS
(Rises, goes to stand at east of central alter, facing west)
I am the voice of Polaris, I am the still point of the heavens around which spins the mighty wheel of the stars. Let us invoke the powers of the constellations in this place.
(Returns to place
Note. The following Officers rise and speak from place)

ARIES
I am the voice of the constellation of Aries, I stand at the gate of the astrological year, first of the signs of the zodiac. Mine is the sign of spring and the first out-flowing of new life. My emblem is the Ram, symbol of rebirth and renewal.
Manifest in this place the energy of new beginnings, the hope of youth, the fire of enthusiasm and joy in living.
(Lights candle and is seated)

MARS

I am the voice of Mars, ruling planet of Aries. I am the warrior who destroys the old, fights injustice and oppression and defends the weak.

Manifest in this place action, energy and rightfully directed force.

(Lights candle and is seated)

TAURUS

I am the voice of the constellation of Taurus, mine is the sign of verdant luxuriant nature, of Earth in generation. My emblem is the Bull, symbol of fertility and strength.

Manifest in this place the harmony and beauty of nature and all earthy things.

(Lights candle and is seated)

VENUS

I am the voice of Venus, ruling planet of Taurus. I am the goddess of love and of beauty.

By my powers is the Earth regenerated and renewed.

Manifest in this place the love of Earth and of humankind.

(Lights candle and is seated)

GEMINI

I am the voice of the constellation of Gemini, I hold the balance between the polarities of manifestation and human existence. My emblem is the Twins, duality in action. I stand between the light and dark pillars and form a bridge leading to their union.

Manifest in this place the perfect balance of the Middle Pillar.

(Lights candle and is seated)

MERCURY

I am the voice of Mercury, ruling planet of Gemini. Mine are the tasks of the messenger, the mediator between the higher and the lower self and between the higher and lower worlds.

Manifest in this place the ability to gain and store knowledge and the wisdom to use it well.

(Lights candle and is seated)

CANCER

I am the voice of the constellation of Cancer, I am a collector of precious things, the riches, arts and treasures of humanities creativity. I am too the seeker of the pearl of great price of spirituality. My emblem is the Crab which ever seeks the safety of its home.

Manifest in this place security and wealth of experience.
(Lights candle and is seated)

MOON

I am the voice of the Moon, ruling planet of Cancer. I bring the qualities of understanding and compassion to relationships. I am the ruler of the oceans of time and of tide in which we dwell. Mine is the still small voice of intuition which speaks in the inner silence.

Manifest in this place the ability to listen.
(Lights candle and is seated)

LEO

I am the voice of the constellation of Leo. I bring the warmth of the summer sun and the peak of nature's flowering. My emblem is the Lion, symbol of strength and energy.

Manifest in this place enthusiasm, confidence and zest for life.

(Lights candle and is seated)

SUN

I am the voice of the Sun, ruler of the sign of Leo. I bring the powers of the conscious ego, the self and its expression.

Manifest in this place creativity, spontaneity, health and vitality.

(Lights candle and is seated)

VIRGO

I am the voice of the constellation of Virgo. I am the bearer of the rich fruits of the harvest, I bring abundance and plenty from the Earth.

My emblem is the Virgin, the eternal feminine in nature. I am Vesta and Ishtar, Persephone, Aphrodite and Mary.

Manifest in this place the power of the feminine.

(Lights candle and is seated)

MERCURY

I am the voice of Mercury, ruling planet of Virgo. I am the communicator, I garner wisdom and transmit it to the Initiate.
I am the scribe and the recorder, mine are the words of Hermes Trismagistus and all sages and teachers.

Manifest in this place the power of the word.
(Lights candle and is seated)

LIBRA

I am the voice of the constellation of Libra. I hold the balance between the head and the heart, intelligence and feeling, the physical and the spiritual.

My emblem is the scales on which the heart is weighed against the feather of Maat.

Manifest in this place balance and harmony in mind and heart.
(Lights candle and is seated)

VENUS

I am the voice of Venus, ruling planet of Libra. I bring the qualities of tact, courtesy, consideration, equilibrium and concord. I balance personalities and create good relationships.

Make manifest the love between us in this place.
(Lights candle and is seated)

SCORPIO

I am the voice of the constellation of Scorpio. Mine is the time of harvest, the garnering of the grapes of the vine and of wisdom. My emblem is the Scorpion, so beware my hidden sting.

Manifest in this place my qualities of determination and persistence.
(Lights candle and is seated)

PLUTO

I am the voice of Pluto, ruling planet of Scorpio. Mine are the hidden qualities of the subconscious mind, the instincts and soul consciousness.

Manifest in this place the transformative powers of the

mind.
(Lights candle and is seated)

SAGITTARIUS

I am the voice of the constellation of Sagittarius. I seek to overcome the limitations of the physical world by aiming thought into the divine realms. I am the hunter of ideas and experiences that bring greater awareness. My emblem is the Archer who always aims high.

Manifest in this place new experiences and a new philosophy.
(Lights candle and is seated)

JUPITER

I am the voice of Jupiter, ruling planet of Sagittarius. I am the seeker. I seek knowledge, expansion and wisdom. I am also the teacher and guide to those who follow me.

Manifest in this place the lessons it is good for us to learn.
(Lights candle and is seated)

CAPRICORN

I am the voice of the constellation of Capricorn. I am the industrious worker, efficient and organised. I am scrupulous with detail, dedicated to my ideals and patient in their attainment.

My emblem is the Goat, who is able to climb high by his own efforts.

Manifest in this place perseverance and tenacity.
(Lights candle and is seated.)

SATURN

I am the voice of Saturn, ruling planet of Capricorn. I bring the qualities of caution, persistence and authority to life tasks and persistence in their completion.

Manifest in this place the patience and fortitude which brings success.
(Lights candle and is seated)

AQUARIUS

I am the voice of the constellation of Aquarius, I value unconventionality and intellectual independence. I am the explorer and the instigator of new ways of thought and action, the visionary and the humanitarian.

My emblem is the Water Carrier who freely shares his water with all who are thirsty.

Manifest in this place generosity and tolerance.

(Lights candle and is seated)

URANUS

I am the voice of Uranus, ruling planet of Capricorn. I bring the qualities of curiosity and an enquiring mind and work for science, technology and humanitarian causes. I fight for and defend the right of individuals to personal freedom.

Manifest in this place tolerance and understanding.

(Lights candle and is seated)

PISCES

I am the voice of the constellation of Pisces, I bring the qualities of ambition, enthusiasm and energy. I follow the paths of mysticism, mystery and the spiritual worlds. I explore the unknown ways of the mind.

My emblem is The Fishes swimming in opposite directions.

Manifest in this place the ability to dream on both the outer and the inner levels.

(Lights candle and is seated)

NEPTUNE

I am the voice of Neptune, ruling planet of Pisces. I bring the qualities of spiritual understanding and awareness. Under my influence tolerance of belief grows and freedom of thought is encouraged.

Manifest in this place expansion of consciousness and spiritual knowledge.

(Lights candle and is seated)

THE VOID

The Temple of the Zodiac is established. The constellations are ablaze. Let the stars shine forth.

ALL
(All light their candles)
    (NOTE Officers remain seated for the following visualisation speeches)

THE VOID
Let us now move from this outer Temple we have created into the Inner Temple where its power resides.

As we relax and close our eyes a pathway appears before us which leads to a majestic building, this is the Inner Temple of the Zodiac. A graceful staircase leads to a large wooden door on which is emblazoned a circle of twelve golden stars.

As we approach the door swings slowly open and we know we are permitted to enter.

The light is so dim within we are temporarily unable to see, the sun of life has not yet risen, for this is the Hall of Aries, the first of the Halls of the Constellations.

MUSICIAN
(Ring bell)

ARIES
Here we are as new born, we are souls at the beginning of a new life journey. We are greeted by a young woman, she is veiled and symbolises our innocence and inexperience. In her hand she holds a small light which she hands to us telling us that this is the small flame of our spirit which will light our life's journey. We walk down the hall admiring the spring like landscapes which adorn the walls all around us.

At the end of the hall is a door, guarded by a warrior who we recognise as Mars. He asks us what our purpose is in being here and we reply "To learn". He nods in acceptance then turns and opens the door for us to pass through.

MUSICIAN
(Ring bell)

TAURUS

We walk into the Hall of Taurus, second of the Halls of the Constellations. Before us is a rich and verdant landscape. There are orchards laden with all kinds of fruits, fields of golden grain dance in the light breeze and all kinds of animals and birds dwell here. Seated on a small rise is a most beautiful woman, she is at the peak of her maturity and power. She beckons us to approach, then asks us what we seek. We reply that we are at the beginning of a new life journey and wish to have a new body, one which will be healthy and strong and serve us well in the natural world. She smiles kindly then says "It will be so." The Lady Venus, for it is she, bids us approach and kneel before her for her blessing.

We rise and approach the next door we can see in the distance. A small child we recognise as Venus's son Eros opens the door for us and we walk through.

MUSICIAN
(Ring bell)

GEMINI

The third hall of the constellations, the Hall of Gemini, is very formal yet imposing. It is dominated by two majestic pillars, one white one black which are topped respectively by two globes, one of the Sun and one of the Moon. Between the pillars stand two figures, identical copies of each other. They address us in unison – "This is the hall where you become two, your spiritual self which you have always been and your material self which builds within your new physical body. These are your vehicles in the realms of polarity." Then each takes us by the hand and draws us forward between the pillars to the next door.

The figure guarding this door is winged on heel and helmet and we recognise him as Mercury the messenger. He says "I am the still small voice within you, the messenger between your higher and lower selves, listen and heed me well." Then he turns and opens the door to the next hall.

MUSICIAN
(Ring bell)

CANCER
Before us is the Hall of Cancer, fourth Hall of the Constellations. It is bathed in a soft and mystical light. Everything shimmers as if under water. We do not see a Presence in this hall but we feel it, a warm, protecting, all enveloping feeling which reminds us of our childhood. Then we remember that this is the hall of Mara, the ocean Mother of us all. Emotion wells up in us and we realise we have awoken to another new level of experience.

The next door draws us onward, the guardian here is a woman clothed in shining silver whose name is Selene. She holds up a hand to bid us stay and says "I am the guardian of the doorway to your spirituality; and your emotions are the power which drives it. Be wary how and when you open my doorway and learn how to be emotions master not its slave."

MUSICIAN
(Ring bell)

LEO
Selene turns and opens the door into the Hall of Leo, fifth Hall of the Constellations. We walk forward into an intense golden light, the sunlight of a high summer's day. Walking towards us is a figure, it seems familiar then we realise that we are seeing ourselves reflected in a large mirror. For this hall is where we blossom into full consciousness of self, we are fully expressing the spiritual and material aspects of our being.

The guardian who stands before the door to the next hall is magnificent, he glows with power and might. He is called Sol Invictus, the Unconquered Sun. He is the representative of the solar gods, the saviours of the world and the willing sacrifices. His voice sounds in our heads, "Take heed your self-esteem grows not too great, remember thou art mortal."

MUSICIAN
(Ring bell)

VIRGO
The door opens and we walk though into the Hall of Virgo, sixth Hall of the Constellations. The scene before us is one of rich harvest, there are laden fruit trees on either hand, crops growing

in the fields and a sea of ripe golden corn shimmers in the sunlight at our feet. Walking towards us we see two beautiful women surrounded by a group of children. They are Demeter and her daughter Persephone. Demeter holds out her hands to us in invitation and we approach her with awe. Holding her hand above our head she says; "I give you my blessing, reap well the harvest of your journey and your maturity."

We walk on and soon come to the next door, the Guardian here is a man of mature years but tall and strong dressed in a plain white robe. His name is Hermes Trismegistus. In his hands he holds a book, he says "I hold the garnered wisdom of the ages, read my writings well that you too may become wise."

MUSICIAN
(Ring bell)

LIBRA
We enter the Hall of Libra, seventh Hall of the Constellations. This is the hall of balance and completion. The floor before us is covered by a black and white squared carpet. In the centre stands a large set of scales, on one side stands jackal headed Anubis and on the other Ibis headed Thoth.

Both turn to look at us as we approach. Thoth speaks; "Know that this hall represents the equal development of your higher and lower self, a balance between head and heart, intellect and feeling. Mine is the voice of your knowledge and learning, the practical application of skills and arts. Use them well." Anubis speaks; "Mine is the voice of the spirit, I am the Opener of the Ways between the inner and the outer, between the body and the soul and the mediator between you and the gods. Be still and heed my voice."

At the end of the hall stands the next Guardian, she is tall and elegant, robed in pristine white. Her name is Maat and she is balance, order, law, morality, and justice. To meet her eyes is to look into every hidden aspect of ourselves with nothing veiled but seen in stark truth. Look deep into her eyes. *(pause)* Maat breaks the contact first, then she holds out her hand and gives us a scarlet feather saying; "See that your heart weights true with this when the time of judgement comes."

MUSICIAN
(Ring bell)

SCORPIO
We pass through the door and enter the Hall of Scorpio, eighth Hall of the Constellations. This is a hall of strong contrasts, its symbols reveal its nature. The scorpion represents the power of the material self with all its challenges. But here too the spirit stirs and begins to seek the awakening of higher consciousness, the flight of the eagle. It is too in this hall that the painful poisons of possessive passion are transformed into a higher consciousness based on universal love and the soul flies on the mystic wings of the dove. We must choose the symbol we follow, choose well.

The guardian who stands at the next door is tall, dark and very powerful, a strong man at the height of his physical powers. His name is Pluto. He holds the keys to the hidden realms beneath the earth, the treasures stored in the subconscious mind and the path which leads to the transformation of consciousness. He holds out three keys to us, each emblazoned with one of the symbols of Scorpio, the Scorpion, the Eagle and the Dove, and bids us choose.

MUSICIAN
(Ring bell)

SAGITTARIUS
Passing through the door we come into the Hall of Sagittarius, ninth Hall of the Constellations. For those who have chosen the key of the dove this is the next stage of our spiritual quest. Here is sought synthesis of the instinctive with the spiritual, the higher with the lower self and consciousness with soul.

Dominating the hall is a very large centaur and about him is luxuriant nature of which he is guardian. But this is Chiron who is so much more; this centaur is very wise, a great healer and teacher much sought after for his oracular powers. Seek his advice and his prediction for your continuing journey. *(pause)* As we turn to leave he says "Aim high that you may gain the greater prize."

At the end of the hall is a huge golden statue, this is

Jupiter king of the gods. He is the lord of the sky and of thunder. His qualities are abundance, freedom, growth and fertility. It is under his influence that we broaden our horizons and cease to view the world in narrow, constricting terms. He moves us to explore, think and act with greater power of our own self-will. The door to the next hall is between his huge feet, we move forward and pass through.

MUSICIAN
(Ring bell)

CAPRICORN
Now we are in the Hall of Capricorn, tenth hall of the Constellations. In this hall we begin to see our goal, the pinnacle of our achievements. It still rises far above, but here we have the tenacity, perseverance and the best kind of stubbornness to take us to the very top. The mountain goat is our symbol in this hall and we must continue to climb with the same tenacity and sureness of purpose as that with which he overcomes obstacles and difficulties.

In this hall we are walking in the darkness and bleakness of winter, yet in the darkest winter there is always the promise of spring. The ruler of this hall is Saturn, the great teacher and initiator, whose influence brings patience, prudence, determination, reliability and discipline. The guardian at the door to the next hall is an old but upright man whose name is Chronos, he who governs time. He says "Haste not to the future, neither linger in the past, for in the moment of the now is the essence of life."

MUSICIAN
(Ring bell)

AQUARIUS
We have passed through the door and find ourselves in the Hall of Aquarius, eleventh Hall of the Constellations. Having reached this hall we have attained to a level of union of our higher self with our lower self, we have experienced and learned. Now we may choose to go further on the path of the mystic, seeking ever deeper union with the Divine. But there is too the call of those

who are still toiling up the mountain, who reach out to us for help. To respond is to choose the path of the Teacher and pause and continue the journey at their side.

A tall and beautiful lady comes walking down the hall towards us, she is not young yet is somehow ageless, her name is Sophia. In her hands she carries a shining chalice which she holds out to us and says; "To drink from my chalice is to become wise, to offer it to another is to become blessed."

Two Guardians stand either side of the next door, on the right hand side is Uranus, ruler of the world and sky and on the left Gaia his wife, lady of Earth.

Innovative, unpredictable, resourceful, imaginative and experimental, Uranus creates sudden-even radical-change. Uranus always works in sudden ways, and is called the Great Awakener. Be prepared to take the opportunities he creates.

MUSICIAN
(Ring bell)

PISCES
Passing through the door we enter the Hall of Pisces, twelfth hall of the Constellations. This is the hall of completion, the finale of our journey through the halls of the Constellations. The bodies we have used must return to their elements but our spirit moves on, richer and wiser, to return to the beginning to start another quest on the ascending spiral of existence.

Approaching the final door we are met by Neptune, Lord of the Sea. In his gift are intuition and spiritual enlightenment and he will aid us to hold in memory the lessons of the halls and take them forward into our future. He is the giver of dreams – dream clear and dream true.

MUSICIAN
(Ring bell)

THE VOID
Leaving the Hall of Pisces we once more see before us the great entrance door, we walk forward into the sunshine and down the elegant staircase and following the pathway find ourselves back in our outer Temple of the Zodiac.

SUN
(Rises. Takes candle. Goes to east of altar, faces east)

I am the voice of the Sun. I am the day star whose messenger rises above the eastern horizon. Soon my day will cloak the stars of night.

I am the light of the world and the great spirit of the Sun behind the sun. I will share my Light with you.

MUSICIAN
(Play music) (Sir John Tavener. Track 1. Song for Athene)

(Sun goes to stand in front of Winged Man, facing each other, Sun says;)

I share my Light with you.

(Winged Man rises. Sun hands candle to Winged Man saying "I share my light with you" then Winged Man gives his candle to Sun. Sun then goes to Void and repeats words and they exchange candles. Winged Man then goes to Void, says words and they exchange candles. This is continued until all have exchanged candles and Sun arrives back at own place and is seated. Each circles the Temple back to their own place.)

SUN
(Rises, goes to east of altar, faces east, raises arm and points to the east, gradually raising arm above head as speaks)

Behold the dawn breaks, my vehicle of Light rises.

Hail to great Ra, *(pause)* Apollo *(pause)* Helios *(pause)* Lugh *(pause)* Sol Invicata. Hail. Hail. Hail.

The constellations fade, the night is done, let the Temple of the Zodiac be closed.

(Returns to place and is seated)

(Each speaker rises to speak from place and remains standing)

(NOTE Each officer extinguishes their candle when they have spoken)

NEPTUNE
I thank the powers of the planet Neptune and veil them in the light.

PISCES
I thank the powers of the Constellation of Pisces and veil them in the light.

URANUS
I thank the powers of the planet Uranus and veil them in the light.

AQUARIUS
I thank the powers of the Constellation of Aquarius and veil them in the light.

SATURN
I thank the powers of the planet Saturn and veil them in the light.

CAPRICORN
I thank the powers of the Constellation of Capricorn and veil them in the light.

JUPITER
I thank the powers of the planet Jupiter and veil them in the light.

SAGITTARIUS
I thank the powers of the Constellation of Sagittarius and veil them in the light.

PLUTO
I thank the powers of the planet Pluto and veil them in the light.

SCORPIO
I thank the powers of the Constellation of Scorpio and veil them in the light.

VENUS
I thank the powers of the planet Venus and veil them in the light.

LIBRA
I thank the powers of the Constellation of Libra and veil them in the light.

MERCURY
I thank the powers of the planet Mercury and veil them in the light.

VIRGO
I thank the powers of the constellation of Virgo and veil them in the light.

SUN
I thank the powers of the Sun and veil them in the light.

LEO
I thank the powers of the Constellation of Leo and veil them in the light.

MOON
I thank the powers of planet Moon and veil them in the light.

CANCER
I thank the powers of the Constellation of Cancer and veil them in the light.

GEMINI
I thanks the powers of the Constellation of Gemini and veil them in the light.

VENUS
I thank the powers of the planet Venus and veil them in the light.

TAURUS
I thank the powers of the constellation of Taurus and veil them in the light.

MARS
I thank the powers of the planet Mars and veil them in the light.

ARIES
I thank the powers of the Constellation of Aries and veil them in the light.

POLARIS
I thank the powers of the Polar Star and veil them in the light.

ALL
(All remaining candles are extinguished)

WINGED BULL
I thank the powers of the Element of Earth and the World of Assiah, may peace and harmony abide between us.

WINGED LION
I thank the powers of the Element of Fire and the World of Yetzirah, may peace and harmony abide between us.

EAGLE
I thank the powers of the Element of Water and the World of Briah, may peace and harmony abide between us.

WINGED MAN
I thank the powers of the Element of Air and the World of Atziluth, may peace and harmony abide between us.
(Winged Man, Winged Lion, Eagle, Winged Bull and Void go to altar, Void standing in front of Winged Man in East facing west.
Void draws large banishing pentagram above altar pausing at each point as the Officer speaks.)

WINGED BULL
Earth.

VOID
Spirit.

WINGED LION
Fire.

WINGED MAN
Air.

EAGLE
Water.

VOID
(Extinguishes three large candles)

The Temple of the Zodiac is now closed, all may depart in peace.

(Officers pick up the four Holy Creatures and all return to their places)

MUSICIAN
(Play exit music (Sir John Tavener. Track 2. Today the Virgin)

GUARDIAN
(When the Officers have returned to their places see that all depart)

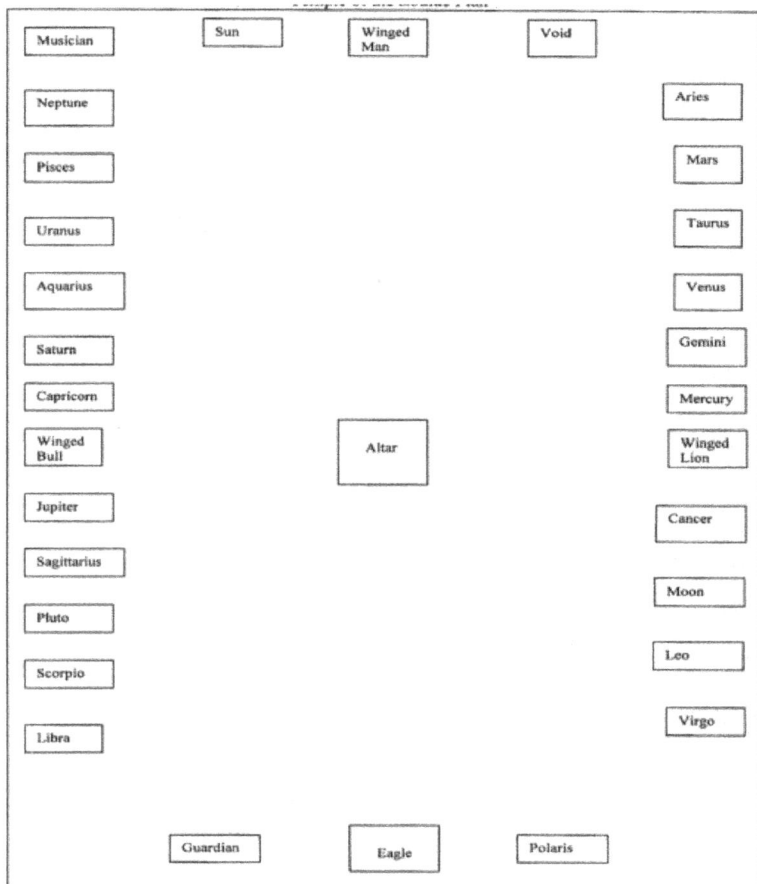

Musician	Sun	Winged Man	Void
Neptune			Aries
Pisces			Mars
Uranus			Taurus
Aquarius			Venus
Saturn			Gemini
Capricorn			Mercury
Winged Bull	Altar		Winged Lion
Jupiter			Cancer
Sagittarius			Moon
Pluto			
Scorpio			Leo
Libra			Virgo
	Guardian	Eagle	Polaris

The Inner Temple Ritual

OFFICERS
Officer of the Inner Temple
Officer of the Holy Creatures
Officer of the Archangels
Officer of the Planetary Spirits
Officer of The Elements
Two Inner Guides
One Outer Guide
Seven Bearers of the Thread

TEMPLE ARRANGEMENTS
There are seats for the two Guides either side of the entrance, however they remain standing, one each side of the entrance facing each other, until all have been admitted.
There is a seat in the North for the Officer of the Elements.
In the North East for the Officer of the Planetary Spirits.
In the South East for the Officer of the Archangels.
In the South for the Officers of the Holy Creatures.
In the Centre for the Officer of the Inner Temple.
Seats are arranged in a circle around the Officer of the Inner Temple for all participants, leaving an entrance in the West.

REQUIREMENTS
Thin rope of sufficient length to go right round the Temple from each Station to the centre.
Single candle at North, North East, South East, South West and Centre.
A crystal for each participant for the Guides. Bowl to hold these.
Small bowl of Earth and Water for Officer of the Elements.
Small cards or other symbols for the Officer of the Planetary Spirits.
Four coloured filters for Officer of the Archangels-- blue, red, green and yellow-- also the symbols of the Archangels.
Sword for Officer of the Archangels.
Four Holy Creatures for Officer of the Holy Creatures.
Music and CD player.

Ritual

The two Inner Guides enter first and switch on music for entry, this plays softly in the background while all are entering.

The Guides then take their place either side of the entrance.

The Officers enter in order;

Officer of Inner Temple, Officer of the Holy Creatures, Officer of the Archangels, Officer of the Planetary Spirits and Officer of the Elements. They circle the Temple to their places and are seated.

The Bearers of the Thread enter, go to their places and lift the Thread. They are responsible for keeping the Thread in place and seeing that all follow it correctly.

The Outer Guide sees that silence is maintained in the waiting area and admits participants one at a time as each moves on from the Inner Guides.

As each participant enters they are stopped between the two Inner Guides who draw them into the Temple by the hand.

The Guides may alternate the speeches and actions as convenient.

GUIDE

Who are you that approaches the boundary of the material world?

SEEKER

(Replies in a manner that must satisfy the Guide)

GUIDE

If you cross this threshold you leave behind the familiar realm of the senses and consciousness of the outer world – are you ready for this?

SEEKER

(Replies in a manner that must satisfy the Guide)

GUIDE

The way of the inner worlds is tortuous and deep, there you may encounter dangers and difficulties such as reflect your deepest fears – are you ready for this?

SEEKER
(Replies in a manner which must satisfy the Guide)

GUIDE
What do you seek?

SEEKER
(Replies in a manner that must satisfy the Guide)

GUIDE
Then take this crystal of Earth as a reminder of your place in the world of practical experience and pass onward into the deep paths of inner consciousness.
(Guide gives Seeker a crystal)

GUIDE
(Placing the Seekers hand on the Thread)
I place your hand upon the Thread of Consciousness which will lead you safely through the Inner Worlds. Follow it and you will find other Guides upon your way who will help and instruct you in your quest.

GUIDE
(As the Seeker passes to the Officer of the Elements the Guides admit the next Seeker ensuring that the Seekers pass in a steady procession round the Temple. The Bearers of the Thread assist in ensuring this)

SEEKER
(Follows the Thread to the Officer of the Elements)

OFFICER OF THE ELEMENTS
Welcome Seeker in the Inner Worlds. I am the Guide of the realm of the Elements. Know that I have the power to confer the blessing of the Elements upon you.

Before you is the symbol of Fire *(points to lighted candle)* the symbol of Air *(lightly blows across hand towards Seeker)* the symbol of Water, *(points to cup containing water)* and the symbol of Earth *(points to bowl of sand)*

You, who are no stranger to these symbols, know their hidden meanings and their purpose. You know your own strengths and your weaknesses – say, which blessing will you choose to empower and strengthen you upon your quest?

SEEKER
(Answers choosing one of the Elements)

OFFICER OF THE ELEMENTS
Then I confer upon you the blessing of ……….. (*The Officer as appropriate moves the candle before the Seeker/places a few grains of sand in the Seekers hand/touches the Seeker with some water or blows gently across their own hand towards the Seeker*) Follow the Thread and pass onward and may the power of …………. sustain you.

BEARER OF THE THREAD
(Assists the Seeker to hold the Thread and pass onward)

OFFICER OF THE PLANETARY SPIRITS
Welcome Seeker in the Inner Worlds. I am the Guide of the realm of the Planetary Spirits. Know that I have the power to confer their blessing upon you.

Before you are the symbols of the Seven Lords;
(Points to the symbols of the Planetary Spirits)

Saturn- Guardian of the Threshold, Jupiter- the Joy-bringer, Mars- the Warrior, the Sun- Lord of Light, Venus-Goddess of Love, Mercury- the Cosmic Messenger and The Moon- Queen of the Deep.

You, who are no stranger to these symbols, know their hidden meanings and their purpose. You know your own strengths and your weaknesses – say, which blessing will you choose to empower and strengthen you upon your quest?

SEEKER
(Answers choosing one of the Planetary Spirits)

OFFICER OF THE PLANETARY SPIRITS
(Officer holds the symbol in one hand and briefly places the other hand on the Seekers head)

Then I confer upon you the blessing of……….

Follow the Thread and pass onward and may the power of …………..sustain you.

BEARER OF THE THREAD
(Assists the Seeker to hold the Thread and pass onward)

OFFICER OF THE ARCHANGELS
Welcome Seeker in the Inner Worlds. I am the Guide of the realm of the Archangels. Know that I have the power to confer the blessing of the Archangels upon you.

Before you are the symbols of the mighty Archangels, Raphael, Michael, Gabriel and Auriel.

You, who are no stranger to these symbols, know their hidden meanings and their purpose. You know your own strengths and your weaknesses – say, whose blessing will you choose to empower and strengthen you upon your quest?

SEEKER
(Answers choosing one of the Archangels)

OFFICER OF THE ARCHANGELS
(The Officer holds the appropriate coloured filter between the Seeker and the candle then touches the sword to the top of the Seekers head and says)
Then I confer upon you the blessing of ………..
Follow the Thread and pass onward and may the power of …………..sustain you.

BEARER OF THE THREAD
(Assists the Seeker to hold the Thread and pass onward)

OFFICER OF THE HOLY CREATURES
Welcome Seeker in the Inner Worlds. I am the Guide of the realm of the Holy Creatures. Know that I have the power to confer the blessing of the Holy Creatures upon you.

Before you are the symbols of these great powers, The Eagle, The Lion, The Bull and the Man.

You, who are no stranger to these symbols, know their hidden meanings and their purpose. You know your own strengths and your weaknesses – say, whose blessing will you choose to empower and strengthen you upon your quest?

SEEKER
(Answers choosing one of the Holy Creatures)

OFFICER OF THE HOLY CREATURES
(Officer gives the appropriate Holy Creature to the Seeker to hold briefly saying)
>Then I confer upon you the blessing of ………...
>Follow the Thread and pass onward and may the power of ………….sustain you.

BEARER OF THE THREAD
(Assists the Seeker to hold the Thread and pass onward)

OFFICER OF THE INNER TEMPLE
Welcome Seeker in the Inner Worlds. I guard the door of the Inner Temple and it is by my will that you may enter therein.
>Tell me – do you come well prepared?

SEEKER
(Must answer to the satisfaction of the Officer)

OFFICER OF THE INNER TEMPLE
Tell me then which blessings you have received and under whose protection you seek to enter the Inner Temple?
>Your Element? Your Planetary Spirit? Your Archangel? Your Holy Creature?
>You have followed the Thread well to this sacred space, I confer upon you the blessing of those I represent, please close your eyes. *(Officer touches hand to centre of the Seekers forehead)* As you have journeyed hence by the aid of physical light, so let the Inner Light rise up and illuminate your inner mind. Go now and find your place among us.

BEARER OF THE THREAD
(Indicate to the Seeker that they now are to be seated in the circle)

INNER GUIDES
(When all the Seekers have been admitted the Outer Guide is admitted.
>*The two Inner Guides follow in turn to the Officer of the Elements.*
>*The Bearers of the Thread then carefully lay the Thread on the*

floor around the circle of chairs of the Inner Temple.

Beginning with the Bearer nearest the entrance they then circle the Temple so each visits the Officers of the Elements, Planetary Spirits, Archangels and Holy Creatures. This should be timed so there is only one Bearer with each Officer at a time.

Finally the Officer of the Elements, having made his/her own choice of Element, goes to the Officer of the Planetary Spirits)

OFFICER OF THE ELEMENTS
You, who are no stranger to the symbols of the Elements, know their hidden meanings and their purpose. You know your own strengths and your weaknesses – say, which blessing will you choose to empower and strengthen you upon your quest? Will you choose Fire, Air, Water or Earth?

OFFICER OF THE PLANETARY SPIRITS
(Answers choosing one of the Elements)

OFFICER OF THE ELEMENTS
Then I confer upon you the blessing of.........   May its power sustain you on your quest.

OFFICER OF THE PLANETARY SPIRITS
You, who are no stranger to the symbols of the Planetary Spirits, know their hidden meanings and their purpose. You know your own strengths and your weaknesses – say, which blessing will you choose to empower and strengthen you upon your quest? Will you choose Saturn, Jupiter, Mars, the Sun, Venus, Mercury or the Moon?

OFFICER OF THE ELEMENTS
(Answers choosing one of the Planetary Spirits)

OFFICER OF THE PLANETARY SPIRITS
Then I confer upon you the blessing of ....

OFFICER OF THE ELEMENTS and OFFICER OF THE PLANETARY SPIRITS
(Both Officers go to the Officer of the Archangels, the Officer of the Planetary Spirits having made his/her own choice of Planetary Spirit)

OFFICER OF THE ELEMENTS

You, who are no stranger to the symbols of the Elements, know their hidden meanings and their purpose. You know your own strengths and your weaknesses – say, which blessing will you choose to empower and strengthen you upon your quest? Will you choose Fire, Air, Water or Earth?

OFFICER OF THE ARCHANGELS

(Answers choosing one of the Elements)

OFFICER OF THE ELEMENTS

Then I confer upon you the blessing of …………

OFFICER OF THE PLANETARY SPIRITS

You, who are no stranger to the symbols of the Planetary Spirits, know their hidden meanings and their purpose. You know your own strengths and your weaknesses – say, which blessing will you choose to empower and strengthen you upon your quest? Will you choose Jupiter, Mars, the Sun, Venus, Mercury or The Moon?

OFFICER OF THE ARCHANGELS

(Answers choosing one of the Planetary Spirits)

OFFICER OF THE PLANETARY SPIRITS

Then I confer upon you the blessing of …………

OFFICER OF THE ARCHANGELS

You, who are no strangers to the symbols of the Archangels, know their hidden meanings and their purpose. You know your own strengths and your weaknesses – say, whose blessing will you choose to empower and strengthen you upon your quest? Will you choose the companionship of Raphael, Michael, Gabriel or Auriel?

OFFICER OF THE ELEMENTS and OFFICER OF THE PLANETARY SPIRITS

(Each answers choosing one of the Archangels)

OFFICER OF THE ARCHANGELS
Then I confer upon you the blessing of .... And upon you the blessing of.............

OFFICER OF THE ELEMENTS, OFFICER OF THE PLANETARY SPIRITS AND OFFICER OF THE ARCHANGELS
(The three Officers go to the Officer of the Holy Creatures, the Officer of the Archangels having made his/her own choice of Archangel)

OFFICER OF THE ELEMENTS
You, who are no stranger to the symbols of the Elements, know their hidden meanings and their purpose. You know your own strengths and your weaknesses – say, which blessing will you choose to empower and strengthen you upon your quest? Will you choose Fire, Air, Water or Earth?

OFFICER OF THE HOLY CREATURES
(Answers giving choice of Element)

OFFICER OF THE ELEMENTS
Then I confer upon you the blessing of ....

OFFICER OF THE PLANETARY SPIRITS
You, who are no stranger to the symbols of the Planetary Spirits, know their hidden meanings and their purpose. You know your own strengths and your weaknesses – say, which blessing will you choose to empower and strengthen you upon your quest? Will you choose Jupiter, Mars, the Sun, Venus, Mercury or The Moon?

OFFICER OF THE HOLY CREATURES
(Answers giving choice of Planetary Spirit)

OFFICER OF THE PLANETARY SPIRITS
Then I confer upon you the blessing of ...."

OFFICER OF THE ARCHANGELS
You, who are no strangers to the symbols of the Archangels, know their hidden meanings and their purpose. You know your own strengths and your weaknesses – say, whose blessing will

you choose to empower and strengthen you upon your quest? Will you choose the companionship of Raphael, Michael, Gabriel or Auriel?

OFFICER OF THE HOLY CREATURES
(Answers giving choice of Archangel)

OFFICER OF THE ARCHANGELS
Then I confer upon you the blessing of …………

OFFICER OF THE HOLY CREATURES
You, who are no strangers to these symbols, know their hidden meanings and their purpose. You know your own strengths and your weaknesses – say, whose blessing will you choose, The Eagle, The Lion, The Bull or The Man to empower and strengthen you upon your quest?

OFFICER OF THE ELEMENTS, OFFICER OF THE PLANETARY SPIRITS AND OFFICER OF THE ARCHANGELS
(Each answers giving one of the Holy Creatures)

OFFICER OF THE HOLY CREATURES
Then I confer upon you the blessing of……….. And upon you the blessing of……… and upon you the blessing of …………

OFFICER OF THE ELEMENTS, OFFICER OF THE PLANETARY SPIRITS, OFFICER OF THE ARCHANGELS AND OFFICER OF THE HOLY CREATURES
(The four Officers go in line to the Officer of the Inner Temple, the Officer of the Holy Creatures having made his/her own choice of Holy Creature. They move in order, Officer of the Elements leading, Officer of the Planetary Spirits, Officer of the Archangels and Officer of the Holy Creatures)

OFFICER OF THE INNER TEMPLE
Welcome Officers of the Holy Powers. I guard the door of the Inner Temple and it is by my will that you may enter therein. Tell me – do you come well prepared?

OFFICER OF THE ELEMENTS, OFFICER OF THE PLANETARY SPIRITS, OFFICER OF THE ARCHANGELS AND OFFICER OF THE HOLY CREATURES

(The four Officers must answer such as satisfies the Officer of the Inner Temple)

Tell me then which blessings you have received and under whose protection you seek to enter the Inner Temple?

(Asks each in turn in order, Officer of Elements, Officer of Planetary Spirits, Officer of the Archangels and Officer of the Holy Creatures)

Your Element? Your Planetary Spirit? Your Archangel? Your Holy Creature?

You do indeed come well prepared to this portal.

I confer upon you the blessing of those I represent, please close your eyes.

(Officer touches hand to centre of the Officers forehead)

As you have journeyed hence by the aid of physical light, so let the Inner Light rise up and illuminate your inner mind. Go now and find your place among us.

(When all are seated music is turned off and a few minutes of silence follows)

OFFICER OF THE ELEMENTS

We have journeyed long and far to reach this place and before us is the entrance to the Inner Worlds. It is not grand or imposing, rather is it one we could almost overlook. Go forward and enter.

The landscape before us is dusk dark, there is still just enough light to see we are standing on a wide plain, in the distance rise majestic mountains which surround this place making it secure and secluded. In the midst of the plain there stands a mighty pyramid, which gleams softly in the twilight and the first beams of the rising moon. An almost magnetic pull draws us towards the pyramid and we find ourselves walking swiftly towards it.

Before us is an almost concealed door which leads into the side of the pyramid, it stands ajar and we know we are welcome to enter.

Inside we find ourselves in a vast hall, shimmering with rainbow light. Each of the four walls is of a different colour, one for each of the four elements. Remember the Element you chose for this journey and walk towards the wall that shines with its colour. As you approach the wall seems to dissolve, it has no solidity, you just keep walking until there is nothing but the colour surrounding you – it is like being in a coloured mist which swirls and floats about you. Remember why you chose this particular Element – was it because you felt the need for a strength it could give you? Or did you feel some lack within yourself you felt it could help you to overcome? Whatever the reason, you are here to draw from this Element whatever you need. Take time now to commune with the Element, let its representative speak to you, ask for what you need in your Earth life and know that you receive it.

(Allow meditation time, sufficient for everyone to receive their gift)

OFFICER OF THE PLANETARY SPIRITS
The time has come to make your farewells to your Element, give thanks for what you have received and lock it securely in your memory, then turn and make your way back into the rainbow hall of the pyramid.

(Pause to allow everyone time to give their thanks and return)

As you stand in the shimmering rainbow light of the great hall, the walls seem to be constantly changing colour, then slowly above your head the pyramid opens like a flower and above you is the velvet blackness of the night sky. As your eyes become accustomed to the darkness the pattern of the stars becomes visible – and there, shining in splendour, is the planet of the Planetary Spirit you chose to empower and strengthen you. Feel it draw you upwards, faster and faster until nothing else exists except the light of the planet and the all-enveloping aura of its Planetary Spirit. Remember why you chose this particular Planetary Spirit, was it perhaps because you felt the need to make your life more focussed with the help of the restrictions of Saturn, or for the strength and stability of Jupiter; are you too fearful in the face of aggression and need the input of more Mars in your nature; are you lacking in warmth and enthusiasm towards the direction of your life and need more of the energy of the Sun; are your relationships lacking in true emotion and need some help from Venus; has your life become sluggish and in need of the swiftness of Mercury to move on in a new direction; or are you not listening to your deeper self and need the light of The Moon to illuminate your inner life?

Whatever may be your need, allow the feeling of your chosen Planetary Spirit to flow into you, to seek out and know where you need help and draw that strength deep within you. Let the influence of the Planetary Spirit become part of you, then lock this experience in your memory so you may draw on that influence whenever you have need.

(Allow meditation time, sufficient for everyone to receive their gift)

OFFICER OF THE ARCHANGELS

Slowly you feel the energy of your Planetary Spirit withdraw from about you, once more you become aware of the night sky and the light of the planet becomes again a point of light taking its place in the vast panorama of the night sky.

Gradually the darkness becomes less dense and a golden glow begins to light the sky, then you are floating in the brightest light you have ever seen and far below you the Sun and its accompanying planets spin in the eternal dance of the heavens. Then out of the brilliance of the morning sky a figure comes, tall as the heavens and clothed in majesty. You have asked for this Archangel's companionship and help – yet the reality of this Presence fills you with awe and a great sense of inadequacy – almost the desire to escape and not be seen! Yet there is no hiding place in this realm of light and you know your presence has been noted and recognised.

The figure is now so close you are embraced within the shadow of its wings, enfolded within the glory of its power. Then you know there is no need for fear, nor any place nor need to hide, this Presence is aware of you and the touch of its compassion soothes your heart. To this Presence you may tell your deepest need, your fears and doubts, indeed your every guilt and old regret.

This Presence you may know as Raphael, or Michael, as Gabriel or Auriel. Yet these are but names we place upon our image and in reality the four are one.

Ask and you will receive that which you need – then take the memory deep within your heart and hold it close.

(Allow meditation time, sufficient for everyone to receive their

gift)

OFFICER OF THE HOLY CREATURES
It seems as if you have slept for a time or that your hold on consciousness has slipped away and when you come once more to awareness of your surroundings you are alone, still floating in the brilliant light. You see the Earth far below you and it seems to reach out to you, calling you home. Yet you know that where you are now is as much your spirit's home as the familiar places where your body dwells.

About you the light intensifies and all sense of place is gone, now there is no Earth below or sky above – there is just this place in which you ARE.

Then there is a sense of no longer being alone and about you the Holy Creatures stand. They are great and vast, both insubstantial and yet vivid in their imagery.

Which did you choose to empower and strengthen you?

Do you seek to rise with the Eagle and fly closer to the source of Light? Or would you fight the battles of life and seek the Lion's strength? Perhaps you need to learn of nature's ways and seek the powers the Bull can give? Maybe humanity has called to you from its deep need and you seek to walk the Earth in the ways of Man until each man and woman too is truly Winged.

Approach the Holy Creature of your choice and take the gift they freely give to you. So shall you carry back to Earth the power you need to meet your destiny.

(Allow meditation time, sufficient for everyone to receive their gift)

OFFICER OF THE INNER TEMPLE
The images of the Holy Creatures fade and once more you are floating in a sea of Light. You feel the pull of your body's call and know that soon you must return and once more take up your tasks in the outer world. Yet now you bear the gifts you have been given and they will sustain and strengthen you in your daily life.

Remember that you can return to the Inner Worlds whenever you choose, all you need to do is to be still, turn your consciousness inwards and enter your own Inner Temple. This

Inner Temple is as small as a corner of your mind or as great as the vast reaches of the Cosmos. It has no dimension and encompasses everything. It is both your private personal retreat and an entire world and universe. It is your refuge and your strength for it is here you may know the touch of the Divine.

Within your Inner Temple you may explore the many dimensions and levels of the Inner Worlds, meet other forms of intelligence and consciousness, know the truth of the illusion which is earthly life and discover the expansion of your own consciousness which is as the explosion of a super nova in the physical world.

Create for yourself this sacred place where you can store the gifts you have been given and in time give them back in service in the Great Work.

(Pause for everyone to visualise their Inner Temple)

We have embarked on a great journey, upon an adventure greater than any undertaken in the lands or seas or skies of Earth. We are explorers who seek to know the mysteries concealed behind the veil of life. We seek to know and dare and understand, that the darkness of ignorance may pass away and the dawn of the light of wisdom may shine upon ourselves and upon all humanity.

Now go aboard the Ship of Light and receive your garland of glory and return to your kingdom and rejoice with all the Aeons.

Depart with the blessing of those I represent.

(Pause for a few minutes for everyone to return then switch on music for exit)

Know yourself back in your body in this outer Temple. When you are ready you may rise and leave the Temple.

(Outer Guide sees that everyone leaves the Temple and then switches off the music)

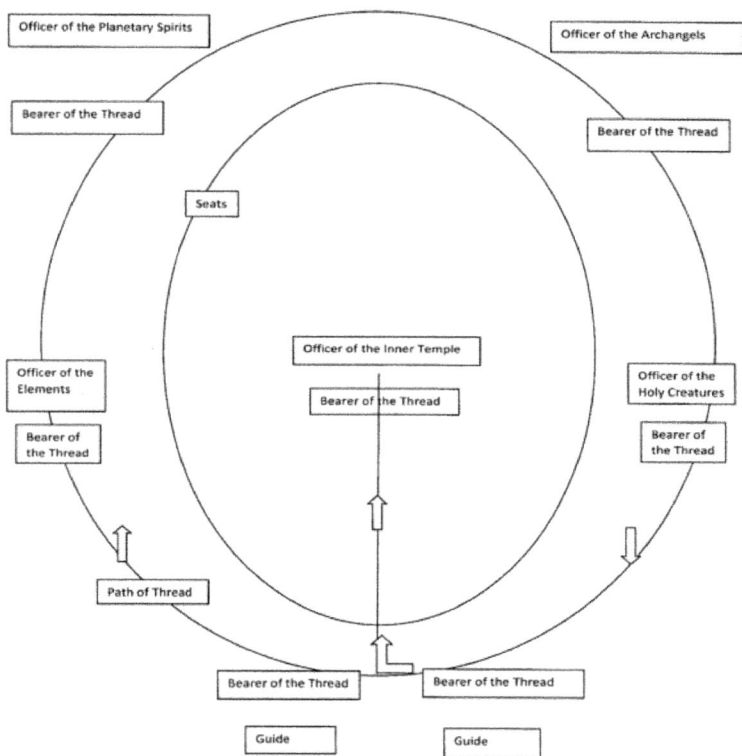

Officer of the Planetary Spirits

Officer of the Archangels

Bearer of the Thread

Bearer of the Thread

Seats

Officer of the Inner Temple

Bearer of the Thread

Officer of the Elements

Officer of the Holy Creatures

Bearer of the Thread

Bearer of the Thread

Path of Thread

Bearer of the Thread

Bearer of the Thread

Guide

Guide

Rothley Ritual
Messages of the Priestess of the West

One

The Chapel is still and quiet about us, an oasis of calm in our hurried twentieth century world. As we relax and close our eyes the quiet steals over us and we feel at peace.

Slowly the image of the Chapel changes, it becomes misty and difficult to see in detail, strange, but the chairs and people have faded away, even the light of the candles has disappeared and we realise we are alone in the empty Chapel. It is familiar yet subtly different, there are rush lights on the walls and the Altar has a golden cloth draped over it with a finely wrought silver chalice in the centre.

There is a faint noise near the doorway and we turn to see a figure watching us quietly. It is a young man, but he looks unfamiliar to our eyes, he wears a long roughly woven robe of deep brown with a white tabard like over cloth emblazoned with a scarlet cross which stretches from mid chest to thigh. He smiles shyly and slowly approaches, he asks if we are newly arrived for the May gathering. We hesitate, then realising that all is a little strange, think it best to be cautious until we know his identity. Yes, we say, we are here for the May gathering. The young man asks if we have been allocated our quarters and when we reply that we are but newly arrived he offers to attend to our needs. Feeling slightly relieved we follow him out of the Chapel. We emerge into a very different world outside the Chapel. The scene before us is one of busy activity, farm animals crop the grass which grows close up to the Chapel and house. Here a young man leads two cows into a nearby shed, there a tall strong youth mounts his horse with sword ringing metallically against his strange attire.

This is no twentieth century world and we realise we are seeing Rothley of the 13th Century and these people about us are members of the Holy Order of the Knights Templar. Our young companion bids us wait while he goes to arrange for our reception and invites us to wander at will while he is gone. Eagerly we look about us, the house is smaller than we thought but solid and attractive. Walking over the grass for a few yards we then turn and look back towards the house and Chapel. To the right of the Chapel we see a large circular building, at first we are mystified as to its use but it is not long before we notice doves emerging from its sides and several more returning from flight. This is the dovecote which was an important part of a large community providing an essential item of diet. Behind the dovecote is the large rectangular orchard, a high wall surrounds it to provide some protection for the fruit trees from the worst weather. Even now the trees are gnarled and old and we realise that while to us Rothley at this time is young, it has in fact already stood here for many years.

Looking to the left we see the grass slope down gently to a fast running river, no doubt there are fish in the clear waters which also help to make the community self-sufficient. We are surprised to see a watermill lazily turning for this has long disappeared from the Rothley of our time. Looking behind us we can just see the arms of a windmill beyond the trees and we realise that everything which is needed the community can provide and process for themselves.

Suddenly we become aware of someone standing quietly at our shoulder and turn, to see the young man returned to fetch us. He bids us follow him into the house and leads us to a small room, Spartan but adequately provided with a table and chair and means of washing. He bids us refresh ourselves and indicates a platter containing some rough brown bread and cheese with a pitcher of water which has a slight fragrance of herbs.

Our guide tells us that, in a short time, we will be summoned to meet the Master of the Temple. We take advantage of the opportunity to rest and refresh ourselves and it is not long before there is a knock on the door. Obeying the summons we are guided to a large oak door on the first floor of the house. Our guide knocks and we are bidden to enter. Seated at a large wooden table is a man of immense stature both of body and bearing. He commands our instant respect and admiration. He wears the same simple brown robe and emblazoned tabard as our young guide in the Chapel, but on this man it is a robe of regal splendour. Rising to greet us he bids us be seated facing him across the table.

The Master resumes his seat and looks at us with eyes full of steel and kindliness and above all wisdom. "Welcome" he says, "you have travelled no space but an immensity of time to visit us on this day. We welcome you to our home, our Chapel and our ceremony on this special day. Our Order, though venerable, is not as yet old, but I fear it will not live to enjoy old age. The political clouds are gathering about our sanctuary and the day is not far ahead when its harsh hand will fall upon us. It is ever so when men are afraid and the King fears our power and independence. It was an ill day when the Holy Father granted us his papal Bull, Omne Datum Optimum, making us subject to his rule alone; for what King can tolerate a group of his subjects who are not bound by his authority? Neither is our wealth, now grown mighty since we spend it no more fighting for the Holy Land, any longer a protection. Rather is it a threat to our security and the eye of envy, greed, and hatred is turned upon us and our days are surely numbered." Our hearts are heavy at his words with our knowledge of what lies ahead for his Order. The Master's face for a moment reflects our feeling. Then he smiles and says, "But today we welcome you to our May gathering and I would invite you to join us in our Festival of Unification Ceremony. Our Order is dedicated to the protection of the Holy Places and our Rule is Chastity, Poverty and Obedience. But we are also Guardians and Custodians of the Ancient Wisdom and our teachings are deep and concealed. For this also we bear the shadow of the hatred of the orthodox. On this day we have a very special guest to our Ceremony, a Priestess of the old religion whose school on the Sacred Island in the West now guards in utmost secrecy the teachings of the wise until another time will need them and bring them forth. Come now my friends, the hour is near and we must attend the Chapel - my young Brother will escort you."

He rises and bows his head briefly to us in farewell. We rise, bow also and follow our guide who leads us out of the house and to the Chapel showing us to our seats.

The Chapel is arranged with two banks of seats facing each other over a central Altar on which burns the Sacred Flame. Before the Altar in the East there is an impressive, elaborately carved chair, and facing it in the West of the Chapel a plain unadorned chair, both are unoccupied.

Some of the seats are already occupied by the Brothers. Slowly the seats are filled, some Brothers in the robes we have already seen, others in full armour with swords about their waists. At last we are all present. A silence and a stillness descends on all present. Suddenly three strikes on a deep resonant gong swell in sound through the Chapel. With great dignity the Master of the Temple enters ceremoniously clasping the hand of a woman, tall and full of grace, her white robe falls in gentle flowing folds about her and her long hair is caught back and makes long coils to her waist. Dark, wise and very intelligent eyes take in the assembly. The Master bows to her as they reach the West, then advances alone to his chair in the East. Both are seated and there is a brief silence.

The Ceremony commences and we are swept upwards on a tide of sound and light and emotion. The candles blaze and the Brothers chant strange magical hymns and psalms. After a long time there is silence and the Master of the Temple speaks, much he says which we cannot remember but his final words go deep into our consciousness.

"In the beginning God made the heaven and the Earth. That is, in the beginning God made the heavenly Mind of God and the Universal Matter. In sacred tradition this first and fundamental condition of BEING has been described as the Holy Trinity; the Heavenly Father (the Divine Mind), the Earthly Mother (Divine Matter) and the Son (the relationship between the Divine Parents). All three are ONE, and came into BEING together, simultaneously from Non-Being. No one person of the Trinity has precedence over either of the other Two Persons, but all three are co-existent and co-eternal each dependent upon the other and together constituting the whole BEING that we call GOD, the All-Good. This first existing, absolute Being, that we call God contains the basic Three Principles of Creativity known as Power, Wisdom and Love, all three being inherent in the Son, the relationship of the Divine Parents, but of the Three, Love is the first to be expressed, as an emanation from the ubiquitous heart.

Non nobis, Domine, non nobis, sed nomini tuo da gloriam. Not unto us, O Lord, not unto us, but to Thy name give the Glory."

There is total silence, then the Master invites the Priestess to give her message.

Her voice soft and low fills the Chapel, much she tells of old ways and wisdom - teaching not heard except in such a place of safe security among those who love truth. Of star wisdom she speaks and the healing arts, of knowledge of the hidden ways of Earth and the long journey of the soul. And of much else she speaks. Finally she recalls the Eternal Laws of the Hidden Ways and bids us observe them always. She continues, "All things at our level of being operate in accordance with the laws of polarity. Positive and negative, masculine and feminine, are the necessary conditions for manifestation. Balance the polarities within your own nature so that you neither think nor act in either poverty or excess. Remember that effects WILL follow causes, therefore in all your actions weigh the causes you set in motion.

Project not anything you would not wish to receive for be assured a superior force will always rebound a lesser force and an evil action reflect back to its source. Strive to hold all forces in equilibrium. See that when one force does give way to another the result is towards the positive polarity. Use all energies at their own level, using physical means for physical results and psychic means for psychic results. In all things act with generosity, hold nothing to yourself in possessiveness or greed. Challenge all dreams and visions, examine all inner experiences with the reason and with the intellect so that you are able to separate inspiration from delusion. Remember that all contacts with the subtler dimensions are made through the channels of consciousness, the mind and all its faculties, and the psychic nature or soul force.

Above all dwell in love that in all your work whether with you own kind, the animal or elemental kingdoms or any forces within the created universe, none may be the less for contact with you. Let Love be your guiding power and service your action." Her voice ceases, then rising she lifts her hands high as if to embrace us all and gives us her benediction:

"May the Power of the Light abide with you always and Light your way to the Paths end."

We gaze in wonder as she resumes her seat and the

Ceremony moves to its closing. Perhaps emotion clouds our eyes but the Priestess shimmers and we can no longer see her clearly, indeed the whole scene begins to break into tiny points of light until our eyes are dazzled and bewildered. Slowly all begins to clarify, but the Brethren no longer wear dark robes with scarlet crosses and the Chapel has a different air. We realise we are returned to our own time and place and sit quietly for a little time letting our senses readjust to our own time.

Two

The Chapel is still and quiet about us, an oasis of calm in our hurried twentieth century world. As we relax and close our eyes the quiet steals over us and we feel at peace.

Slowly the image of the Chapel changes, there is the sound of male voices chanting a beautiful anthem. Looking about us we recognise the rush lights upon the walls and the finely wrought silver chalice upon the golden altar cloth. Once more we have slipped back in time to the Rothley Temple of the 13th Century. But this time it is no empty Chapel we have entered but a full assembly of the Brethren of the Knights Templar. In the East of the Temple sits the Officiating Priest, to his right we see the tall impressive figure of the Master of the Temple clad in his simple brown robe with white tabard emblazoned with the scarlet cross of the Templars. Before him he holds the mighty sword of his Office which shines softly golden, the jewels on its hilt glinting in the candle light.

We sit quietly in our seats and realise that our presence is no surprise for our places had been prepared for us before our coming. The ceremony is beautiful and profound and our hearts are moved by the depth of devotion of these men. At last the final prayer is said and a deep silence fills the Chapel.

The Master of the Temple rises and his eyes, which we remember as being so full of kindliness and wisdom, sweep over each of us, but now the wisdom is veiled by a deep and bitter grief.

"My Brethren, join me in bidding welcome to our guests, far have they journeyed in time to be with us on this day. We welcome them but grieve at the necessity which called them here. When last they visited us I spoke of my fears that dark clouds were gathering about our Sanctuary, alas those fears have proved too well founded. The news from France is dark indeed, our Brethren have been seized and imprisoned, their properties confiscated and their very lives put at danger. Our enemies are strong about us and no scruples modify the charges made against our Order. All manner of evil they bring to our attack, vile practices they accuse us of and no depravity that the mind of man can conceive but they think to use the accusation of it to our destruction. The time is now upon us when these evils will come to pass in England also, therefore must we ensure the safety of those things we hold most dear. Tonight a small number of our Brethren will travel north and take our books and such of our treasures as they safely may, to the kingdom of the far north where we have loyal friends who will guard them well. But the greatest of our treasures cannot thus be sent away to safety, they are with us always, yet if we perish then are they like to perish with us also and the Light of Wisdom vanish from this land. Brethren of another time, will you accept our treasures into your hearts and memory that they may sleep within your souls until a future age shall call them forth to light again the Pathway to the Stars?" The Master's voice ceases and for long moments there is total silence, our hearts too heavy with emotion and aching sadness to answer if we would.

Then one of our Companions rises and slowly walks forward to stand before the Master of the Temple, dropping on one knee he bends forward and touches with his lips the Ring of Office on the right hand of the Master, then silently rises and returns to his place. One by one we follow his example and when all are again seated there is a deep warmth lightening the grief in the eyes of the Master. Rising to his full height the Master addresses us all:

"My Brethren, Brothers and Sisters both, we thank you with all our hearts. Now we would ask that you make a journey with us, for we also must leave Rothley this night. There is no safety here and we must be swift away. Horses will be ready within the hour and we will make what distance we may before the night is upon us."

The Master raises his hand and speaks a Benediction then passes to the West and leaves the Chapel.

The next hour is full of orderly haste and activity as the

Brothers prepare for our departure and those who are to accompany us. The Master of the Temple and four of the Brethren are to travel with us, all the remaining Brethren are leaving also but we are not told of their destination or when they will all meet again. There is little time for farewells at our parting but we feel the unspoken grief at the knowledge that never again will the Brethren meet in Rothley Temple.

Soon we find ourselves mounting the horses, feeling a little apprehensive at the journey ahead of us. We ride for what seems a long time after the sun has disappeared below the western horizon until at last we ride into the courtyard of a large house and friendly faces bid us welcome and minister to our needs and comfort. Even before first light we are away and once more upon our journey. Days blur into a haze of fatigue and we lose count of time. Our way is ever westward and the land becomes rougher and more sparsely populated. Then there are mountains and our horses are changed more frequently at our places of rest. We marvel that so many are willing to help us on our way and gratefully accept the food and rough comfort of our quarters.

At last we are through the mountains and follow a broad river down a fertile valley. Then we see before us a panorama of sea and sky, the mountains behind us rising majestically into a crown of clouds. Our guides lead us down towards the sea and we see before us a broad stretch of water, grey and forbidding, swirling currents revealing the hidden dangers in its depth. Our hearts go cold at the sight and we silently pray we will not have to cross this water. But the Master calls us to him and tells us that the island across the water is our destination and that there will soon be boats to row us across the sea.

Our journey has been full of discomforts but this passage to the island is full of fear, the water swirls and drags at the boats and it seems even the strong arms of the oarsmen cannot prevail against it. The boats sway and dip and our senses swim, the journey seems endless, yet miraculously it does end and we are once more on firm ground. Thankfully we stumble up the beach and once more find welcoming hands to lead us and minister to our needs. Now at last we are allowed to rest and recover our strength and energy.

For several days we rest in what proves to be a religious

house which is sympathetic to the Knights Templars. As we recover from our journey we find there is a small Chapel in the house and here the Brethren meet at intervals throughout the day for services according to their faith. We too join with them and find the experience refreshing and uplifting. Then there are long conversations with the Master and he tells us much of their wisdom, bidding us bury these things deep within our memories and carry them back to our own time where they may once more bring Light into the minds and hearts of men and women.

Then one evening the Master tells us that on the morrow we are to visit the Priestess whom we last saw in the Temple at Rothley on the day of the May celebration ceremony. A ripple of excitement flows through us for we had not realised this is her island home.

At first light we are ready and find small hardy ponies ready and awaiting us. We ride for some time until the morning is well advanced, then coming through a small woodland area we find ourselves once more near the sea. At a small stone house we are asked to leave our ponies to rest and feed, from here the remainder of our way is on foot.

Climbing and sliding we cross the high sand hills, strands of sharp spiky grass providing the only handholds to check our wild slide down the sand. At last we arrive on a shore of golden sands, recently clean swept by the sea, a line of seaweed marking the high water mark so recently left dry. The sands sweep away to our right in a graceful perfect bay. At the end of the crescent of sand we see the dark outline of a small island. The walk along the sands is further than we had expected but at last we draw near to the island, then we can see that only a small channel still keeps it an island as the tide recedes. A few more moments and there are rocks appearing in the channel, then the sands appear and we walk through the now shallow water to the soft sand of the shore of the island. Climbing the small cliff we find ourselves on a wide grassy path, bracken and gorse grow thick along the slopes of the shallow sides of the hillocks on either side of the path. Following the pathway we are amazed to suddenly see a small stone built Chapel almost across our path. The Master bids us wait at the door and enters ahead of us. After a short time a young maid in a long dark blue robe opens the wooden door and bids us follow her. Silently we pass into the Chapel one by one and the sight which meets our eyes makes us catch our breath in wonder and reverence. This Chapel has no decoration by the art of man, but is a bower of flowers complete with strange shapes of seaweed draped in fantastic coils, the gleam of seashells catching the light of the several candles about the walls in exquisite patterns and subtle colours. So small is the Chapel there is little room to accommodate us all. Two seats only there are within the Chapel, seated in one is the Master of the Temple and in the other the Priestess we remember from the ceremony at Rothley. Yet it seems our memories have failed us totally for her beauty and magnetic aura are such that we feel we are seeing her for the first time. As before she wears a white robe of gentle graceful folds, her long hair caught back which emphasises the clarity of her features. Her dark eyes smile into ours and bid us welcome.

Cushions and rugs cover the floor and we are bidden to be seated. Then we notice there are other women present as well as the young maid who admitted us and all wear the same dark blue robes. They sit quietly about us. The Priestess sounds an instrument in her hand, half bell, half gong, and the strange sweet sound sends a swift excitement through our hearts. Then the Priestess begins to intone a chant, very low at first, then the other women join in and the sound swells until it is like the echo of the sea, a deep throbbing rhythm from the depths of Earth. Suddenly there is silence and the air quivers with vibrating power. The Priestess spreads her hands towards us and speaks:

"Brothers and Sisters of another time, we welcome you and thank you for your presence here. Much has the Master taught you and there will come a time when you will remember how to remember and all his wisdom will be available to you. For now we would give you of the Ageless Wisdom which we have long guarded, remember well our words." The atmosphere of power in the Chapel is almost tangible so intense is our emotion, the silence is total apart from the soft and distant murmur of the sea.

The Priestess speaks: "Remember every human personality is absolutely and unqualifiedly dependant on the Universal existence. The Universe is an orderly, rhythmic manifestation of life which is determined and operates by fixed laws. The True Self of man has a consciousness above our intellectual level and it is our birthright to have access to and guidance from this Higher Consciousness. Nature is the Teacher and She unveils herself to man when man approaches Her in right meditation.

Evil is the appearance presented to us by natural processes that we do not understand. It is the veil of terror hiding the beautiful countenance of Truth. Whatever exists is a form of spiritual energy. Higher levels of this energy flow through the mind of man by the means of conscious imagery. The conscious mind of man is the mediator between that which is above and that which is below. The Universe is rational and its reasoning may be read in nature. There are means of cognition beyond the ordinary forms of human experience. Direct perception of reality may be received through intuition. These perceptions are never contrary to reason, they provide correct solutions to particular problems, but every solution is also the revelation of an eternal principle. Man and human intelligence are an essential link in the chain of the manifestation of the Life Power.

It is the energy of the Life Power which enables man to contact super conscious levels of experience. Man progresses by the realisation that the personal life is a manifestation of the action of the Life Power. Knowledge of the action of the Life Power is gained by listening with profound attention for the instruction of the Inner Voice. Mental imagery is the door to the higher knowledge. Human life is not limited to the physical world.

All the activities of the Universe are held in equilibrium. The thoughts, words and deeds of man are the sum total of the operation of Cosmic Forces and Laws. All manifestation arises in the Original Creative Power. Nothing happens by chance because all things arise from Cosmic Causes. The Higher Self is enthroned above the level of personal consciousness, and from that superior station directs by its infallible word those who have ears to hear. The Universal Sub-consciousness produces mental images and from those images all forms on all planes have their origin, hence all forms are mental images. The dissolution of form is a fundamental tendency of the Cosmic Process. All things change. All conditions pass away. No form ever remains fixed. Existence is a stream, a series of waves, an eternal movement. The Cosmic Process is a meditation of the conscious energy of the Life Power. The Life Power is perfectly successful at every stage of the Cosmic Process and has always some definite objective from the beginning of a cycle of manifestation to its completion. Every human being is under the direct guidance of the one identity. Human imagination is, in kind, though not in degree, the same as the imagination that forms the Universe.

Human personality is a synthesis of all Cosmic processes. Man summarises all that precedes him and is the point of departure for the manifestation of a new creature. The natural man is the seed of the spiritual man."

"Brothers and Sisters of another time, take these things and hold them in your hearts for they are the keys which will open to you the portals of wisdom."

A profound silence fills the small Chapel as we sit in meditation. The words of the Master and the Priestess sink deep into our minds and we marvel at the depth of their understanding in an age when to speak of such knowledge is to risk persecution and a cruel death.

Slowly we begin to feel the pull of our own time and realise the moment of return is drawing near. The sounds of the sea grow fainter and fainter and our inner vision tells us the Chapel is fading and changing. Soft music calls gently to us and we quietly allow ourselves to float gently back into our twentieth century and our physical selves here in our own time and space.

Three

The Chapel is still and quiet about us, an oasis of calm in our hurried twentieth century world. As we relax and close our eyes the quiet steals over us and we feel at peace.

Our awareness of the Chapel slowly fades and we are aware only of a swirling mist, shafts of light form strange patterns and almost we think there are forms which twist and weave about us, half teasing, half tender. It seems we wander in this world of shifting shapes for a long time, a dreamy sense of peace lulling our senses so that we neither sleep nor wake. Slowly the mist thins and we begin to see a pathway before us; it winds across a shallow valley and we feel the rough grass springing beneath our feet. Through the last swirls of mist we see the outline of a building before us and recognise the small Chapel of the Priestess - a thrill almost of homecoming shoots through us as we realise we are once more upon the Island. We become aware of the sound of the sea and the sweet melancholy crying of the seagulls. As we draw nearer to the Chapel we notice a light glowing behind the small windows, even before we can knock upon the door it opens and we recognise the young maiden in her dark blue robe. Smiling, she greets us and bids us enter. The soft glow of candlelight illumines the interior of the Chapel; as on our last visit the light falls upon a wealth of natural beauty, but this time the colours are the golds and red of autumn, scarlet leaves and golden corn and the warm glow of summer's fruits in rich profusion.

Before us sits the Priestess, robed on this occasion in a robe of darkest blue which emphasises the startling beauty of her skin and features. Dark eyes watch us gravely, then a slow smile of welcome lights their depths and she extends a hand in welcome and bids be seated on the rugs and cushions on the floor. The Priestess speaks, "Brothers and Sisters of another time, we welcome you. I have called you here once more because the time of our communion is growing short and there are things I would say to you and doorways which I would ensure are open unto you. Today I would take you to our Temple but first I would have you understand its nature. Although we meet within the Inner realms, this Chapel is as a mirror of your outer world, form and shape it has and a reality parallel with your own. But the Temple to which I would take you now has no such form or substance of the worlds. Built of the Light of Thought are its walls and all that is most sacred to us all is held within its Sanctuary. Here do our hearts take wings and mind commune with mind where Wisdom dwells."

As the Priestess falls silent the atmosphere in the Chapel is calm and still, we watch the gently flickering candles and our hearts are full of peace.

After a time the Priestess rises and one of the maidens sets a cloak about her shoulders. As we too rise we also are given a warm cloak, then one by one we quietly leave the Chapel and follow the Priestess into the open air.

The pathway we follow winds further along the shallow valley in the centre of the Island, golden bracken clothes the slopes of the valley sides and short green grass marks out the path we follow. We do not walk for long before the faint sound of the sea, of which we had hardly been aware, grows into an insistent roar of waves crashing on a nearby shore. The beach comes suddenly into view and we see a small cove with a sand and shingle beach. But the cove does not hold our attention long, for to our right a flight of steep stone steps go sharply upwards to a small round building set upon the pinnacle of a rocky promontory. The Priestess walks slowly up the steps and we follow her not knowing what to expect when we pass through the doorway.

We enter the small building wondering how we will all find room within, but our eyes open wide in amazement for this is no small room in which we stand. Before us is an immense hall, upon the floor an intricate and beautiful mosaic of the constellations of the Zodiac in all their symbolic splendour. At either hand a wide and graceful staircase sweeps upwards, each curving towards the other as they disappear from sight far above us. The Priestess smiles at our astonishment and says, "In this place there are no dimensions such as you know on Earth, here all things exist without limitation of time or space. You have but to think and it is so, you have but to desire and it is to see."

The Priestess indicates that we should climb the staircases and we glide effortlessly upwards to find ourselves on a wide balcony. Before us are golden doors on which are set in bold relief the figures of the great Archangels. On the right hand door are Raphael and Michael and on the left hand door Gabriel and Auriel. The mighty doors swing gently open and we follow the Priestess within. Our senses swim with the almost overwhelming force of the vibrations within, the subtle perfume of incense, the glow of numerous candles and the dazzling brilliant light which radiates above the central sanctuary. And such a Sanctuary as we have never seen meets our dazzled eyes. Upon a raised dais stands a rectangular altar of purest crystal, cut and faceted so that the light from the candles dances from them in a thousand hues. At the four corners stand the figures of the Guardians of the Sanctuary in the form of the four Holy Creatures, a Man, a Lion, a Bull and an Eagle. So lifelike are they we do not know whether we are looking at carved statuary or indeed the living creatures. Above the Altar shines a brilliant blazing Light which seems to radiate into space from no visible source, as a Star shining in the heavens. The Temple is immense, or rather there is space about us and we cannot perceive any walls which limit its extent. The air glows and shimmers about us and sweet sounds fill the air which are like no music we have ever heard on Earth.

The Priestess bids us stand to the North of the Altar, then moves away from us towards the East. From the deep shadows comes the figure of a man. Something about him seems familiar, perhaps his height and bearing which is full of power and dignity. Slowly the realisation grows, indeed we know him, but he is changed from our last meeting. The Templar robe has been replaced by a simple robe of purest white and all the evidences of age and care have dropped from him. The Priestess holds out her hand to him then turns and together they advance towards us.

He whom we know as the Master of the Temple smiles at us in welcome then speaks to us:

"Brethren of another time I bid you welcome. From this day we will no longer keep our ties with Earth, our destiny lies far beyond and we must hasten to it. Glad are our hearts that you will keep the light we lit aflame and it is with deep rejoicing that we pass to you our trust.

Much have we taught you in our meeting times and you will remember when you have need of it. Now we would give you further of the Ageless Wisdom that you may be prepared and ready for the tasks which lie ahead for you. Remember well our words. "The world every man lives in is the world he forms within his mind. The nobler his inner life, the nobler his outer life.

Every man must come to perceive that all activity within the range of personal experience is really the one spiritual energy in action. Everything which comes into manifestation in the world must first be perceived as a seed idea, yet must these ideas be seen as actual realities in the living present. Since natural man is the seed of spiritual man, he who would scale the heights of adeptship must resolve to become more than man. Spiritual man rises from the limitations of time and space into a higher dimension. He is changed from mortality into immortality. Everything which happens in earthly life is a means towards this transformation, it is the operation of a perfect law having beauty and evolution for its foundations. Man must become Master of the forces of dissolution and integration, for only he who can dissolve forms may master the art of constituting them. Conscious transformation is an act of self-consciousness. By the use of mental imagery man directs the forces behind form. Mental direction of the life power as it flows from super conscious levels, through self-conscious levels, enables man to control, modify and alter the mental images generated by sub-consciousness. Self-consciousness is the point of control. Mental control and equilibrium may be achieved by exercising the opposite of any evil by its corresponding good. Human self-consciousness, seemingly poised between an infinity above and an infinity below, is really an aspect of the ONE of the Universe. That ONE sees through our eyes, hears through our ears and speaks through our lips. The life power is ready to impart its higher knowledge to any man. Always it dwells at the centre of the Temple of human personality. Always it is ready to speak. We have only to listen. The One is the Sun of life and light, the spiritual sun of which our daystar is the external manifestation and symbol. He who would know will understand eventually that his personality has no existence apart from the shining of the spiritual sun. The highest manifestation of the spiritual solar energy is the constituting intelligence that makes, frames, and composes everything in the Universe. That intelligence is an actual presence in every human personality. Every human personality is a centre for the expression of that intelligence, this is the real truth about man. A great adept is one who fully realises this truth. Remember these things Brethren that you may be way showers and Guardians of the Light in your own time." Their voices cease and a profound silence fills the Temple.

Then smiling at us, the Priestess says that she has one more place to show us before we part and bids us follow her. Priest and Priestess lead the way from the Sanctuary and we find ourselves ascending a wide spiral staircase. We climb for what seems a long way then emerge into a small circular room. The walls are entirely transparent and we can see a vast panorama spread below us. It seems we can see the entire island and far along the coast looking over the sea also to the mountains of the mainland. The Priest and Priestess stand in the centre of the room then bid us form a circle about them facing outwards and joining hands. When we have done so and are looking out over the beautiful view of mountains, sea and sky we become aware of a light behind us. The light is shining forth from the Priest and Priestess and they bid us join our light to theirs.

The view before us changes, widens, it seems there are no limits to our vision, forests, deserts, mountain ranges, cities, towns, and all the surface of the Earth seem to be open to our view. Then from us all the Light beams forth. In long pulsating rays of power it carries strength and healing over Earth. We are no longer separate from the Light but part of its living energy and power. For a long time we radiate within the Light then slowly it dims and we become aware once more of the room about us. The Priestess bids us turn towards the centre of the circle, we do so and find the figures of the Priest and Priestess are but a shimmer of form within the fading light. With one last bright blaze the light is gone and echoing in our minds we hear the words "farewell, farewell". We know the time has come for us too to leave this place, but we know too with a deep certainty that we are free to return whenever we wish to assist in sending forth the Light.

In silence we descend the stairs and find they have brought us back into the entrance hall. Passing out of the building we find ourselves once more on the steps of the little building on its rocky promontory. We walk down the steps once more onto the beach and make our way back down the pathway to the little Chapel. Knowing we will find it empty, we still cannot pass without going once more within. The candles still burn and the autumn colours glow. We sit among the rugs and quietly allow our minds to return from the heights we have so recently visited.

Then the Chapel begins to seem a little indistinct, perhaps the candles are burning low. Slowly the image fades and we begin to feel the pull of our own time, fainter and fainter becomes the Chapel and we quietly allow ourselves to float gently back into our twentieth century world and our physical selves here in our own time and space.

Four

The Chapel is still and quiet about us, an oasis of calm in our hurried twentieth century world. As we relax and close our eyes the quiet steals over us and we feel at peace.

Suddenly we become aware of a loud rhythmic noise which is at first puzzling. Then we recognise it as the sharp sound of horse's hoofs ringing on hard road-way. Looking about us we realise that the Chapel is no longer as it was when we closed our eyes but is in the now familiar form of its Templar time. Rising to our feet we start towards the doorway, but before we have gone many paces a wild figure comes rushing into the Chapel. His rough cloak of dark woven wool is grimed with the mud and dust of the road and his face shows too the marks of long travel and little pause for rest. A look of relief crosses his face as he sees us and comes forward to speak to us. "We had news that you planned to return", he says, "but it is no longer safe for you within these walls, much has changed since last you were here. I was sent with all speed to meet you and conduct you to our nearest house of safety. Come follow me before your presence here is known."

The urgency of his tone fills us with some alarm and we follow him in silence from the Chapel. Once outside we note with some surprise that it is night and only the faint starlight gives us light enough to follow our guide. Swiftly and silently we cross the outer courtyard and soon are out upon the road. With swift pace our guide leads us towards the small village of Rothley then, suddenly turning, disappears through a high wall. We realise that he has passed through a small and hidden gate and hasten to follow him. Beyond the gate we see the outline of a long low house then notice movement within the shadows of its walls. Several dark clad men come towards us each leading a large and sturdy horse. They hand us each a dark warm cloak, which we are glad to wrap around our shoulders, then bid us mount the horses and with some difficulty we do so. We file silently away from the house into the night, the unfamiliar feel of riding the horses taking all our concentration. We ride for what seems a long time but can in fact be little more than an hour. At last we approach another large house where we are greeted with light and warmth and generous hospitality.

After we have eaten and rested, we gather in the large hall of the house and here we are greeted by a tall strong faced man dressed in a plain dark robe. There is something familiar about him which teases the memory - "Welcome", he says, "my Brother told me of your visit and of your shared journey to the Island of the West. You surely know that he was taken from us some time ago and we know you must indeed share our sorrow at his passing." His voice turns the key to the last door of memory and we know him for Brother to the Master of the Temple. "There has been much sadness since your last visit here," he continues. "The Brethren are all fled and Rothley Temple no longer is a place of light and worship. Yet does the flame still blaze in remote and secret places in this land and if you will we would ask your company to visit where it dwells." A deep joy floods through each of us and not one thinks to refuse the invitation.

We sleep deep through the night and with the dawn set out upon our journey without question where it leads or how long it may last, for we know it is a quest our hearts must follow to its end. Our way is ever northwards and we travel many days till we are saddle-sore and weary. The year is far advanced and autumn has just laid its hand upon the land. We pass through valleys rich with harvest gold, through woodlands beginning now to hint at the rich golden colours soon to blaze with gold, and mountains still showing purple heather on their heights.

For many days we travel, each brief night pausing in some friendly house to catch what sleep we may, and rest and change our patient horses. Then comes a time when we have left the last rolling vistas of England far behind and Scotland's hills surround and guard our way.

Now we no longer stay in inns and houses, but are welcome guests at Abbeys along the way.

At last we reach a small country town dominated by the tall towers of a beautiful graceful Church, surrounded by the numerous buildings and fields of a prosperous and large community. Weary as our horses, we pass slowly through the arched entrance and gratefully dismount to a warm welcome and hospitable rest. A plain but satisfying meal and we are shown to our sleeping quarters to fall almost at once into the deep slumber of exhaustion.

We awake to bright sunlight and a world fresh with the smell of overnight rain. Rising we prepare ourselves for whatever the day may bring. Soon a young Brother comes to summon us and guides us to a beautiful room whose panelled walls are almost covered by rows of ancient books. A tall man rises from his chair behind a table laden with books and papers. He wears the plain brown robe and white tabard emblazoned with the scarlet Templar Cross stretching from mid chest to thigh which we remember from our first visit to Rothley Temple. He smiles and stretches out a hand in greeting and bids us be seated. After asking of our welfare and comfort in our quarters he tells us more of the purpose of our visit. "You will remember," he says, "that the Chalice of Rothley was brought north for safe keeping. Here it has dwelt in safety and seclusion. Now is the time come when it will once more serve the Light and we would bid you join us on this day. Far have you travelled to be with us, yet must you be strong to complete your journey on this quest. For now it is only your own strength which will bring you to the dwelling place of the Chalice. Prepare yourselves swiftly for we leave within the hour." Within a short time we are ready and gather before the Abbey Church together with many of the Brethren who also have come from many distant places.

Our Guide leads us out of the arched entrance and turning left walks briskly through the small town which clusters about the Abbey. Soon the road becomes a pathway across fields and through a small wood of dark conifers. The pace is gentle and we have time to look about us at the beautiful countryside which glistens in the bright sunlight of the morning. Emerging from the wood we see a small bridge curving over a swift flowing stream and beyond three hills rise steeply into the sky. Their slopes are steep but the grass upon their sides give a gentle air to the otherwise imposing sight. Many of our Companions are already across the bridge and beginning to climb the narrow path which quickly steepens. The way is not difficult for there are natural steps in the more difficult places. But gradually the climb becomes sharper and we pause now and then to regain our breath. As we do so we look back and see the Abbey building and town gradually unfolding far below. The air is sharp and fresh and we feel invigorated, there is a haunting fragrance which drifts across our senses like a sweet strange incense on the slight breeze. Looking closely, we see small flowering plants and herb-like shrubs which grow low upon the ground and are the source of this sweet scent. The way becomes still steeper and we climb in silence for some time, our eyes fixed upon the ground at our feet as we choose our way with care. Then suddenly we have reached the crest of the hill and find ourselves on a broad flat area stepping on short springy grass. The scene is awe inspiring. On either side the rounded hills still tower above us and we are sheltered safe between them as if we lay at Nature's breast itself. Before us stretches far below the rolling hills and sweeping planes of England's northern borders, and behind us the valley of the Abbey and the vast panorama of Scotland's majestic mountains as far as eye can see.

Suddenly we become aware the rest of our group has moved well ahead and almost disappeared within a copse of trees. We hasten to re-join them and pass quickly into the small wood. But it is not trees we see about us, instead we stand before a wall of rock with a narrow opening immediately in front of us. There is no sign of our Companions and a shiver of apprehension ripples down our spines. Surely they must be ahead of us for there is no other way they could have taken. We summon our courage and step within the rock. A narrow passage stretches ahead of us and we catch a brief glimpse of one of the Brethren just ahead. Hastening forward we follow the passage which slopes very gently downwards. Then to our amazement we step out into a natural Cathedral whose crystal studded walls gleam and sparkle in the dancing light of innumerable large candles. We see with some relief that the rest of our Companions are all gathered here, some already seated on the shelving rocks.

Long pink coloured stalactites hang from the roof, and reaching up as if they would join hands, beautiful stalagmites stretch upwards to meet them. And in the centre of this hidden Sanctuary there stands an Altar of shining, snow white quartz. Upon the Altar gleams the Silver Chalice of the Templars and all the radiance from the countless candles pales beside the Light which shines about it.

Then from the shadows a tall figure comes, his long white robe unadorned save for a golden cord about his waist. In total silence he approaches the Altar then turns and raising high his hands he gives a blessing to us all. "Brothers and Sisters in the Light", he says, "welcome to our Sanctuary. Long have we waited for this day and it is with deep joy we greet your presence here. Time was the Mysteries of the Light were taught and practised from this place. But dark times came when we could only wait and set guard upon the Treasures of the Light until the land once more was safe to send them forth. Now indeed is that time come when you may take the Light from this timeless place and once more send it forth within your outer worlds. To each is given knowledge fitting to their need and strength and wisdom to their task. From this our Sanctuary receive the gift of Light and take it forth with love into your life."

Then taking the Silver Chalice in his hands he turns and from a small stream of water flowing from the wall he fills it to the brim and holds it out to us. One by one we come forward to stand in front of this Guardian of the Mysteries and from his hands receive the brimming Chalice. We raise it reverently to our lips and drink deep of the pure cool water. As each one drinks the Chalice remains full, though all have taken according to their need.

When all have taken of the Chalice, the Guardian of the Mysteries lifts his hands in a gesture which embraces us all. Then with a look of great love and wisdom he says: "From the loneliness of your spirit you have reached out to your Mother/Father God, seeking to lean upon the love and protection of your Great Parents.

But you who have reached this place have chosen the Way of the Priest/Priestess and for those who walk this Path such comfort is no longer accessible, though that love and protection are ever about you. You have chosen the Path of Service and it is therefore your task to comfort rather than to be comforted. Know that the Priest/Priestess is not one who seeks the favour of God by seeking to be the servant of God, but one who is the servant of all men and women and thereby becomes the true instrument of God in their service. Out of the fullness of your life extract the nectar of wisdom from your experience in the Eternal. Then will you truly be the Servant of the Mysteries. Know yourselves as vessels of the Power which is Life. In all your acts and thoughts know yourself as the Silent Watcher on the

Heights of Being who orders and directs the actions of the lesser self in Earth. For the lesser self is servant to the Greater Self and it is in the blending of these two into one that the purpose and the mystery of life is attained. Carry the Light of this place back with you into your world and the work of those who walked this Path before you will not fail."

The silence is total as his voice ceases, then as we watch his form shimmers and where he stood we see first the form of the Priestess in his place which slowly changes into the image of the Master of the Temple. Then do we understand that they only appeared to pass from our reach, for all the Guardians of the Mysteries are one Guardian and are ever with and about us.

Slowly the images fade and we become aware once more of our surroundings. The time has come for us to return to our outer world and we see that already our Companions are leaving the great cavern. We follow them back down the passageway and find ourselves once more passing through the small opening in the rock face out into the wood.

In quiet companionship we walk back down the mountainside enjoying the warmth of the sun now high above our heads. At last we reach the little bridge and the path back into the village. The Brethren have prepared a warm meal for us and it is not long before we seek our beds and drop gratefully into a warm secure sleep.

The night passes quickly, now we are aware of returning wakefulness, we feel our bodies welcome our return and awake from our long dream of an inner journey to full awareness of ourselves here in our twentieth century world in our own time and space.

Five

The Chapel is still and quiet about us, an oasis of calm in our hurried twentieth century world. As we relax and close our eyes the quiet steals over us and we feel at peace.

Slowly we drift into a deep quiet place where only vague shifting shapes fill our inner vision. Soft hues of colour dance and blend and as we watch the gentle movement lulls our senses deeper into a soft sense of peace.

Then in the centre of our vision a form takes shape, a

woman robed in midnight blue. Slowly the image deepens until we see before us the familiar form of the young maiden who serves the Priestess of the Island. The beauty of her face and the graceful lines of her body are just as we remember them. Her deep blue eyes watch us, waiting for our recognition. The faint hint of a smile spreads from eyes to lips and she raises her hand in greeting and welcome.

"The time has come for you to once more visit our Temple and to bring those new to your Company to join in our communion there" she says.

The shifting colours about her slowly steady and behind her grows a scene we recognise. A deep blue sky with small drifting clouds meets a white capped sea of even deeper blue and mighty waves rush onwards to the shore. Far on the horizon high mountains meet the clouds which wreath and dance about their peaks. To our left we see a small cove with a sand and shingle beach and then the air is full of the roar of the crashing sea as it spends its power in majestic curling breakers, foaming white and green, which seem to compete in reaching ever higher on the shore. Then to our right we see a flight of steep stone steps which go sharply upwards to a small round building set upon the pinnacle of a rocky promontory.

The Maiden beckons us then turns and slowly climbs the steps, pausing she turns and speaks to us again: "For those of you to whom this place is new, I would have you understand that the Temple to which I take you now has no form or substance in the worlds. Its walls are built of the Light of Thought and all that is most sacred to us all is held within its Sanctuary. Here Mind communes with Mind and we can touch the place where Wisdom dwells." Then turning she opens the door and bids us follow her. We enter the small building, our newcomers wondering how we will all find room within, but their eyes open wide in amazement at the immense hall in which we stand.

Before us the floor is decorated with intricate and beautiful mosaic of the constellations of the Zodiac and at either hand a wide and graceful staircase sweeps upwards, each curving towards the other as they disappear from sight far above us.

Again the Maiden explains - " In this place there are

no dimensions such as you know on Earth, here all things exist without limitation of time or space. You have but to think and it is so, you have but to desire and it is to see."

Following the Maiden we climb the left-hand staircase to a wide balcony Before us are golden doors on which are set in bold relief the figures of the great Archangels. On the right hand door are Raphael and Michael and on the left hand door Gabriel and Auriel. The mighty doors swing gently open and we follow the Priestess within.

Our senses swim with the almost overwhelming force of the vibrations within, the subtle perfume of incense, the glow of numberless candles and the dazzling brilliant light which radiates above the central Sanctuary. And such a sanctuary as we have never seen meets our dazzled eyes. Upon a raised dais stands a rectangular altar of purest crystal, cut and faceted so that the light from the candles dances from them in a thousand hues. At the four corners stand the figures of the Guardians of the Sanctuary in the form of the four Holy Creatures: a Man, a Lion, a Bull and an Eagle. So lifelike are they we do not know whether we are looking at carved statuary or indeed the living creatures. Above the Altar shines a brilliant blazing Light which seems to radiate into space from an invisible source, as a Star shining in the heavens. The Temple is immense, or rather there is space about us and we cannot perceive any walls which limit its extent. The air glows and shimmers about us and sweet sounds fill the air which are like no music we have heard on Earth.

Then in the West of the temple we see a mighty window which looks out on a vast panorama of sea and sky, blue and green the colours gleam and sinking in its depth the scarlet setting sun draws a path of gold across the sea from far horizon to the island shore. Then down this Path two figures come, walking side by side straight through the window into the Sanctuary.

A surge of joy sweeps over us as we recognise them - the Priestess of the West and the Master of the Temple. They are as we last saw them, transformed into Light, yet does our memory clothe them in the form we knew. For those who see them for the first time they take the form of those who come to us as Teachers in the Light. Then standing before the window they smile their welcome to us and both raise a hand in greeting to each one.

The Priestess speaks: "Greetings our Brothers and Sisters of another time. We welcome you once more to our Sanctuary. We have watched over your work since last we met and it is well. All ties of time and place are now healed and it is time for each one to go forward in the Light. Therefore we will give you further of our Teaching and our Blessing."

The Master of the Temple now steps forward and speaks: "Remember - all activity is spiritual activity and the centre of all spiritual activity is the One Self. The Limitless Light condensing Itself in a single Point, begins a whirling motion. The small Point is within. It is the Point of consciousness, the centre of expression for the ONE, the ALL. It is for every human being the point of contact with Absolute First Cause. This Indivisible ONE depends on nothing whatever. It itself does not act, but from It action proceeds, there is no limitation to its power to initiate cycles of expression. The Initiate is one whose Will aligns itself with, and becomes one with, the originating Will of the Universe, who has become a free channel for the expression of Omnipotent Spirit. This is your goal and your Path upon which we are ever your Guides and Counsellors - follow it well."

Then the Maiden comes to each of us in turn and taking our hand, leads us before the Priest and Priestess. We kneel before them and each in turn touches us in blessing. Then we are led quietly from the Sanctuary and make our way in silence out on to the balcony and down the stairs to the great hallway.

Here we pause for a few moments to collect our thoughts and take this experience deep into our inner selves.

The door stands open and slowly we walk through and back down the steps and become aware once more of the sound of the sea on the shore of the cove.

Our view becomes misty as if the sea spry fills the air with hazy light, then the mist thickens the colours swirl, then slowly clear and we become aware of ourselves sitting once more in our physical bodies here in our own time and space.

Six

The Chapel is still and quiet about us, an oasis of quiet in our hurried twentieth century world. As we relax and close our eyes the familiar appearance of the Chapel changes. The out-lines blur and blend and for a few moments, we feel disoriented and unsure of our surroundings. Then everything steadies and clears. We are still sitting in Rothley Temple but now the scene has changed. Bright banners hang above our heads and the walls gleam as new cut stone. In the East the Altar stands, but now draped in pure white and upon it two candles, one on either side of a silver chalice, undecorated but of such exquisite shape that we are dazzled by its beauty. Behind the Alter the form of the Chapel is difficult to see, there seems to be a misty haze through which we cannot quite be sure whether the walls are there or not. Then in the haze we slowly perceive two figures form, one on each side of the Altar. With deep joy we recognise the familiar forms of the Priestess and the Master of the Temple and feel their welcome as they notice each one of us.

On the left the Priestess stands, tall and full of grace, her white robe falling in gentle flowing folds about her, her long fair hair caught back and making long coils to her waist. Her dark, wise and very intelligent eyes survey us all.

On the right stands the Master of the Temple, a man of immense stature both of body and of bearing. He wears the brown robe and white tabard emblazoned with the Templar Cross and gives to this modest attire the dignity of the richest robe. Each raises a hand in greeting and in blessing, then the Priestess speaks: "We welcome you once more our Brothers and Sisters of Another Time and come to share your companionship upon this day. We bring you gifts to help you in your work and quest. These gifts are potent in the Inner Worlds and will give you strength and balance much needed for your future tasks.

When come the times, as come they will, when it seems your way is barred and every path is blocked with fences, too high for you to climb, or difficulties which cloud your view. Then take these gifts and from them draw the inspiration to renew your strength and feel within your hand the instrument with which to cut a new clear way, Come - receive them from our hands."

Then one by one we go forward to stand in front of the Priestess and the Priest. Clasping each other's hands they extend their other hand to us and bid us join with theirs. With beating hearts we place our hands in theirs and feel a vibrant Power pulse round the triangle we make. "Remember this" they say, then break the contact. The Priestess smiles at us, then holding her hands together she slowly extends them towards us and as she parts them, cupped between her palms there glows a brilliant sphere of Light, " Use this well and by its Light judge all that happens in your life. Look into its depth and you will see Truth and Understand." Thus saying she places the Sphere between our hands and we receive it and take it into ourselves.

Then at his command we turn and face the Priest and see he holds a Sword. The Light glitters and gleams upon the metal of the blade and makes it seem as if it were made of Living Flame. The Priest holds high the Sword above our heads and says "They who bear this Sword stand solitary in their strength. Yet is this not the loneliness of the outsider but the aloneness of those who lead and serve." Then lowering the sword, with a swift movement he turns it and offers it to us by the hilt. With slightly shaking hand we reach out to take it , for this sword is two edged and we wonder if we have the strength to carry it. "Use this with caution and hold the scales of judgement always in true balance," he says and places the sword in our hands. When each has received their gift and returned to their place the Priest and Priestess raise their hands in blessing and farewell. We hear their voices ring within our minds - " Walk in strength and remember who you are."

Then their image shivers, breaks and slowly fades, and we are alone once more within the Temple. We sit for a short time allowing the gifts we have been given to become absorbed and part of our being, then the Chapel shimmers and we are back in our twentieth century world in our own time and space.

Seven

The Chapel is still and quiet about us, an oasis of quiet in our hurried twentieth century world.

As we relax and close our eyes we let go of our outer world and begin to attune to the inner Temple which has built up for us in Rothley Chapel. Slowly the images rise. The walls of the Chapel gleam about us, the stone new cut and clear, and above our heads the bright banners hang. In the East the Altar stands, now draped in pure white and upon it two candles, one on either side of a silver Chalice, undecorated but of such exquisite shape we catch our breath at its beauty.

To the right of the Altar we notice a mistiness through which we cannot quite discern the details of the wall. Then almost as if he has walked through the solid stone, the Master of the Temple is standing there, tall and powerful in the brown robe and white tabard of his Templar Office. Slowly he walks to the front of the Altar and surveys us all.

"Greetings once more my Brothers and Sisters of another time" he says. "I come to-day to aid you in your work and give to you some guidance for your thoughts. As you well know my tradition is one of both spirituality and military strength. These things do not seem to be compatible to those who see spirituality only as the path of prayer and meditation. But I say to you that spirituality is in every aspect of our life within the world and our inner life must be the font from which our strength and action springs so that our whole life becomes the basis of our spirits growth.

For each one of us the wheel turns each time we come into incarnation and we will walk each pathway that the Earth can give. For some the warrior's way is long in the past and it may be we walked it side by side and shared its horrors - and its glories too.

The Warrior's Way may, in action, be the way of peace, but peace held only through the strength of arms held ever in readiness to defend. The warrior too controls his fate in life and is the master of his material world. When Man first walked the world and Earth was young the instinct of survival made defence of himself, his territory and his family a vital part of his experience. The tools of Earth, the stones and wood of trees were weapons to his hand. Then Man discovered Fire and by its aid, forged mighty swords to keep his freedom safe. Thus is Fire the symbol both of our life force and of its defender and destroyer.

It is the responsibility of the Initiates of the Mysteries to hold the Sword of Fire, to wield it in defence of freedom of body, mind and soul, and to use it always in justice and purity of purpose." Thus saying he extends his hand in blessing towards us and slowly fades from our view.

We think deeply on his words and see that the violence of battle is indeed sometimes necessary to defend the Light.

Then as we watch the Chapel darkens as if night fast approaches, until in a few minutes we are unable to discern any of its features. Perhaps we are no longer in the Chapel? We look up and the darkness is just as deep, then far above we see tiny specks of light and realise we are gazing upwards into the starry night sky. A figure forms among the stars and we sense rather than see the figure of the Priestess arched across the sky. The stars are shining jewels amidst her hair and on her brow sits, like a diadem, the crescent moon. We look about us and realise we are floating just above a dark and silent sea. The waves below us gently rise and fall and the reflection of the crescent Moon grows larger and larger in our view as the Priestess bends down and folds us in her arms.

In soft and gentle voice she speaks and we hear it like a whisper in our ear. "Remember that all things flow like the tides and seasons of the sea," she says. "Be not too quick to wield the Sword of Fire but look also to the waters of compassion and the endless tides which ebb and flow through humanity and nature. Remember for every warrior who falls in battle a hundred weep in desolation at their loss. To destroy is easy yet the work of one moment's strife is instantly beyond recall. Look only to destroy that which you can undertake to re-create."

We briefly feel the touch of her hand upon our head in blessing then she too fades and vanishes from our view.

We feel alone and somewhat sad and desolate at the feelings and thoughts she leaves behind. We look up once more into the dark sky and watch the twinkling lights of the stars. Then it seems the stars grow bigger and bigger in our view until we are surrounded by their light. Then each one takes on shape and we realise that their light concealed the form of one of our Companions, we reach out our hands and clasp that of the Companion nearest us. The ring of well-known faces grows and a surge of love and companionship sweeps over us and its force rushes round the circle we have formed. We let the energy throb through us all and feel our strength grow and our minds expand. We are part of an eternal company, we are companions upon a vast adventure amid the stars and we will be together until the journeys end. This knowledge starts to sing a song of joy within us and its melody and rhythm swell out over sea and sky until we have become one with Creation.

Slowly the song fades into silence and we see above the horizon the first gleam of the returning sun. As it climbs into the sky we find ourselves once more in the full light of day and become aware once more of the Chapel image and then reality about us where we sit in our physical bodies here in our own time and space.

Eight

The Chapel is still and quiet about us, a haven of quiet in our hurried twentieth century world. We see about us the familiar Officers of the Ritual and the colours and lights of the candles. Then we close our eyes and begin to tune in to the Chapel on a deeper inner level. This Chapel is still familiar to us for we have visited it many times in our past path-workings. The only difference from the physical Chapel is that we see everything in the strange light of the inner worlds.

The sunlight is shining through the windows in the East and forming patterns of colour on the stone floor. Then, as we look upwards at the windows, the light seems to grow brighter and brighter, it elongates until it fills all of the eastern wall - the light is so bright we can hardly bear to look. Then slowly two mighty doors form in the light and as we watch they swing gently open on an inner landscape. Before us we see a broad green valley with a meandering river flowing down its centre. It is spring time, all is green and fresh and beautiful. On either side of the river are lush meadows bordered by woodlands which slowly thin as the land rises to soft rounded hills. The morning sun shines brilliantly directly before us, bathing the whole landscape in its glory, its power is irresistible and we find ourselves drawn forward towards the great doors. We hesitate upon the threshold feeling we should not enter without invitation, then a voice sounds within our heads which tells us this land is open to all, we are part of it as it is part of us. Reassured and with joy in our hearts, we pass between the doors and find ourselves in a little valley. At our feet a small stream flows over shining rocks, little fish dart in and out of the shadows, and the sound of the rippling water fills the air. Just above where we stand, the stream comes tumbling over a small waterfall.

We climb the short rise and follow the stream as it winds its way deeper into the valley. Gradually the valley narrows until we come face to face with a high cliff. There is an opening in the rock face from which the stream flows and hoping to find the source of the stream we step into what is little more than a crack in the rock, its walls press close about us - rough and moist to the touch. After a few moments our eyes become accustomed to the dim light, enough to enable us to see we are in a short natural tunnel, it is only about nine feet long and at the far end we can just see a dim light. Curiosity spurs us on to explore further and we cautiously walk forward towards the light- to emerge into a high cavern. It is circular in shape and the roof towers some thirty feet above our heads. In the roof is an opening through which a beam of brilliant sunlight streams down to illuminate a great stone slab which stands in the centre of the cavern. The slab is shaped like a triangular table held up by three supporting stones and on it lies a sword in an ornately embroidered scabbard. All is in shadow in the cavern apart from the sunlight on the stone, and the only sound is the drip and ripple of the water of the stream. Then there is a sudden sound, someone is there in the darkness, we feel a presence - but before we can feel alarmed our attention is caught by the sword lying on the stone. Surely we were mistaken - but no, the sword DID move. Then from the shadows comes a young girl, her green and blue dress clinging about her as if she has just emerged from water. She pays no attention to our presence and we realise she is the spirit of the cavern and this is her domain. The sword by now has risen a good two feet above the stone and as we watch it begins to turn, the girl reaches out and draws off the scabbard to reveal the shining blade. Now the sword is upright as if an invisible hand held it by the hilt, it hovers in the air then begins to move. Fascinated we watch its progress then find ourselves following just a few feet behind it as it moves across the cavern, illuminating our way as it does so. We are led deeper and deeper into the hill until at last we come into another cavern. This place is no longer dark but glows with phosphorescent colours. In this strange light we see the figure of a man seated on a stone throne, his dress is of a time long past. He wears a loose chain mail over rough woollen shirt and trousers, a dark purple cloak hangs from his shoulders and ranged about him are the weapons of the warrior and the emblems of sovereignty. He stretches out his hand and the sword somersaults in the air and then in a flash the hilt is grasped firmly in the man's hand. He looks straight at us and smiles, a strange enigmatic smile which nevertheless succeeds in putting us at our ease. It is on the tip of our tongue to pour out a steam of questions - but we feel just a little too much in awe of him for that. As if he had read our thoughts and knows quite well what we wish to ask he starts to speak. "I am he whom men call the Sleeping King, I am the Guardian and Defender of the Land. I am its strength and its vitality. In my hand is the sword of truth and justice which brings light into the dark places. When the attacker strikes then will my sword be strong and mighty to restore peace and rightful rule. When evil ones threaten then will my sword be as a scythe for their pruning. I sleep only in your peace, yet is my dreaming a watchfulness and a waiting for your need. In your knowledge of my being is my power and in your action is the security of my rest. Go forth and be my Watchers."

So saying he beckons us forward and as each approaches and falls upon one knee, he touches us upon the head with his sword. As he does so a spark of light leaps from the sword and shoots down through our bodies. We rise knowing ourselves empowered and changed. As the last one rises the Sleeping King opens his hand and the sword leaps forward into the air resuming its role of guide. Dazed, we follow its light down dark passageways until at last we emerge once more through a fissure in the rock and find ourselves standing on the hillside in bright sunlight.

To our right is a meadow filled with long grass which waves gently in the slight breeze. Grazing in the meadow is a white mare, she looks up, sees us and whinnies softly then trots towards us. She is not very large, in fact little more than a large pony, but strong and well made with a full coat and long shaggy mane. In the strange way of the inner worlds we each feel as if we alone mount the white mare and yet that we are still in company. No sooner are we astride the mare than she gallops off down the valley, we hurriedly clasp our arms about her neck and hold tight to her mane. Faster and faster we ride - then we are not riding on the ground any more - we are climbing higher and higher and the ground recedes and we see the scenery flashing by.

Below us we see fields and rivers, villages and farms, in the distance the hazy mass of a town, there are hills and valleys, all crystal clear to view yet blending into a panorama of the land below. Then we can see a coastline, the sun reflecting on a still calm sea and a large rocky island just off the shore. There is a building of some sort on the island, it is like a small castle or a village enclosed within strong surrounding walls. Then we realise we are descending and as we land our mount vanishes leaving us standing in the middle of a large courtyard filled with a medley of people - dogs, hens and ducks - and many other animals, trees and plants, like a market within the castle.

We wend our way through the crowd which is large and cheerful and nobody pays us any attention at all. There is an archway in one of the buildings leading through to some steps, we hesitate trying to work out which way to go. There is somewhere in the buildings we need to be but we cannot see the way to get there or even why we need to find it. But we are not left long in doubt; a woman comes towards us down the steps and beckons us to follow her. We feel relieved to do so and find ourselves led through spacious rooms and hidden courtyards until at last we arrive at the door of a small stone building. Our guide gestures for us to enter. We do so and find ourselves in a beautiful Chapel. It is all decorated with flowers and fruits, tall bundles of wheat and many other gifts of nature. A woman, robed and crowned, kneels before the central altar which holds only a plain earthen chalice. We wait in silence until at last the woman rises and smiles at us. Taking the chalice in both hands she comes towards us, then in a deep and melodious voice she say; "Welcome my children. I am the Lady of the Land, wife to the Sleeping King. I bring life and fertility to all, in my hands is the care of all living things and the blessings of all nature. Come my children, drink of my cup that it may impart my love and healing through you to Earth and all humankind." So saying she blesses the chalice then lifts it in both hands and offers it to each of us.

As we drink its contents it tastes like sweet warm honey and we are aware of its glow of love and warmth spreading out through every part of our being. The glow does not fade but remains as a source of light within us. But as we look up we see that it is the Lady who is fading, she no longer seems real and is becoming just a shimmering image - almost an illusion. Then she is gone and only the memory of our experience remains. The chapel is still and quiet and as we look towards the brilliant light flooding through the east windows we see a pair of mighty doors slowly forming. We walk towards them and see beyond our familiar Rothley Chapel. We walk through the doors and find ourselves back in our bodies in our own world in our own time and space.

Nine: The Element of Air

The Chapel is still and quiet about us, a haven of quiet in our hurried twentieth century world. We see about us the familiar Officers of the Ritual and the colours and lights of the candles. Then we close our eyes and begin to tune in to the Chapel on a deeper inner level. This Chapel is still familiar to us for we have visited it many times in our past path-workings. The only difference from the physical Chapel is that we see everything in the strange light of the inner worlds.

The sunlight is shining through the windows in the East and forming patterns of colour on the stone floor. Then as we look upwards at the windows the light seems to grow brighter and brighter, it elongates until it fills all of the eastern wall - the light is so bright we can hardly bear to look. Then slowly two mighty doors form in the light and as we watch they swing gently open on an inner landscape.

We are standing on a shingle beach, it is late evening and only the last faint glow of twilight still lingers in the sky. The sea is breaking in small wavelets at our feet with just a faint and whispering sound. We see the narrow line of foam at the water's edge as the swell gently breaks on the shore. Above our heads there are great clouds sailing slowly and majestically against the ever darkening sky. Then, from behind one of the clouds the Moon appears, it is full and shining brilliantly. Then as the clouds pass over, one by one the stars appear until the whole heavens are gleaming in a vast canopy of twinkling light. We look out across the surface of the sea and see the whole splendour of the heavens reflected in its surface. A second Moon dances in the water and we stare down at it fascinated by its motion created by the restless sea. Then suddenly we are no longer standing on the beach but falling into the image of the Moon, the stars whirling about us in a mighty Cosmic dance. Straight into the light of the Moon we fall, but we do not hit a hard surface as we land, there is no gravity and we float gently as if caught within a bubble which supports and holds us. "Greetings my children" says a strange deep voice. We look about us to see who spoke, there is nobody, yet the voice seemed to come from just below us. "You are most welcome to my element" continues the Voice. Then just below us we notice a large Eagle which dips and weaves in harmony with the bubble in which we are floating. Surely it was not the Eagle who spoke? "Of course it was," the Voice answers our thought. "When you come visiting the inner worlds you must expect the unexpected. I am here to help you to experience the power and the wonder of the air, to show you the freedom of riding on the wind and to introduce you to some of my Brethren. Come, lie along my back and spread your arms along my wings, blend with me and we will fly the west wind."

Obeying his instructions we begin to feel the air supporting us, the movement of each feather as his wings beat to take the extra weight. Then we are soaring high into the sky, we meet a thermal of warm air and shoot upwards, faster and faster with an exciting and exhilarating speed. Then just as suddenly the temperature changes and down we swoop, the earth hurtling towards us at an alarming speed, but our Eagle gives a strong beat of his wings and our flight straightens then climbs once more. "The West Wind is sister to the element of water" says our Eagle, "hold tight now for there is a storm coming, the elements are not always calm and gentle, they can be fierce and savage also." No sooner has he given us the warning than we notice dark storm clouds gathering on the western horizon, the breeze begins to freshen then swiftly gathers strength, our Eagle turns his flight so that he is flying with the wind. We are caught in a wild turbulence, then the rain begins and we surrender to the excitement of the storm. We climb, and fall, are tossed and turned about and the wild song of the wind is all about us, we feel its irresistible strength and power. Slowly the storm passes and we can see the earth beneath us once more. The gale has carried us far to the East but also North. Below us now are snow-capped mountains whose sides are clothed in dark pine forests. "This is not my territory," the Eagle informs us with a not very pleased note in his voice. " I will leave you to the care of my Brother the Snow Goose and he will show you how to ride the North Wind." Before we have time to either thank him or say good-bye we find our companion has changed. Our arms are clasped around the neck of a beautiful snow goose, pure white feathers beneath our fingers and a different rhythm to our flight. "Welcome to my territory," says the Snow Goose in a silent communication which rings in our thoughts.

"The North Wind is Sister to the element of Earth, hold tight now and we will see how they work together." Once more we are flying swiftly but now with a strong steady beat of heavy wings. Below us are high mountains cleft by deep ravines, we swoop down and the Snow Goose bids us notice the strange shapes of the rocks which look as though they were carved into fantastic whirls and slender pinnacles. He tell us that this is the work of the North Wind through countless storms and soft persistent breezes. Then we are flying over a vast white wonderland of snow and ice. But it is not just flat; beautiful castles of ice tower into the air, high walls of snow twist and turn in endless convolutions with tops which curve over in gravity defying scrolls, mighty swords of ice rise from sculptured hands - and all the work of the wind carving with ice and snow. Over all the low winter sun shines, striking diamonds and rainbow colours which shift and change with every movement of our flight. We are quite overwhelmed by the beauty of it all. Then we feel a change in our flight, the wind has strengthened and we are aware that our Snow Goose is changing direction. We turn into the wind as it grows to a howling gale and snow whips up into a blinding blizzard which whites out the world, we ride on its force and are carried swiftly southwards.

At last the storm abates and we are flying once more in calm air. The cold is far behind and we see below us the vast waters of the southern seas. So engrossed had we been in riding the storm that we had not noticed a change in our guardian. Still the feathers are a snowy white but now the wings which bear us onward have a mighty span, the neck we clasp is shorter and we can just see a massive curved beak which looks fierce enough to deal with even the largest fish. As if he sensed our recognition of him our guide thinks his welcome to us. "I am the Wandering Albatross and the southern seas are my home, only rarely do I come to land, for I am the companion of the mariner and the restless voyager of the oceans. The South Wind is the sister of the element of fire for she brings warmth on her breath, yet too is she the mother of hurricane and typhoon. Life and destruction she bears in her wings, gentle and fierce are her ways for she is searing heat in the desert and summers blessings in the fertile lands. But the sea is her constant home and the source of her power." For a long time we fly with the Albatross and experience all the moods of the South Wind, from the soft gentle breeze to the unearthly calm in the eye of the tropical storm. We are carried at last far to the East and the Albatross tells us that he must return south once more but that he will leave us in the care of the guardian of the East Wind. Then he is gone and we think we must go crashing to the earth for it seems we are no longer supported. But it is not so, beneath our hands are soft grey feathers and we have adjusted ourselves to the size of our new guardian and a small grey Dove bears us on. High into a bright morning sky we climb on the wings of a light and pleasant breeze. Beneath our hands we feel the heart-beat of the Dove and deep within our minds we hear her welcome and her love. "The East Wind is Sister to the Element of Air ", she thinks to us, " it is stillness and storm, the icy blast of winter and the cool air which brings relief to high summer's heat. Breathe deeply of this clear fresh air which is the fuel of your life force, the sustainer and restorer of all life forms upon the planet." We do as we are bid and feel new energy and vitality course through our being. The Dove is now flying due east and ahead of us we see the morning Sun rising over the horizon. As we fly it climbs higher and higher into the sky. Then we are going straight into its Light, larger and larger, brighter and brighter it becomes until there is nothing else in our vision. We are completely dazzled and illuminated by it. Then within the light of the Sun two mighty doors slowly form and we recognise them as our entry back into our own world and physical bodies in Rothley Temple. Go through the doors and become aware of your body closing around you. The light of the Sun is still flooding your consciousness and your recent experience of Air is sharp and clear in your memory. The Light begins to contract, it becomes smaller and smaller until it is like a small brilliant star in the centre of your head. Let this become absorbed into your consciousness as a gift from the Element of Air which you can recall whenever you wish to do so. Now become fully awake and open your physical eyes and be back in Rothley Temple.

Ten: The Element of Water

The Chapel is still and quiet about us, a haven of quiet in our hurried twentieth century world.

As we relax and close our eyes we see before us a light mist which swirls slightly as if in a slight breeze and glows with light as if the sun were just about to break through the mist.

As we watch we see a small movement deep in the mist which slowly forms itself into a figure walking towards us. With a leap of joy deep within us, we recognise the tall slender figure of the Priestess, her long golden hair swings out behind her and is lifted in rippling waves by the gentle wind. She wears a gown of soft floating material in a colour which is a mixture of the soft blue of the summer sea and the green of the first leaves of spring. As she draws near to us she smiles in recognition then holds out a slender hand to us and beckons us to follow her.

We walk forward into the mist, hastening our pace as the Priestess seems about to disappear from view. Then the mist suddenly clears and we are standing on a long sandy beach a few feet from the water's edge. The sea rolls towards the shore in white capped waves which glitter in the bright sunlight. It looks so inviting we want to plunge into the water and let it refresh and cleanse us. But the Priestess calls to us and beckons us to follow her. She leads us over the beach towards a rocky cliff, then round a large rock - and there before us is the opening to a cave. Without pausing the Priestess enters the cave and disappears from our sight. It is dark and cool within the cave and yet in a strange way we can see the black rock of the walls and the sandy pebbled floor beneath our feet. Deeper and deeper we go into the cave which has narrowed now into a passageway we can just touch on either side. We walk for what seems a long time, then ahead in the gloom we see a small light which becomes a high curved opening into the light as we approach. Then we are once more in the open air and the Priestess is just ahead of us, she half turns and smiles at us over her shoulder then walks on. We are on another beach which curves away on our left. To our right it is short and ends in a narrow channel of sea which ebbs and flows over a rocky floor. On the other side of the channel is the small beach and green grass of an island.

The Priestess stands at the water's edge and calls us to her. We gather about her, eager to see what she will show us. She bends in a swift graceful movement and splashes her hands in the sea, sprinkling the water over us as she straightens. She laughs as we shake the droplets from our hair. Then lifting her hand she points out to sea "Look well" she says " there is my domain in the West, the vast waters of the endless sea; the life blood of planet Earth. The rains are but the tears torn from her heart by the fierce hand of the storm and the rivers naught but their swift flowing home. I am the daughter of the sea and Priestess of the Waters, mine are the rites of her marriage with the Sun; I it is who govern the Mysteries of the birth and the death of her children, the rivers, the streams and the pools. Sacred is her life giving power, for she is the womb of all life and the sustainer thereof." As she falls silent we hold our breath, caught in the magic of the moment. Then a slight breeze ripples across the water and gently lifts the Priestess's hair as if in caress and acknowledgement of her reverence.

The Priestess turns and gives us a small smile then steps into the water and walks across the channel onto the island. We follow her. The moment we feel the island beneath our feet we know it for a sacred place. Energy seems to flow upwards from the land and the sense of Presence is strong and clear. It enfolds each one of us, taking us into its own space and dimension.

The Power of the land and the magic of the elements is all about us, we feel ourselves swept up in the dreamlike quality of the experience of the island. Our feet flow over the grass finding no fatigue or difficulty in climbing the hills, it is as if we are born onwards by an energy greater than our own.

The island is not large and we soon come to its highest point from which viewpoint we can see the pathways which criss-cross it and the many small bays and beaches of its coastline. As we descend once more we are surprised to see a small copse of trees which we had not previously noticed. Perhaps they too are part of the magic of the island. Indeed it may well be so for the Priestess is standing waiting for us just within the shadows of the trees. Though not very tall they are of a dense dark green foliage through which the sunlight only fitfully filters. The Priestess leads us along a narrow path which seems to go on for far longer than we would have thought possible from our first view of the wood. Then we emerge from the gloom of the trees to find ourselves in a clearing in which there is a green mound about thirty feet high. The path passes round the base of the mound - then sheer enchantment meets our eyes. Before us is a small dell in which grows every kind of wild and cultivated flower in a dazzling medley of natural beauty. In the centre of the dell is a grotto of old, wind shaped stone. The Priestess comes and invites each of us in turn to enter. We pass through the hanging vines, honeysuckle and deep purple clematis which serves for a doorway. Within it is cool and quiet. At our feet there is a small pool which is fed from a crystal clear stream which bubbles straight from the rock face and ripples down a short waterfall. The Priestess points to a flat stone near the edge of the pool and bids us kneel and look into the water. "Look well and long," she says, "for in this mirror of the Waters you may see much that you desire to know. Look well and remember what you see, for the Powers of Light speak thus to humankind and you will see that which it is fit that you should know. Look well - and remember". (Pause)

The images shimmer and dissolve and we are once more looking down into the pool. As we rise to our feet the Priestess is beside us, her hand resting lightly on our shoulder. "Now is the time to pay homage to our Mother," she says, "you will return to your own time and place through the pool. Have no fear for you will swim as a fish and be at one with the water as if it were your own natural element." So saying she gives us a slight push and we fall into the water. The slight chill makes us gasp, then the water is above our heads and we find we are swimming quite naturally. A kick and we fly through the water, a turn of the head and we change direction. This wonderful underwater world is totally magical. We dart between the swaying seaweed, catch fishes in our hands and feel them slip through our fingers and away, chase crabs and lobsters across the sandy floor of the pool and marvel at the endless variety of life and colour of this underwater world.

Then the Priestess is with us in the form of a beautiful mermaid, her golden hair rippling out behind her as she swims. We know we are to follow her once more. She leads us to the side of the pool, then dives to the bottom and slips through a narrow opening. We follow and after a very short time we find ourselves out in the ocean. Different fishes swim with us here, then a large dolphin appears and we clasp hold of a fin and we are taken on an exhilarating ride back to the shore. The dolphin leaves us in the shallow water and we splash and half swim to the beach, clumsy in our return to human form. We walk back up the beach, our clothes drying swiftly in the hot sun, then a light mist begins to blow off the land and the scene shifts and changes before our eyes.

Outlined against the mist is the figure of the Priestess, the light forms a halo about her and the water droplets in the air scatter the light and create a rainbow of colours which shimmer and dance for several feet around her. The sight is so beautiful we stand spellbound watching her. Then we see she is holding a beautiful crystal chalice in her hands, she bids us approach and as we do so, we too become enveloped in the rainbow colours. "Come, drink of the Waters of Life," she says, holding out the chalice towards us. "This Cup is ever full, its water flows from the heart of creation, it is cleansing and healing, it is the solace of sorrow and the fountain of joy".

She holds out the Cup once more and each of us in turn goes forward and drinks from the Cup in her hands. The cool fresh water tastes of mountain springs and sweet summer rains. It feels clean and wholesome in our mouths and then its vitality courses through every particle of our being as if it were living fire. When each has drunk their fill the Priestess turns and gives the Cup into unseen hands. Then facing us once more she lifts both arms in blessing, then becomes one with the Light and disappears.

We walk into the mist and find ourselves back at the entrance to the cave. We enter and slowly make our way back along the rock passageway. At last we emerge into the mist at the other end, we walk forward then watch it slowly clear and we return back into our physical bodies in Rothley Temple where we sit quietly in meditation allowing this experience to become part of our consciousness.

Eleven

The Temple is still and quiet about us, an oasis of quiet in our hurried twentieth century world. As we relax and close our eyes we feel ourselves sinking deeper and deeper into a warm, comfortable, relaxed feeling which seems to enfold and surround us. There is no form to this place in which we float, it is almost as if we are sinking down through the ocean, supported and safe within this strangely familiar element.

We do not seem to have any physical form here, we just ARE. As we look about us seeking our companions we see only bright sparks, like stars in a midnight sky, floating about us and keeping pace with us as we drift softly downwards. Then we realise that we too are just another spark in this glittering company.

Then, as if we are caught in a strong current within this mysterious sea, we feel ourselves change direction. Faster and faster we go, swept irresistibly on within the current. Then suddenly we break through the surface of the ocean and in a mighty fountain of shooting stars we are thrown out into the vast darkness of cosmic space. Yet this is not the space of our material universe, it is pulsing with energy and constantly moving and changing. We too flow with its power. In a strange way we feel totally at home here.

Then, from each of the four corners of this Universe, we sense rather than see, four mighty Beings speeding towards us on wings of flame. So brilliant are they, it is as if four great suns illumine the heavens and we are bathed in their glory.

The four Beings meet and then stretch out their hands to each other to form a circle of intense light. As we watch a sphere forms in the centre of the circle and to our amazement we see an image form within the sphere - it is a child, perfectly formed and full ready for its birth..

Stranger still we realise that we and the child are one, we are looking at the very beginnings of our own physical vehicle.

As we watch the child stirs, the sphere turns, and together we begin to swirl round and round in a dizzying dance through the space of becoming.

Suddenly the scene changes and we find ourselves in a place which is half Temple, half workshop. The floor is made of black and white squares and if we could but count them they number the days of our life which is about to begin. In the centre of the Temple stands an altar, but this is no earthy altar for it is also a work table and a creative cauldron. Before the altar stands a workman who is busily employed in making a beautiful sword over the creative fire which burns within the cauldron.

Behind the workman we notice a pair of heavy dark doors surmounted by arches of elaborately worked stone. Then one of the doors swings open and from it steps the figure of a Priestess, clothed in white, her golden hair falling about her in cascading waves of shimmering light. She smiles at us in greeting then steps forward to stand beside the workman who turns and gives the sword into her hand.

The Priestess bids us come forward and with a graceful gesture turns the sword and holds it out for us to take. As our hand closes over it the Priestess tells us that this is the Sword of Will, that with it we may fashion and rule our coming life. She bids us use it well and to remember that, since it is given of the Gods, it is too our protector but also our destroyer should we misuse its power.

Now the workman hands her a golden staff which she gives to us with the warning that while it carries the power to bestow worldly authority it also can corrupt and blind us to the true purpose of our life.

Then the Priestess turns and from the northern altar of the Temple she brings a chalice from which a golden stream bubbles yet never falls. She bids us take the chalice and drink from it, telling us that it is the cup of human happiness and pleasure. She tells us that the cup is always ours to drink from and only by our own actions can we cause it to turn bitter and run dry.

Now the workman hands the Priestess a silver platter on which are three perfect golden spheres, she holds out the platter towards us and we gaze at the spheres in fascination. Again as we watch an image forms within the sphere and we see once again the babe awaiting birth. Then within the other two spheres we see the images of our Parents of this lifetime, young and fresh as they were when they brought us through into manifestation. For a time we watch them as they change and we review our feelings towards them and then see them as two individuals like ourselves with their own path to tread and their own mistakes to make and lessons to learn. For the first time we see them, not as our parents but as a Brother and Sister with whom we have long links of lifetimes shared. The Priestess smiles at our absorption in the images then tells us to remember the lessons which this vision has taught us. She says too that we should learn also from this insight that we have been looking at the most potent and powerful combination in the whole of Creation. For three is the number of creation. Just as two parents bring forth a child so also is everything which exists the result of two causes blending. With this Key, she tells us, we can unlock many Mysteries.

The Priestess lays the platter of the spheres upon the altar and takes between her hands the sphere in which we saw the vision of the babe. She bids us gaze upon it until the image is once more clear, then holds out her hands and places the sphere between our waiting palms. We clasp the sphere tightly and hold it close knowing that it contains our future as well as our past.

The sphere expands and seems to take us in, then we are once more floating deep in space. And then we see the four mighty Beings of Light still holding hands below us, but now in their midst we see the Earth, our home planet, shining like a jewel among the stars.

The Beings begin to spin, faster and faster round the Earth until at last the circle breaks and we are looking down at a silver Moon which shines down on our planet home. As sparks of Light we blend into the Moon's light and slide down a moonbeam back to Earth to find ourselves standing in a woodland glade. About us the trees are decked in the freshness of spring's new growth. Beneath our feet the grass is tender sweet and green. Everything is fresh and new and full of promise of new life. We too feel new born and full of eagerness to meet the coming days.

A soft sound makes us turn to see a woman walking towards us through the trees, her long gown of green and brown making her seem almost a part of the land. She smiles in greeting and as we look into her eyes we recognise the Giver of our Gifts. She signs for us to gather about her, then she tells us that the journey we have just taken and the visions which we have seen are also a precious gift which we should treasure and use well, they are an insight into the meaning and purpose of our lives. Then she reminds us that the Guardians we have seen are ever present near the Earth to support and protect us as we go through the experiences of life. She tells us to call on them should we have need for we are children of the Cosmos and in their care.

We bow our heads for her blessing and when we open our eyes once more we are alone in the wood. There is a small pathway which leads out of the clearing and we feel impelled to follow it. It is a pleasant and relaxing walk through the wood and we enjoy the sights and sounds of spring and all the life about us. At last the path opens out into a meadow and we see before us the familiar sight of Rothley Temple. We approach the Chapel door and quietly enter the Chapel and then return to our physical bodies and become fully awake in our own time and space.

Twelve

The Chapel is still and quiet about us, a haven of quiet in our hurried twentieth century world.

As we close our eyes and begin to relax a light mist begins to form in front of us.

You walk slowly forward into the mist curious to see what it will reveal. From above your head a narrow sunbeam begins to shine, it penetrates the mist which slowly dissolves and disappears in the suns warmth. Before you are two large vertical stones. They are about six feet tall and four feet apart. They stand like a gateway into another world. But the way is barred to you by two heavy staves which are crossed between the stones. Obeying an inner prompting you walk forward and place your hands upon the staves and with an authority which surprises you command them to allow you entry in the name of the Light. The staves fall to the ground and you walk forward between the stones.

You find yourself in a lush landscape, you are standing in a meadow bright with summer flowers and here and there is the pleasant shade of ancient trees. As you look about you and take in the beauty of this place you see that you are not alone, all your Companions from the Chapel have also arrived in the meadow.

They are walking away into a small wood over to your left and you hasten to follow them. The shade is pleasant as you enter the trees and almost too soon for your liking, you have emerged again on the other side of the wood. Before you the ground rises into a small but steep hill. You can see the others already ahead of you climbing the hill and realise they are making for the top where you can just see the heads of a ring of tall standing stones.

Gathering your energy you begin the climb, hastening a little to try to catch up with the others. The effort makes your legs ache and your breathing somewhat laboured - but at last the final effort brings you to the top.

The ring of stones is small but very beautiful, the stones are tall and slim and of a beautiful dark grey-blue colour with little shining specks of quartz which glisten like diamonds in the bright sunlight. Everyone is gathered in front of two particular stones which are obviously marking the entrance to the circle. As you watch a tall robed figure begins to take shape between the stones, he wears a long brown robe and his face is concealed behind the folds of his hood. He gestures you to enter the circle and you walk forward between the stones into the circle. But it is not a circle of stones which you have entered.

Before you is a magnificent Temple, it is open to the sky and formed only by four majestic pillars which stand one at each corner, towering upwards towards the heavens. The floor is made of black and white marble squares which are cool beneath your feet. In the centre of the Temple is an altar which looks as if it is made of black obsidian with silver veins which run through it like comet trails across a midnight sky. Upon the altar burns a sacred flame which flickers and dances as if alive.

But it is the atmosphere of the Temple which impresses itself most deeply on your consciousness. It is ancient and familiar, alien yet known, and above all it is sacred and holy.

In the East of the Temple sits a figure; he too wears a simple brown robe but the hood is thrown back and we can study the face of this man. He is of mature years yet strongly built and has an air of intense vigour about him. His short beard is well trimmed and only slightly tinged with grey. He raises a hand and gestures for us to come closer. Everyone goes forward in a group to stand before him - in curiosity and not a little awe. Suddenly he smiles in welcome and any fear is instantly dispersed. His eyes are grey and very very wise - they seem to see right down into the deepest corners of your mind. The Master of the Temple rises and as he does so we see he holds a mighty sword before him. His hands rest lightly on the hilt of the sword and its tip rests upon the white square at his feet. Then he begins to speak;

"Brothers and Sisters of another time, I bid you welcome. I greet you as fellow workers in the service of the Light. My time is now long past and even my work at this level of being is drawing to a close. I greet you as the heirs to the Tradition which I served and builders of the vessels through which its future now must flow. You stand before a doorway between that which is not and that which is to be. I know you think you are not worthy of the task but the greatest Temples are built on one small stone. To make a start is to set your feet towards the goal. Be clear and sure in your intent, then build steadily and proceed with care and caution but a brave heart. Be steadfast in your purpose and proceed with wisdom. You are the parents of the future time and upon your dependability and dedication rests the perpetuation of our Truth and Light. This Sword is fashioned for the coming time – re-forged in Fire for the era now to be. Defender and Servant of Light, it is born of courage and tempered with will. Into your care I pass its future, Warriors of the Spirit, you who are both magicians and guardians, wield its power well in defence of right and the causes of the Light."

He looks straight into your eyes and holds out the sword towards you, you hesitate but his gaze demands your response and you go forward to take the sword from him. It is heavy in your hands and you feel the weight also of the task which lies ahead.

The Master of the Temple holds out his hand in blessing, you bow your head and receive it like a great charge of energy. Then when you lift your head once more - he is gone.

You turn to leave the Temple and see that now there is a figure seated in the West between the Pillars. It is a woman robed in blue. Her face is silver veiled and yet you can just see the long golden hair which flows about her and your heart leaps to think her face would not be unknown if you should see behind the veil. In her hand she holds an ancient scroll and with the other she beckons you come near. You stand before her, bowing your head in homage and leaning lightly upon the sword in your hands. The Priestess bids you come closer then holds out the scroll towards you and speaks:

"Bearer of the Sword of Truth and Will, look well upon this scroll. Within it are contained the secret Teachings of all Time, these are the words of power which will light the future way. Look deep within your mind and you may read its Mystery. Temper the sword with knowledge and mercy and build with wisdom."

The Priestess holds out her hand in blessing and again you bow your head and feel her compassion and her love flow over you. When once more you raise your eyes she too is no longer there. Within your heart there is a sadness and yet an exhilaration and a great hope for the new direction and work of the future years. You turn and going to the altar, place the sword there by the sacred Light, knowing you may return and claim it at any time you have need of it.

Then without another look back you leave the Temple and find yourself once more outside the ring of stones. But now night has fallen and the stones glimmer in the soft light of the crescent moon which shines brightly among the stars. Slowly and carefully you descend the hill to find a swift flowing river beyond which lies your path of return. The waters of this river carry no threat to you, they are refreshing and rejuvenating. The land on the other side of the river is a new world waiting to be discovered and conquered; new work waiting to be done. The land beyond offers new opportunities and new successes - the work of the world goes on. With courage and determination you plunge into the river, only to find you do not need to swim and the water is pleasant and easy to wade through. At last you reach the further shore and the familiar Path which leads back through the wood to your own world. You realise that your Companions are still about you, you all join hands and in continuing companionship walk back through a gathering mist into your own time and space and new work in the Light.

About the Author

Born in Colwyn Bay, North Wales, U.K. Elizabeth Anderton spent her early years in Wales and later in Cheshire. By profession an Ophthalmic Optician she is now retired from active practice.

Having an interest in spiritual and psychic matters from an early age, Elizabeth joined the Ancient Mystical Order Rosae Crucis in 1962 and followed their system of home study until 1990. In 1979 she first made contact with local groups and soon became actively involved in the work of the Order serving as a Chapter and Grand Lodge Officer until her resignation in 1990.

From the beginning of the Order Militia Crucifera Evangelica in the United Kingdom in 1991, Elizabeth served as Marshal of the U.K. Priory until her appointment to the Sovereign Priory as Magister Templi of the Order in 1996. She retired from this Office in October 2009 having worked extensively with OMCE groups world-wide.

In 1981 she was Initiated into the Traditional Martinist Order. Her Martinist work continues now within the British Martinist Order as a 4th Degree Initiator.

In 1985 she was Initiated into Co-Masonic Free Masonry, Le Droit Humane, an International Order of Free Masonry open to both men and women, in which she continues to participate.

Since becoming a student of the "Servants of the Light" School in 1982, Elizabeth has worked extensively within the School and has been a supervisor for the SOL course work since 1985.

During 1980 she met John A.B. Fox. From 1982 onwards they shared a working partnership of lectures and workshops which led to the eventual formation of their own "Sirius" title in 1990, under which they presented workshops and seminars both personally and organizing them for many of to-days fore-most Teachers. John and Elizabeth were married in 1992. After a short illness John died on 27 January 2002 which brought to a close their long partnership in esoteric work.

From 2002 until 2015 Elizabeth was co-presenter with Dolores Ashcroft-Nowicki, Director of Studies of SOL, in their series of thirteen annual Ritual with Purpose workshops.

Elizabeth now lives in Milford Haven, south west Wales, and while largely retired from group work, continues to be involved in teaching and some Lodge work within the SOL, OMCE, CR+C, BMO and Co-Masonry, now International Freemasonry for Men and Women.

Get More at Immanion Press

Visit us online to browse our books, sign-up for our e-newsletter and find out about upcoming events for our authors, as well as interviews with them. Visit us at

http://www.immanion-press.com and visit our publicity blog at http://ipmbblog.wordpress.com/

Get Social With Immanion Press

Find us on Facebook at
http://www.facebook.com/immanionpress

Follow us on Twitter at

http://www.twitter.com/immanionpress

Find us on Google Plus at
https://plus.google.com/u/0/b/104674738262224210355/

9 780099 551736